THE
ARMS
OF HIS
LOVE

THE
ARMS
OF HIS
LOVE

TALKS FROM THE 1999
WOMEN'S CONFERENCE
SPONSORED BY
BRIGHAM YOUNG UNIVERSITY
AND THE RELIEF SOCIETY

DESERET BOOK COMPANY
SALT LAKE CITY, UTAH

Library of Congress Cataloging-in-Publication Data
  Women's Conference (1999 : Brigham Young University)
    The arms of His love : 1999 Women's Conference.
      p. cm.
    Includes bibliographical references.
    ISBN 1-57345-632-2 (HB)
      1. Women in the Mormon Church—Congresses.   2. Mormon women—
    Religious life—Congresses.   I. Title
    BX8641 .W73 1999
    289.3'32'082—dc21
                                                          99-462078

Printed in the United States of America   72082-6634

10   9   8   7   6   5   4   3   2   1

Contents

Preface

We are delighted to offer this volume, the fourteenth in the series, of selected presentations from the 1999 Women's Conference, which was sponsored jointly by Brigham Young University and the Relief Society of The Church of Jesus Christ of Latter-day Saints. We appreciate the time, prayer, and thought the authors put into preparing their presentations for the conference, and we are pleased that we can share some of their ideas and feelings with an even greater audience by means of this volume.

We have taken an exciting new approach for this year's book. For the first time, several "how to" sections have been created to include highlights of a number of excellent presentations. We believe these "how to" articles will be a blessing to the many sisters who can take only a couple of minutes at a time for uplifting reading and renewal.

We are indebted to the wonderful conference planning committee. Their selfless efforts and dedication made both the conference and this volume possible. We appreciate, too, the work of our editorial team—Dawn Anderson, Suzanne Brady, Dlora Dalton, and Susette Green—in putting the volume together.

Our theme, found in Doctrine and Covenants 6:20, speaks to the longing we each have to be encircled in the arms of the Savior's love: "Be faithful and diligent in keeping the commandments of God, and I will encircle thee in the arms of my love." What reassurance and comfort that passage brings! What possibilities open up to our minds and hearts as we live to receive the encircling of his love!

Wendy L. Watson
CHAIR, 1999 WOMEN'S CONFERENCE

In Mercy's Arms

ARDETH G. KAPP

This is a historic time. I can almost hear the friends I've worked with over the years say, "She always says that," and yes, I do. But consider where we stand today. Looking back, just a short time ago, we commemorated and celebrated those faithful early Saints who gave so much that we might have the blessings we enjoy today, who gave us the foundation of the Church on which we now build. Looking ahead, there is a great work for us to do.

President Spencer W. Kimball spoke of our time with these prophetic words: "Much of the major growth that is coming to the Church in the last days will come because many of the good women of the world (in whom there is often such an inner sense of spirituality) will be drawn to the Church in large numbers. This will happen to the degree that the women of the Church reflect righteousness and articulateness in their lives and to the degree that they are seen as distinct and different—in happy ways—from the women of the world."[1] He further said, "To be a righteous woman during the winding-up scenes on this earth, before the second coming of our Savior, is an especially noble calling. The righteous woman's strength and influence today can be tenfold what it might be in more tranquil times."[2]

Did not our very souls burn within with the call from a prophet, President Gordon B. Hinckley, in a recent general Relief Society

Ardeth Greene Kapp, former general president of the Young Women organization, received her bachelor's degree from the University of Utah and her master's degree in education from Brigham Young University. She was a member of the BYU College of Education faculty and served on Church curriculum planning and youth correlation committees. Sister Kapp is the author of six books. She is married to Heber B. Kapp.

1

meeting? Hear again his words: "Rise up, O women of Zion, rise to the great challenge which faces you."[3] On another occasion he called for "a little more effort, a little more self-discipline, a little more consecrated effort. . . . You can do better than you are now doing."[4]

Is this in any way a chastisement? No, I think not. Rather, it is a testimony of a prophet concerning our potential, our divine nature, our ability to make a difference at this historic time. Could it be he knows us and our circumstances better than we know ourselves?

We might hear in our minds the familiar words from another time and season: "And who knoweth whether thou art come to the kingdom for such a time as this?" (Esther 4:14). This is our time, my beloved sisters, our challenge and our opportunity, whoever we are, wherever we are. Our Father in Heaven knows us and is counting on each one of us to do her part. And we can. We are given strength and power through our covenants, which provide a special relationship with our Father in Heaven. Through the bounteous mercy and love of Jesus Christ and our obedience, we receive an enabling power to do things we could not otherwise do on our own.[5]

What lies behind us and what lies before us are not as important today as what lies within us. We can expect opposition, but we can rise to the challenge. Our Father in Heaven is with us all the way, and he has set the pattern for us. It is a pattern that does not change. It is a pattern based on love and obedience, sacrifice and service. It is a pattern made possible through the atoning sacrifice of Jesus Christ and realized when we make and keep sacred covenants.

The Pattern of Love and Obedience

I have heard the story told of a mother who, wishing to encourage her son's progress at the piano, bought tickets to a Paderewski performance. When the evening arrived, they found their seats near the front of the concert hall and eyed the majestic Steinway waiting on the stage. Soon the mother found a friend to talk to, and the boy slipped away. At eight o'clock, the lights in the auditorium began to dim and the spotlights came on. Only then did they notice the boy up on the piano bench, innocently picking out "Twinkle, Twinkle, Little Star" on the Steinway. His mother gasped, but before she could retrieve her son, the master appeared on the stage and quickly moved to the keyboard. He whispered to the boy, "Don't quit; keep playing." Leaning over, Paderewski reached down with his left hand and began filling in the bass part. Soon his right arm reached around the other side and improvised a delightful obligato. Together the old master and the young novice held the crowd mesmerized.

In our lives, unpolished though they may be, the Master surrounds us. God is our Father. We are his children. He knows us. He knows our needs and invites us to come to him and be encircled in the arms of his love. He wants us to know him and experience his love. We have his word: "I will go before your face. I will be on your right hand and on your left, and my Spirit shall be in your hearts, and mine angels round about you, to bear you up" (D&C 84:88).

We do not wait until the end of our performance or the end of our life for someone to take up the slack when we find ourselves falling painfully short because of our weaknesses, our imperfections, and even our sins. The doctrine of grace and mercy through the Atonement is an ongoing, hourly, even moment-by-moment process.

Elder Bruce R. McConkie, speaking at the funeral of a friend of mine some years ago, helped me better understand this concept. He said: "We don't need to think everlastingly about God our Eternal Father as being an omnipotent, almighty, glorified person. . . . We might do better to think of God our Father as just that—as a father . . . as a personal being whose face we have seen and in whose household we have dwelt, whose voice we have heard, whose teachings we have learned before ever we were born into this life."[6]

Whatever your feelings at this time—whether joy, gratitude, excitement, optimism, and peace in your heart, or discouragement, depression, even despair, whether concern for a wayward child or a troubled relationship or a seemingly unanswered prayer, anxiety for the life of a loved one, sorrow for sin, feelings of unworthiness, or just feelings of inadequacy—whatever may be the burden on your shoulders at this time, hear in your heart and your mind these words from a loving Father in Heaven: "I have spoken unto thee because of thy desires; therefore treasure up these words in thy heart" (D&C 6:20). Being active members in his Church surely suggests something of our desires. And what are the words he would have us treasure up in our hearts? "Be faithful and diligent in keeping the commandments of God, and I will encircle thee in the arms of my love" (D&C 6:20). Through obedience to a loving God's commandments, given to bring us peace and happiness, we can feel his warm embrace.

The Lord has set the terms for the rewards and the promised blessings of exaltation. Discipleship requires effort—not a particle more than we can handle, but not anything less. He wants us to become like him. We are a covenant people. President George Q. Cannon explained: "When we went forth into the waters of baptism and covenanted with our Father in heaven to serve Him and keep His commandments, He bound Himself also by covenant to us that He would never desert us, never leave us to ourselves, never forget us, that in the midst of trials and hardships, when everything was arrayed against us, He would be near unto us and would sustain us."[7]

The Lord never stops loving us or desiring to help us and bless us. In the words of Isaiah, "For I the Lord thy God will hold thy right hand, saying unto thee, Fear not; I will help thee" (Isaiah 41:13).

Oh, if only we could possibly understand the breadth and depth, the length and reach of his arms of mercy and all the blessings within our reach. We must not become impatient or discouraged but rather listen with our hearts for the encouraging message: "Don't quit; keep playing."

Bruce C. Hafen has written: "The person most in need of understanding the Savior's mercy is probably one who has worked himself to exhaustion in a sincere effort to repent, but who still believes his estrangement from God is permanent and hopeless. . . .

"I sense that an increasing number of deeply committed Church members are weighed down beyond the breaking point with discouragement about their personal lives. When we habitually understate the meaning of the Atonement, we take more serious risks than simply leaving one another without comforting reassurances—for some may simply drop out of the race, worn out and beaten down with the harsh and untrue belief that they are just not celestial material."[8]

When those feelings creep into our hearts like termites that can erode the very foundation of our faith and diminish our righteous influence, let us turn to the scriptures. I have often referred to my scriptures as my letters from home. If you could go out to the mailbox on a very dreary day, when the clouds of life hang heavy, and pick up a letter addressed personally to you, would it have greater meaning? Consider this letter from the Lord. Type it up with your name in the introduction if needed, but read it the way you would read a letter from someone who loves you very much: "Behold, ye are little children and ye cannot bear all things now; ye must grow in grace and in the knowledge of truth. Fear not, little children, for you are mine, and I have overcome the world, and you are of them that my Father hath given me; and none of them that my Father hath given me shall be lost" (D&C 50:41–42).

Consider the similar message in a favorite sacred song:

> The King of love my Shepherd is,
> > Whose goodness faileth never;
> I nothing lack if I am His,
> > And He is mine forever.
>
> . . . .
>
> Perverse and foolish oft I stray'd,
> > But yet in love He sought me,
> And on His shoulder gently laid,
> > And home rejoicing brought me.[9]

On his shoulders, encircled in his arms, at his side, wherever we stand in relationship to him, he is our Savior, our Redeemer, and our Judge. President Joseph F. Smith gave us these comforting words: "God does not judge men as we do, nor look upon them in the same light that we do. He knows our imperfections—all the causes, the 'whys and wherefores' are made manifest unto Him. He judges us by our acts and the intents of our hearts. His judgments will be true, just and righteous; ours are obscured by the imperfections of man."[10]

Elder Richard G. Scott describes the attributes of God in these words: "God is not a jealous being who delights in persecuting those who misstep. He is an absolutely perfect, compassionate, understanding, patient, and forgiving Father. He is willing to entreat, counsel, strengthen, lift, and fortify."[11] He marked the path and led the way and invites us to follow. This clearly marked path begins and ends with love. If we follow, we find along the way the markers that secure our safe travel, through our ordinances and covenants.

The Pattern of Sacrifice

In the Great Council in Heaven, our Father called for help to carry out the plan of salvation. The Savior, knowing what would be required, was willing to pay the price for our sins and our souls. He said in the council, "Father, thy will be done, and the glory be thine forever" (Moses 4:2). He came to earth, the Son of God, to do the will of the Father and become our Savior. And he asks us to remember the covenant: "Behold the wounds which pierced my side, and also the prints of the nails in my hands and feet; be faithful, keep my commandments, and ye shall inherit the kingdom of heaven" (D&C 6:37).

Speaking of this great act of redemption, President Boyd K. Packer tells us: "Save for those few who defect to perdition . . . , there is no habit, no addiction, no rebellion, no transgression, no offense exempted from the promise of complete forgiveness."[12]

This plan of happiness calls for our obedience and our sacrifice.

The sacrifice we are to offer unto the Lord in righteousness is that of a broken heart and a contrite spirit (see D&C 59:8). It is all we really have to lay on the altar, a consecration of self, a willingness to submit all to the will of the Lord, to make his wants our wants, to sacrifice anything that could come between us and him, to keep our covenants even when it may not be convenient or popular or comfortable, when at times it may even seem impossible. Let us reach out to others, to minister to one another, to open our circle and our arms and be an extension of his arms. May we learn to love one another as he loves us.

In the words of Mother Teresa: "Do not search for Jesus in far-off lands. . . . He is in you. Just keep the lamp burning and you will always see Him." And she also said: "Give Jesus not only your hands to serve, but your heart to love. Pray with absolute trust in God's loving care for you. Let Him use you without consulting you. Let Jesus fill you with joy that you may preach without preaching."[13]

How grateful I am for the preaching of my great-grandmother Susan Kent Greene. When her family was driven from Nauvoo to Mount

Pisgah in the summer of 1846, her husband, Evan, pitched their tent and then returned to the main camp to help others who had no means of transportation. As soon as Evan had left her and their five young children, their eleven-month-old baby became ill. The child rapidly grew worse and soon died in its mother's arms. Susan had to prepare the baby for its last rest herself. Years later, on 3 February 1875, she recorded in her journal: "I make this covenant to do the very best I can, asking God for wisdom to direct me in that I may walk with him in all righteousness and truth. I much desire to be pure in heart that I may see God. Help me Lord, to overcome all evil with good." Signed: "Susan K. Greene."[14]

How thankful I am for her testimony, a witness "written not with ink, but with the Spirit of the living God; not in tables of stone, but in the fleshy tables of the heart" (2 Corinthians 3:3).

As another example of sacrifice and love, let me share with you a letter I received from one of our dear sisters, truly a disciple of the Lord. This letter was sent to me after I spoke publicly of a family in the Philippines who had been saving every penny they could for two long years, anxiously looking forward to the time they would have enough money for a one-way trip to the Manila Temple to be sealed as an eternal family forever. Though it might take another two years in Manila to earn enough money to return to their home, they believed the blessings of the temple far outweighed the sacrifice.

The back of the envelope reads: "Dear postal worker, I know this address is not complete, but *please* do all you can to deliver this. Thank you." Her letter reads in part, "I've been struggling lately with what seems to me like a great burden of financial difficulties and my usual ability to count my blessings hasn't been seeing me through, making it more difficult to bounce back emotionally from each blow. But then I looked around and found blessings everywhere, some half hidden." She continues, "My children are sealed to me, though their father has removed himself from the eternal family through his agency. So with gratitude for all I have, I give what I can spare to that family. Maybe in their country five dollars will go further than it does here. Please try to get it to them. If not, to someone else in need."[15] What price would you put on the value of her offering to someone she doesn't even know?

The Pattern of Sacred Covenants

We are blessed with a cleansing of our thoughts through our covenants. President Ezra Taft Benson explained, "When we take the sacrament we commit to 'always remember him.' And thinking Christlike thoughts helps us shape Christlike lives."[16]

The sacrament helps us weekly to remember the Savior's atonement and our sacred covenants, the highest of which are available only in the temple. In many parts of the world, in many languages, I have heard young women repeating with great feeling their baptismal commitment to "stand as witnesses of God at all times and in all things and in all places," followed by the last part of the Young Women theme: "We will be prepared to make and keep sacred covenants, receive the ordinances of the temple, and enjoy the blessings of exaltation." It is in the temple that we receive a review of the entire plan of salvation. We learn something of our premortal life and the purpose of our temporary separation from our Father and his Son Jesus Christ. In the temple, we may find peace concerning matters for which our mind has no answers. From the blessings of the temple, we learn that we may be healed spiritually as well as physically.

There are times when we feel unworthy, perhaps even uncomfortable, about carrying his holy name. We have a keener sense of our imperfections, of those moments when the flesh is weak and our spirits suffer disappointment for our errors and our sins. At such times, we might feel a sense of withdrawal, a pulling away, a feeling of needing to set aside, for a time at least, that divine relationship with the Savior until we are more worthy. But at those very moments, even in our unworthiness, the offer is again given to us to accept the great gift of the Atonement—even before we change.

When we feel a need to pull away, let us reach out to him. Instead of feeling the need to resist, let us submit to his will with a broken heart and a contrite spirit. With his help we can make a profound difference. We can participate in the fulfillment of prophecy. We can pull down the blessings of heaven through obedience to law. The Lord has said, "On my servants and on my handmaidens I will pour out in those days of my Spirit; and they shall prophesy" (Acts 2:18).

Is it any wonder that the adversary would try every conceivable means to contaminate and if possible control our thought processes, polluting the conduit through which the Spirit flows into our minds and hearts? It is wonderful, but not surprising, that after the admonition to "be faithful and diligent in keeping the commandments of God," the Lord tells us how this is to be in these few simple and compelling words: "Look unto me in every thought; doubt not, fear not" (D&C 6:20, 36). Doubt and fear are enemies that can enslave us in prison walls of our own making. Thoughts don't have to be sinful, only distracting enough to weaken the communication so we don't hear the whisperings of the Spirit. Looking unto him in every thought will eradicate thoughts that fuel the fires of jealousy, envy, pride, and related attitudes that distract and destroy.

We are instructed, "Let virtue garnish thy thoughts unceasingly; then shall thy confidence wax strong in the presence of God" (D&C 121:45). President David O. McKay said, "No principle of life was more constantly emphasized by the Great Teacher than the necessity of right thinking."[17] The attempt of the destroyer to fill our minds with negative, unrighteous thoughts is no small attack but a major confrontation. It has been said, "Man is made or unmade by himself; in the armory of thought, he forges the weapons by which he destroys himself."[18] Knowing what we do, would we ever admit into our homes movies, television programs, videos, music, advertising, or tantalizing entertainment of any kind that would, if possible, hold us and our families captive by polluting our minds?

I recall a lesson I heard as a child in which my Primary teacher emphasized with considerable effort the danger of letting bad words get into our minds. That was long before television, internet, R-rated movies, and the like. I left that class sobered. The two worst words I knew, which would barely be considered slang today, grabbed my attention and played across my young mind. I recall sitting in my desk at school the next day burdened. The harder I tried not to think of those two words, the more constant they seemed to be. They refused to let go of my attention. The following week, as I recall, one of the memory gems we used to repeat in Sunday School each week came to my mind as a rescue to my thoughts:

Purify our hearts, our Savior,
Let us go not far astray,
That we might be counted worthy
Of thy Spirit, day by day.[19]

When our hearts are right, our thoughts are right. And God knows our thoughts and the intent of our hearts (see D&C 6:16). For years after that day, when an unwanted thought grabbed my attention, I repeated the words of that old memory gem.

You will have your own memory gem, and it may change from time to time. For me at this time, I repeat over and over again, "Look unto me in every thought; doubt not, fear not."

Being mortal, as we are, we have embarked on a journey through a life in which many different things happen to us, and each moment we have a choice concerning our response. We can nurture negative thoughts and feelings, playing them repeatedly on the screen of our minds like old-time movies, reliving the experiences over and over again with the same emotions, nursing our self-pity and misfortune. Or we can change our thoughts. We must not trifle with thoughts that at first appear trivial and in the end become tragic. Negative and distracting thoughts, however just they may seem, are too heavy a load to carry. Some may try to escape responsibility by saying, "I can't help how I feel; it is just the way I am." In case we are ever tempted by that kind of thinking, let us consider the words of President George Q. Cannon: "It is true that some have greater power of resistance than others, but everyone has the power to close his heart against doubt, against darkness, against unbelief, against depression, against anger, against hatred, against jealousy, against malice, against envy.

"God has given this power unto all of us, and we can gain still greater power by calling upon Him for that which we lack. If it were not so, how could we be condemned for giving way to wrong influences? . . . God has given us power to resist these things, that our hearts may be kept free from them and also from doubt; and when Satan comes and assails us, it is our privilege to say, 'Get thee behind me, Satan, for I have no lot nor portion in you, and you have no part in me.' "[20]

I have a book on my shelf at home given me by a friend with a fun sense of humor. She wrote a note in the front suggesting that I might find the content useful. The title of the book is *How to Make Yourself Miserable*. There is one chapter on the power of negative thinking and another on how to change your worries into anxieties. It gives instruction for optimum brooding conditions. There is information on how to make yourself miserable about the future (what if) and another chapter on how to make yourself miserable about the past (if only). I confess, I've tried it all, and I don't recommend it—none of it!

Expect Opposition

Could there ever be a time in our lives when we are striving to keep the commandments, to be obedient, yes, even to sacrifice in our small way, yet we cannot feel his arms of love and mercy? Could it ever be that he would reach out but we wouldn't let him in? He says to each of us every day of our lives, "Behold, I stand at the door, and knock: if any man hear my voice, and open the door, I will come in to him, and will sup with him, and he with me" (Revelation 3:20). Do we ever refuse to open the door, maybe because we are too busy or too tired, or because we don't hear the knock, or because we even question on occasion that he is there?

In my own life, I remember a very difficult time when I, not realizing it, refused to let him in. It was Mother's Day. At the close of the Sunday School meeting, a young woman participating in the traditional tribute to mothers tried to push a little potted geranium, not yet in bloom, into my clenched-tight fist. The clenched fist was symbolic of my heart and my mind, uptight with a myriad of unanswered questions. Why? Why?

Something about the innocence of this young girl's face softened my heart enough to at least make me open my hand and accept the gift. I took the little plant home. In time, the rays of the early morning sun released the buds, which gradually came into bloom and opened up into bright pink blossoms. From this little plant I had wanted to refuse came a message: "If you will just open your hand and your heart, the Son, the Son of God, will come to you." I bear testimony that if—instead of wrapping our empty and aching arms around ourselves—we will open our arms, he will encircle us in his arms, his arms of mercy, his arms of love and understanding, and we will be able to open our arms to others. If through doubt and fear we clench our fists, he can't get through.

Looking back on that experience, I can more fully appreciate that some of my most fervent prayers have been answered only after I have returned again and again, yes, even for years, and in the process have become acquainted with the voice of the Lord in my mind and in my heart. In my meager attempt at poetry I recently penned these few lines while sitting on a log by the creek in our neighborhood:

> There is a place I walk not far from home,
> Off the highway where I can be alone.
> A quiet place, in solitude.
> An invitation for a sacred mood.
> The rocks and water make a perfect setting,
> The symbols of His life resist the forgetting.
> A place for sorting, for sifting, for clearing the vision,
> And knowing my weaknesses, He's made restitution.
> In my meditation, a form of prayer,
> I think and ponder and feel Him near.
> When a cleansing is needed, and surely it is,
> I remember His love and know I am His.
> I've been bought with a price that only He can redeem.
> My Savior He is, I carry His name.
> In this quiet place like a Heavenly shrine,
> I hear in my heart, Daughter, you're mine.

Is there anyone who has not had occasion to cry out at some time and plead with a burning desire to reach and stretch far enough to connect with God? He tells us, "Draw near unto me and I will draw near unto you" (D&C 88:63). After periods of fasting and prayer, have we not asked, "But Father, what more can I do?"

A day will come in our progress when we learn to hang on and to let go. We learn which things we must hold to tenaciously and which we must let go of if our faith is to grow. Differentiating between the two is a mighty step forward in our spiritual development.

We no longer need to have things our way, not now, not ever. We don't need all the answers, and we don't need additional promises. We have come to trust in the words of the Psalmist, "Cast thy burden upon the Lord, and he shall sustain thee" (Psalm 55:22).

You recall the account of Mary Magdalene burdened with grief as she stooped to look into the empty tomb. Her whole heart consumed by the anxiety of the moment, she did not recognize the person standing next to her. In the quiet of that garden setting, in the springtime of the year and the freshness of a new day, the Savior spoke her name: "Mary" (John 20:16). One word turned her grief to joy. She recognized his voice. She recognized him.

To each of us he says, "Be still, and know that I am God" (Psalm 46:10; D&C 101:16). If we allow our doubts and fears to swallow up faith and hope, we might find ourselves in the predicament described by C. S. Lewis: "The time when there is nothing at all in your soul except a cry for help may be just the time when God can't give it: you are like the drowning man who can't be helped because he clutches and grabs. Perhaps your own reiterated cries deafen you to the voice you hoped to hear."[21]

A father told me of the anguish he and his wife felt for a wayward son. It consumed their total attention, of course; not for a moment was that child out of their thoughts. They kept repeating over and over the statement, "No success compensates for failure in the home." They were weighed down, burdened by what seemed evidence of failure.

They did not remember the comforting words of Elder Marvin J. Ashton: "We only start to fail when we give up on a son, daughter, mother, or father [or self]."[22] We must never give up, but we must try to let up. We need to let up on our feelings of anguish and doubt, to trust in the Lord with all our hearts to do what we cannot do for ourselves. Then, with our hearts full of faith, not fear, our arms will be open wide and our hearts will be filled with love, a power that can penetrate the prodigal.

Rise to the Challenge

Sisters, as we rise to the great challenges that face us, may our afflictions, our adversities, our trials and tests cause us to reach up, reach out, reach far enough to touch the hem of his garment. I don't know what the circumstances are when you reach and may not touch. I do know that many times I reach and seem not to make the connection, but I have also come to realize that he is there, always there, although sometimes I must walk by faith. Never let those times of not connecting weaken your testimony of those occasions when you have felt and recognized the Spirit. The Lord said to Oliver Cowdery, and to us, "Verily, verily, I say unto you, if you desire a further witness, cast your mind upon the night that you cried unto me in your heart, that you might know concerning the truth of these things. Did I not speak peace to your mind concerning the matter? What greater witness can you have than from God?" (D&C 6:22–23).

I must tell you about my dear Aunt Alice and a night when peace came to her mind. Oh, I wish you might have known this woman with her indomitable spirit. At age ninety-three, she attended a stake dance, and danced, of course. After she had retired for the night, she awakened. Her leg swollen, her heart pounding, she was afraid she was going to die. She told me that she couldn't be found dead in bed looking as she did, so she got up, made her bed, changed into her newest nightgown, put on fresh makeup, combed her hair, and, looking nice, went out to die on the living room couch. She said she was quite surprised to awaken in the morning still alive. She has since passed on, but let me tell you more about this remarkable woman, that we might learn from her journey.

Not long before her passing, she was asked to speak in stake conference on the subject, "To learn the capacity to love as our Savior loved." She sent me her beautiful handwritten copy of her address and gave me permission to share it. She begins: "Our Savior's love is beyond comprehension. When I became a wife I thought that to be the most perfect love that ever could be." In time she tells of her husband being called to a foreign mission. After he had been in the mission field about a month, their first baby was born. She says, "He became the center of my love and existence for two long years. When my husband returned, our lives were filled with love and thanksgiving for this adorable child. When he was five years old, he was accidentally killed. It seemed all the light went out of the world for us. As I walked the streets at night unable to sleep, hoping to see that dear little face in a cloud somewhere, I came to love my Heavenly Father more as I pondered His words, 'Take time to be still and know that I am God.'"

She goes on to tell of another son who grew to young manhood and went on a mission. Shortly before his release from his mission, she received word from his mission president that her son was critically ill. He had cancer of the lung. "It seemed unbelievable," she said. "We had great faith that he would be healed through fasting and prayer, but it wasn't to be."

She comments that at that time their life was anything but what the life of a Latter-day Saint family should be. She doesn't say more about this, but I will add that her husband had failed to keep his covenants, which resulted in tragic, addicting habits. Concerning that time, she writes, "As I put my dear baby down for the night and the two older children had gone to bed, I dropped on my knees by the couch and poured out my heart to Heavenly Father as I had never done before. I thought my heart would break with the sorrow that possessed me. I said, 'Father, if things can't change, if I only knew that my prayer was heard, then with the love I have for these dear children, we will survive.' While I bowed there in humble prayer, a warm feeling enveloped me, that sweet peace that passeth all understanding, and although I didn't see anyone I knew, there was a holy presence there."

She continues, "I most likely will never walk where Jesus walked in this life, but I knew I had walked and felt His presence there. I had never knelt in the Garden of Gethsemane where all alone He prayed, but I knew I had knelt and prayed and I wasn't alone. Some divine presence was there. I was able to pick my heavy burden up and with Him by my side I climbed the hill of Calvary where on the cross He died for my sins and yours. My heavy burden was gone, and I lived, I lived as I had never experienced life before.

"The sweet peace filled my soul, and as the love for my Savior grew I recalled the words in John 17:3, 'And this is life eternal, that they might know thee the only true God, and Jesus Christ, whom thou has sent.'"

This is our time and our season as we enter a new millennium. Let us go forth with the faith, the vision, and the decision to follow the pattern the Savior has given us. It ensures blessings not only for ourselves and our families but for all of God's children everywhere. Let us each feel deeply the power and strength and influence for good of our individual and united resolves. With renewed confidence and commitment to the covenants we have made, we shall become, in every way, women of God. Let us respond to the call of our prophet to rise up as women of Zion.

Let us rise to the great challenge that faces us, using the words of Paul for our pledge: "Who shall separate us from the love of Christ? shall tribulation, or distress, or persecution, or famine, or nakedness, or peril, or sword? . . . Nay, in all these things we are more than conquerors through him that loved us. For I am persuaded that neither death, nor life, nor angels, nor principalities, nor powers, nor things present, nor things to come, nor height, nor depth, nor any other creature, shall be able to separate us from the love of God, which is in Christ Jesus our Lord" (Romans 8:35, 37–39).

As we share time together, in small gatherings or large, let us feel the powerful bond of sisterhood and the righteous influence that emanates from gathering through love, obedience, sacrifice, and service. As we go forth, let us carry in our hearts the tender words from the song "Mercy's Arms," written by Julie de Azevedo and sung by Sister Gladys Knight:

> The mighty fortress walls
> I have built around my foolish heart
> How they crumble and they fall
> As I surrender all
> To Mercy's Arms
>
> . . . .
> Sweet the surrender
> Sweet the embrace
> Sweet the forgiveness
> To one forever undeserving of His grace
> Safely encircled
> Rested and warmed
> Sweet is the taste
> Of love that awaits in Mercy's Arms [23]

Of these eternal truths I bear testimony, knowing that what lies behind us and what lies before us are not as important as what lies within us.

NOTES

1. Spencer W. Kimball, *My Beloved Sisters* (Salt Lake City: Deseret Book, 1979), 44.

2. Kimball, *My Beloved Sisters*, 17.

3. Gordon B. Hinckley, *Ensign*, November 1998, 99.

4. Gordon B. Hinckley, "The Quest for Excellence," Brigham Young University Devotional, Provo, Utah, 10 November 1998.

5. See LDS Bible Dictionary, s.v. "grace."

6. Bruce R. McConkie, address at funeral of Florence Johnson; typescript in author's possession, 27.

7. George Q. Cannon, *Gospel Truth: Discourses and Writings of George Q. Cannon*, comp. Jerreld L. Newquist (Salt Lake City: Deseret Book, 1987), 134.

8. Bruce C. Hafen, *The Broken Heart: Applying the Atonement to Life's Experiences* (Salt Lake City: Deseret Book, 1989), 5–6.

9. Henry W. Baker, "The King of Love My Shepherd Is," 1914; quoted in *Best-Loved Poems of the LDS People*, ed. Jack M. Lyon, Linda Ririe Gundry, Jay A. Parry, and Devan Jensen (Salt Lake City: Deseret Book, 1996), 181.

10. Joseph F. Smith, *Journal of Discourses*, 26 vols. (London: Latter-day Saints' Book Depot, 1854–86), 24:78.

11. Richard G. Scott, *Ensign*, May 1995, 75.

12. Boyd K. Packer, *Ensign*, November 1995, 19.

13. *Love: A Fruit Always in Season, Daily Meditations from the Words of Mother Teresa of Calcutta*, sel. and ed. Dorothy S. Hunt (San Francisco: Ignatius Press, 1987), 67, 29.

14. Personal journal; copy in possession of the author.

15. Letter in possession of the author.

16. Ezra Taft Benson, "Think on Christ," *New Era*, April 1994, 4.

17. David O. McKay, *Gospel Ideals* (Salt Lake City: Improvement Era, 1970), 38.

18. Quoted by Joseph B. Wirthlin, *Finding Peace in Our Lives* (Salt Lake City: Deseret Book, 1995), 211.

19. *Hymns of The Church of Jesus Christ of Latter-day Saints* (Salt Lake City: The Church of Jesus Christ of Latter-day Saints, 1985), no. 183.

20. Cannon, *Gospel Truth*, 16–17.

21. C. S. Lewis, *A Grief Observed* (New York: Bantam Books, 1980), 53–54.

22. Marvin J. Ashton, "Love of the Right," *Ensign*, June 1971, 32.

23. From the song "Mercy's Arms," written by Julie de Azevedo. ©1996 Mohrgüd Music (BMI), a subsidiary of Excel Entertainment Group, Inc. Used by permission.

That Summer Home in Babylon

Sharon G. Larsen

Let me invite you to move beyond casual acquaintance with a familiar scripture to a deeper understanding of what the Savior offered when he said: "Come unto me, all ye that labour and are heavy laden, and I will give you rest. Take my yoke upon you, and learn of me; for I am meek and lowly in heart: and ye shall find rest unto your souls. For my yoke is easy, and my burden is light" (Matthew 11:28–30).

The dictionary says a yoke is a frame fitted to a person's or an animal's shoulders to carry a load in two equal portions. A burden that is overwhelming or impossible to bear by one person could be equitably and even comfortably borne by two bound together with a common yoke: their combined effort is more than the two working separately. But the idea of being yoked may be intimidating. You are not fully free to move around. You must be in step with someone else, always moving together, step by step.

What do we know about Christ's yoke? How can it be easy and light? Let us consider five questions relating to this magnificent invitation from the Lord:

Who loves us more than Christ loves us?

Who knows our burdens better than Christ does?

What makes Christ's yoke easy and his burden light?

What disqualifies us from accepting Christ's generous offer?

What qualifies us to be yoked to Christ?

Sharon Greene Larsen serves as second counselor in the Young Women General Presidency. She has taught in the public schools, on educational television, in seminary, and in institute. She and her husband, Ralph Thomas Larsen, are the parents of two children and the grandparents of two.

Who Loves Us More Than Christ Loves Us?

Ponder what we may learn about Christ's love from the following four sources.

First, from the experiences of Elisha the prophet: Elisha was the prophet for Israel when Israel was at war with Syria. Every battle, Syria lost. The Syrian king was frustrated and troubled, until his servant told him Israel's secret to success—Israel had a prophet who, as a seer, always knew Syrian battle plans and could relay them to Israel's king. The Syrian king could see an easy solution to that problem: kill the prophet.

When Elisha and his young servant (possibly the age of a deacon's quorum president) awoke one morning and walked outside, they saw the Syrian army with horses and chariots surrounding the city—a daunting sight for a smaller, weaker army; an impossible circumstance for two people!

The fledgling servant was overwhelmed with the predicament they were in and said, "Alas, my master! how shall we do?"

To which Elisha answered: "Fear not: for they that be with us are more than they that be with them."

At that moment, all the young man could do was count heads. What did Elisha mean, "They that be with us are more than they that be with them"? Elisha then prayed that the boy could see what he saw. The Lord opened the boy's eyes, and he too saw that round about them "the mountain was full of horses and chariots of fire" (2 Kings 6:8–17).

The Lord will rally whatever help is necessary to sustain us. We never need worry that he will ever run out of resources to bless us. "Come, cast your burdens on the Lord / And trust his constant care."[1]

Second, from President George Q. Cannon: "When we went forth into the waters of baptism and covenanted with our Father in Heaven to serve Him and keep His commandments, He bound Himself also by covenant to us that He would never desert us, never leave us to ourselves, never forget us, that in the midst of trials and hardships, when everything was arrayed against us, He would be near unto us and would sustain us."[2] To be bound that way is something only the Lord can or would do.

Third, from the Savior himself: "Ask, and it shall be given unto you;

seek, and ye shall find; knock, and it shall be opened unto you. For every one that asketh, receiveth; and he that seeketh, findeth; and to him that knocketh, it shall be opened. Or what man is there of you, who, if his son ask bread, will give him a stone?

"Or if he ask a fish, will he give him a serpent? If ye then, being evil, know how to give good gifts unto your children, how much more shall your Father who is in heaven give good things to them that ask him?" (3 Nephi 14:7–11).

Fourth, from Psalms: "When I consider thy heavens, the work of thy fingers, the moon and the stars, which thou hast ordained; What is man, that thou art mindful of him? and the son of man, that thou visiteth him? For thou hast made him a little lower than the angels, and hast crowned him with glory and honour. Thou madest him to have dominion over the works of thy hands; thou hast put all things under his feet" (Psalm 8:3–6).

In answer to the question, "Who loves us more than Christ loves us," we answer resoundingly: No one! No one in this world or galaxy or the whole universe loves us more. "I worry that many sometimes . . . fear that God in his heaven, with all of his urgent national and international, galactic and intergalactic business, is certain to be occupied with things other than your hopes and happiness," said Elder Jeffrey R. Holland. "My testimony is that *nothing* in this universe is more important to him than your hopes and happiness."[3]

When days are harder to bear than you can endure, know that God has not forsaken you, nor will he ever. He will not trick you or hurt you. He will never leave you or forsake you (see Hebrews 13:5). He is eternally committed to your happiness. "Thy days are known, and thy years shall not be numbered less; therefore, fear not what man can do, for God shall be with you forever and ever" (D&C 122:9).

Who Knows Our Burdens Better Than Christ Does?

Wherever you are, wherever you've been, he has been there before you. He has known you for eons of time—your sorrows, your weaknesses, your sins, your idiosyncrasies, your joys, and your triumphs. "His personal knowledge, his great love, and his atoning powers combine in tailoring his assistance to meet your peculiar needs," said Elder Merrill J.

Bateman. "The Atonement involved more than an infinite mass of sin; it entailed an infinite stream of individuals with their specific needs."[4] He was sent to heal the brokenhearted. Trust him.

Alma tells us that Jesus took upon himself the pains, afflictions, temptations, and sicknesses of his people; he did this, experiencing our every weakness, so that he would know how to help us (see Alma 7:11–12).

"Surely he hath borne our griefs, and carried our sorrows. . . . He was wounded for our transgressions [and] bruised for our iniquities" (Isaiah 53:4–5). No one knows our burdens as intimately as Christ does.

Are you hurt and disappointed by people in your life? Jesus has been there. He was rejected and run out of his hometown by the very people he should have been able to trust: his neighbors and friends in Nazareth (see Luke 4:28–29). He even asked his disciples if they were also going to leave him. He was a "man of sorrows, and acquainted with grief" (Isaiah 53:3).

I own a long red carpet that I use on occasions such as missionaries coming home, marriage proposals, and prom invitations. Last week, for instance, seven young men borrowed the carpet to pick up their prom dates. As each boy knocked on his date's door, the other six rolled out the carpet and then stood at attention as the couple walked to the waiting limousine. One occasion stands out above all others in my mind. A mother called whose son had left home when he was sixteen. For three years she had had no idea where he was. She had just received a call from him; could he come home? For his homecoming, she wanted to know, could she borrow that red carpet? The Lord helps us carry our burdens, and he helps us to love and forgive.

We have a son who is making choices that are self-destructive. I know that many sisters, like the mother who borrowed my red carpet, understand all that that means. At one period of time I felt the burden was heavier than I could bear. But I knew I couldn't quit or give up because I didn't want Heavenly Father to quit or give up on me. My constant challenge is to stay connected and loving—to resist the impulse to wash my hands clean and say, "I've done enough." Only the Lord can say it is enough. So we hang in and we hang on, and the Lord understands.

Over a period of time, which has seemed like an eternity, the Lord has eased my burden. Even though the situation has not changed, he has changed my ability to carry the load. The Lord tells me, as he told Alma and his people: I will ease the burdens which are put upon your shoulders, so that you cannot feel them upon your back, even though your circumstances have not changed, that you may know of a surety that I, the Lord God, do visit you in your afflictions (see Mosiah 24:14). Christ knows my burdens, all of them, and he knows how to succor me—and each one of you.

Perhaps you are weighted down by certain ideas, commitments, or people. Perhaps emotions such as envy, despair, or resentment burden you. Or you find yourself yoked to chafing habits of materialism or perfectionism. Perhaps you don't even realize these are burdens that you don't need to carry.

Can you identify with this story?

"Esther was trying to be the perfect [Latter-day Saint] wife and mother. Every morning she woke up announcing to herself: 'This is the day I will be perfect. The house will be organized, I will not yell at my children, and I will finish everything important I have planned.' Every night she went to bed discouraged, because she had failed to accomplish her goal. She became irritable with everyone, including herself, and she began to wonder what she was doing wrong.

"One night Esther knelt in prayer and asked for guidance. Afterward, while [she was] lying awake, a startling thought came to her. She realized that in focusing on her own perfection, she was focusing on herself and failing to love others. . . . She was being . . . essentially selfish. She was trying to be sweet to her children, not freely, out of love for them, but because she saw it as a necessary part of *her* 'perfection.' Furthermore, she was trying to get a feeling of righteousness by forcing her husband and children to meet her ideal of perfection. When her children got in the way of her 'perfect' routine, she . . . became irritated with them." Esther finally realized that "being perfect even as our Father in Heaven is perfect" includes loving, above all, and that she had been pursuing the wrong goal.[5]

Another undesirable trait we may be yoked to is the desire to show the world how competent we are. We take on projects to aggrandize ourselves, which keeps us consumed with ourselves. Paul warned us not to be entangled with the yoke of bondage (see Galatians 5:1). I remember throwing myself into committees and boards and causes, I suppose as some sort of self-validation, and showing my dad my overscheduled planner. When I finally ended my tirade about how very, very busy and stressed I was, he smiled and said something I will never forget: "You know, Sharon, it doesn't take much to keep some people busy." Yoking ourselves with the Lord is not complicated. It's resisting his yoke and insisting that we can do it ourselves that makes us feel weary and heavy-laden.

Christ knows all the yokes we are carrying instead of his, and he stands ready to help us make the change.

Several years ago I asked a very dear friend who had left the Church, "Do you ever think you will come back?"

"If I do come back," he said, "I think I could take the faith part of the Church, but I could never take all those absolutes: you have to do this; you can't do that."

"But you haven't looked beyond to see what living those absolutes can do for you."

He looked at me skeptically. "What in the world could living absolutes do for me?"

"When I'm doing what I know I should be doing," I assured him, "I have a peace within me that I know who I am, why I'm here, and that with the help of God, I can handle anything."

A shadow of sadness passed over his face and he said, "I don't have that peace."

And the Lord said, "Peace I leave with you, my peace I give unto you: *not as the world giveth*, give I unto you. Let not your heart be troubled, neither let it be afraid" (John 14:27; emphasis added).

Rose Kennedy, the matriarch of the Kennedy clan, was a mother who had every reason to be troubled and afraid. She said, "If God were to take away all his blessings, health, physical fitness, wealth, intelligence, and leave me but one gift, I would ask for faith—for with faith in him, in His goodness, mercy, love for me, and with belief in everlasting life, I believe I could suffer the loss of my other gifts and still be happy—trustful, leaving all to His inscrutable providence."[6] The world cannot give us that kind of peace. Only Christ can do that. He knows our sorrows, our weaknesses, our heart's desires, and he is ready and qualified to comfort and console us.

What Makes Christ's Yoke Easy and His Burden Light?

Christ's presence with us is the gift he offers. His constant succoring, forgiveness, and encouragement not only make our burden light but increase our own capacities. His commandments are not rigid laws to catch us when we mess up. They are an instruction sheet to tell us how we can become like him and adopt his qualities, goodness, and way of life. His commandments are the instruction sheet for the great plan of happiness. It's like following the instruction pamphlet to put together a bicycle piece by piece and then rolling down the road with the wind in our hair and the soft, warm rain on our face, singing as we go.

His yoke is easy when we choose good over evil, when we get rid of pettiness—upstaging, ignoring, criticizing, self-serving, interrupting—especially with those who are difficult for us to love. How difficult is it to listen attentively to an acquaintance who is feeling lonely? Or pay attention to those whom no one else notices? Can we pause a moment to hold the door for someone as we rush along intent on our own agenda? Or forgive a friend who is overlooking our needs?

The gospel is intended to lighten our burden. In the gospel covenant, we are in partnership with the Savior. That is what makes his yoke easy. When we are yoked with him, Heavenly Father accepts our combined total worthiness. Christ makes his yoke easy for us, but do we believe him when he tells us that he will? Do we believe he really is who he said he is and will do for us what he said he would do?

In explaining this empowering grace, Stephen Robinson compares it to tithing. In the gospel covenant, "the Savior requires from each of us a specific percentage: all that we have, or one hundred percent. Yet each individual's one hundred percent will be a different quantity from everyone else's. . . . [H]e never requires more than I am able to give, and what he does require of me is always appropriate to my knowledge and circumstances."[7]

"All too often . . . my vision of Christ [is] as a type of spiritual advisor," BYU religion professor Robert L. Millet admits, "a sort of celestial cheerleader who stands on the sidelines and whispers encouragement but not the Lord God Omnipotent who came to earth to make men and women into new creatures by empowering them to do what they could never do for themselves."[8] Only the Lord has this kind of power and this kind of love. When he says his yoke is easy and his burden light, he does not mean that his burden would cause no pain, no suffering, no staggering under its load, no sacrifice. In fact, it calls for the greatest sacrifice of all—our old selves, our natural selves that are an enemy to God (see Mosiah 3:19).

According to the great Christian theologian C. S. Lewis, Christ says, "Give me all. I don't want so much of your time and so much of your money and so much of your work: I want You. . . . Hand over the whole natural self, all the desires which you think innocent as well as the ones you think wicked—the whole outfit. I will give you a new self." Lewis goes on, "The terrible thing, the almost impossible thing, is to hand over your whole self—all your wishes and precautions—to Christ. But it is far easier than what we are all trying to do instead. For what we are trying to do is to remain what we call 'ourselves,' to keep personal happiness as our great aim in life, . . . to let our mind and heart go their own way— centered on money or pleasure or ambition—and hoping, in spite of this, to behave honestly and chastely and humbly. And that is exactly what Christ warned us you could not do. . . . When he said, 'Be perfect,' He meant it. He meant that we must go in for the full treatment. It is hard; but the sort of compromise we are all hankering after is harder—in fact, it is impossible." And Lewis explains why it's impossible: "It may be hard for an egg to turn into a bird: it would be a jolly sight harder for it to learn to fly while remaining an egg. We are like eggs at present. And you cannot go on indefinitely being just an ordinary, decent egg. We must be hatched or go bad."[9]

Taking Christ's yoke upon us is the vital step we take toward god-hood. We can't skip this step on the ladder. It is receiving the incomprehensibly exquisite gift of the Atonement. Elder F. Enzio Busche warned us, "We will not be satisfied until we have surrendered our lives into the arms of the loving Christ, and until He has become the doer of all our deeds and He has become the speaker of all our words."[10]

When you decide it's Christ's yoke you want, you will quit resisting his love, and the weight of your burden will be equalized by his yoke. You will find that your half of the yoke, your own capacity, has taken an exponential leap. He is saying to us, "Let me arrange your burdens so you can carry all the opportunities life has to offer."

His yoke is easy for us, but it wasn't for him. Not at any time in his mortal life was it easy—from his birth in a lowly stable to his cruel death on Golgotha.

His atonement was infinite. It covered everything that is not perfect from the beginning of this world to the end. His atonement was intimate because in that garden in Gethsemane, the Redeemer of the world somehow completely paid for our own personal burdens of disappointment, sin, and guilt. That's why his yoke is easy for us—and so heavy for him. He paid the awful price of justice so we could rest in mercy's arms with him forever.

What Disqualifies Us from Accepting Christ's Generous Offer?

I'm sure if I asked you to take out a piece of paper and list all of the reasons you don't qualify to be yoked with him, you could go on and on. But wouldn't everything you list fall under one heading: earth stains? We long to live in Zion, but we want to keep a summer home in Babylon!

In *The Great Divorce*, C. S. Lewis tells a story about some folks living in hell who take a bus ride to heaven. When they get there, they may choose to either live in heaven or go back to hell. However, if they choose heaven they must give up their sins, even their most favorite. They cannot keep even a small souvenir from hell![11] Many of us can relate to Lewis's insights into our individual struggles over this offer.

To prefer our sins over the changes that we would have to make to qualify for heaven is far too easy. Spurred on by twentieth-century technology, we are developing an endless appetite for entertainment. This "pleasure binge" is among the destroyer's most effective ammunition. We have begun to expect fun out of every experience and may even view entertainment as an entitlement rather than a luxury. Nearly sixty years ago, President J. Reuben Clark Jr. cautioned: "The constant multiplication of amusements should not continue. The world is more than a funhouse."[12]

Lamoni's father understood the price. He said, "I will give away all my sins to know [God]" (Alma 22:18). We can't keep that summer home in Babylon, not even for weekends, if we want to accept Christ's offer. But those "favorite souvenirs from hell" keep raising their ugly heads.

I discovered to my horror one day that I was saving souvenirs of anger and impatience.

A few years ago, I deliberately picked up a burden and strapped it on my back. We were building a patio on the back of our home and were anxious for it to be finished before our missionary daughter returned. The contractor did not feel our urgency. To me it seemed that he and his crew were constantly taking breaks, lying in the shade of our trees to smoke and drink beer, and using the facilities in our house, including the telephone. I pulled out those souvenirs of anger and impatience and denounced their careless, overly casual attitude and their infringement on my privacy by closing all the shutters and curtains and locking the doors. I even refused to answer the doorbell. (I disqualified myself for sharing Christ's yoke in a hurry right there and then!) After several days passed, I became aware that anger had become a heavy burden. In a few more days, I also realized it was keeping me from being happy about anything. But even worse, I didn't *want* the Lord to soften my heart. It was as though I thought I deserved to feel this way.

Finally one morning, after several pleadings with the Lord to help me want to repent, I knew this was the day I needed to act. My heart pounded as I heard the trucks driving up and the men arriving for work. I took a deep breath, opened the shutters and curtains, unlocked the doors, and went outside. "I owe you an apology," I said. "I have been very rude."

The contractor put his hammer down and replied, "I could tell something was wrong."

"I have been angry that the patio is not going to be finished on schedule. But I finally realized that there are more important things than patios—like people for instance—like you!" Then I asked him where he lived.

"We live just a few blocks from here," he told me. "I think my wife knows you."

I held my breath. "Who is your wife?"

When he told me, I recognized the name of a sister that a nearby ward was trying to welcome into fuller activity. I was her stake Relief Society president! While the ward was trying to bless and strengthen this family, I was locking them out of my house and my life.

Allowing ourselves to indulge in anger is destructive. "Whether it draws blood or wears a civil face, strife among us divides us, takes away our spiritual breath, sweeps us into spirals of retaliation and misery, and gradually addicts us to resentment and revenge."[13] I am grateful the Lord took that burden from me and gave me a new heart and a new friend. They came to our patio party when it was finished, and a few months later their bishop told me they had accepted his invitation to attend the temple preparation class.

It takes no brains or talent to find fault with others.

Could ingratitude also be another "souvenir from hell" that we are saving? President Gordon B. Hinckley said, "Our society is afflicted by a spirit of thoughtless arrogance unbecoming those who have been so magnificently blessed. How grateful we should be for the bounties we enjoy."[14]

At times I have been consumed with my own broken dreams, ready to retaliate or quit. I have felt unappreciated by my children—at times even hurt and despitefully used. (Those of you who have raised difficult children know about this.) Then the Spirit whispers to me: "How many times have you taken from the Lord and never acknowledged it? How many times has he interceded for you and you haven't even noticed? Yet how often does he keep giving, blessing, forgiving, and carrying your burden?" His love is extended all the day long. He may have to withhold blessings (see D&C 130:20) but never his love. He causes his sun to rise on the evil and on the good, sending rain for the sustenance of both the just and unjust (see Matthew 5:45). And that includes me.

Another favorite sin that too often disqualifies us from his generous offer to share our burdens is living the law of Moses—an eye for an eye and a tooth for a tooth. As Tevya from *Fiddler on the Roof* observed, "If everyone were still living that law, the whole world would be blind and toothless." When I judge too quickly, saying, "Why can't they see? Why do they keep shooting themselves in the foot?" I can almost see the Lord shake his head and hear him say, "Why can't *you* see? Why do you keep shooting *yourself* in the foot?" Elder Neal A. Maxwell reminds us, "The heaviest load we feel is often from the weight of our unkept promises and our unresolved sins, which press down relentlessly upon us."[15]

Speaking from experience, the Lord asked us to love our enemies and do good to them that hate us. But how do we do that? How can we love our enemies? Only by putting off the natural man and becoming a Saint through the Atonement (see Mosiah 3:19). Only with help from the One on earth who did it can we reach this level of charity. When he pulls alongside us, yoked with us, our capacities are augmented far beyond ourselves. We find ourselves absorbing all the wrong done to us with love—always love. We do, in fact, become Saints. By yoking ourselves to the Master, we rid ourselves of the burdens of Babylon and find rest. Rest from competition and self-promotion. Rest from exhausting hypocrisy and insincerity. Rest to our souls. Life is happier, more meaningful, rewarding, and invigorating when we put another ahead of self, listen instead of talk, give credit instead of taking it, and forgive instead of judge. Life is happier when we drop our burden at his feet and bear a song away.[16]

We alone, independent of others or circumstances, determine for ourselves if we will accept his offer of time and all eternity and be changed into new creatures.

What Qualifies Us to Be Yoked to Christ?

The answer is: When we make time in our lives to become acquainted with him. You remember that when Christ appeared to the Nephites after his resurrection, he invited the multitude to come one by one to feel the prints of the nails in his hands and feet. He already knew every individual Nephite, but he wanted them to know him.

How long has it been since you've poured out your whole soul to God? "Prayer feeds the soul," Mother Teresa reminds us. "As blood is to the body, prayer is to the soul—and it brings you closer to God."[17]

Do your prayers bring you closer to God? Or do your prayers sound like this fictional prayer dialogue:

"My dear Father in Heaven . . .

"*Yes?*

"Don't interrupt me. I'm praying.

29

"But you called me. You said, 'My dear Father in Heaven.' Here I am. What do you have on your mind?

"But I didn't mean anything by it. I was just saying my prayers for the night. I always say my prayers. It makes me feel good—like getting my duty done.

"All right. Go on.

"Bless the missionaries to be led to the doors of the honest in heart.

"You mean people like Margaret?

"Margaret?

"Yes. The woman around the corner.

"That Margaret? But she smokes and never goes to church.

"Have you had a look at her heart lately?

"Of course not. How can . . .

"I've looked, and hers is one of those honest hearts that you were just praying about.

"Well then, get the missionaries over there. Do you think I like having a nonmember for a neighbor?

"You're supposed to be a missionary. Everyone is a missionary.

"Hey, wait a minute. What is this, 'Criticize Me Day'? Here I am, doing my duty, keeping your commandment to pray; and all of a sudden, you break in and start reminding me of all my problems.

"You called me. And here I am. Keep on praying. I'm interested. Go on.

"Please forgive me of all my sins, and help me to forgive others.

"What about Bill?

"See! I knew it! I knew you'd bring him up! Listen, Father, he told lies about me, and I lost a job. Everyone in that office thinks I'm a first-class creep, and I didn't do anything. I'm going to get even with him.

"But your prayer. What about your prayer?

"I didn't mean it.

"Do you enjoy carrying that load of bitterness around?

"No, I don't. But I'll feel better as soon as I get even.

"Do you want to know something?

"What?

"You won't feel better. You'll feel worse. Listen to me, you forgive Bill, and I'll forgive you.

"But, Father, I can't forgive Bill.

30

"Then I can't forgive you.

"No matter what?"

"No matter what. But you're not through with your prayer yet. Go on.

"Look, I need to finish up here. This is taking a lot longer than usual. Please help me not to fall into temptation.

"Good. I'll do that. But you stop putting yourself in all those places where you can be tempted.

"What do you mean by that?

"Stop hanging around the magazine racks and spending so much time in front of the TV. Some of that material will get to you sooner or later. You'll find yourself involved in some unfortunate things before long.

"I don't understand.

"Yes, you do. You find yourself in a crisis situation, and then you come running to me. 'Father, help me out of this mess, and I promise I'll never do it again.' It's amazing how the quality and intensity of your prayers improve when you are in trouble. Do you remember some of those bargains you've made with me?

"Wait a minute. I want to ask you a question. Do you always listen to my prayers?

"Every word. Every time.

"Then how come you never talked back to me before?

"How many chances have you given me? There's not enough time between your 'amen' and your head hitting the pillow for me to draw a breath. How am I supposed to give an answer?

"You could, if you really wanted to.

"No, I could if you really wanted me to. I always want to.

"Father, I'm sorry. Will you forgive me?

"I already have. And thank you for letting me interrupt. I get lonely to talk to you sometimes. Good night. I love you.

"Good night. I love you, too."

Do your prayers help you get acquainted with your Father in Heaven? Find the right way to pray—the way that works for you. This is a very personal matter. He stands at the door and knocks, but he will never kick it in. We must open the door.

"Be prayerful," President Gordon B. Hinckley counsels. "You can't do it alone. You know that. You cannot make it alone and do your best. You need the help of the Lord. . . . The marvelous thing about prayer is that it is personal, it's individual, it's something that no one else gets into, in terms of your speaking with your Father in Heaven. . . . Be prayerful."[18]

We also become better acquainted with the Savior and qualify to be yoked with him when we care about each other. "It may be possible for each to think too much of [himself]; it is hardly possible for him to think too often or too deeply about [his neighbors]. The load, or weight, or burden of my neighbour's . . . should be laid on my back, a load so heavy that only humility can carry it."[19]

The war against evil is fought with one act of love at a time. There is no "time out" or sidelining in life. We move on, regardless. Everything we do or say or feel makes a difference.

Elder Vaughn J. Featherstone grew up in difficult circumstances. His father was an alcoholic and his mother worked two jobs. One Thanksgiving when he was a young boy, his mother decided to cook a wonderful Thanksgiving banquet and invite everyone—aunts, uncles, cousins. It was a magnificent feast with turkey and all the trimmings. After dinner, loved ones sat around the table enjoying the conversation and each other. The day turned into night and the hours passed. Young Vaughn got up and went to the kitchen for a drink of water. When he opened the door to the kitchen, what a sight met his eyes. There were pots and pans of leftovers still left out. Splashes of boiled-over vegetables and sauces covered the stove top. Plates and serving dishes crusted with drying food were piled high on the cupboard. He looked at that mess and thought, *After everyone goes home tonight, my mother is going to have to come in here and clean this all up and then go out to work.*

He rolled up his sleeves and dug in. He had every dish and pot and pan washed and put away and was on his hands and knees mopping the kitchen floor when his mother walked in. "I will never forget the look on my mother's face as she surveyed the clean kitchen," Elder Featherstone remembered. "I decided right then that I wanted to be the kind of person who would put looks like that on people's faces."[20]

> Truly he taught us to love one another.
> His law is love and his gospel is peace.

Chains shall he break for the slave is our brother.
And in his name all oppression shall cease.[21]

Every day we have opportunities to cease oppression.

At O'Hare International Airport, a severe storm had caused delays and cancellations of flights. "Among [the thousands of people stranded] was a woman, a young mother standing in a long line at the check-in counter. She had a two-year-old child who was on the dirty floor at her feet. She was pregnant with another child. She was sick and weary to the bone. Her doctor had warned her against bending and picking up anything heavy, so as she moved slowly with the line she pushed her crying and hungry child with her foot. People who saw her made critical and cutting remarks, but none offered to help.

"Then a man came toward her and with a smile of kindness on his face said, 'You need help. Let me help you.' He lifted the dirty, crying child from the floor and held her warmly in his arms. Taking a stick of gum from his pocket, he gave it to the child. Its sweet taste calmed her. He explained to those in the line the woman's need of help, took her to the head of the line, spoke with the ticket agent, and soon had her checked in. He then found seats where she and her child could be comfortable, chatted for a moment, and disappeared into the crowd without giving his name. She went on her way to her home in Michigan."

Gordon B. Hinckley, who tells this story, identifies the man as Spencer W. Kimball, then an apostle. President Hinckley added this sequel to the story: "Years later there came to the office of the President of the Church a letter which reads as follows:

"'Dear President Kimball:

"'I am a student at Brigham Young University. I have just returned from my mission to Munich, West Germany. I had a lovely mission and learned much. . . .

"'I was sitting in priesthood meeting last week, when a story was told of a loving service which you performed some twenty-one years ago in the Chicago airport. The story told of how you met a young pregnant mother with a . . . screaming child, in . . . distress, waiting in a long line for her tickets. She was threatening miscarriage and therefore couldn't lift her child to comfort her. She had experienced four previous miscarriages, which gave added reason for the doctor's orders not to bend or lift.

"'You comforted the crying child and explained the dilemma to the other passengers in line. This act of love took the strain and tension off my mother. I was born a few months later in Flint, Michigan.

"'I just want to *thank you* for your love. *Thank you* for your example!'"[22]

Prophets are not too busy to minister to us. Despite incredible schedules, they make time for the individual. If we want to be yoked to the Savior, we must emulate this charity.

We must think seriously about whether we are willing to take Christ's yoke upon us because it is rarely convenient. That is part of the test. Will we live by our planners or by the promptings of the Spirit? It is not an easy matter to undertake to be a Latter-day Saint, nor is it possible at the same time to keep that summer home in Babylon.

Some may say his yoke is restricting, we are not free to go wherever we want to go. That is true—unless where we want to go is where he is. Then we will always want to be in step with him.

To answer the five questions, we say:

No one loves us more than Christ loves us.

No one knows our burdens better than he does.

His yoke is easy for us when we put off the natural man.

We disqualify ourselves from Christ's offer when we try to keep that summer home in Babylon.

We qualify ourselves to be yoked to him when we make time to become acquainted with him and his other children.

"God, our rich, Heavenly Relative" (as Stephen Robinson calls him) does not offer us a summer home. He offers us his whole kingdom. He offers the most loving and constant invitation that has ever been given or ever will be given since the beginning of time: "Come unto me, all ye that labour and are heavy laden, [I think he knew that would include all of us at some point during mortality] and I will give you rest. Take my yoke upon you and learn of me. . . . For my yoke is easy, and my burden is light" (Matthew 11:28–30). His yoke is the incarnation of Love—all kinds of love for all kinds of people. Wherever you are, wherever you've been, wherever you're going, come unto him first, and you will have the riches of eternity.

NOTES

1. *Hymns of The Church of Jesus Christ of Latter-day Saints* (Salt Lake City: The Church of Jesus Christ of Latter-day Saints, 1985), no. 125.
2. George Q. Cannon, *Gospel Truth; Discourses and Writings of George Q. Cannon*, sel. and ed. Jerreld L. Newquist (Salt Lake City: Deseret Book, 1987), 135.
3. Jeffrey R. Holland and Patricia T. Holland, "Considering Covenants: Women, Men, Perspective, Promises," in *To Rejoice as Women*, ed. Susette Fletcher Green and Dawn Hall Anderson (Salt Lake City: Deseret Book, 1995), 96–97.
4. Merrill J. Bateman, "One by One," in *Speeches of the Year, 1997* (Provo: Brigham Young University, 1998), 9 September 1997, 15–16.
5. From *Teach Them Correct Principles: A Study in Family Relations* (Salt Lake City: The Church of Jesus Christ of Latter-day Saints, 1987), 7.
6. Rose Fitzgerald Kennedy, *Times Remembered* (Garden City, N.Y.: Doubleday, 1974), 520.
7. Stephen E. Robinson, *Believing Christ* (Salt Lake City: Deseret Book, 1992), 49.
8. Robert L. Millet, "After All We Can Do: The Meaning of Grace in Our Lives," in *May Christ Lift Thee Up: Talks from the 1998 Women's Conference* (Salt Lake City: Deseret Book, 1999), 58.
9. C. S. Lewis, *Mere Christianity*, rev. ed. (New York: Macmillan, 1960), 153–55.
10. F. Enzio Busche, *Ensign*, November 1993, 26.
11. See C. S. Lewis, *The Great Divorce* (New York: Macmillan, 1946).
12. J. Reuben Clark Jr. Papers, *Memorandum of Suggestions*, 29 March 1940, address to auxiliary presidencies, transcript, Historical Department Archives, The Church of Jesus Christ of Latter-day Saints, Salt Lake City, Utah.
13. C. Terry Warner, "Honest, Simple, Solid, True," in *Speeches of the Year, 1995–96* (Provo: Brigham Young University, 1997), 133.
14. Gordon B. Hinckley, *Teachings of Gordon B. Hinckley* (Salt Lake City: Deseret Book, 1997), 247.
15. Neal A. Maxwell, *Ensign*, November 1989, 85.
16. See "How Gentle God's Commands," *Hymns*, no. 125.
17. Mother Teresa, *A Simple Path* (New York: Ballantine Books, 1995), 7.
18. Hinckley, *Teachings*, 468.
19. C. S. Lewis, *The Weight of Glory and Other Addresses* (New York: Simon and Schuster, 1996), 18.
20. Used by permission.
21. M. Cappeau de Roquemaure, "O Holy Night," trans. John S. Dwight.
22. Gordon B. Hinckley, "'Do Ye Even So to Them,'" *Ensign*, December 1991, 5; see Hinckley, also *Teachings of Gordon B. Hinckley*, 240–41.

Saved by Hope

JANET S. SCHARMAN

"For we are saved by hope" (Romans 8:24). These words, written by Paul to new converts of the Church, interest me because of what they say but also because of what is not said. Paul did not say that we are saved by obedience, good works, a willingness to sacrifice, or love of our neighbors. He said, "We are saved by hope." I believe Paul's message is one not of exclusion but rather one of order. It is not that those other things are not important to our eternal progression—they are. But without hope, finding the motivation to obey the commandments of the Lord, to do what is needed, and to extend ourselves to others is difficult. If we have hope that our Heavenly Father is aware of us, that he cares about what we are experiencing, if we have hope that the Holy Ghost will guide us in important life decisions and comfort us in times of need, if we have hope that the experiences we are having in this life—no matter how challenging—are designed to prepare us for exaltation, then we will gladly do those things which will make us worthy of our Savior's redeeming sacrifice.

A few years ago, while I was working in the Brigham Young University counseling center, a dozen roses arrived from my husband for a special occasion. A day or so later our office manager, Connie, dropped by my office and offered to take the flowers and change the water in the vase. Although I told her that wasn't necessary, she was quite persistent and left my office with the vase in hand. A few minutes later she

Janet S. Scharman is the dean of students and assistant vice-president of student life at Brigham Young University. She and her husband, Brent, have a blended family of one son and nine daughters. She serves as Gospel Doctrine teacher in her ward.

returned with eleven roses, not twelve, and an earnest apology. In the restroom she had encountered a young student, eyes swollen, makeup smeared, who clearly had been crying and was still quite upset. Connie struggled with a sudden thought to give the young woman a rose. After all, it wasn't hers to give. But the thought remained and finally she pulled a flower from the vase, handed it to the young woman, and said simply, "This rose is for you." The woman mumbled a word of thanks and quickly exited. That was it—an interchange that took only seconds. Of course, I didn't mind my dozen roses being one short. Connie left and I quickly put the story out of my mind and continued with the tasks at hand.

About an hour later, the front desk secretary e-mailed a request to all the people in the offices on our floor of the building. A letter had been left on her desk addressed to: "The lady who gave me a rose in the restroom today." If anyone understood what that meant, she should claim the letter. Soon after, Connie dropped by to share the rest of the story with me. In the letter, the young woman had spoken of the many problems she had recently been experiencing. As she was walking through our building that day, the number and intensity of all her troubles suddenly overwhelmed her, leaving her feeling out of control and very alone. She felt she just could not go on, and as a flood of tears streamed down her cheeks, she quickly sought refuge in the nearest restroom. She prayed sincerely and fervently to her Heavenly Father, begging him to let her know somehow that he knew and that he cared about what was happening to her. As soon as she was able to muster a little composure, she turned to leave. And there was Connie, the rose in hand, given with the simple message that this young woman understood to be an answer to her prayer. A single flower and a simple phrase, "This rose is for you," offered by someone who, by following a prompting, had been privileged to act as the Lord's emissary. This event was life-changing for this young woman not because her circumstances had improved but because from that moment on she knew that Heavenly Father had not deserted her and that he would be at her side as she struggled and ultimately triumphed.

I find two strikingly important truths in this one simple event. The first concerns the power of hope. With hope we feel the courage, strength, support, and desire to face almost any challenge. Hope gives purpose to our experiences, a sense that something good will be gained because of our struggles. Without hope, our very existence may seem pointless. The second truth concerns Connie's part in the exchange. I believe that we, as women of the Church, by our very nature, divine calling, and deep understanding of true principles, are uniquely qualified to be agents of hope, to understand promptings as they come to us, and then to act on them in ways that may have eternal consequences.

Another woman, Arabella Smith, along with her husband, Stanford, faced some challenges that I can only begin to imagine. Shortly after this pioneer couple arrived in the Salt Lake Valley, Brigham Young asked them to pack up their belongings and move to the Colorado River basin to help establish a new settlement there. BYU religious education professor Brent L. Top tells their story:

Stanford "had been one of the most active leaders in helping blaze a trail through a treacherous canyon in southern Utah that became known as 'Hole-in-the-Rock.' On January 26, 1880, Stanford spent the day helping all of the wagons in the company get down through the notch in the rocky canyon. Using ropes and pulleys as well as logs tied to the backs of wagons as a braking system, each wagon was carefully lowered through the rocky crevice and driven to the banks of the river and then ferried across. When word came that all of the wagons were safely down and across the river, Stanford looked for his wagon—but it was nowhere to be found. It was still up at the top of the canyon. It had been moved back while the others were being taken down, and now it had been overlooked. His wife, Arabella, and his children were waiting for him at the top of the canyon.

"For a moment Stanford's face flushed with rage. He threw his hat on the ground and stomped it—as was his habit when he was angry.

"'With me down there helping get their wagons on the raft, I thought some one would bring my wagon down. Drat 'em!'

"'I've got the horses harnessed and things all packed,' Belle breathlessly assured him as they ran toward the wagon.

"Stanford unlocked the brakes; checked the team; tied old Nig, the mule, to the back axle as a brake; and cross-locked the wheels with chains.

"They walked to the top of the crevice, where hand in hand they looked down—10 feet of loose sand, then a rocky pitch as steep as the roof of a house and barely as wide as the wagon—below that a dizzy chute down to the landing place. . . . It was that first drop of 150 feet that frightened him.

"'I am afraid we can't make it,' he exclaimed.

"'But we've got to make it,' she answered calmly. . . .

"'If we only had a few men to hold the wagon back we might make it, Belle.'

"'I'll do the holding back,' said Belle, 'on old Nig's lines.'

"She then busied herself getting the children to a safe place back from the crevice. Three-year-old Roy held the baby, and sister Ada sat in front of them and said a little prayer as Belle kissed each of them and tucked quilts snugly around them. 'Don't move, dears. Don't even stand up. As soon as we get the wagon down, Papa will come back for you!'

"Stanford braced his legs against the dashboard and they started down through the Hole-in-the-Rock. The first lurch nearly pulled Belle off her feet. She dug her heels in to hold her balance. Old Nig was thrown to his haunches. Arabella raced after him and the wagon, holding to the lines with desperate strength. Nig rolled to his side and gave a shrill neigh of terror. . . .

"[Belle] lost her balance and went sprawling after old Nig. She was blinded by the sand which streamed after her. She gritted her teeth and hung on to the lines. A jagged rock tore her flesh and hot pain ran up her leg from heel to hip. The wagon struck a huge boulder. The impact jerked her to her feet and flung her against the side of the cliff.

"The wagon stopped at the end of the chute. Stanford jumped off the wagon and first noticed the bloodied, bruised, and almost lifeless mule that had been dragged most of the way down. There, holding onto the reins, blood streaming from her leg, and covered from head to foot with dirt, was Arabella. She had been dragged down along with the mule—but she wouldn't let go. She had hung on for all she was worth. Miraculously they made it down and were safe.

"'Darling, will you be all right?'

"'Of course I will. Just leave me here and go as fast as you can for the children.'

"'I'll hurry,' he flung over his shoulder and began the steep climb up the incline they had just come down.

" . . . He slowed down, and looked around. He had driven a wagon down that fearful crevice, and dragged his wife behind. . . . God bless her gallant heart! He kicked the rocks at his feet and with tears streaming down his face lifted his hat in salute to Arabella, his wife."[1]

Arabella hung on to the rope. But more important, she hung on to her faith. When the mule, Old Nig, fell and rolled as the wagon plunged down, she held on to the reins. And even when she too stumbled and fell, a point which for most would have been one of terror and despair, she refused to let go. Stanford would never have attempted the descent with only the two of them had Arabella not encouraged him forward. When Stanford thought all was lost, it was Arabella who calmly offered words of reassurance. It was Arabella who lovingly tucked quilts around her three little babies as she left them alone on the edge of a cliff with a promise that their father would return for them. It was Arabella who faced unbelievable terror and certain physical harm as she was flung through the air almost immediately after starting, dirt and sand scouring her face, rocks tearing her flesh.

In truth, none of this was fair. The two of them should not have had to attempt so dangerous a journey on their own. They had given their share, and likely much more, and they deserved the help and considera-tion of the others in their group. How many more times would they be asked to give more than was humanly possible? But Stanford and Arabella were not coming from a worldly perspective. They understood the value of the gift of the atoning sacrifice, a price that was paid not just for their sins but also for those times when what they personally had to offer—physically or emotionally—was not enough. The promise they understood and which gave them the courage to continue on was not that the journey would be easy but that it would be worth their best effort and sacrifice.

I know some of you are going through your own treacherous journeys which may be unfair. In fact, I believe that every one of us during our lifetimes will experience our own modern-day versions of the Hole-in-the-Rock. And, as with Stanford and Arabella, those absolutely crucial events may take place without group acknowledgment or any obvious support. They can be terrifying and excruciatingly painful—physically, emotionally, and spiritually. But the message is for us to hang on. Remember who is encouraging you and what the messages are. The whisperings of Christ are always those of comfort, peace, and hope. The Lord will not desert you. Think of the words in Alma 36:3: "Whosoever shall put their trust in God shall be supported in their trials, and their troubles, and their afflictions."

Satan is the one who stirs up our fear, self-doubt, and feelings of abandonment. Elder Howard W. Hunter once said, "Satan may have lost Jesus, but he does not believe he has lost us."[2] If he can confuse us, distract us, or encourage us to let go of what we know to be true, then he has won a very powerful victory not only over us but over all those we can influence. I believe lack of hope to be Satan's most powerful tool. We are most often not tempted to major sins. But if, over time, we can be pushed to the point of giving up, of believing that what we have been asked to do is either not reasonable or really not very important, then all else becomes meaningless to us and Satan has won. As with Arabella, women are often the ones who are able to look beyond the obvious to a greater strength and power which is there and then use that insight to encourage and support those around them. Our hearts are tender as we naturally reach out to those we love and to those for whom we are responsible. Patricia Holland, at the Women's Conference in 1988, said, "If I were Satan and wanted to destroy a society, I think I too would stage a full-blown blitz on its women."[3] We don't have to wonder if that might be Satan's approach. The war is well under way, the blitz has started, and we are right in the middle of it. This is not a cheery thought; but recognizing that it is indeed how things are, we can then defend ourselves with the armor of Christ. That understanding alone can bring great peace to our souls.

It seems that one of Satan's most effective weapons in this battle is to confuse us with counterfeits. Mormon warned, "Take heed . . . that ye do not judge that which is evil to be of God, or that which is good and of God to be of the devil" (Moroni 7:14). Other prophets have echoed this same warning, and never more than now have we needed to be on the alert, to catch ourselves being lured into false beliefs. How often have we been tempted to think that financial security, material possessions, or good health are signs of God's love for us? Conversely, have we ever questioned why the Lord does not seem to listen to our prayers, or direct our children to make good decisions, or help us avoid life's pitfalls? Satan's message is to equate God's love with a problem-free life. Nothing could be further from the truth. We would not be confused if we understood our real purpose for being here on earth.

Let me explain with an example from my experience as dean of students at BYU. One of my responsibilities is to oversee student leadership. Most often this task is very enjoyable, but at times the responsibility seems overwhelming because of this current generation's exceptionally high caliber of students. They are much more capable, intellectually and spiritually, than I was at their age. It is our charge, as their advisors, to provide training programs which will enhance the skills they already possess and to further prepare them for future leadership in their homes, businesses, communities, and the Church.

A few months ago, two of our student groups planned events which, for each group, were the highlight of the year's activities. The student leaders for each group had done an excellent job of planning, preparing, delegating, and following through with assignments. In both cases, off-campus visitors had been invited to be involved, and one group of presenters was scheduled to fly in from Canada to participate. One of the student groups had built an elaborate stage specifically designed to fit the Wilkinson Student Center's Garden Court. The other event, because of the large number of people involved, could only be accommodated in the ballroom of the same building. The advertising for each had been high quality, prepared well in advance, and widely distributed. Only days before the events, someone noticed a critical problem. These two events were scheduled for the same time and the Garden Court and ballroom are right next to each other. This was problematic for two reasons. First, the numbers expected to attend each event were large enough that there were potential traffic flow problems. The second, and more severe problem, was that one event revolved around a fashion show and its accompanying dialogue; the other was a drum and bagpipe show to take place right across the hall, the sounds of which would fill the building. Careful examination of every alternative made it clear that there was simply no way to give one group exactly what it had planned without negatively affecting the other.

Struggling with difficulties provides a wonderful opportunity for learning and growth. That's not usually our first thought when problems arise, however, and rarely do any of us purposely pursue trouble. Difficulties surface on their own, but what we choose to do on such occasions fashions our lives. In this instance, a complicated, real-life dilemma had presented itself. Compromises and adjustments had to be made. No one was to blame, but even if someone had been, the only way for either side to have any measure of success would be through negotiation, problem solving, and a desire to do what would be fair and right.

As mentors we structured the student negotiations, giving them clear options and outlining potential consequences for each possibility. The students knew we were available if they got stuck, but in the end the final decisions would be theirs. This process was difficult, and the students struggled with it. Having more experience and perspective, we could have stepped in and pushed through to a resolution more quickly, saving them from the arduous task of struggling to a solution. We did not intervene, and eventually the students emerged from their meeting with a plan, a plan for which each individual took ownership and which each group supported. The compromises they chose were reasonable and both events were very successful. The process had not been easy, but, as we had hoped, the benefits were twofold. Not only had the problem at hand been solved but also those who were involved had formulated a framework to use in future encounters.

What these students experienced is not unlike what we experience every day as mortals on earth. Problems arise, not always because of someone's mistake, or anyone's intention to hurt, or because our Heavenly Father has forgotten we are here. They are just part of living in an imperfect world. We have been given guidelines and commandments, which, if followed, will in the end result in our happiness. Because we can't always see the end from the beginning, we need to trust in what we do know and be willing to proceed with faith. When we are willing to do that, the next time we have a challenge, it becomes easier, and then even easier again.

As university mentors for student leaders, we regard problems such as the scheduling dilemma to be lab experiences. Students are taught the theory, but in the lab they actually put the theory into practice. We hope these leadership labs help our students prepare for life in the real world. I often think that our Heavenly Father, in much the same way, sees the challenges and dilemmas we often face as his training lab for us. He has given us a structure, guidelines to follow, and he is not far away when we really need help. At any point in time, he could probably step in and resolve the conflicts or solve our problems, but then we would lose the benefits of the struggle. As we learn in these labs of life, we prepare for mastery for the eternities.

Our ability to learn from these experiences often depends on the amount of hope that we feel. Daniel Goleman, a Harvard graduate, researcher, and author, wrote the best-seller *Emotional Intelligence*. In his book he refers to the work of University of Kansas psychologist C. R. Snyder who has researched the relationship between hope and academic success. In one experiment Dr. Snyder presented the following hypothetical situation to college students:

"Although you set your goal of getting a B, when your first exam score, worth 30 percent of your final grade, is returned, you have received a D. It is now one week after you have learned about the D grade. What do you do?"

The students described to him how they would handle that situation. Dr. Snyder carefully examined their responses and then compared the final grades of those students who exhibited high degrees of hope with those who were low on hope. Here are five main points from his findings, summarized by Daniel Goleman:

Dr. Snyder "discovered that hope was a better predictor of their first-semester grades than were their scores on the SAT, a test supposedly able to predict how students will fare in college (and highly correlated with IQ). Again, given roughly the same range of intellectual abilities, emotional aptitudes make the critical difference. . . .

"'Students with high hope set themselves higher goals and know how to work hard to attain them. When you compare students of equivalent intellectual aptitude on their academic achievements, what sets them apart is hope.' . . .

"Hope, in a technical sense, is more than the sunny view that everything will turn out all right. Snyder defines it with more specificity as 'believing you have both the will and the way to accomplish your goals, whatever they may be.' . . .

"People with high levels of hope . . . share certain traits, among them being able to motivate themselves, feeling resourceful enough to find ways to accomplish their objectives, reassuring themselves when in a tight spot that things will get better, being flexible enough to find different ways to get to their goals or to switch goals if one becomes impossible, and having the sense to break down a formidable task into smaller, manageable pieces.

" . . . People who are hopeful evidence less depression than others as they maneuver through life in pursuit of their goals, are less anxious in general, and have fewer emotional distresses."[4]

This research reaffirms what the apostle Paul taught almost two thousand years ago about the importance of hope. A Pharisee educated in Jerusalem who devoted his life to the persecution of Christians, Paul was respected and comfortably well off by the standards of his day. By all accounts, people would have considered him to be very blessed. One day, when Paul was journeying to Damascus to continue his work of persecution, the resurrected Lord spoke to him in a vision. This vision brought about a mighty change of heart, and Paul's life changed dramatically. Foreordained to serve his Lord as a mighty missionary to the Gentiles, Paul was baptized in Damascus, and after a brief period of preparation with the disciples, "straightway he preached Christ in the synagogues" (Acts 9:20). Hundreds of years later the Prophet Joseph Smith referred to Paul's powerful message of hope and faith in the thirteenth Article of Faith: "We follow the admonition of Paul—We believe all things, we hope all things, we have endured many things, and hope to be able to endure all things" (see 1 Corinthians 13:7). The hope Paul must have had in the redeeming love of his Savior was great enough that he was willing to devote the remainder of his life to serving him, even though that also meant suffering ridicule, hardship, imprisonment, and eventual martyrdom.

When we ponder on times so long ago, it might be easy for us to think of Paul in idealistic terms. Someone of Paul's stature would, of course, be able to summon the courage needed to give everything he had to the Lord. But the truth is, the greater hope of eternal life Paul felt was based on the day-to-day hope he relied on throughout his travels. Think, for example, of the time Paul placed a bundle of sticks on a fire and was bitten on the hand by a viper, or snake (see Acts 28:3–6). His faith in Christ could be very strong, and although the venom did not harm him, still his hand would have hurt then and perhaps for several days after. He likely hoped that his hand would heal properly, that it would not hinder his work, that he would have enough to eat, that he would be able to find a safe and comfortable place to sleep, and so on. Hope is what motivates us to do the little things in our lives which then enable us to do the more notable, consequential acts.

As a young boy my father was one who seemed to lack a sense of who he was and what he could become. Although not a troublemaker, he was also not particularly motivated to achieve, academically or in many other ways. This pattern continued until he served a mission. While on his mission, the Spirit touched his soul, he learned that he was smart, that he had a gift for teaching, and that he had a testimony of the gospel—and his testimony began to burn within him. From that time on, he ascribed to this motto: "You can do anything in this life, if you are willing to pay the price, and if you really want to do it, the price is worth it." His hope that this really was true moved him in unbelievable ways. He learned that if he wanted to do something—virtually anything—and was willing to devote the necessary studying, experimenting, and time, he could succeed. In addition to earning a Ph.D. in educational psychology from the University of Utah, he eventually built three houses from scratch. That meant he prepared the foundations, did the framing, plumbing, painting, electrical, and detail work—all of it himself. He built a twenty-foot boat, an electric car, a grandfather clock, and a freezer. He taught himself German, French, and Spanish. That hope inspired him to touch the lives of others as well. I remember as a young child riding in the car with him while we practiced vocabulary words or played math games. I thought we were just having fun, but he hoped that our time spent together engaged in learning would build my confidence and plant in me the love for learning that he had not developed until he was an adult. His hope for me is the same hope my husband and I have as we do similar things with our children and grandchildren.

Having hope does not mean that everything will be easy, even when our intentions are good and noble. As mentioned earlier, challenges are just a part of this life. Throughout the Doctrine and Covenants we read reminders from the Lord to Joseph Smith for him to be patient in his afflictions; that although terrible, from an eternal perspective of time his persecutions would last but a small moment; and that all his trials would give him experience (see D&C 31:9; 121:7; 122:7). Henry Fielding once said, "Adversity is the trial of principle. Without it, a man hardly knows whether he is honest or not."[5] It is easy to do the right thing when the right thing is easy. Those are not the times, however, when we learn and grow the most. It was during the struggles of his mission that my father was able to decide who he was, what was important to him, and what he was going to do about it. And what he did was based on the hope that those actions would produce the results he desired.

Every day people must make decisions and take action based on hoped-for outcomes. For our son and his wife at the University of Virginia Law School, deciding which school to attend was not easy. They researched schools, examined the pros and cons of each option, and weighed potential benefits against costs, both financial and emotional. They hope that the money and effort they are investing now will benefit their family in the future. One of our daughters and her husband are currently moving to Boston, while another daughter and her husband have just moved back from there; again, both families hope that the career decisions they have made are good ones. In each case, there has been some agonizing, much careful exploration of difficulties, prayers that have been answered, and positive experiences.

In my immaturity, I often wish that I could just enjoy all the good parts of life and avoid altogether anything which may create some discomfort. Elder Bruce C. Hafen, speaking to the Association of Mormon Counselors and Psychotherapists, said: "To miss the misery is to miss the joy. And to miss the joy is to miss it all."[6] That, sisters, is the whole point to our existence here. Our Heavenly Father wants us to be happy, and genuine happiness comes through growing and stretching, and through yearning for something and then rejoicing at its accomplishment.

Think of joyful times in your life and how you have known how happy you were. If you have sent off a missionary, think of the day you took that son or daughter to the Missionary Training Center. I will never forget the moment when the missionaries were instructed to exit out one door and family members to leave by another. I thought my heart would break. I could not have been more thrilled to have a son who both desired and was worthy to serve a mission, and yet, at the same time, two years away from home, starting that very moment, sounded impossibly long. We were willing to send him far away because we hoped that he would be safe, that his mission president would watch over him, that he would be filled with the spirit of the Holy Ghost and be able to share the truth in a way that others could hear it. We hoped he would learn and grow and then come back safely to us. The day he returned filled me with joy. We had missed him so much, and yet his absence was what made his return feel so good. Similar moments occur all the time in our lives—a difficult child who offers a spontaneous hug and says, "I love you"; a good grade in the most difficult class at school; even finally reaching the bottom of a laundry pile. To miss the misery *is* to miss the joy. To miss the challenge is to miss the opportunity to look to Christ for hope and love and encouragement. Each experience we have as we progress through various levels of development further defines who we are and what we are learning from this earthly lab.

In junior high school, I, along with hundreds of thousands of other girls throughout the world, was madly in love with the Beatles—every single one of them. I had visions of us meeting and, if all went as planned, eventually marrying. Although Paul McCartney was my favorite, any of them would do. Of course, there was one little problem—somewhere along the way, they would have to hear about the gospel and become converted. When I was fourteen, the lucky break came; Ringo Starr had become ill and needed an operation. A friend and I did some sleuthing and actually came up with an address where we could send flowers. This was my golden opportunity to contact a Beatle. I carefully wrapped up a Book of Mormon and attached an endearing note, bearing my testimony and adding in clear, perfect handwriting (which took several attempts to achieve) my home address. I may have been immature and naive, but I was sincere. Much to my surprise, I heard nothing. Not even one word of acknowledgment. Ever. Fortunately, I eventually grew up, and my broken heart mended.

Years later, I am now older, more educated, more experienced, and more mature. In most ways that's good. But I wonder if I still have the same innocent faith that propelled me to action then. I know the Church is true. I know lives are blessed when individuals receive the doctrines that will lead them to exaltation. And yet, at times I shy away from doing the very things I could do to help our Heavenly Father's children, including me, return to him. I doubt Ringo ever read the Book of Mormon and my accompanying testimony. In all likelihood he never even received it. That doesn't mean it wasn't a good thing for me to have sent it. Many, many times we will never see the fruits of our labors, even after we have invested a great deal. There will be other times when something as simple as a rose given to a young woman in the restroom may bring life-changing results. Even if we, in our efforts to reach out to others, are the only ones who have gained from an experience, that is good enough.

President Thomas S. Monson tells of a man who had the kind of unreserved trust in the Lord that I desire to have. Irving Wilson was the branch president of a small area in the Canadian Mission over which President Monson presided from 1959 to 1961. President Monson described his first meeting with Irving Wilson following Church services held in the basement of a lodge hall. Only twelve of the approximately twenty-five members had attended.

"At the conclusion of the services, the branch president, Irving Wilson, asked if he could meet with me. At this meeting, he handed to me a copy of the *Improvement Era*, forerunner of today's *Ensign*. Pointing to a picture of one of our new chapels in Australia, President Wilson declared, 'This is the building we need here in St. Thomas.'

"I smiled and responded, 'When we have enough members here to justify and to pay for such a building, I am sure we will have one.' At that time, the local members were required to raise 30 percent of the cost of the site and the building, in addition to the payment of tithing and other offerings.

"He countered, 'Our children are growing to maturity. We need that building, and we need it now!'

"I provided encouragement for them to grow in numbers by their personal efforts to fellowship and teach. The outcome is a classic example of faith, coupled with effort and crowned with testimony.

"President Wilson requested six additional missionaries to be assigned to St. Thomas. When this was accomplished, he called the missionaries to a meeting in the back room of his small jewelry store, where they knelt in prayer. He then asked one elder to hand to him the yellow-page telephone directory, which was on a nearby table. President Wilson took the book in hand and observed, 'If we are ever to have our dream building in St. Thomas, we will need a Latter-day Saint to design it. Since we do not have a member who is an architect, we will simply have to convert one.' With his finger moving down the column of listed architects, he paused at one name and said, 'This is the one we will invite to my home to hear the message of the Restoration.'

"President Wilson followed the same procedure with regard to plumbers, electricians, and craftsmen of every description. Nor did he neglect other professions, feeling a desire for a well-balanced branch. The individuals were invited to his home to meet the missionaries, the truth was taught, testimonies were borne and conversion resulted. Those newly baptized then repeated the procedure themselves, inviting others to listen, week after week and month after month.

"The St. Thomas Branch experienced marvelous growth. Within two and one-half years, a site was obtained, a beautiful building was constructed, and an *inspired dream became a living reality. That branch is now a thriving ward in a stake of Zion.*"[7]

There are many who treasure Paul's message, "We hope all things" (1 Corinthians 13:7). They believe it, and as with branch president Wilson, it motivates them to act. Sadly, many others do not understand his message and are unable to get in touch with the very feelings which could bring them comfort or move them to act. They may need to share our testimony for a time. Being a member of a Zion community means that we work together, that we are willing to share another's burdens, and that we care about each other's success. We cannot get to the celestial kingdom by ourselves. This means that, even when it's difficult, we reach out to our neighbors, we teach our children, we offer support to a spouse. Sometimes, in order to do that we must step back, slow down our pace a bit to be where they are, and try to understand the world from their perspective.

Our family lived in Germany from 1983 to 1986. We knew we had only three years, so we decided to take every occasion we could to see Germany and learn its history. Typically, I would pull out the tourist guide before we left and read to the children about what we would be seeing that day. These excursions were extremely pleasant for me, and so one morning as we were preparing to leave, I was puzzled when our seven-year-old daughter seemed unhappy. Amie had been curious from almost the moment she was born; I had assumed that she was enjoying the many castles, cathedrals, and museums just as much as the rest of us were. As I was combing her hair that morning, she stomped her foot and said, "I don't want to go today."

"Tell me why not," I responded with surprise.

"Well, I just don't feel like looking at a lot of people's bottoms today." We had been on many outings, and it had never before occurred to me what a beautiful, old cathedral looked like to a child scarcely three feet tall, standing in a room full of adults. Suddenly seeing the world from her viewpoint helped me adjust our future outings to meet her needs. Changing perspectives made all the difference—for her and for me. Sometimes that's all that is needed.

Besides trying to understand the viewpoint of another, gaining an accurate perspective for ourselves is also vital. We feel compelled to action having a prophet who is so active and productive. Clearly, there is a great deal of work to be done in building God's latter-day kingdom, and we are the ones to do it. But just being busy is not the answer. We must ask ourselves *why* we are doing the things we're doing. The question should be: Are our efforts moving us closer to the Savior, or further away from him? Do we find ourselves too tired to read the scriptures, too busy to hear the Spirit, too frustrated to listen to our children, or too weary to court our spouse?

As Church members who care about others, who want to do what is right, and who understand how very much there really is to be done, we can mistakenly talk ourselves into believing that we need to be doing it all and all the time. We may even justify being overinvolved with this scripture in Matthew 5:41. "And whosoever shall compel thee to go a mile, go with him twain." Even in good works, however, we can lose hope if we take on too much or become overwhelmed. Listen to the Joseph Smith Translation of that very same verse. "And whosoever shall compel thee to go a mile, go with him a mile." We are asked to give 10 percent of our income for tithing. Ten percent is enough. We know we should attend all of our meetings on the Sabbath, and yet, just recently the Brethren have cautioned us not to schedule unnecessary additional meetings on that sacred day. More is not always better. If your bishop calls you to a ward position, accept it, do your best, and then enjoy the feeling of a job well done. It benefits no one for you to worry needlessly or to experience excessive guilt. There will always be more to do than can be done. One of life's great learning experiences is for us to figure out how to do as much as we can without overburdening ourselves or neglecting the ones for whom we are primarily responsible and who are most important to us.

We read in the Book of Mormon that King Benjamin had a tower built so that his final words could be heard by the multitudes of faithful families who had gathered to hear him. In his speech he included what he considered to be the very most important messages that he could leave with the people he had loved and served during his lifetime. This was a man of great wisdom and experience who loved the Lord and who wished to fill the hearts of his people with the hope they would need to carry on in righteousness. Consider this counsel from that final address: "It is not requisite that a man should run faster than he has strength" (Mosiah 4:27). That seems obvious enough. And yet, there must have been a reason King Benjamin felt compelled to say that to a group of righteous, hard working, and caring individuals. And there is a reason that his counsel was preserved for us today. Life is a process, a progression of experiences. We must "run with patience the race that is set before us" (Hebrews 12:1). Learning to pace ourselves will help us to make it to the finish line.

Each baptized and confirmed member of the Church receives a special gift; this gift, called the Holy Ghost, entitles us to personal revelation as we seek to find balance in our lives and discern among many choices what is most important for ourselves and for our loved ones. This gift can help us with important life decisions such as choosing a career, dealing with relationships, discovering personal talents. This gift can also be a comforter, blessing us with calm and peace as we struggle with life's challenges. The deliverer of hope during times of our deepest despair is most often the Holy Ghost, a member of the Godhead, and we may have his constant companionship if we remain worthy. Blessed with this companionship at the time of our baptism, we can renew it every week as we partake of the sacrament: "That they may *always* have his Spirit to be with them" (Moroni 4:3; emphasis added). What a wonderful promise. We have a Father who loves us, who believes in us, and who wants to help us accomplish all that he asks of us.

Corrie ten Boom in *The Hiding Place* describes from firsthand experience some of the great atrocities of Nazi Germany. I believe the Holy Ghost must have touched her heart in order for her to overcome personal humiliation and hardship and a desire for revenge, and to help others do the same. Not long after the war ended, she spoke at a church service in Munich. She did not notice seated in the audience the former S.S. man who had stood guard at Ravensbruck where she had been held captive and where her sister, Betsie, had died. Not recognizing Corrie, he came forward afterwards to express thanks for her message—that his sins had been washed away. This is her report of that experience.

"His hand was thrust out to shake mine. And I, who had preached so often to the people in Bloemendaal the need to forgive, kept my hand at my side.

"Even as the angry, vengeful thoughts boiled through me, I saw the sin of them. Jesus Christ had died for this man; was I going to ask for more? Lord Jesus, I prayed, forgive me and help me to forgive him.

"I tried to smile, I struggled to raise my hand. I could not. I felt nothing, not the slightest spark of warmth or charity. And so again I breathed a silent prayer. Jesus, I cannot forgive him. Give me Your forgiveness.

"As I took his hand the most incredible thing happened. From my shoulder along my arm and through my hand a current seemed to pass from me to him, while into my heart sprang a love for this stranger that almost overwhelmed me.

"And so I discovered that it is not on our forgiveness any more than on our goodness that the world's healing hinges, but on His."[8]

The Holy Ghost is there to bless hearts that are turned to God. The moment Corrie saw the former S.S. man must have been as full of anguish as any she had experienced throughout the entire war. Seeing him brought it all suddenly back, "the roomful of mocking men, the heaps of clothing, Betsie's pain-blanched face." And yet, without that, she may have missed the intensity of the healing power she felt as the Lord's love passed through her in forgiveness of this man. How lucky for her, and for him, that she was able to hang on, having hope in a God who could help when what she had to offer on her own was not enough.

Although without a doubt Satan is working at full force in these latter days, we know what to do to protect ourselves from succumbing to his influence. I am inspired, encouraged, and refocused by the words of President James E. Faust:

"We stand on the brink of the next century. From this vantage point, we need to remember that the most significant events in the last 2,000 years were not the marvels of science, technology, and travel. They were the Savior's Atonement and the restoration of the gospel, with the priesthood keys and authority. These two singular events will continue to be of transcendent importance to mankind as we move forward in time. The past, present, and future pivot on these marvelous divine interventions. . . . We should seize every opportunity to move forward in faith, looking beyond the year 2000 into a future bright with hope, acknowledging that all good gifts come by divine providence."[9]

I know we will seize every opportunity to make our lives richer and fuller, moving forward in faith, when we understand who we are and what great gift from God we have been given. President Gordon B. Hinckley has said, "Wherever the Church is organized its power is felt. We stand on our feet and say that we know. We say it until it almost appears to be monotonous. We say it because we do not know what else to say. The simple fact is that we *do* know that God lives, that Jesus *is* the Christ, and that this is their cause and their kingdom."[10]

Sisters, I *do* know those things. I also know that if we can hang on to that knowledge, just as Arabella did, if we can act in ways that demon-strate our hope in the Savior Jesus Christ, we will have the privilege to act as the Lord's emissary to strengthen and encourage those we love. What a blessing it can be to feel that hope in our lives.

NOTES

1. Brent L.Top, "It Still Takes Faith," *Brigham Young University Speeches of the Year, 1996–1997* (22 July 1997), 336–37.
2. Howard W. Hunter, *Ensign*, November 1976, 18–19.
3. Patricia T. Holland, "Many Things . . . One Thing," *A Heritage of Faith*, ed. Mary E. Stovall and Carol Cornwall Madsen (Salt Lake City: Deseret Book, 1988), 17; also in *Best of Women's Conference* (Salt Lake City: Deseret Book, 2000), 194.
4. Daniel Goleman, *Emotional Intelligence* (New York: Bantam, 1995), 86–87.
5. Henry Fielding, quoted in Marvin J. Ashton, "Adversity and You," *Hope* (Salt Lake City: Deseret Book, 1988), 15.
6. Bruce C. Hafen and Marie K. Hafen, "Covenant Marriage," Spring 1999 AMCAP Conference (1 April 1999), Salt Lake City, Utah, tape number 10.
7. Thomas S. Monson, *Ensign*, November 1990, 69; emphasis added.
8. Corrie ten Boom, *The Hiding Place* (New York: Bantam, 1971), 238.
9. James E. Faust, *Ensign*, May 1999, 17, 19.
10. Gordon B. Hinckley, *Ensign*, May 1998, 70.

The Cost of True Discipleship

CAMILLE FRONK

When I consider the scripture "be faithful and diligent in keeping the commandments of God, and I will encircle thee in the arms of my love" (D&C 6:20), my eyes and heart leap toward the concept of being encircled in the Lord's love. The Lord's promises instill fervent hope and glorious anticipation. I own several sets of scriptures. In one of my sets, I have underlined God's promises in a separate color. Then during scripture study, I will at times read only those promises, one after the other. Reading them rejuvenates me to again face life's multiple demands.

Recently I have also become very interested in the teachings that immediately precede these promises as I have come to recognize the tremendous power inherent in the *requirements* associated with a particular blessing. Even before I respond to the promised blessing of being encircled in Christ's love, I am now learning to feel gratitude for the portion of the verse which reads: "be faithful and diligent in keeping the commandments of God."

These requirements of obedience, upon which all blessings are predicated (see D&C 130:20–21), I refer to as the cost of true discipleship. I believe that as our reverence and gratitude for the costs connected with being true disciples of Christ deepens and increases, it will instill in each of us a greater faith and willingness to do what he wants us to do, say what he wants us to say, and be what he wants us to be.[1]

Camille Fronk is an assistant professor of ancient scripture at Brigham Young University and a counselor in her stake Relief Society presidency. She has served as a member of the Young Women General Board, as dean of students at LDS Business College, and as a seminary and institute instructor.

Discipleship

Let's first consider the meaning of discipleship. Most simply defined, a disciple is not only one who follows Christ after accepting his gospel but one who also spreads his good news to others. The goal of a disciple is not to be different from everyone else but to be more like the Master. Likewise, discipleship is not to pray that God be for us but to pray that we be for him.

Consequently, being a disciple is not a single event but a spiraling process that begins at baptism and continues throughout our lives. Years ago, one of my seminary students observed: "Simply going to Church on Sunday does not make a disciple out of you any more than sleeping overnight in the garage will make a Chevrolet out of you." Also, it is not enough to have once had our lamp filled with oil, or to have once felt to sing the song of redeeming love; we must be able to sing it now, to have our lamp full today (see Matthew 25:1–13; Alma 5:26).

Having full lamps does not mean disciples are without weaknesses. Their mistakes, however, neither paralyze nor preclude them from serving. Similarly, disciples do not require perfection from those they serve or serve with. True disciples know that only once in mortality was a sinless life realized. Their faith in that perfect one, Jesus Christ, is what fills them with hope and commitment to carry on and find good in others.

During his mortal ministry, Jesus often spoke to the costs or requirements of blessings and discipleship. Matthew 11:28–30 is probably one of the most frequently cited scriptures on this subject, mainly because we feel so strongly the inherent promise as we hear or read it.

Come unto me,	*The invitation*
all ye that labour and are heavy laden,	*Our condition without the Savior*
and I will give you rest.	*The blessed promise that attracts our souls like a magnet*
Take my yoke upon you, and learn of me; for I am meek and lowly in heart:	*The cost*

and ye shall find rest unto your souls. *The promise repeated*
For my yoke is easy, and my   *A contrast to burdens we are*
    burden is light.   *currently carrying*

In this scripture, the cost is found not at the beginning but in the very center of the passage, flanked on either side by the promised blessing, which in turn is surrounded by the reminders of our condition if we ignore the Savior's invitation, "Come unto me," which prefaces the entire passage.

I want to explore each phrase of this invitation to discipleship.

Come unto Me

The scriptures are replete with teachings that Christ is "no respecter of persons" (Acts 10:34; see also 1 Nephi 17:35; Romans 2:11; Acts 15:9). We are often touched by his compassion to both Jew and Gentile, the physically ill as well as the physically whole. He healed men and women, Samaritan and Pharisee, publican and harlot. This invitation to enter into his "rest" was extended to people in every station of life and in every era of time. His invitation was to all.

At times, the Savior expanded the invitation "Come unto me" to "Come and see," underscoring the need for each individual to experience, or "see," his message firsthand. We can never know him, trust him, and willingly follow him if we do not first come to him and see what he alone can offer us. John the Baptist understood this critical step in discipleship. For example, some months after baptizing Jesus, when he was in prison, John the Baptist sent his disciples to Jesus with instructions to ask, "Art thou he that should come? or look we for another?" (Luke 7:19). In answer, "that same hour [Jesus] cured many of their infirmities and plagues, and of evil spirits; and unto many that were blind he gave sight" and then "said unto them, Go your way, and tell John what things ye have seen and heard" (Luke 7:21–22). These disciples of John could never recognize the superiority of Jesus if they did not come to the Savior and see for themselves. They could then return to John and report the miracles that they had seen and heard, as the Spirit bore them personal witness that Jesus was the Messiah and John his forerunner.

Before we make covenants with the Lord, each of us will have occasion to "see" the Savior and witness that he is the Redeemer of the world. In other words, before we are baptized or enter one of the Lord's temples, each one of us is asked whether we know and have felt, through a personal witness from the Spirit of God, that the teachings of Jesus are true. We cannot become true disciples, let alone benefit from the costs, unless we have first come to Christ and received a testimony of his divinity and goodness. He never requires us to commit to discipleship before we first have an established trust in him.

A footnote to Matthew 11:28 in the LDS edition of the Bible directs the reader to an entry in the Topical Guide, "Problem-Solving." The Savior invites us to come unto him for solutions, not temporary, Band-Aid treatments. His answers are eternal solutions. Of course, we all carry burdens, problems that yearn for resolution. In this scripture, each of us is personally called to come unto him to have our problems solved. That is where the cost, or "yoke," comes in.

The Yoke

A yoke was a wooden beam worn on the shoulders of a pair of oxen or other draft animals. With their massive, broad shoulders working together, a team of oxen can pull extremely heavy loads, such as the wagons that carried our pioneer ancestors and their belongings across the plains.

Recently, I visited some high school friends, Eli and Carol Anderson in Bothwell, Utah. Eli has an impressive and extensive collection of wagons and horse-drawn carriages. After showing me all his wagons, including some yokes made for animals to pull those wagons, I asked Eli his thoughts about the scripture in Matthew 11. He took me into their home to a wall where he had hung for display numerous archaic tools. Among them was a yoke designed to be worn by a human. This yoke is a crossbar designed to rest on a person's shoulders with ropes or cables at each end from which hang buckets or baskets to hold the loads. Yokes allowed the bearers to carry—or endure—heavy burdens for a longer period of time by distributing the weight of a balanced load over the broadest and strongest part of the body—the shoulders. An individual may then use the rest of his body, braced by the spinal column, to support the shoulders in their labor.

Compare the superiority of a yoke to other ways we sometimes carry weighty and cumbersome commodities: holding a loaded basket by a handle, or a heavy sack slung over one shoulder or on a strap passed around the neck. These methods quickly become uncomfortable and taxing to hand, arm, shoulder, or neck. In each case, all the weight is concentrated at one point, placing painful stress on that one part of the body. A yoke was an ingenious, useful device.

Historically, yokes were used for cruel purposes, however. Conquering armies placed yokes on their captives to humiliate and brutalize them in forced labor. A tongue connected to a wagon or other load could be attached to the yoke requiring the captive to assume the dehumanizing role of a work animal in heavy labor. The Israelites, as slaves in Egypt, probably wore such yokes to build massive monuments and buildings for Pharaoh's glorious cities. From pictoral reliefs commemorating the Assyrians' many victories, we know that the Assyrians used yokes on their captives. During the time of Assyrian conquest of the northern kingdom of Israel, Isaiah in Judah, the southern kingdom, powerfully testified, "The Lord of hosts hath sworn, saying, . . . I will break the Assyrian in my land, and upon my mountains tread him under foot: then shall his yoke depart from off them, and his burden depart from off their shoulders" (Isaiah 14:24–25).

Yokes, then, may symbolize either on the one hand, slavery and oppression, or on the other, empowerment beyond natural abilities. In reality, every one of us wears a figurative yoke in our attempt to carry our important but at times overwhelming responsibilities and burdens in life. We are among those whom Jesus described as "all ye that labour and are heavy laden." But we are not left alone to bear these burdens; in Matthew 11, the Lord teaches us how to carry our burdens successfully.

All Ye That Labour and Are Heavy Laden

Let's take a closer look at these burdens we are carrying. What causes us to be heavy laden? I can't begin to name all of humankind's burdens in a finite list, but several examples make this fact clear: the Savior is talking to each one of us in this scripture. Arguably, the heaviest burden to weigh us down is sin. When we know "to do good" but we "do it not"

(James 4:17) or when we knowingly commit evil, we offend the Spirit of God and are left to our own strength.

But noxious burdens of other sorts may cumber us. Financial concerns are particularly weighty, whether we have spent more than we can repay, or have never had enough to adequately care for our own, or have too much and do not know how best to use it. Other burdens may include fear of the future, worries over being alone in life, attempts to live up to others' expectations, or browbeating ourselves for falling short of our own impossible expectations. We may become heavy laden comparing ourselves to a neighbor who appears to have it all together when we are filled with uncertainty, ignorance, and doubt—ever learning but never able to come to the truth (see 2 Timothy 3:7). We are weighed down when we get sucked into the relentless pursuit of status or wealth. And we are burdened when—as a new convert in the Church—we feel inferior and lost because we can't understand or speak the LDS cultural lingo.

Among the heavy laden are also those who have not yet received the saving and exalting ordinances of the gospel, as well as Saints who suffer from illness, from betrayal, or persecution, or unreciprocated love, or from concern for a loved one residing in a nation at war. Our burdens are heavy when we are bent under the pressures of time, having perhaps lost perspective on how best to use our time and talents. In certain circumstances, even service in the Church, care and time for our families, and worship of God can become cumbersome.

In Matthew 11, the Savior was addressing a group of Jews who were weighed down with the minute particulars of what had become the redefined law of Moses. The law's demands, reshaped and embellished by scribes and Pharisees, had become impossibly complex. No one could successfully live the law. Even Peter, as head of the Church after the Lord's resurrection, referred to the law of Moses as "a yoke upon the neck of the disciples, which neither our fathers nor we were able to bear" (Acts 15:10). Jesus chastened the scribes and Pharisees of his day who continued to subject the Jews to their interpretation of the Law yet refused to help them bear up under the burdens of compliance. He warned, "For they bind heavy burdens and grievous to be borne, and lay them on men's shoulders; but they themselves will not move them with one of their fingers" (Matthew 23:4).

To the humble Jews who heard Jesus teach in mortality, and to us who are heavy laden today, the Lord calls, "Come, . . . every one that thirsteth, come ye to the waters; and he that hath no money, come buy and eat; yea, come buy wine and milk without money and without price" (2 Nephi 9:50; see also Isaiah 55:1). These great promises are ours for free as far as money or material possessions are concerned, but they are not without cost as far as our priorities and desires are concerned. When we realize we have too much to carry alone, the Lord asks us to willingly take *his* yoke upon us. That requires an exchange. We will have to set aside the faulty, yet by now very familiar, yoke we have been using to carry our burdens, and with utmost trust in the Lord replace it with his yoke and all the additional cargo that goes with it.

Take My Yoke upon You

Willingly taking his yoke with its cargo upon us at first appears ludicrous when we obviously have too much to carry already. Perhaps, we may reason, Christ promises that our burdens will become light with his yoke, because, like an Aesop's fable, he will eventually remove his yoke, making our problems feel comparatively light. Or maybe we hope it means that we simply deposit all our responsibilities and cares upon the Lord and leap off to play, never turning back to see if all is well. We hope we can be irresponsible, and he will atone for our misdeeds and weakness. But that is not at all what the Lord is offering to us. He sees much greater potential strength in us than we ever do in ourselves. He also knows what is necessary to help us reach that potential.

What, then, makes his yoke different from the others? He told us that his "yoke is easy" and his "burden is light." In Greek, the word translated *easy* means "kindly." One way for a yoke to be more kindly is for it to fit properly. Ill-fitting, roughly hewn yokes would chafe the neck and gouge shoulders. A yoke that was too long would concentrate too much weight on the ends of the shoulders. Jesus was a carpenter by trade and undoubtedly made yokes for both animals and humans. He would know that the most kindly yoke would be sanded smooth so as not to chafe where it touched the body and cause sore spots. He would know that a choice of strong yet flexible wood could be a designed to bow slightly in the center when heavier burdens were attached, relieving pressure from the neck. Jesus also knew about the importance of having a load perfectly balanced when it is attached to the yoke. The Savior knows a lot about perfect balance.

Elder Spencer H. Osborn, a former member of the First Quorum of Seventy, observed yokes in use by humans in the Philippines. He passed a farmer "carrying an enormous load of vegetables and produce hanging from both ends of a wooden yoke carried across his shoulders." After Elder Osborn stopped and photographed the farmer, the man lowered his burden to visit. Elder Osborn reported their conversation: "I asked my friend if his load wasn't really too heavy to carry a great distance. He replied, 'No, it isn't, because it's balanced.' 'Doesn't that yoke hurt?' I asked. 'At first it did, but I carved and sanded it with a rough stone, and now it fits and is comfortable.'"[2]

When my friend Eli showed me the yoke from his collection, he invited me to put it on my shoulders. The yoke had been hollowed out to fit around the shoulders of the wearer and was carved and sanded smoothly to go behind the neck without rubbing. I was surprised at how comfortable it was. When he pulled down on the two ropes that were attached to the ends of the yoke, I could instantly feel the added weight, but it didn't dig into my neck or press uncomfortably anywhere along my shoulders.

My brother who is a mechanical engineer helped me to understand the optimum design of a yoke, as I have described, including the importance of a balanced load. When the load attached to the yoke is not balanced, the person is also thrown off balance by the uneven pull of gravity and required to use extra energy to compensate for the torque forced upon the spinal column. This torque causes instant and sustained discomfort, requiring extra steadying exertion on our part to counterbalance the load and restore equilibrium.

A knowledgeable carpenter could design and create an individualized yoke, one that fits a particular person's frame precisely, and he could calculate a balanced load for that person's specific height, weight, and strength. Jesus Christ, the Master Carpenter, will do this and more. He will design a yoke for each of us that considers our personality, talents, and personal circumstances. The Lord is sensitive to the personalized loads we carry. "Obviously, the personal burdens of life vary from person to person, but every one of us has them," explained President Howard W. Hunter. "Furthermore, each trial in life is tailored to the individual's capacities and needs as known by a loving Father in Heaven. . . . Whatever the reason [we are weighed down], none of us seems to be completely free from life's challenges. To one and all, Christ said, in effect: As long as we all must bear some burden and shoulder some yoke, why not let it be mine? My promise to you is that my yoke is easy, and my burden is light."[3]

The Lord's yoke perfectly equalizes our individual responsibilities and personal burdens and distributes the weight so that it is not only bearable but "easy." His yoke isn't harsh, sharp, or debilitating but accommodating, encouraging, and enabling.

Will a good yoke in some way actually diffuse the weight of the load, transferring part of the weight someplace away from the person, freeing the person from bearing part or all of the burden? I had hoped that might be so, but I am sorry to report that I found no such magical solution—in physical fact or in metaphor. But what I did find is even better.

The Father did not send us to earth to learn the best ways to escape burdens and responsibility. He sent us to decipher which of our burdens are unnecessary and debilitating, to learn how to divest ourselves of that extra baggage, and how to successfully carry our God-given loads. We are here to learn to become more like the Savior, and we don't do that by having someone else carry our pack for us. The Lord's yoke not only enables us to carry the load he has called us to assume but allows us to carry it for as long as he requires. As one biblical scholar described it: "The weight of Christ's yoke is wings to the soul."[4]

My Yoke Is Easy and My Burden Is Light

I have identified five reasons that the Lord's burden is light when we use his yoke.

1. *We dispose of unnecessary baggage.* When we assume the Lord's yoke, we discover immediately that some things we carry must be left behind. Often, these things we almost insist on packing with us never help us and take up needed space for important cargo. Sins against God are the heavies that first come to mind. Once we repent of all our sins, even

those favorite small sins that we think aren't adding much weight, we will be amazed at how light the overall load suddenly becomes.

Next, we must discard those sins for which we have already sought and received the Lord's forgiveness. They are dead weights on the soul. If we continue to cling to them, our load becomes overwhelmingly burdensome and heavy, as though we were wearing a massive medallion of guilt. Through his atonement, Christ has already assumed these burdens and has authorized us to let them go.

In addition, we need to jettison burdensome attitudes. If we are to wear the Lord's yoke, we must take care not to persist in doing things our way or the world's way rather than the Lord's way. Besides adding excess weight, seeking approval from others turns our load immediately topsy-turvy, much like a washing machine shaking radically out of balance. President Spencer W. Kimball taught: "When you do not worry or concern yourself too much with what other people do and believe and say, there will come to you a new freedom."[5]

Christ clearly taught that a person cannot "serve two masters: for either he will hate the one, and love the other; or else he will hold to the one, and despise the other" (Matthew 6:24; see also 3 Nephi 13:24). He also said, "They who are not for me are against me" (2 Nephi 10:16). President Brigham Young identified the chaos caused by insisting on carrying unnecessary burdens, whether burdens of our choosing or burdens chosen by someone other than the Lord: "they who try to serve God and still cling to the spirit of the world, have got on two yokes—the yoke of Jesus and the yoke of the devil, and they will have plenty to do. They will have a warfare inside and outside, and the labor will be very galling, for they are directly in opposition one to another. Cast off the yoke of the enemy, and put on the yoke of Christ, and you will say that his yoke is easy and his burden is light. This I know by experience."[6]

Christ's yoke becomes easy and his burden light when we dispose of unnecessary baggage, including the yoke of Satan. The apostle Paul encouraged us to "lay aside every weight, and the sin which doth so easily beset us, and let us run with patience the race that is set before us" (Hebrews 12:1). From this perspective, eliminating Satan's yoke of bondage makes our burden so light we can even run while carrying our load.

2. *We find sustaining power through covenants.* Covenants are the primary source of power in our lives. When we make covenants with the Lord, he promises us his strength to support us in carrying our loads, making our burdens lighter. At baptism, we covenanted to willingly take Christ's name upon us, or figuratively speaking, take his yoke upon us. In return, the Lord promises that his Spirit will always be with us. In all reality, we could not possibly handle the total weight of mortality without the Lord's support. The psalmist therefore counseled us to "cast thy burden upon the Lord, and he shall sustain thee" (Psalm 55:22). The fact that he sustains us suggests that we still carry his yoke but not alone. Neither are we merely appreciative spectators while he does all the work. Because the demands on us are real, he promised that he would not leave us comfortless (see John 14:18). President Howard W. Hunter reasoned: "Why face life's burdens alone, Christ asks, or why face them with temporal support that will quickly falter? To the heavy laden it is Christ's yoke, it is the power and peace of standing side by side with a God that will provide the support, balance, and the strength to meet our challenges and endure our tasks here in the hardpan field of mortality."[7]

To missionaries in the early days of the Church, the Lord promised, "And whoso receiveth you, there I will be also, for I will go before your face. I will be on your right hand and on your left, and my Spirit shall be in your hearts, and mine angels round about you, to bear you up" (D&C 84:88). That is a tremendous assurance of sustaining help with our burdens!

3. *We mutually support one another.* In the covenant of baptism we promise that we will watch out for each other and help whenever there is need. The Lord's yoke is easy and his burden light in part because we help each other to carry our loads. When we work together, we create a synergism. Each participant is strengthened, more is accomplished, and, when we work together rather than alone, significantly less stress or pressure rests on everyone's shoulders. In addition, when we vicariously feel the heartache of another, we often gain the strength and wisdom from a particular trial without having to experience that trial ourselves.

The Lord never intended us to face the burdens of mortality alone. Essential to God's plan, Eve is to be "an help meet for [Adam]" (Moses 3:18; Genesis 2:18). In the original Hebrew, the first word, *'ezer,* translated as *help*, combines the meanings "to rescue or save" with the idea of *strength*. The second word, *kenegdo*, translated as *meet*, means "equal." These words, considered together as one term, *helpmeet*, suggest one who has equal strength to rescue. In other words, the Lord provided Adam the partnership of Eve, who was given equal capacity to help him as he was given to help her. [8]

Not everyone has a spouse, or has a spouse who is a helpmeet. Fortunately, the Lord has organized his Church so that we help each other with our burdens in additional ways. Consider the people of Alma who desired to come unto Christ. In taking his yoke upon them, they covenanted "to bear one another's burdens, that they may be light; . . . to mourn with those that mourn; yea, and comfort those that stand in need of comfort" (Mosiah 18:8–9). With baptism, we become members of a community of Saints who have all made this same covenant. If we faithfully keep that covenant, every individual in our ward or branch will feel that lift, or boost, that comes from the larger community. When we forget that covenant, individual brothers and sisters may feel overwhelmed and discouraged, and some will leave the yoke of Christ to search in vain for an easier way to carry their load.

4. *The Lord increases our strength as we serve him.* Wearing the Lord's yoke gradually strengthens our back and shoulders so that we become capable of carrying greater loads and with greater ease. Spiritual, as well as physical, muscles that are consistently used and stretched become stronger whereas those not in use quickly atrophy. At a fitness gym, if you want to increase your upper body strength, the trainer will start you off on relatively light weights. After you have mastered those, the trainer is unlikely to say, "Okay, you're done now. You're strong." She will add another five or ten pounds and encourage you to lift that. The same principle applies when the Lord commissions us to carry beneficial burdens or responsibilities. A new mother, feeling overwhelmed with all her new responsibilities, wonders how she will ever have the energy or wisdom to nurture this baby to adulthood. She notices a mother with five children at church and is astonished. How does she do it? "I got them one at a time," explains the mother of five. As we mature in the Lord's service, he increases the weight of our responsibility, and our

overall strength increases correspondingly. In the process, we are becoming more like him.

Let's return to Alma and his covenant-keeping community of Saints. They were warned to depart from the waters of Mormon. They traveled into the wilderness, and there they settled in a "beautiful and pleasant land," which "they called . . . Helam" (Mosiah 23:4, 19). They prospered in a Zionlike society for a time but were eventually discovered by an imposing band of Lamanites and Alma's former associates, the wicked priests of Noah. Amulon, the chief of the wicked priests, immediately put these good people into bondage, "exercis[ing] authority over them, and put[ting] tasks upon them, and put[ting] taskmasters over them" (Mosiah 24:9).

But Alma and his people who had prospered and been strengthened under the yoke of Christ, knew from whence their strength would come, and they "began to cry mightily to God," "pour[ing] out their hearts" in silent prayer when Amulon stationed guards to stop them from praying (Mosiah 24:10–12).

"And it came to pass [that suggests some time has passed without any sign of divine assistance] that the voice of the Lord came to them in their afflictions, saying: Lift up your heads and be of good comfort, for I know of the covenant which ye have made unto me; and I will covenant with my people and deliver them out of bondage" (Mosiah 24:13). Their complete release from bondage, however, was not imminent. First, the Lord told them that he would "ease the burdens which are put upon your shoulders, that even you cannot feel them upon your backs" (v. 14). Note that the Lord did not ease their burdens by removing them from bondage. The enemy yoke remained on their shoulders for a while longer. Again, the Lord has greater things in store for them than a way to escape hardship. Then we read: "It came to pass [more time passes] that the burdens which were laid upon Alma and his brethren were made light; yea, *the Lord did strengthen them that they could bear up their burdens with ease,* and they did submit cheerfully and with patience to all the will of the Lord" (v. 15; emphasis added).

What a stunning example of how the Lord incrementally strengthens us with his yoke and thus lightens our burdens. The Bible Dictionary teaches us that through the grace of Jesus Christ not only does he provide his divine support and strength but *we* actually "receive strength and assistance to do good works that [we] otherwise would not be able to maintain if left to [our] own means" (s.v. "grace"). The burden is light because we become stronger.

5. *Christ teaches us how to carry burdens.* In Matthew 11:29, he explained how to make his yoke easy. He said, "Take my yoke upon you, and learn of me; for I am meek and lowly in heart." Prepositions are the key here. In the Greek, the Lord did not say "learn of me" but "learn *from* me." One biblical scholar comments: "The yoke . . . symbolized discipleship. When our Lord added the phrase 'learn from me,' the imagery would have been familiar to Jewish listeners. In ancient writings, a pupil who submitted himself to a teacher was said to take the teacher's yoke."[9] Jesus is our teacher when we wear his yoke. What does he want us to learn from him on the subject? How to be "meek and lowly of heart."

Christ showed us the way. If we follow his example of meekness, we will *never* be weary of well-doing. We will be patient in times of tribulation, and we will submit our will to the will of the Father in all things. Jesus knows what it is to carry a yoke, one that is not easy, and bear a burden that is anything but light. He carried his yoke without complaint and with absolute trust in his Father. Consider the terrible cross, much like a yoke, that he carried on his remarkable yet mortal shoulders so that our burden would be light. Consider also that he allowed another to assist him in carrying that burden (see Matthew 27:32). That is the kind of meekness we need to learn from him to ease us as we carry our burdens.

The scriptures also give us examples of disciples who have learned to be meek under divine tutelage. Consider Peter hearing the cock crow thrice that dreadful morning after Christ's arrest. Consider Paul's lesson in humility on the road to Damascus. Consider Moses whom Stephen, a disciple of Christ, described as "learned in all the wisdom of the Egyptians, and was mighty in words and in deeds" (Acts 7:22). That is not the way we typically remember Moses—mighty in words. Wasn't he the one who said, "I am not eloquent, . . . but I am slow of speech, and of a slow tongue" (Exodus 4:10)? And in Numbers 12:3, Moses is described as "very meek, above all the men which were upon the face of the earth." That was at a time when Moses might have been glorying in his accomplishments. He had just delivered the children of Israel out of bondage, brought them through the Red Sea, and was camped with them in the wilderness.

What happened to change Moses from being mighty in words to being the meekest of men and slow of speech? I don't think Moses' speech necessarily changed as much as his standard of greatness changed. In latter-day revelations, we learn that Moses was taught by the Lord himself, a level of learning a bit beyond even "all the wisdom of the Egyptians." After this period of instruction, Moses exclaimed, "Now, . . . I know that man is nothing, which thing I never had supposed" (Moses 1:10). If we turn to worldly powers for instruction on how to carry burdens, we will become either arrogant and proud or self-deprecating and depressed. If we learn discipleship from Christ, we will become even as he is, meek and humble.

Meekness is seldom listed among traits people hope to acquire, and it is even less likely to be recognized by the world as a means to success. President Howard W. Hunter wisely observed: "In a world too preoccupied with winning through intimidation and seeking to be number one, no large crowd is standing in line to buy books that call for mere meekness. But the meek shall inherit the earth, a pretty impressive corporate takeover—and done *without* intimidation! Sooner or later, . . . everyone will acknowledge that Christ's way is not only the *right* way but ultimately the *only* way to hope and joy. Every knee shall bow and every tongue shall confess that gentleness is better than brutality, that kindness is greater than coercion, that the soft voice turneth away wrath."[10]

King Benjamin described meekness with closely related words. Listen for the cost of true discipleship in this list: "submissive, meek, humble, patient, full of love, willing to submit to all things which the Lord seeth fit to inflict upon him, even as a child doth submit to his father" (Mosiah 3:19). As this scripture suggests, children often model traits of a true disciple. Through our association with little children, we can learn of him and of his ways. Most children are trusting, curious, eager to learn, instantly willing to volunteer to help—all characteristics that make the yoke of Christ easier.

Compare scenes from two Church classes. Imagine yourself leading Sharing Time in Primary. You ask the children for a volunteer to say the prayer. What happens? You ask for someone to help you during Singing Time. What happens? Arms fly up and wave enthusiastically. Eager voices plead, "Choose me! Choose me!" Now let's peek in the Gospel Doctrine class. Again, imagine you are the teacher. You ask for a volunteer to say the prayer. You ask for help in reading a scripture. What happens? Heads go down; eyes look anywhere but at you; eventually the uncomfortable silence nudges out a volunteer.

Two summers ago at Brigham Young University, I taught a young man whom I will not soon forget. The first day of class, I asked for a volunteer to offer the prayer. His hand immediately shot up. The second day, I made the same request. Again, this young man instantly raised his hand. The same thing occurred the third and fourth days. Finally, I asked him, "Why? What motivates you to volunteer every day? In all my years of teaching religion classes, I have never had a student so quick to volunteer." His reply was simple. Years ago his deacons quorum advisor taught them that every chance they had to volunteer to serve would be a tremendous blessing in their lives. He had obviously never forgotten. That day, I saw in this student a type of Christ. In premortality, the Father asked, "Whom shall I send?" There was one who did not hesitate. He reverently volunteered, "Here am I, send me" (Abraham 3:27). Christ is meek; therefore, he submits his all to the Father. "Trust in the Lord with all thine heart; and lean not unto thine own understanding. In all thy ways acknowledge him, and he shall direct thy paths" (Proverbs 3:5–6). When I lack meekness, I do not trust the Lord in what he requires of me. I lean to my own understanding and consequently add many unnecessary burdens to my load.

Consider the Savior as the greatest example of meekness in yoke-carrying. When we learn meekness from Christ, we submit our all to God and gladly serve wherever and whenever he calls. As a result, the yoke becomes easier and the burden light.

Let me review those five things that make Christ's burden light:

1. Taking his yoke prompts us to eliminate our sins and all unnecessary burdens.

2. Through covenants the Lord supports and sustains us in our responsibilities.

3. As a covenant people, we lift one another's burdens and they become light.

4. The Lord increases our strength and our ability to carry our load.

5. We learn to be meek and lowly of heart from Jesus Christ himself.

And I Will Give You Rest

In many ways, in pondering the cost of discipleship, the cost of putting on his yoke, I almost forget about the promise. There are so many powerful blessings in the cost, I realize that he has already showered me with promises. Even so, to those blessings he adds one more, the covenanted promise when we willingly take his yoke upon us and learn from him by shouldering our responsibilities.

In addition to the miracles that occur in our life by willingly taking upon us the yoke of Christ, he promises us "rest." Alma directed his son Helaman to teach his people "to never be weary of good works, but to be meek and lowly of heart; for such shall find rest to their souls" (Alma 37:34). The promise of rest is not restricted to the next life; the Lord promises us "peace in this world, and eternal life in the world to come" (D&C 59:23). President Joseph F. Smith explained: "To my mind, [rest] means entering into the knowledge and love of God, having faith in his purpose and in his plan, to such an extent that we know we are right, and that we are not hunting for something else, we are not disturbed by every wind of doctrine, or by the cunning and craftiness of men who lie in wait to deceive. . . . The man [or woman] who has reached that degree of faith in God that all doubt and fear have been cast from him, he has entered into 'God's rest.' "[11]

Rest—being rested, finding rest—will actually restore the strength and energy we need to carry our life's burdens, to continue on sustained by the power of the yoke of Christ. In other words, with the yoke of Christ and his blessing of rest, we are empowered to endure to the end.

As we come to understand what it means to bear Christ's enabling yoke, we will begin to love the cost as well as the promise. Christ has designed a kindly yoke for each of us, made to fit our particular abilities and circumstances. It will not chafe and gouge but fortify and protect. From bearing his kindly yoke, we will learn in a most powerful manner that he indeed loves us and is teaching us in every possible manner to become like him.

May we remember his yoke when next we renew our covenant to keep his commandments, take his name upon us, and always remember him. It is his yoke alone that carries the guarantee "[you] cannot fall" (Helaman 5:12) as we strive to stay true and upright in an impure and increasingly disoriented world.

NOTES

1. *Hymns of The Church of Jesus Christ of Latter-day Saints* (Salt Lake City: The Church of Jesus Christ of Latter-day Saints, 1985), no. 270.
2. Spencer H. Osborn, *Ensign*, November 1984, 76.
3. Howard W. Hunter, *Ensign*, November 1990, 18.
4. George Arthur Buttrick, *Interpreter's Bible*, 12 vols. (New York: Abingdon Press, 1951–1957), 7:391.
5. Spencer W. Kimball, *Teachings of President Spencer W. Kimball*, ed. Edward L. Kimball (Salt Lake City: Bookcraft, 1982), 236.
6. Brigham Young, *Journal of Discourses*, 26 vols. (London: Latter-day Saints' Book Depot, 1854–1886), 16:123.
7. Howard W. Hunter, *Ensign*, November 1990, 18.
8. See Jolene Edmunds Rockwood, "Eve's Role in the Creation and the Fall to Mortality," in *Women and the Power Within*, ed. Dawn Hall Anderson and Marie Cornwall (Salt Lake City: Deseret Book, 1991), 51–52. Nowhere in scripture does the term *helpmate* appear. That term suggests the Lord gave Adam a subordinate companion, as a servant, who would carry his load for him—quite a different meaning from that communicated by *helpmeet*.
9. John F. MacArthur Jr., *The Gospel According to Jesus* (Grand Rapids, Mich.: Zondervan, 1988), 112.
10. Howard W. Hunter, *That We Might Have Joy* (Salt Lake City: Deseret Book, 1994), 9.
11. Joseph F. Smith, *Gospel Doctrine*, 5th ed. (Salt Lake City: Deseret Book, 1939), 58.

The Power of Remembering

VIRGINIA H. PEARCE

I like words. Some people like seashells, some people like Beanie Babies, and some people like stamps. I like words. One of my earliest memories is of sitting on the floor in the hallway of our home while my older brother and sister were taking turns reading out of a book to me. I very clearly remember becoming aware for the first time that I could connect the words they were saying with the printed words on the page. It was a wonderful moment. The magic code had been broken! Ever since, I have felt nourished and sustained by words.

Some words' sounds are in perfect synch with their meaning, and these words are a particularly good variety to collect one by one. *Remember* for me is one of those collectible words. It's nice to say. The rhythm of the three syllables, the easy way it causes your lips to pop lightly together, its abundance of soft vowels and consonants—no harsh or abrupt ones—seem to echo and reinforce its meaning. *Remember. Remember.* Do you like it, too? Because of the poetry of its sounds and the emotions it so easily evokes, it's a favorite for lyricists:

> Try to remember the kind of September
> When life was slow and, oh, so mellow.
>
> . . . .
>
> Try to remember, and if you remember,
> Then follow, follow, follow, follow . . .[1]

Virginia H. Pearce, former first counselor in the Young Women General Presidency, received a master's degree in social work from the University of Utah. She and her husband, Dr. James R. Pearce, are the parents of six and the grandparents of twelve. She serves as the Relief Society president in her ward.

Doesn't everyone associate the word *remember* with this song?

Some words are not particularly lovely by themselves, but when they are put together, they paint a beautiful picture that enlivens our minds and emotions. These words masterfully put together by Norman Maclean in his book *A River Runs through It* draw a vivid picture of a man against the rivers of Montana casting a fishing line. You might even remember the scene from the movie and recall how ably the cinematographer translated the words into images:

"He waded into the water and began to cast again . . . a man with a wand in a river. . . .

" . . . His big right arm swung back and forth. Each circle of his arm inflated his chest. Each circle was faster and higher and longer until his arm became defiant and his chest breasted the sky. . . . The air above him was singing with loops of line that never touched the water but got bigger and bigger. . . .

" . . . He was going to let the next loop sail . . . [and his] body pivoted as if he were going to drive a golf ball three hundred yards, and his arm went high into the great arc and the tip of his wand bent like a spring, and then everything sprang and sang."[2]

Do you remember that picture? When we saw it on the screen and heard the words read aloud, the beauty of it opened our hearts and made them bigger.

Let me take you back now to 1829. A young man in his twenties went to board with the Smith family in Palmyra, New York. From the Smiths, he heard the story of the golden plates, and he determined to go to Harmony, Pennsylvania, to meet the man in question and decide for himself about the truth or falsity of his claims. Joseph Smith opened the door to Oliver Cowdery on April 5th. Two days later, Oliver began writing as Joseph Smith translated from the plates, now able to take up the work that had been abandoned when Martin Harris lost the 116 pages.

But before they began this important work that would continue until June, the Lord spoke to Oliver through Joseph Smith on the morning of April 6th. His counsel to Oliver, which became Doctrine and Covenants 6, includes this verse: "Verily, verily, I say unto you, if you desire a further witness, [Oliver,] cast your mind upon the night that you cried unto me in your heart, that you might know concerning the truth of these things. Did I not speak peace to your mind concerning the matter? What greater witness can you have than from God?" (D&C 6:22–23).

Indeed, Oliver had received a witness while still in Palmyra, but he had told no one of it, not even Joseph, until these words were spoken. Reading that he was to "cast his mind back on that night," I can almost see that beautiful line circling, springing, and singing back to a quiet sacred moment in Palymra.

Casting and remembering. Casting, then, is about more than catching fish, and remembering is more than a cozy-quilt word. In fact, I believe that *remember* is a holy word. I believe it is one that prophets have used to move us more surely to our Heavenly Father. Those amazing computer programs reveal that the word *remember* appears 136 times in the Book of Mormon. Like *verily, verily*, it becomes one of those reassuring words, a familiar rhythm in the scriptures. But unlike *verily, verily*, the word *remember* is a wake-up call.

Remembering can build faith. As with Oliver Cowdery, it is a beginning place when you begin to feel doubt. The mental act of casting our minds back—of remembering—has become a subject of great interest to me.

Some time last May or June, I sat in Sheri Dew's office at Deseret Book. Piled between us on her desk were stacks of remembrances of my mother written by friends and acquaintances. Sheri was trying to figure out a way to help the women of the Church become better acquainted with Mother. She had asked me to read the papers the previous weekend so that I could help her decide what to do with them.

After we had talked about several possibilities, she looked at me and asked, "Virginia, what would it take—what would I have to do—to get you to take on this project?" In one of those absurdly clear and direct moments—one of those times when your mouth moves and you hear the words coming out, but you feel the calmness of being directed by another power—I said to her, "Sure. I'll do it if you'll teach me how and hold my hand. Yes, I'd like to do it." I want you to know how many times in the ensuing months I had to cast my mind back on that very moment to remember its calm, decisive clarity. Remembering the clearness of my response was a lifeline that I had to keep in place.

That is a long way around to tell you how I came to begin casting, circling and circling with the line, and reeling in memories of my mother from the past. Deciding which to keep and then casting again. It was a marvelous exercise. Many of you have had the same experience writing personal histories or family biographies. Like Oliver Cowdery, I began to remember times that were of great value and importance to me in the present and for the future—times when my line went high in a wide arc, bent like a spring, and then everything "sprang and sang" for me. Often, these were events that I had either forgotten or had not fully understood until I began to remember and write.

Let me share one of those times when the line for me sprang and sang. "I was a little freckled ten-year-old, sitting at the dining-room table helping my mother get ready for her Primary leadership meeting. She was the stake leader for the Seagulls [the eleven-year-old Primary girls] and it was her job to arrive that night with posters and enrichment material that the ward Seagull teachers would use during the coming month. So we were cutting out four or five of everything. I got to choose the people for the posters, cutting them out of the array of old sewing pattern envelopes before me. Each poster began with a little girl and ended up with a mature woman. Each was attached to some kind of string. At the end of each string was the appropriate phrase: 'Thoughts become words, words become actions, actions become habits, habits become character, and [then at the end with the adult,] character is what we really are.' The first little person held a thread, the next dental floss, the next a string, the next heavy twine, and the last a piece of rope. I've never forgotten the poster or the message.

"My parents taught the gospel mostly by example, but the actual talking about gospel principles often happened in the context of mother's Church callings.

"The dining room table would sprout more and more books and papers each day as her Relief Society lesson approached. She would sometimes be studying when I came in from school—so excited about the material that she was a magnet for my attention. I shuffled through her notes and posters and I absorbed it all. Most of all, I absorbed in a deep, deep place her love of Church work. It's where I saw her mind and heart come alive with all of her immense talents focused on the lesson or event of the week.

"When I was in high school she was the ward Relief Society president. I remember that year because, unlike most of my life, I would often come home to an empty house. I knew where Mother was. Our ward stretched from 2700 East to the top of Mill Creek Canyon. There was a couple who were the caretakers at Tracy Wigwam Boy Scout Camp up the canyon. The wife had cancer of the stomach, and Mother was her Relief Society president. I was always a little deflated [and sometimes a little irritated] to come home from school to an empty house, but that feeling quickly evaporated against what I felt as I watched my mother on those days when she had been taking care of her Relief Society sister. She would come home so sad and so full of pure love—describing the terrible tumor growing larger and larger, and this woman's courage.

"The sister died that year. I never met her. Now that I think of it, I wonder why. Was she a member? Was she less active? Maybe they couldn't leave their post to attend meetings. Maybe she was quiet, and I just never noticed her at church. I don't know, but even her invisibility was a powerful testimony to me of Relief Society compassion. Had she been Mother's best friend, perhaps the lesson of gospel service wouldn't have been so sweet.

"I love Church work. Is it any wonder, with a mother like that?"³

I had forgotten about that time until I began to cast my line. Recollecting it became immensely important to me as I reflected on that experience in view of what I was doing at the moment and of what I would be doing in the future—that is, accepting callings—and thinking of what my doing so might mean to my children.

Remembering: What? So What? Now What?

I have been talking of poetry, of beautiful words, such as *remembering* and *casting*, *springing* and *singing*, but allow me to give you a much simpler, much less poetic, formula. This formula is a tool for looking back and appreciating the significance of what memory reels in.

I want you to ask just three questions. The first one is "What?" The second is "So what?" And the third is "Now what?"

First, what happened? You recall the event. In this case, the event was my mother's Church work and, more specifically, remembering in detail those posters that I helped her with—that's the "what" part. When I remembered Mother's visits to the sister with cancer, that was the "what" part. The "what" is simply the event itself.

Then comes the "So what?" The "So what?" is how the "what" attaches to gospel or eternal truth and takes on personal meaning. The "so what" is why we remember an event. We remember because there is some lasting, vital truth in the experience that affects our lives forever and always will. When I began to look back, the truths that I began to see in my mother's Church service were about working in the kingdom with all your soul and the fact that when you do that—serve with your whole soul—everything around you becomes more instead of less. Your children become more, you become more, the people you serve become more. Those are some of the eternal truths attached to what happened to me in that experience.

The third question is "Now what?" After I cast back, I can look forward by asking, What do I do now? For me, the "Now what?" in my mother's story is that I will keep serving. I will do so because to serve is so monumentally important to me. Because of that remembrance, because of that line springing and singing backward in time, I have experienced a renewed commitment in the present and the future. The formula: What? So what? Now what?

Remembering: A Tool for Building Relationships

Remembering can help build relationships. Think about someone in your life—your husband, your sister, a woman in your ward, a close friend. Picture that person and see if you can cast a line back to one specific moment in time. If you were sitting around a kitchen table, for instance, recall what you were feeling and what you were seeing. Snag the moment solidly before you reel it in for a closer look.

You may be thinking about your children. I can remember one moment in my children's life so clearly that it is like a photograph in my mind. I don't think I had a camera that day, but in my mind I have this wonderful picture from a hike to Red Pine Lake up Little Cottonwood Canyon. The children were fairly young. My husband and I had just started hiking together quite a bit, and we decided to take the family to Red Pine Lake. It's a day-long hike so we left the baby with my sister, but we took the other five children, the youngest of whom was about five. My memory is from our arrival at Red Pine Lake. In my mind is a picture of my children walking ahead of us around the path that follows the lake's edge. All of them laughing and talking together in that beautiful Utah mountain setting, the sun high overhead, the water dancing with light. As I look back, that's the "what" part. The "so what" was the incredible feeling I had, perhaps for the first time, as I realized that these children were going on ahead of us—into their future. I had a vision of what it meant to be in that family forever, a vision of happy, interdependent comradeship—all of us going forward. The "now what" part is that I will keep doing whatever I can to support that vision of their independence and their friendship with one another. Even now, when I recall that picture and think about it, the magic happens again. I'm happier being a mother, I like my children more—and don't we all need days like that?

But what if the memories aren't very happy? After all, nobody has 100 percent happy memories. As with any principle that has great power in it, Satan knows how to use this one against us. He will want us to count up and dwell on all the bad times. He'll want us to think about them, remember them, and carry them on our backs, so that we speak and act out of those instead of the good memories. I know of a woman who struggled with a wayward son, one who had done terrible things and who eventually disappeared. Her memories of him were full of grief, anxiety, and anger. After two or three years she heard from him again. He was going to be home for a brief time. No repentance had taken place. She said, "I was afraid to have him come home. I was just so afraid to have him come home." She became increasingly anxious as the day grew near. "I decided to get out his scrapbook," she said, and like me, she didn't have it completed, so it took some time to put things together. "As I sorted the pictures and pasted them onto the pages," she explained, "something changed. I began to remember all of the good things, all the positive things, all the wonderful qualities that, frankly, were still part of him." She foiled the adversary, didn't she? She foiled him by deciding for herself what she would choose to remember and what she would choose to think about. That decision changed in an unexpected, almost miraculous way what took place between mother and son in those few days that he was home.

Now what if the memories are even more painful than that? What if they are memories of abuse, memories from childhood or other times that are so hurtful that they color almost everything you do and every way you behave—and you can't forget them? With terrible abuse, a person can't ignore or cover up the hurt by simply saying, "Oh, I'll just remember the good things." It may be possible, however, that the same formula will help us work through bad memories when we find ourselves thinking about them. We confront the facts—"yes, that happened"—and then ask, "so what?" meaning, "Is there an eternal truth, even from abuse, that I have learned?" Of course there is. One truth that an abused person understands better than anyone else is how wrong it is to behave in ways that damage another person's agency and inner sense of worth. The "what now" could be that you will never, ever do that to anybody. And, more urgently, you will not allow the hurt to continue isolating you from the love of good people. Can using the formula to process a bad memory help us make a tool of that memory rather than another brick in a wall that keeps us trapped? I hope so. In cases of abuse, however, we may need professional support to help us deal with the hurtful memories. But they can be dealt with. I've seen people do so, in magnificent ways, because they are more than mere mortals. They have the help of the Holy Ghost.

Remembering: A Tool for Building Our Relationship with the Lord

Last February I was in Los Angeles with friends to attend a temple session. Getting ready that morning, I realized suddenly that the Los Angeles Temple was the very first temple I had ever been in. I was eleven years old at the time. As a member of the temple dedication committee, my father was invited to attend. Because California was within driving distance of Salt Lake, my parents thought it would be a convenient way to take a family vacation as well as giving those of us who were old enough an opportunity to attend a temple dedication. I'd never been in the Los Angeles temple since, so I was curious to know what memories it would activate after forty-three years.

With only nine people in the eight o'clock session, it was a very quiet morning. As I stood in the celestial room after the session, I had the most amazing experience. Have you ever gone back to your grade school and compared how small the halls look to how you remember them? Places that I have returned to from my childhood always feel diminished. But my return to the Los Angeles celestial room was just the opposite. It felt bigger, lighter, more magnificent than I remembered. Sitting there thinking about that, I realized that the largeness, the light and grandeur, reflected all the temple experiences I have had in the intervening forty-three years. Many subsequent experiences in temples had taught me about what really happens there—things I had no way of knowing when I was eleven. When I returned home that Monday, I needed to concentrate on writing a talk on an assigned topic, but I could not get this experience out of my mind. I kept casting back, and that line just kept circling. As it would circle and I would let it go drifting back in the flow of memory, I kept picking up and reeling in temple moments from all those years. It was as if a corridor opened up, and I could see straight down a brightly lit hallway of wonderful experiences and understandings that had come to me because of temples. That day— the one I had blocked out to prepare the talk—was my birthday, so I said to myself, "This is a birthday gift for me. I'm going to write these things down, and I will just give a talk tomorrow not on the subject they expect but on temples, because it's my birthday." So I did that, and I don't know if my talk benefited anyone else, but my faith was rekindled.

Alma used remembering to rekindle faith in a people who were drifting. More than once he told the story of his conversion—of how he came to know God. His own personal encounter with the Lord became a touchstone of his life from that day forward. He told the story to spark in the people renewed faith, and I believe he also sought to renew his own faith in his Father's mercy and long-suffering and his trust in the atoning sacrifice of Jesus Christ. You and I will have our own moments of drifting and of doubting. Can we choose to rekindle our own faith— or that of our loved ones—through remembering?

In every family there are miracles, family stories of when the Lord rescued us, times when he stretched out his arm to our families and preserved us. Tell those every so often and write them down. One sister I know purchased a wooden box made in the shape of a book, which she calls "the small plates of Christensen." In it are accounts written by family members of how the Lord has intervened in their lives. What a source of faith!

Times come for each of us when we need to go back and methodically reconstruct our faith. One friend who went to a foreign country to serve as the wife of a mission president told me that when she arrived, without any of her children, without the familiar background of places and friends or any of the things that had made her life work before, a day came when she sat down and thought, "Maybe I don't believe this stuff. What am I doing here? Maybe none of it is true." She then began to methodically reexamine her belief. "I would say to myself, 'Okay, maybe it isn't true, but don't forget the time when . . .'" She kept methodically casting that line and reeling in those experiences until there was enough inside for her to go forward again. By remembering, she was able to reweave the fabric of her faith, and with the reweaving it became stronger.

Let me tell you about a touchstone event in the life of my mother. She says, "When I was a mother with young children, we had a monthly leadership meeting on Thursday nights. On one particular Thursday I was tired. I had children to get to bed and dishes to wash. I did not want to go to the meeting. But I went.

"When the recently called stake president stood up, the first thing he said was, 'Brothers and sisters, Joseph Smith either had a vision or he didn't.' He said that he didn't know what he could say to encourage us in our efforts other than the fact that Joseph Smith either had a vision or he didn't. If he did not, then we were engaged in a tremendous hoax, but if he did, then it behooved each of us to give all the time, money, effort, and energy we could muster to promote the kingdom of God.

"That is all it took to remind me that this is the work of the Lord, and the most important thing we can do is to serve in every way we can. I have recalled this stake president's words many times, particularly when I have thought that perhaps the Church requires too much of my time and energy."[4]

How many times would the average Church member have to recall that? All the time, and Mother has done that over a lifetime. That touchstone took place in her life probably sixty years ago, and yet she continues to remember it to rekindle her faith.

Also extremely important for us to remember is the Lord's goodness to us as a people. From Exodus on, the prophets are constantly reminding the people to remember how the Lord "brought your fathers out of Egypt" (Joshua 24:6). That message becomes a refrain in the Old Testament. Lehi and then Nephi were still saying that when they were trying to bolster their family's faith (see, for example, 1 Nephi 17:24–34). Alma was still saying it when he was trying to bolster the Nephites' faith. Alma would methodically start with the Lord's rescuing Israel in Egypt and bringing them across the Red Sea. Then he would tell them about how the Lord took their fathers out of Jerusalem and rescued them. "Do ye not remember that our father, Lehi, was brought out of Jerusalem by the hand of God?" (Alma 9:9). He would then remind them of how often they had been rescued since. "Have ye forgotten so soon how many times he delivered our fathers out of the hands of their enemies?" (Alma 9:10). Even now, he would say, we are here because of the goodness of God. Something about the recital of the Lord's continuing goodness to his people, even beyond acknowledging blessings in our own individual lives, is bolstering. It makes us bigger than we were before, part of something great and good.

In the 1997 sesquicentennial celebration of the pioneers' arrival in the Salt Lake Valley, that was what we were doing. We were remembering the Lord's goodness to us as a latter-day covenant people. For our dispensation, the trek across the plains is our rescue from Egypt. That's why we talk about it so often. We need a touchstone in this dispensation to affirm our relationship, as a people, with God. Honoring our pioneer ancestors who gathered from Nauvoo, and pioneers from throughout the world who continued to gather, says, "The Lord rescues us. He upholds us; he sustains us; we rise to the occasion; we are his chosen people." Remembering the pioneers increases our faith and our sense of a higher purpose as we cast our line back, some of us to family members, some not. When we honor the pioneers, it really doesn't matter whether or not we have direct ancestors who crossed the plains. Lehi had no immediate family member that crossed the Red Sea, nor did Alma, but that touchstone point of the ancient world was magnificently important as they began to remember and then to build on the past. We can do that with our children; we can tell them pioneer stories, even if we're not from pioneer stock. We can tell them our family stories of faith. We can tell them our personal stories. Remembering their heritage of faith will build within them a reservoir of shared memories from which their line can go springing and singing back in time.

Remembering: The Power of the Writing Process

Writing is hard, just plain hard. Not being writers by profession, however, doesn't mean we are off the hook, because there is something almost magical about writing that is truly important. Somehow when we focus ourselves hard enough to find just the right word to describe an experience or idea, we discover things. I have never in my life written anything when I did not discover more than I knew at the beginning. The process of writing isn't just writing down what you already know in your head. It is a process of discovering. As you write, you will say, "I'm learning things that I didn't know I knew." I believe in the power of writing.

President Spencer W. Kimball encouraged us to write journals for this reason: "Those who keep a personal journal are more likely to keep the Lord in remembrance in their daily lives."[5] When we need to rekindle our own resolve and our own faith, and that of our family, we will have our written record to help us, to remind us of our deeper thoughts and feelings. President Kimball promises us, "If you will keep your journals and records they will indeed be a source of great inspiration to you, each other, your children, your grandchildren, and others throughout the generations."[6]

Also, in the process of writing, we discover the "so whats" and the "what nows." I've seen journals of only the "whats." That works, too. Whether you keep a daily or weekly diary of only the "whats," or you keep an every-so-often journal of "whats" with an occasional "so what" thought or two, record keeping of any sort will serve the purpose of leading you to take the next step into the "so whats" and the "what nows." Some people keep learning logs with the "what" on one side of the page ("I went to Women's Conference" and a phrase or two of what was said) and the "so what" on the other (not what the speakers said, but some of what happened to you on the inside, where you connected with eternal truth).

I believe in the power of writing, but I must confess that I have no journal. I feel a little better about that after working on my mother's book, however, and for all those of you who aren't journal keepers, let me share the reason why. My mother never kept a journal. My father has journals that go on and on and on, but my father had a secretary and a Dictaphone—my mother never did. There is not one line of a journal entry in this woman's life. My sister said to me one day, "Do you feel bad that there wasn't a journal? Do you feel like there was something missing?" I thought about her question for days, but the answer I finally came to was no. In the course of her living, in the course of her being a member of the Church, in the course of her being a family member, so much was written. I had innumerable talks she had given to draw from. I had notes from lessons, letters back and forth to children, letters to other people. In addition, there were other people's journal entries of encounters with her. In sorting through all that, the written record of my mother's life was abundant. The wonder of it to me was that all she did was just live and do the daily work of life, and it happened. The little notes you write to your children may contain your values more clearly than a self-conscious essay. The little PSs on the end of my mother's notes told us the "what" and the "so whats" and the "now whats." The talks and the lessons were there, although they weren't all in perfect written form, if that makes you feel better. They were on little scraps of paper everywhere, and it took us a while to put it all together in sequence—but she's there.

My own goal is to have twenty little vignettes written by the end of my life. My children don't have time to read journals anyway. Twenty vignettes of moments such as the hike to Red Pine Lake, because in that are all the best parts of how I feel about being a mother. It may not be the daily stuff, the dishes and laundry, car pools and music lessons and games, but that isn't the important thing for me, and I want my children to understand that. In fact, I want to understand myself, but I won't really be able to until I write it down. For example, one of my daughters wrote this vignette about my mother—Grandma—last year after she went to women's conference. It was written not because she was so disciplined that she went right home and wrote about her women's conference experiences in her journal. She went right home to babies and other trauma, picking up the pieces at home like most of us do. But—

and this is another hint—she had to speak in sacrament meeting on Mother's Day in her ward, so this is what she chose to write about. Listen for the "what," listen for the "so what," and listen for the "now what." It's all there.

"When each of the granddaughters is married, Grandma gives us a priceless treasure. It is a framed collection of portraits showing seven generations on our maternal line, back to the first woman on that line who accepted the gospel in Cambridge, England. They are: Sarah Jarold Hyder (1800–1897); her daughter, Charlotte Hyder Evans (1834–1906); her daughter Martha Elizabeth Evans Paxman (1866–1954); her daughter, Georgetta Paxman Pay (1888–1980); her daughter, Marjorie Pay Hinckley (1911–); in my case, her daughter, Virginia Hinckley Pearce (1945–); and then a portrait taken at the time of my marriage, Laura Pearce Jenkins (1969–). Along with the framed portraits are short laminated biographies of each woman, written by Grandma.

"Recently, my cousin Celia and I were at the Women's Conference in Provo. We had been to a few classes that were hopefully going to make us wonderful mothers who would rear incredibly talented, bright, and faithful children. We noted the accomplishments of the panelists and their parenting strengths. We began discussing what our children will think of us when they look back. Will they say, 'My mother was a great pianist who brought a love for music into our home'? Well, that wasn't it. Will they say, 'She was incredibly bright and a gifted teacher at home and in her profession'? or 'She was uniquely creative. Mom could make a fun experiment out of anything'? No to both of those.

"Later that evening, we went to visit my sister in Orem. She pulled out two beautiful Easter dresses she had made with smocking and ribbon embroidery, along with an exquisite blessing dress she was sewing for her new baby daughter. Celia and I looked at each other. Well, our children would definitely not look back and call us seamstresses. But we kept thinking. It would be so nice to decide on that one special thing now, so that we could focus on it while rearing our children. But we couldn't come up with anything that seemed to fit our personalities and that seemed to come quite naturally.

"I continued to think about this dilemma until one day I glanced at Grandma's gift hanging on my wall. I sat down with the little biographies and reread them carefully. Each woman had special gifts and talents, but I began to notice a strong golden thread—a thread repeated over and over as Grandma recorded the lives of those good women. Every one of them was full of faith. Every one had made and kept temple covenants.

"Suddenly I had my answer. If I could choose only one thing for my children, I would want them to develop faith in our Heavenly Father. I want my children to say that their mother was a faithful member of the Church who kept her covenants. I want to show them by example how to be faithful themselves. I want them and their children to become part of the legacy of faith that Grandma has given to me.

"When I made this startling discovery, I wrote to my sister, who was serving a mission. She wrote back enthusiastically: 'You're right, Laura. We may be duds, but we can be faithful duds!'

"We certainly can. Thanks for the gift, Grandma."[7]

That was Laura's record of some of what she heard at Women's Conference and how it affected her—some of the "whats" and then some "so whats," and after pondering, some important "now whats."

In our lives, we can tap into tremendous power by remembering—by casting our minds back to moments of faith, of love, of revelation. If we will circle with that line when we feel low and need encouragement, or even when we feel happy and are counting our blessings, if we will circle and then cast that line and let it go, it will spring and sing, and our lives will be richer for it.

NOTES

1. Tom Jones and Harvey Schmidt, "Try to Remember" (Chappell and Co., 1960); used by permission.

2. Norman Maclean, A River Runs through It and Other Stories (Chicago: University of Chicago Press, 1976), 96–98; or see A River Runs through It, directed by Robert Redford, 124 min., 1992, videocassette.

3. Virginia H. Pearce, ed., Glimpses into the Life and Heart of Marjorie Pay Hinckley (Salt Lake City: Deseret Book, 1999), 29–31.

4. Pearce, Glimpses, 6.

5. Spencer W. Kimball, President Kimball Speaks Out (Salt Lake City: Deseret Book, 1981), 59.

6. Spencer W. Kimball, Teachings of President Spencer W. Kimball, ed. Edward L. Kimball (Salt Lake City: Bookcraft, 1982), 349–50.

7. Pearce, Glimpses, 14–16.

I Want It All

EMMA LOU THAYNE

A title and suggested session abstract came by mail: "What I Have Learned from This Chapter of My Life: As a daughter of God and a Latter-day Saint, there are transitional times of great learning that continue from one phase to the next, adding rich and meaningful chapters to one's book of life."

I called. "I think you want me to talk about aging. Is that right?"

"Yes."

I thought, *Well, I can understand why that's my category*. I said, "Maybe we could change the title and the abstract a little bit?"

Since that time, how many more chapters have there been? These life chapters that keep coming and coming remind me of a Robert Browning poem:

> Grow old along with me!
> The best is yet to be.
> The last of life, for which the first was made.[1]

Curious, I checked my Browning book. He was fifty-two when he wrote that. I thought, *Robert, my friend, wait 'til you're ninety*. At any rate, my title is "I Want It All." And my abstract reads, "No matter the season, the age, the circumstance, life offers choices too succulent or imperative to resist, and impossible to ignore."

I've always said that for me, every decade has been easier—if I can

Emma Lou Thayne, poet and author of more than thirteen books, has been a part-time English teacher at the University of Utah for thirty years. She has also served as a member of the MIA General Board and the Deseret News board. With her husband of fifty years, Melvin E. Thayne, she has a family of five daughters, five sons-in-law, and nineteen grandchildren. She considers her present Church calling the best ever: a greeter in her ward.

stay upright. So far I've only had twenty-seven surgeries, plus a couple of broken bones here and there. My husband says that when he married me he should have asked for a certificate of health from my father. Actually, I'm remarkably healthy in between catastrophes. I grew up in a family of boys. I played their games, and oh, my, it was wonderful. I got the best of two worlds all the time. I'm accident prone, I suppose, but I'm also thrill prone, and when I say I want it all, I really do.

I'm nearly seventy-five, and I'm glad to be. I wouldn't go back a syllable. In every age, in every season, in every week, there are changes—chapters that keep coming. I like this wonderful old joke about changes: "There are five stages in a woman's life: to grow up, to fill out, to slim down, to hold it in, and to heck with it." Each stage in our lives is something of a challenge, especially when you just get out of the bathtub and happen to glance in the mirror. But along the way we have to learn to get along with ourselves, with life and with the changes. My mentor and friend Lowell Bennion said if something bad happened to him—and some bad things did happen along the way for this marvelous man—he refused to be defeated twice, once by circumstances and the other time by himself, by getting bitter.

So how do we recognize and capitalize on our own capacities? How do we realize the full measure of our creation. I find that the thing I have to watch out for is to maintain my own identity—not to be lost in a prepositional world where I am "the daughter of, the sister to, the mother of." Even "the friend of" and most notably "the lovely wife of." The prepositions can take over. I'll never forget when Ruth Hinckley Willis, the president of our Relief Society, invited everyone to come up to the pulpit and introduce herself by her maiden name. (Our Relief Society was so large we had to meet in the chapel.) As the women filed by that microphone and shared their maiden names, it was an introduction to a whole different group of women. It is remarkable to think that that identity is still inside us. Keep track of it. Know that you're a person, that you were born as one person, that you will die as one person. We all need to know who that person is.

Ruth also asked us that day to tell what we were best at. We had only a minute (she clocked us), and we marched on through. I watched all those dear sisters whom I had lived among for forty-one years march past and say their names and what they were best at—a docent at the zoo, a good listener, a maker of dolls—all things I didn't know. From then on, every one of us in that Relief Society, I'm sure, saw each other in a different way. We had reclaimed a part of our identity.

We need to be made whole along the way. There are always divisions in life, things that fracture us—good and not so good. At one point in life I had five little girls under ten. Now they are between thirty-seven and forty-seven and no longer under one roof. When they were, I wrote this poem called "Goodnight."

> Softly aging here
> I move from bed to bed
> and measure out my tired time
> in lengths along their languid,
> covered legs.
> Five daughters, sleeping to my touch are
> spread across the pillows
> honeyed to their hair
> and take my kiss in ways as
> different
> as their eyes and ages.
>
> Eight rolls up tighter,
> nudges me, and sighs.
> Fifteen startles wide and then
> collapses into quiet recognition,
> smiling. Seventeen hardly stirs
> but breathes against my cheek some
> gentle sound. Twelve tenses, turns,
> and pulls me down in fierce
> acknowledgment. And nineteen rolls
> away to cover up my brazen tattoo
> on her cheek.
>
> I move toward the stairs
> vulnerable, divided into fifths,
> and come to you
> to be made whole.[2]

91

My committee has now grown up. I call them my committee because of all those years that we bumped bottoms in the kitchen. We did and discussed everything together in that kitchen and elsewhere. I like the notion that they were my committee.

I think of my oldest friend, Corinne Miles. We've been best friends since first grade. She was my beautiful friend that I always stood in awe of. She had ten children while I had five, and now she has fifty-six grandchildren. We often lunch with some of our friends we went to school with. A couple of weeks ago, Corinne said that one of her grandchildren had asked to see a picture of her when she was getting married. She got out one of those pictures—remember, she was beautiful—and this little four-year-old looked at her, looked at the picture again, and said, "Grandma, do you ever miss you?" Things do change.

Years ago I asked a friend of mine who is a counselor what one quality she would want most for success in marriage or what one quality she would suggest cultivating to the people she counsels. Without a moment's hesitation, she said, "The ability to change." When you think about that, it means we have to stay flexible. I like the idea of staying flexible because it keeps you from getting bent out of shape. I think of that wonderful serenity prayer of American theologian Reinhold Neibuhr, adapted by Alcoholics Anonymous and used in many settings since: "God grant me the serenity to accept the things I cannot change, the courage to change the things I can, and the wisdom to know the difference."

It's hard. Things do change. When I was forty-six, studying for another degree, and the pages seemed foggy, I called my good friend, my doctor of eyes Richard Aldous, and said, "I've been putting all the Visine in the world in my eyes, and it just doesn't seem to do any good."

He laughed and said, "How old are you, Emma Lou?"

"Forty-six."

He said, "Come on in. You're at the age."

So now I put on glasses. I can remember when Red Skelton was master of ceremonies for the Academy Awards years ago. He picked up some glasses, put them on, and said, "It isn't that I need these, it's just that sometimes my curiosity gets the better of my vanity." Oh, that curiosity!

I've also decided that I do not do names anymore. I wrote a frail little verse for *Utah Holiday* years ago when I had just turned fifty. The title was, "A Rose Is a Rose Is a . . . ?" The middle part went something like this:

> Please say who you are, even nephew or daughter,
> Be more than a blotch on my over-blotched blotter,
> 'Cause since I've passed fifty, the best I can do,
> With a name of a something, a someplace, a who
> Is just to hope please, that something subliminal
> Fills in the blanks that max in their minimal.

So I ask myself, What's the matter with "used to"? Both getting "used to" what is now and replaying memories of what I "used to" do. I have to bring my body and my capacities and my seeing and my running and my maintaining my balance all into balance now. Right now. Yes, even my committee has to march in a new time for me. Everything has now become a little bit vicarious. I watch a granddaughter ski a mountain now on a snowboard. I watch another one on a horse that, since an accident, I am not able to ride anymore. I look at my grandchildren as they learn to water ski, and I sit on the bow and relish their being out there jumping the wake as I used to.

Now I have a class of them. My college-age grandchildren and a couple of high school ones wanted me to teach them some English— actually asked me. I was pretty appalled at what they didn't know, but we've had a lot of fun laughing about what they're learning. Six of them, all boys but one, come to our kitchen every Friday afternoon at 4:30, and we have a wonderful time. They didn't even know subjects and verbs, let alone diagramming. Can you imagine an old English teacher's heart pounding with joy as somebody says, "Teach me"—especially when they are these kids who listen with such eagerness to every word I say? Believe me, we get to talk about a lot besides grammar.

Think about Marjorie Pay Hinckley. What a remarkable woman. Talk about keeping your own identity. Not disappearing into "the lovely wife of." In the introduction to her biography, her daughter Virginia Pearce says, "Mother would be the last person in the world to suggest that others should emulate her and her life. She, too, has had her opportunity to

93

answer the questions: 'What is this book?' and 'Why publish it?' She resisted it with her own questions: 'What *is* this, anyway?' and 'Who, besides family, would *ever* want to read it?'

"And so in answer to her and to that first question, 'What?' I submit that this book is not a recipe for others to follow but just one more example of the gospel in action in the life of a fellow sojourner. And to the final question, 'Why publish it?' I respond with what I told Mother, that the gathering and the editing of the material had somehow changed me for the better, and that perhaps the book should be published with the hope that maybe, just maybe, we who read it will be inspired to try a little harder to be a little better—to become the people the Lord knows we can be. She reluctantly agreed, and we much less reluctantly offer you glimpses into the life and heart of a righteous woman."[3]

Virginia, remembering that her mother and I had been good friends, asked if I would write something for the book. I went to bed that night thinking that I really would like to write something about Marjorie Hinckley—my friend Marge. Over the years, I've learned to do what my mother said all through our growing up years: pray at night, plan in the morning. Because night is the place that things happen, that is the time when we get informed, if we listen. *If we listen.* It is so easy to pray and then not listen. Anyhow, I woke up in the morning with a poem that I didn't change a single syllable of. I called Virginia and said, "I have it."

The poem, called "Packed and Ready," begins the book. Any who have read President Hinckley's biography will remember the time when Sister Hinckley asked, "Gordon, do you want me to go with you to Asia tomorrow?" And he said, "Do we have to decide that *right now?*"[4] This poem is inspired by that incident. I've included just the first and last verses here:

> For decades, one of the "lovely wives" obscured by position,
> identity melded into his, only he and she knowing
> her invisible name tag wrought by what hears birds on the
>   morning
> or lifts prayers into dreams into unselfconscious becoming
> . . . .
> for whoever is present in the radiant presence

of this woman, this lovely wife, this forever young woman
replete in knowing exactly how,
abundant in aging, personification of radiant faith,

. . . .

She is a vivid body of good, graced by
a loving God's expectation and surely fulfillment
packed shining and ready for whatever
and when.[5]

I love her "unselfconscious becoming." She never read a how-to book.
She never read *How to Win Friends and Influence People*. She simply has
been and continues to become. I signed the poem, "With outrageous
respect and affection." To get the poem on one page, that was cut off in
the book, and I was very sorry because that's how I feel.

For all the incapacities that come with age, there is still one great big
advantage in being seventy-five: I have three-quarters of a century to
remember and draw on. I wrote another poem when I was away at my
retreat in Sun Valley, "A Walk into 75."

Yesterday on my nippy October walk
        from Sun Valley to Ketchum,
        I picked two dandelions beside the path.
        The first was still a yellow starburst
        barely poking out from under the stiff grass,
        hiding from what the seasons had to say.
        It had fooled the wind and slanted sun so well
        it had staved off turning into a puff of grey
        like the second I picked,
        round, delicate, standing upright on its stem,
        a constellation that might in any wind explode.

I put them on my desk where,
        lying on a yellow aspen leaf,
        they could stay the night.
        Next morning, the yellow dandelion was stiff,
        stem and all, shriveled to no sign of what it was,
        as if discovery of its hiding and picking it had done it in.

The grey is still intact, virtually unchanged by being picked,
>   as if it needed no nourishment except from itself, inside.
>   One edge has lost some wisps, thinned out.
>   But its basics are definable, a constellation still,
>   on a wrinkled but pliable stem.
>   It could yet go with the wind in a hundred directions,
>   drop the bounty of its intricate remainderings,
>   tiny Mary Poppins umbrellas, life to send into spring.

Maybe that's what being seventy implies,
>   what May Sarton says, "I must notice then
>   and write of all the small glories in my life,"
>   especially of those that are life enhancing,
>   as my experiences with the mystical at seventy
>   have so richly been.

>   And then let them scatter as they will.

And maybe that's where aging brings us—to needing no nourishment from outside because our years have stored it up inside.

And for me, I must notice especially those glories that are life enhancing, and let them scatter as they can. So what do we do with this life of ours? It's a jagged course. One day you'll have "the small glories," and the next day you'll have terrible tragedies. For example, I was returning home from a thirteenth annual "Girls' Trip" with my five daughters. Usually we have gone to somewhere close, like St. George for four or five days; this time we went to Ireland. In their hectic, young mother lives (we left eighteen grandchildren with their papas), I wanted them to know the mystic quiet of ten days in that emerald world. After a wonder of a time laughing and being in on each others' lives, we got off the plane at the airport to be met with the news that the son of our former bishop just two days before his eighteenth birthday had committed suicide. We were already reeling from other news: the macrocosm tragedy in Kosovo and the Colorado shooting that happened while we were gone. All macro, out of our control. But then here was this microcosm tragedy with this young boy whom everybody loved, as well as his parents trying to deal with it. I wanted to go immediately to the mortuary. The viewing was supposed to be over at 9 o'clock and it was almost 9, but I thought we could at least say hello to his family and give hugs. I went, still in my uniform, as my daughters call it—the warmups that I've worn forever to travel in, and tennis shoes—knowing there were a lot of things more important than what I was wearing.

So we went to the mortuary, thinking we could slip in. Instead, there were cars parked all around the block. When we got in, we faced rows of people, through the chapel, and clear to the back of the mortuary. Lined up against the walls were, it seemed, all of the students from East High School, each one standing there in the strangest kind of atmosphere for seventeen- and eighteen-year-olds. It was quiet. Everything was subdued. If they talked, they talked in whispers. How long has it been since you've heard an eighteen-year-old whisper? They live in a world of two thousand decibels on everything, and yet here they were, quiet. It took us two hours to get to the room where the bereaved parents were.

During that time, I looked at those young people, and I was reminded of years ago when our children were attending East High School. Five boys, returning from hiking the caves out in Delta, were speeding—130 miles per hour on an empty stretch of back road—and a tire blew out. They rolled. Three were killed on the spot, one survived for two days, and one finally lived. Some years later I wrote about watching those young people at East High trying to make sense of the tragedy. And writing helped me to come to terms with it. The poem is "The Caves." It starts:

> Why it mattered
>> as it did,
>>> probably was mostly age.
> Who dies at seventeen
>> when immortality
>>> is easy fact
>>>> as undeclared as breath?

The poem continues, and we see the incident through the eyes of the

students and Barry, the sole survivor, as well as the narrator. The sole
survivor:

> "Don't ask me. Yeah
> I was there. I saw
> it all. Sure. Wide
> awake the whole time—
> Remember?
> Geez, What a question.
> But I'll forget. They say
> you do. Real soon. So
> just quit asking. OK?"

> [The students:]
> "But Deb, nobody dies yet, not really!
>   Just think of what's ahead." "Some fun at least."
> "Remember Danny—just last Friday he
>   Sang in A Cappella half a beat too fast
> Just to see if Miss Bowman would notice."
>   "And now he's dead. He won't be sitting there
> Tomorrow." "Don't you wonder where he is?
>   I mean . . . Saturday he hiked the caves. Barry
> Says they hiked all day." "They were all alive
>   In the caves and in the car and loving it
> That fast." "And Barry, too . . . how come he lived?"
>   "I wonder if he wishes now he hadn't."
> . . . .
> "If other people really die and end
> And go somewhere or maybe don't, then I
> Could too."

>   "But no. Not me. It takes a fluke—
>   A crazy slip. I'll never really die."

The poem continues in this pattern: the students remembering
moments with the boys; Barry trying to reconstruct what happened,
the caves, the hilarity and exhilaration and fear of speeding along, the

accident, being the only one "awake," bandaging the others with socks and shirts out on a deserted back road; the students trying to comprehend something unthinkable, trying to evade it. The poem ends:

> But empty seats
> gave voice to emptiness
> and tangible excuse
> for tears,
> savored for obscuring in
> their pseudo-salt
> those spaces
> turned to caves
> too deep to look at
> in the sun.[6]

Who can look that deep, in the sunlight of being scarcely seventeen?

I watched different young people now coming in to the funeral home, this time kids who loved this young man who had deliberately taken his life. Nobody could understand—what had happened? Who knew the terrors of depression and what can happen when someone quits taking the medication?

We had been through it with one of our daughters. When she was nineteen, she had a very serious episode of manic depression and then bulimia. In 1970 nobody knew anything about these illnesses. I was on the YWMIA General Board at that time, and we were writing music for June conference. Joleen Meredith, who is a wonderful musician, was on the same committee. We had written other music together, and we said, "Let's write a hymn." At that time, the words came easily to me because my daughter was so sick. I went down into my study in the storage room and wrote the three verses of "Where Can I Turn for Peace?" It was easy to ask that question but hard to really know the answer. When I had finished the lyrics, I called Joleen on the phone. She had a feeling for these words, too; she had a long history in her family of depression, and she was suffering from agoraphobia at that very time. She sat at her piano, and as I read a line, she wrote a line. After the conference, the hymn sort of got lost until the new hymn book came out in 1985.

In between writing the hymn and attending this young man's funeral,

I had a death experience that took me to what I call the place of knowing. While I was driving on the freeway, a big piece of metal became airborne from the freeway and smashed through the windshield to hit me in the face. Luckily I was not driving. The six-pound rod hit my temple, barely missing my eye, and my cheek was blown apart. I couldn't read for seven months, couldn't put my head down. The doctors put me back together, eight fractures screwed to titanium plates, performing the surgery up through my mouth and down through my eye to prevent scarring. And I'm telling about it. I went to that place of knowing and came back with a promise that I would tell of the Light that was there. I think of the word that came to me in a poem about that sacred time when I visited the place of knowing and woke up to write a word in my journal, which I could not read back until months later. That word to describe my state of being—way beyond *bliss*, way beyond *euphoria*, way beyond any of the descriptions I might have come up with—and I love words. The word that was there was *childness*. Not *childish*, not *childlike*, but *childness*. Imagine pictures of the Savior with little children. A little child bursts onto a day with that sense of expectation and, surely, fulfillment. That is *childness*, that is the feeling, that is where I was in that place of knowing.

I wished that night at the mortuary and the next day at the funeral, that I could, by some sacred transfusion, offer that knowing to those students who were standing around with such grief. Last Sunday the A Cappella choir from East High sang in our ward. Some of the boys couldn't sing; they were filled with grief and wondering, "Where can I turn for peace?"

Who of us has not, in this last week even, had a Gethsemane? A time of tragedy, of terror, of disappointment, of distrust? Of feeling what makes us want to say, "Where can I turn for peace?" There is that resource, the ultimate source that we can draw on if we pay attention, if we have the faith of the woman with the flow of blood for twelve years, who touched only the hem of the garment of Christ and was healed. Between the woman and Christ, there was a reciprocity which he recognized when he said, "Thy faith hath made thee whole; go in peace" (Luke 8:48).

All the finding and maintaining of self, the learning and growing and becoming in my life have brought me to this finale, this life-enhancing glory. This is my testimony—what I know to be true—about where to turn with absolute trust:

> Where can I turn for peace? Where is my solace
> When other sources cease to make me whole?
> When with a wounded heart, anger, or malice,
> I draw myself apart, searching my soul?
>
> Where, when my aching grows, where, when I languish,
> Where, in my need to know, where can I run?
> Where is the quiet hand to calm my anguish?
> Who, who can understand? He, only One.
>
> He answers privately, reaches my reaching
> In my Gethsemane, Savior and Friend.
> Gentle the peace he finds for my beseeching.
> Constant he is and kind, Love without end.[7]

NOTES

1. Robert Browning, "Rabbi Ben Ezra," *Norton Anthology of English Literature*, 5th ed., 2 vols. (New York: W. W. Norton, 1987), 2104.
2. Emma Lou Thayne, *Spaces in the Sage* (Salt Lake City: Parliament Press, 1971), 6.
3. Virginia H. Pearce, ed., *Glimpses into the Life and Heart of Marjorie Pay Hinckley* (Salt Lake City: Deseret Book, 1999), xviii.
4. See Sheri L. Dew, *Go Forward with Faith: The Biography of Gordon B. Hinckley* (Salt Lake City: Deseret Book, 1996), 338.
5. Pearce, *Glimpses*, i.
6. Thayne, *Spaces in the Sage*, 52–60.
7. *Hymns of The Church of Jesus Christ of Latter-day Saints* (Salt Lake City: The Church of Jesus Christ of Latter-day Saints, 1985), no. 129; capitalization altered slightly by author.

Year of Jubilee

ELDER L. TOM PERRY

Charles Dickens started his story of A *Tale of Two Cities* with the statement that these were the best of times and the worst of times. Perhaps that is the way we must describe the world's condition today as we approach a new century and a new millennium.

Beginning a new millennium is a significant event because it happens so rarely. Many live out their lives without witnessing the beginning of a new century, and only a few are privileged to see the beginning of a new millennium. Because it is so rare, beginning a new millennium invites us to reflect upon the past, to look to the future, and to remember those things that are of greatest significance.

Remembering is vital to keeping our balance in life. In many places, the scriptures emphasize the importance of remembering. When the Lord instituted the Passover celebration, he told Moses that "this day shall be unto you for a memorial" (Exodus 12:14) and instructed the children of Israel to commemorate that great event each year so they could remember their deliverance from bondage (see vv. 26–27). Adam was instructed to keep a "book of remembrance" (Moses 6:5). Helaman named his sons Nephi and Lehi so that "when you remember your names ye may remember them; and when ye remember them ye may remember their works" (Helaman 5:6).

Anciently, the Lord also used the calendar as another way to help the children of Israel remember important spiritual truths. He taught them

Elder L. Tom Perry has been a member of the Quorum of the Twelve Apostles since 1974. A graduate of Utah State University, he holds a bachelor's degree in finance and was vice-president and treasurer of a Boston department store chain. He and his wife, Virginia Lee, who died in 1974, are the parents of three children. He is married to Barbara Dayton Perry.

of the need to show their devotion to him by designating certain holidays and festivals as times of remembrance, reflection, and rehabilitation. The most important day of remembrance was the Sabbath, the seventh day of each week. The seventh day was set aside as a day of rest and a time for spiritual refreshment. The seventh month of each year was to be a time of celebrating the harvest and a time of thanksgiving to the Lord for his blessings to them. Every seventh year was to be a Sabbatical year. The children of Israel were to sow and reap for six years, but on the seventh year they were to let the land rest. This practice was to help them remember that the land belonged to God. The seventh year was also a time of releasing debtors from their debts.

And after a period of seven sabbatical years, that is, at the end of seven times seven years, or every fifty years, there was a grand year of remembrance. This was called the year of jubilee. It was begun with a joyful shout and the sound of trumpets. Two years in a row (that is, the seventh sabbatical year and the jubilee year that followed) the land was allowed to lie fallow. Agricultural land could not be sold permanently to someone, for during the year of jubilee every piece of land that had been sold would revert back to its original owners or his heirs. Slaves were also granted their freedom as a part of the jubilee celebration. Thus, every fifty years the children of Israel had a grand opportunity to remember who it was who had brought them out of Egypt, who it was who had given them their freedom, who it was who owned the land, and who it was to whom all men would be indebted eternally.

We are ushering in a new millennium. Perhaps we should take a lesson from the Lord's dealings with ancient Israel and make this major calendar event, including the year to follow, a time of jubilee and a time of remembering for us as well. And in remembering, we can renew our commitment to those things which are of lasting value and turn away from those things which cannot bring us "peace in this world, [or] eternal life in the world to come" (D&C 59:23).

What marks these last hundred years as the best of times and the worst of times? As we look back over the twentieth century, we see many things that are remarkable and good. Sadly, we also see much that is bad, that is harmful, and that is destructive. The population on earth in the year 1900 was 1.7 billion. By the year 2000, the population will have

103

more than tripled to about 6.1 billion. More and more of our spirit brothers and sisters have come this past century to experience mortality, and more and more are having a longer time in mortality as our life expectancy continues to increase. In 1900, the average life expectancy was about forty-eight years. Today it is seventy-five years. To bring that about, great advances in medicine and the war against disease have taken place, and much suffering has been alleviated.

With population growth, more and more people have migrated from rural areas to urban centers, with 45 percent of the world's population now crowded into cities. That is a giant increase over the last fifty years, jumping a full 6 percent. Many now have the blessings of modern city life—electricity, transportation, medical help. But large cities are also havens of crime, poverty, degradation, and suffering.

Another great advance in the last hundred years has come in our ability to feed the growing population. In a single lifetime, agriculture in the United States alone has advanced more than in all the preceding millenniums of our history. Not only is an abundance of food being grown but through the miracle of modern transportation, we now enjoy fresh fruits and vegetables at every season of the year. And yet in this time of plenty, many of the underdeveloped nations are still without sufficient food. Our hearts ache for the starving children we see on our television broadcasts, their condition largely a result of political strife or government restrictions. Even though we are rapidly developing a global economy with free trade almost worldwide, we continue to have difficulty getting along one with another. War after terrible war has been the hallmark of this last century, and we have come to know what the Lord meant when he revealed to his prophets that we would live in time of war and rumors of war.

We could reflect on many trends as we remember the twentieth century. I would like to center on just three: the technological advances, the growth of the Church, and what has happened to the family.

First, let us examine the revolution and growth in technology. Never in history has there been an age of such astounding change. As we moved into the twentieth century, marvelous nineteenth-century inventions in travel and communications were becoming available for use by the general population. Morse had developed the telegraph, Marconi the radio, and Bell the telephone. Steam-powered ships crossed the Atlantic, and steam-driven engines pulled trains across the continent. The first motion picture machine had been developed, and the first internal combustion engine powered, at a slower pace, early models of the automobile.

Inspired and creative minds among our Father in Heaven's children were changing forever the way we would live. As we moved into the twentieth century, man moved off the ground and into the air, with the Wright brothers making their first flight in 1903. That remarkable invention developed so quickly that a pioneer who crossed the plains pulling a handcart lived long enough to ride in an airplane.

By 1920, we could communicate by telephone from major city to major city, and by 1929 public phone service expanded overseas. The first commercial radio stations went on the air in 1920. Transportation continued to be easier and faster. The automobile, the railroad, and the steamship all expanded their services.

The thirties, forties, and fifties continued to excite the minds of men. Silent, black-and-white motion pictures developed sound and then Technicolor. Audio grew into video with the introduction of television. Jet engines made worldwide travel possible. The first generation of computers started processing massive amounts of information. The decades of the sixties, seventies, and eighties saw unparalleled growth. With each decade, the pace seemed to accelerate. Our language acquired many new words—*digital technology, stereophonic sound, CDs, fiber optics, fax machines, cellular phones, lasers, satellite dishes, the information highway, silicon chips, electronic bandwidth, the Internet,* and hundreds of others. Computers were using integrated circuitry to organize, employ, and transmit massive amounts of information. Communication satellites circled the globe. With cellular telephones we can now carry a phone almost anywhere, and we can communicate with people all over the world.

But with all of these wonderful advances, the adversary was quick to capitalize on new technological developments and, in his diabolical way, turn them into instruments of corruption and destruction. With his usual cunning, he used technology to wage war on the morals and minds of man. Sadly, at the same time these marvelous developments were improving our lives, two terrifying world wars forced nations into developing weapons of mass destruction that could destroy mankind. Bows and arrows and spears were replaced by machine guns, laser-guided bombs, guided missiles, and nuclear weapons. The powers of devastation increased exponentially, and such tragic words as *holocaust* and *genocide* became part of our vocabulary.

Much that is destructive has also targeted the family and seriously eroded deeply held traditional values. For example, today in America, of all young people who are between the ages of sixteen and nineteen, one in twenty is idle—neither in school, the labor force, the military, nor working as homemakers. One-fourth of all adolescents now contract sexually transmitted diseases before they graduate from high school. Juvenile crime rates have grown alarmingly, with percentages still rising yearly. Gangs make many of our cities urban battlefields. The death rate has risen among teenagers, with suicide now one of the major causes of death. A large proportion of first-born children in America are born into homes where at least one of three major risk factors is present, factors that are correlated with decreased chances of success in life. These risk factors are mothers under the age of twenty, unmarried parents, or mothers who have not completed high school. Twenty-five percent of children under the age of six have both parents or their only parent in the labor force. Twenty-five percent of the children in this country live in single-parent families.

Yes, our technological advances have brought us many blessings and made our lives more comfortable than at almost any other time in the history of the world. But with technology has come a forgetfulness of those things that matter most. When will we as a nation follow the way the Lord has designed for us and live the lifestyle that he would expect of his children here in mortality? As we remember our astonishing progress, let us also remember the values that brought us that progress.

Now let us focus on the second area of change during the 1900s: the growth of the Church during this last one hundred years. On 1 January 1900, there were forty-four stakes in the Church. In the United States, only one was located outside the state of Deseret (as Brigham Young had proposed it when Utah was still a territory), and that stake was in Missouri. Two stakes were located outside the borders of the United States in Canada and Mexico. By 1900, seventy years after the Church was organized in 1830, our membership had grown to 284,000. At that time, there were twenty missions and four operating temples.

Today we have more than ten million members. That means that during the same hundred years, Church membership grew at a rate more than ten times faster than world population grew.

Just as technology dramatically changed the way we live during the last century, in the 1900s we have seen great change in the size and boundaries of the Church. When the twentieth century opened, Heber J. Grant of the Quorum of the Twelve Apostles was in Japan to dedicate the land for the preaching of the gospel and to open a mission there. The Church was continuing the international thrust, which had been present from its beginnings.

On 10 October 1901, President Lorenzo Snow died at his home in Salt Lake City at the age of eighty-seven, and President Joseph F. Smith became the president of the Church. He was the first president to travel outside the continental United States, visiting Europe, Hawaii, Canada, and Mexico. During his administration, the Sunday School introduced Churchwide parenting programs to emphasize the role and responsibility of parents in teaching their children the gospel. He promised great blessings would follow from holding "home evening" activities. Seminaries were started during his administration, and the Relief Society Magazine appeared in 1914. He passed away just eight days after the end of World War I at the age of eighty. Church membership was 455,000 in sixty-eight stakes and twenty-one missions, with still only four temples.

President Heber J. Grant was sustained and set apart as the seventh president of the Church in 1918. Change continued as the Church grew. General conference was now being broadcast over radio. The Hill Cumorah Pageant was started. The welfare program was instituted. During World War II, Latter-day Saint servicemen were scattered around the world; they returned home bringing a new dimension to the Church in understanding the world and world conditions. On 14 May 1945, President Grant died in Salt Lake City at the age of eighty-eight. The Church now had 954,000 members in 148 stakes and thirty-eight missions, and by that time, the number of operating temples had doubled—there were now eight.

George Albert Smith became the eighth president of the Church. He mobilized the great relief effort to help the Saints and others who were suffering in war-torn Europe. President Smith served until 4 April 1951, when he died at the age of eighty-one. President David O. McKay then became the ninth president of the Church. He traveled widely throughout the world as the Church expanded internationally following World War II. Under his direction additional temples were constructed.

President McKay passed away at the age of ninety-six on 18 January 1970, and President Joseph Fielding Smith became the tenth president of the Church. He presided over the first area conference of the Church, held in Manchester, England. He died on 2 July 1972 at the age of ninety-five, and President Harold B. Lee became the eleventh president of the Church. President Lee had devoted a great deal of his Church service to developing correlation programs. He introduced innovations in correlating instructional material so that husbands, wives, and children would all be studying out of the same scriptures in their Sunday School classes, priesthood meeting, and the meetings of other auxiliaries. President Lee passed away the day after Christmas in 1973 at the age of seventy-four.

President Spencer W. Kimball was set apart as the twelfth president of the Church. The Church had 3,400,000 members in 675 stakes and 113 missions, and fifteen temples were in operation. President Kimball was a dynamic leader, immediately calling for the missionary effort to be expanded throughout the world. He called for every young man to serve a full-time mission. The numbers increased almost overnight from 18,000 to nearly 30,000. The missionary force was now in place for expansion of the gospel throughout the world. President Kimball died on 5 November 1985 at the age of ninety.

President Ezra Taft Benson became the thirteenth president of the Church. The Church membership was 5,900,000, in 1,582 stakes and 188 missions. Thirty-seven temples were operating throughout the world. President Benson's great message to the world was that in both our missionary efforts and in our studies to learn the gospel, we should rely on the great power and force of the Book of Mormon. He called on every member of the Church to read and study diligently in the Book of Mormon.

President Benson passed away at the age of ninety-four on 30 May 1994, and President Howard W. Hunter was ordained and set apart as the fourteenth president of the Church. The Church had now reached 9 million in 2,008 stakes and 303 missions, and we had forty-seven temples in operation. President Hunter's great message to the Church was to expand the work being done in the holy temples. He urged every member to strive to be worthy to enter the temple. Under his direction, we saw temple ordinance work grow in leaps and bounds.

On 3 March 1995, President Hunter passed away, and President Gordon B. Hinckley was ordained and set apart as the fifteenth president of the Church. Today more than ten million Church members fill over 2,500 stakes and 330 missions. We can't really specify the total number of temples because with the energy that President Hinckley is pouring into temple building, it is difficult to keep up with the count.

Over this last one hundred years, we see that each president of the Church has made remarkable contributions to its growth. Each helped the Church to focus on particular needs as the Church steadily expanded into a worldwide organization with members in over 150 countries.

As we view the past century, it almost overwhelms the imagination to think what the Church will be in another one hundred years. Yet still, with all the growth, we, like those dealing with the Y2K problem, find ourselves procrastinating until the president of the Church has to remind us that we have a "pearl of great price," the way to eternal life, to offer our Father in Heaven's children. Church members still procrastinate their duty to find souls to whom they can teach these marvelous truths. President Hinckley recently declared that it is every member's responsibility to share the gospel with neighbors. He also called on us to take part in fellowshipping new members that they may grow in understanding, receive their temple blessings, and continue in faithful service. Oh, let us not continue to procrastinate such important duties. Let us remember the great things that have happened in this past century and recommit ourselves to become part of that work.

The final area of remembrance I would like to consider is the family and how it has changed over the last hundred years. We are a family-centered Church. The Proclamation on the Family declares: "The divine plan of happiness enables family relationships to be perpetuated beyond the grave. Sacred ordinances and covenants available in holy temples make it possible for individuals to return to the presence of God and for families to be united eternally."[1]

Chief among the organizational arrangements and foreordinations in the premortal existence was the organization of lineage and family. Church offices and positions are important, of course, but these callings in the earthly kingdom are only for a time and a season, whereas our callings and relationships associated with the family endure throughout the endless eternities. In 1919, Elder David O. McKay, then a member of the Quorum of the Twelve Apostles, said: "Latter-day Saints, the responsibility of saving this sacred institution devolves largely upon you, for you know that the family ties are eternal. They should be eternal. There is nothing temporary in the home of the Latter-day Saint. There is no element of transitoriness in the family relationship of the Latter-day Saint home. To the Latter-day Saint the home is truly the cell-unit of society; and parenthood is next to Godhood."[2]

As I look over the changes that have occurred in family life in this last hundred years, I see many things which have been lost. I remember those things with fondness and wish they were more widely present in our day.

To give you an idea of what I mean, I'd like to use an example from my wife Barbara's family. When they gather together and talk about the "good old days," here is what they refer to. They lived on a ranch two miles outside a small Wyoming town where there was little that competed to draw the family away from the home. In fact, during the cold winter days in Wyoming, there was little incentive even to leave the ranch and go to town. The family had to create their own recreation. Of course, an abundance of farm labor occupied much of their time. Milking cows night and morning was the number one distasteful activity among the boys. The family patriarch always reasoned with his sons this way—that it was character building to do something you dislike every day.

Family dinners were full of exciting conversations. Scripture study was a regular part of family life. Contests were held to see who could memorize the most scriptures. The friendly competitive spirit of various games filled the evening hours along with an abundance of family music. The father played the banjo; the mother, the piano. Added to this were a trumpet, a clarinet, a saxophone, and a trombone. Each child mastered the art of playing the piano. Schoolwork was never neglected, and it was a family tradition for each child to be the class valedictorian upon graduation from high school.

The Sabbath was faithfully observed. Meetings were regularly attended, and Church assignments fulfilled. Church activities were an extension of family life since everyone in the family participated.

The family was self-sufficient in a number of ways. They played together, worked together, made music together, had dinner together, and studied together. My own early childhood was not that much different in that the family was the center of most of our activities.

With the urbanization of America and the great advances in technology, our ability to establish a self-sufficient family life has almost been lost. What else has been lost with that change? I think one of the very most important things is the family mealtime. Early in our century it was a given that families ate all their meals together. With more mobility and more and more work being done away from the home, families began eating only breakfast and dinner together. And then eating together as a family only once a day became more and more common, and even acceptable. Now many families do not have meals together more than once a week. Convenience foods, fast foods, and eating on the run have replaced shared mealtimes in the nurturing setting of a family circle that feeds both body and soul.

With the loss of family mealtime, many have lost the invaluable family tradition of praying together. We have also lost several skills that mothers usually taught their children, such as proper table settings, appropriate table manners, and various other courtesies known simply as the social graces. The ability to properly plan, prepare, and present a meal is becoming a lost art. We have a whole generation of young mothers who do not know the basics of cooking, such as how to make gravy, apple pie, or other common foods. Eating out has replaced regular family gatherings around the dinner table. An ever growing number of children will leave home as adults without ever having the pleasure of arriving home after school to the smell of bread baking or hot cookies. Indeed, many adults these days have never had a homemade birthday cake. Traditional family recipes are no longer passed on from generation to generation, and the secrets of a grandmother's great culinary crafts are being lost. Also lost is the time spent together as parent and child in preparing and passing on special family recipes. I believe that these lifestyle changes are more serious than just a loss of traditions; they represent a weakening in the family structure and a turn from practices that bind families together and strengthen family members.

Another practice that seems to be disappearing is family work time. Our current society all too often focuses on entertainment rather than meaningful work. Children as young as two years old want to help, and that is not too soon to begin to teach them to work alongside other family members. But doing so is a challenge in our modern society. On family farms there was no choice but for all to work and contribute. Even young children had significant work assignments and responsibilities. In addition to learning how to work, another valuable result of working together was a sense of personal worth, of being an important part of the family, and of contributing to society.

Today, most families focus more on play than on work. An abundance of toys, commercial play centers, video games, recreational equipment, and so forth fills our time and is replacing the family's working together. As family work time is lost, so are many of the skills that should be part of the essential fabric of our lives. Few mothers teach their children how to sew these days. Growing a garden together and the important lessons learned from planting, caring for, and harvesting the fruits of our labors are being lost in many family units. Saturday chores have been replaced with soccer games, twirling or dance classes, Little League sports, and all sorts of activities that draw the family away from the home. Watching television has replaced families playing together. That alone is a significant loss, not to mention what the children are watching on television. Few programs these days are proper for families to watch.

High-tech entertainment even encroaches on family outings and vacations. Lost are the habits of visiting with neighbors, making music or reading aloud a story together, or joining efforts on a puzzle, or playing parlor games with other family members.

Here, as with technology, Satan has not been idle. As we reflect on this past century, we can see his successful efforts to weaken the family and disrupt the strong influence of healthy homes and loving families. Note how many times in the media mother's role in the home is blatantly minimized or even ridiculed. The homemaker's role is mocked while women who pursue careers, often in preference to loving and caring for their children, are honored and admired.

In our generation, modern conveniences make housework much easier for the woman in the home. These conveniences, such as the automatic washing machine, food processors, and microwaves, save us time and energy, but are we using that extra time wisely and well? Do we devote ourselves to those things that matter most? Or have we filled that extra time with play or other projects that do not strengthen the family as the basic unit of society? Are we encouraging women to work away from home even when there is no pressing financial need? In some cases the answer is clearly yes. We need to prayerfully reevaluate how we spend our time, establish priorities that will strengthen our families, and carefully plan for meaningful family time that will preserve those essentials of the home and family life that were so much a part of earlier generations.

And so again, as we approach the new century and the new millennium, I suggest that it is a time to remember, a time to look back over the past. Let us rejoice in the marvelous changes that we have seen in this past one hundred years. They have blessed lives, extended health and well-being, and reduced suffering and misery. But in the remembering, let us also be wise enough to identify things of value that have been lost and not ignore trends that are a cause for alarm or situations that can lead to sorrow. Remembering what has been lost as well as what has been gained will benefit us if we, in the remembering, determine to shun those things that lead us away from God and from obeying his commandments.

As part of this time of remembrance, perhaps we can do as ancient Israel did and make the year 2000 a time of rejoicing, of freedom, of turning our minds to things of eternal value. Let us make the year a year of jubilee *in our spiritual lives*. Let us make it a time of celebration, and also a time of mending and repairing that part of society which has strayed from sound principles.

Many look upon the coming new century with fear and gloom,

predicting great calamities and even a possible threat to the stability of our civilization. Let us not be caught up in that pessimistic view of things. We know that God is at the helm. We know that his work is progressing throughout the world as never before. We know that all we see is prelude and preparation for the ushering in of Christ's reign as King of kings and Lord of lords. It is a glorious time to be alive. Let us lift up our heads and be glad for the wonderful gifts we have been given. Let us always remember God's promises, his assurances that he is in charge and that "no unhallowed hand [shall] stop the work from progressing."[3]

Note the words of the Prophet Joseph, written to the Saints at a time when mounting persecution against the Church had forced him into hiding: "Shall we not go on in so great a cause? Go forward and not backward. Courage, . . . and on, on to the victory! Let your hearts rejoice, and be exceedingly glad" (D&C 128:22).

Do you find a sense of pessimism and gloom in our prophet today? No. President Gordon B. Hinckley is filled with a joyous hope for the future. He is happy, upbeat, and positive. Note these words from his first address as prophet of the Church: "May I say that I glory in the wonderful, courageous, victorious past of this great work. I marvel at the present when you and I stand as watchmen upon the towers. *I envision the future with hope, assurance, and certain faith.*"[4]

Let us follow the example of these wonderful leaders and greet the new century with hope and gladness. May we remember the past century that is now coming to a close and both rejoice in its gifts and reverse its errors. And may we enter the coming century with the hope of the gospel burning brightly within our minds and hearts. Let us be faithful and diligent as we strive to become more like our Savior and Master and prepare for his eventual coming.

NOTES

1. First Presidency and Quorum of the Twelve Apostles of The Church of Jesus Christ of Latter-day Saints, "The Family: A Proclamation to the World," *Ensign*, November 1995, 102.
2. David O. McKay, *Gospel Ideals* (Salt Lake City: Improvement Era, 1953), 485.
3. Joseph Smith, *History of The Church of Jesus Christ of Latter-day Saints*, 7 vols., 2d ed. rev., ed. B. H. Roberts (Salt Lake City: The Church of Jesus Christ of Latter-day Saints, 1932–51), 4:540.
4. Gordon B. Hinckley, *Ensign*, May 1995, 53; emphasis added.

Postcards from the Past: What Our Foremothers Wanted Us to Know

CAROL CORNWALL MADSEN

In 1880, the jubilee anniversary of the founding of the Church, a group of women decided to write their life histories and place them in a container scheduled to be opened in 1930, fifty years later, on the one hundredth anniversary of the Church. The histories all specified destinations similar to Mercy Fielding Thompson's: "It is designd for my oldest Female Decendant if such should be living at the time this will be brought forth. If no such individual can be found, I design it to be hand[ed] to the oldest Female decendant of Martha Ann Smith Harris, my sister's Daughter, Daughter of Hyrum and Mary [Fielding] Smith."[1]

What prompted these women to specify only female descendants as recipients of these priceless gifts from the past? Might they have worried that a male descendant would consider their stories trivial and insignificant? Did they want to pass on their stories to those they felt were most likely to appreciate and understand them? Women, it has been said, often hear their own voices in the voices of other women. Perhaps they felt that their voices would resonate across the generations and touch the lives of those who came after them.

Whatever the reason, we are blessed to have not only these life

Carol Cornwall Madsen, author of books and articles on early Mormon women, is a professor of history and a research professor with the Joseph Fielding Smith Institute for Latter-day Saint History at Brigham Young University. She serves as a member of the Church Public Affairs Hosting Committee. She and her husband, Gordon Madsen, are the parents of six children.

writings but many other records and diaries of our foremothers in the Church Archives. Each one opens a window in history to a time long past and to a life with all the lessons which that life reveals. Many are a legacy as yet unclaimed by a female descendant. If not lineal descendants, certainly we are the spiritual descendants of these faithful women. Their writings are part of our heritage as Latter-day Saint women.

The glimpses I will give, usually a single incident or statement from their life stories and writings, will be little more than postcards—brief messages which touch on the essence of what I believe their writers would like us, their spiritual descendants, to know about their rich, complex life experience. Told in full, their life stories are self-inscribed testaments to God's work in the latter days.

If one common characteristic links their lives one to another and threads through their writings, it is the sentiment expressed so well by Evan Stephens, a first-generation Welsh convert: "True to the faith that our parents have cherished."[2] For them, faith was not a static belief or just a hope. It was life's motive force—an energizing power that expressed itself not just in words in a testimony meeting but in every act of life. We can learn what "cherishing the faith" really means when we see the extent to which they sacrificed for it. Nancy Naomi Tracy, for instance, lived with her husband and children in a comfortable home on a thriving farm in New York, with family and friends all about them. Their future prospects were promising. Then two Mormon missionaries came to their village, and their life would never be the same. Unable to deny the truth of what they heard, the Tracys were baptized. They sold the farm, packed up their belongings, bade loved ones good-bye, and made their way with their children to gather with the Saints in Kirtland. From Kirtland, they followed the Church to Missouri, and from Missouri to Nauvoo, each move diminishing their goods and affecting their health.

Nauvoo seemed to promise permanence, a place to rebuild their fortunes and rear their family. They began their life there in a tiny log cabin but soon moved to a more substantial home. However, after losing two sons, Nancy concluded that it was "almost impossible to raise a child there." Then, they once again had to leave nearly everything behind when the Saints were forced to leave Nauvoo for the West.

Winter Quarters and the trail to Utah added to their loss—in goods, in health, and again in lives. The Salt Lake Valley beckoned as a place to start again, but it too brought loss and heartache. Moses Tracy died within a few years, leaving Nancy with several young children to raise and a fledgling farm to manage on her own. Near the end of her long and moving remembrance, Nancy admits: "My life, ever since I became a Mormon, has been made up of moving about, of persecutions, sacrifices, poverty, sickness, and death." These were her trials. But her response to them—what she wants us to know and remember about her—is in this expression that follows: "Through all my sufferings I never doubted, but felt to cling to the Gospel."[3] Her unyielding faith in the divinity of the work for which she suffered so much sustained her through it all.

For those first Mormons, faith required more than just acknowledging Christ as one's savior, doing charitable work, attending Church, or discovering the value of prayer. It meant a life like Nancy's. But in most of the diaries the overriding emotion, either implicitly or explicitly expressed, was gratitude. We marvel at their endurance, their courage, their sacrifice, but to their minds, the great wonder was that somehow they had been in the right place at the right time to hear the message of the restored gospel. They felt that through the grace of God they had been virtually plucked out of a resisting world, chosen to lay the foundation of the new gospel dispensation from among many who were called. Each one of these early converts tried to explain to incredulous relatives feelings similar to those of British convert Ellen Douglas, writing to relatives left behind in England: "I for one feel to rejoice & to praise my God that he ever sent the Elders of Israel to Eng. & that He ever gave me a heart to believe them."[4]

Though by all of its detractors' accounts the Church appeared destined to fail, Ellen Douglas and Nancy Tracy and thousands of others believed, as Nancy expressed, "We are but mortal and liable to err . . . , but this kingdom will roll on and eventually triumph over all others. . . . [W]e shall eventually become the head and not the tail. This is worth living for, and, if needs be, to die for."[5] Consecrating their lives to their faith was the supreme expression of their gratitude. This they would want us to know.

A faith as strong as theirs led naturally to an equally strong commitment to give whatever would be required to establish the kingdom. The model of commitment was Eliza R. Snow who left our generation many postcards in the counsel she gave to the women of her time. Eliza deliberated long and cautiously before committing herself to the Church. Though she was taught the gospel by the Prophet Joseph Smith himself and lived in close proximity to the Church as it settled in Kirtland near her home in Mendon, Ohio, she nonetheless took almost five years before she accepted baptism. She was educated, talented, already acknowledged as a poet of promising talent who may well have gained prominence as a writer and teacher. But when she decided to become a Mormon, she never looked back to any road not taken. The choice she made to be a Latter-day Saint governed her life, consumed her energies, utilized her talents, and deepened her natural spirituality. She explained this all-consuming commitment some time later in poetic form. One of the verses describes her response to the "clarion call":

> It touch'd my heart—I listen'd to the sound,
> Counted the cost and laid my earthly all
> Upon the alter, and with purpose fix'd
> Unalterably while the spirit of
> Elijah's God within my bosom reigns,
> Embrac'd the "Everlasting" Covenant,
> And am determin'd now to be a saint
> And number'd with the tried & faithful ones
> Whose race is measur'd by their life—whose prize
> Is everlasting, and whose happiness
> Is God's approval, and to whom 'tis more
> Than meat and drink, to do his righteous will.[6]

If there was a model of Mormon womanhood in her time, it was Eliza R. Snow. Her childlessness did not preclude her being called "The Mother of Mothers in Israel," and her spiritual nature and leadership brought her encomiums as "the high priestess of the religion of Jesus Christ and as such she ministered amongst the people."[7] One writer expressed what all Church members knew. Her "absolute devotion to the principles of the Everlasting Gospel amounted to a consecration of all her time, talents, and life itself upon the altar of her faith."[8] She indeed personified the words she spoke. A sermon Eliza gave to her sisters might well be a message to us. "I want my feelings absorbed in Zion. I don't call in question am I able? I ask the Lord to give me strength to do what is required of me, but I do not wait for the strength to come before I make the effort, we must start then he will help us. We want a determination as strong as the everlasting hills, to do the will of God."⁹ Whatever hardship that determination required (and for us it usually means inconvenience more than hardship), these women accepted it as an expression of their faith and commitment.

No one expressed this spirit of service and sacrifice more eloquently than Eliza Cheney in a letter to her family from Winter Quarters. As news of the privations and struggles of the exiled Mormons spread throughout the country, Eliza's family wrote and begged her to renounce her Mormonism and return to the security and comfort of the life she had left behind in the East. Her response is, I believe, one of the great testimonies of faith—one to ponder. "I did not embrace this work hastily," she wrote her family. "I came into it understandingly. I weighed the subject, I counted the cost, I know the consequence of every step I took. I have not been disappointed in the least. I compare this Gospel with that which the Saviour and the Apostles preached, and I see what it cost them. I was convinced that the same doctrine must be preached at the same expense. It never did cost anything to support error. Men can propagate error and be popular, but the truth always costs the best blood on earth, not excepting the Son of God, and if I set my standard so high as to aspire to be a joint heir with Jesus Christ, of course I must not shrink from drinking the bitter cup."¹⁰ What is it our hymn says? "In the midst of affliction my table is spread. With blessings unmeasured my cup runneth o'er."¹¹

In their lives, these two Elizas displayed a resourcefulness and self-reliance not always expected of women of their generation. Their level of commitment required such qualities; these early LDS women could not expect to lean on someone else for their faith, for their strength, or even for their livelihood. They could not indulge themselves in living out the popular Victorian image of men and women—the delicate vine clinging to the sturdy oak for shelter and protection. Joseph Smith had told the sisters of the Nauvoo Relief Society that they were responsible for their own salvation. "It is an honor to save yourselves," he said.[12] By necessity these women expanded that counsel to include their temporal as well as spiritual salvation as circumstances so continually demanded it of them.

Emmeline B. Wells learned early the need to be self-reliant and depend on her own resources to make her way through her long life. Deserted by her first husband and bereft of her only son in Nauvoo, she married Newel K. Whitney, only to be widowed six weeks after the birth of her second daughter in 1850. She turned to school teaching, one of the few vocations open to women. Marriage to Daniel H. Wells two years later brought her three more daughters and initially promised her a permanent home and financial security. But a family of six wives and many children, along with a failing business, pushed Emmeline, the last wife, to muster her own resources. The *Woman's Exponent*, a Mormon women's newspaper, which she edited for thirty-seven years, became her means of support, always insufficient and tenuous. It is little wonder that she was "determined to train my daughters to habits of independence so that they never need to trust blindly but understand for themselves and have sufficient energy of purpose to carry out plans for their own welfare and happiness."[13]

Still editing the newspaper at age eighty-two, when she was appointed general president of the Relief Society, she only then considered an offer made earlier by her stake president to provide a monthly stipend to relieve her of depending on the newspaper for her livelihood. At the time of his proposal, her self-reliance had been too well entrenched and she refused. "That seems such a queer proposal to me," she wrote in her diary. She could not imagine the Church paying for the "delicacies of life" and vowed that "not until I can no longer work will I do that, certainly not."[14] It is easy to understand why so many of her editorials in the *Woman's Exponent* urged women to develop their talents, acquire skills, and gain an education, not only because each individual woman deserved, indeed, was responsible to reach her highest potential, but because she needed to be armed for life's unexpected challenges. The gospel taught eternal progression and the Prophet Joseph urged the seeking of knowledge. I believe that Emmeline B. Wells would want us to know that no faithful LDS woman need stifle her will or desire to acquire knowledge or to develop skills and talents. These were—and are—qualities as essential to kingdom building as to personal growth and security.

At one time or another, many LDS women became "missionary widows" left to manage on their own for years at a time, while husbands performed missionary or other church service away from their families. Louisa Barnes Pratt suffered more than most. Obliged to manage on her own for most of her married life while her husband repeatedly served as a missionary, she became both the economic and spiritual provider for her family of four daughters. When the Saints settled in Nauvoo, Louisa and her husband, Addison, acquired a piece of property and had just begun to build a house when Addison was called on his first mission, to Tahiti. By teaching school and carefully trading goods and services, Louisa was able to hire workers to complete the house. She lovingly prepared it for the return of her husband, which she expected within two years.

He had not yet returned, however, when the awful news of the decision to abandon Nauvoo was revealed at the Church conference in November 1845. Louisa was devastated. "No pen can paint the anguish of my heart when I heard the news. It fell on my ear like the funeral knell of all departed joys. What could I do, I thought, with my little means and my helpless family, in launching out into the wilderness. I had no male relative to take charge of my affairs." But surely, she thought, Church leaders will be of help since her husband was serving the Church so far away in the Pacific Islands. But when she made her appeal, she was told, "Sister Pratt, they expect you to be smart enough to go yourself without help, and even to assist others."

Her sound business sense and ability to manage on her own had evidently given her a reputation for resourcefulness. And indeed she was up to the challenge. "The remark," she wrote, "awakened in me a spirit of self-reliance. I replied, 'Well, I will show them what I can do.' "[15] And she did. No man managed better than Louisa. Selling her property at a good price, acquiring a wagon, oxen, and supplies as well as a competent teamster, she supervised her own way west to the Great Basin, and it would be five years, not two, before she was reunited with her husband.

The need for this kind of self-reliance energized the latent abilities of many LDS women. Years later a *Woman's Exponent* editorial confirmed the value of such self-development. "Let [women] shine by the intelligence of their own minds and not by that reflected from man," the editorial began. "Let woman be qualified to stand alone if necessary [as many had and were still doing], and then if she become a wife or mother, she can act with wisdom and judgment; and if her path be in smooth and quiet places, she is none the less womanly because of her innate powers. But should her lot be cast in rough and thorny paths, how great her need of strength from within and without to endure. Remember there are many lonely walks in life, and it is necessary to be well armed with courage and fortitude."[16] That message came out of the reality of experience and is surely a relevant postcard for today's women.

Besides fortifying ourselves temporally, as our foremothers from necessity did, they would want us to seek constant spiritual nourishment, another and ultimately more profound necessity. To do so, they often met in informal gatherings to bear testimony and exercise the gifts of faith in healing and blessing. In their more formal meetings of the Retrenchment Association and Relief Society, they shared experiences with one another, gained instruction, and prayed together. These frequent sharings strengthened their spirituality. But the temple was the spiritual center of their lives, even for those who had little access to it in the early years.

The exodus from Nauvoo did not begin until most of the nearly six thousand people who ultimately received their temple blessings there had been endowed. For Sarah DeArmon Pea Rich, the endowment promised more than eternal salvation. It gave her the courage to face an unknown future when the Saints fled Nauvoo. She felt that it would have been like "walking into the jaws of death" if they had not received the spiritual power given to them in the temple.[17] For the Jolly family, the temple comprised their primary experience in Nauvoo. Sarah Jolly's husband and older sons gave all of their working hours to building the temple, which meant that Sarah was left to provide for the family. Like so many other Saints, Sarah and her family survived on little more than corn bread and water for weeks at a time. "But it was good," Sarah explained. "I don't complain. I had the privilege of going through the temple with my husband so I am paid for all of my trouble."[18]

Some Saints were privileged to receive their endowments and sealings from the Prophet Joseph himself, even before the temple was completed. Fearful that he might be thwarted from fulfilling this essential part of his mission, Joseph taught the temple ordinances to a few of his most faithful, trusted associates. Eliza R. Snow, Mary Ann Young, and Elizabeth Ann Whitney were among the number and became the first female officiators in the Nauvoo Temple when it was later completed. Elizabeth Whitney recalled that she worked in the temple every day until it was closed. "I gave myself, my time and attention to that mission." She felt that her greatest blessing, however, had come a year earlier when she had given birth to "the first child born heir to the Holy Priesthood and in the New and Everlasting Covenant in this dispensation."[19] A cherished birthright for that child, a daughter, whom the Prophet named Mary.

One of the great blessings of the temple to these first generation Mormons was the comfort it gave to those who had left loved ones behind when they accepted the gospel and gathered with the Saints. In early patriarchal blessings, these new converts frequently were promised that because they had accepted the gospel, precious family ties broken in this life could be reconnected forever. Privileged to be "saviors in the midst of their fathers and mothers," they would serve as instruments in reuniting their families as part of God's family, which is the purpose of the temple, President Howard W. Hunter has explained. Cherish the blessings of the temple, this postcard would say. Nowhere else can you receive the assurance of salvation and the perpetuation of precious relationships.

The reverence these women held for the temple made temple service the holiest of all their callings in building the kingdom. Women who were appointed as officiators were honored and respected for this service. But women were needed for many other tasks as well in kingdom building. Only an Eliza R. Snow could face rows of tired women, burdened with both child and farm cares, struggling to make a home in a new settlement, and call them to action. "Let your first business be to perform your duties at home," she admonished Zion's mothers. "But inasmuch as you are wise stewards," she added, "you will find that your capacity will increase, and you will be astonished at what you can accomplish."[20]

For many women their first—and last—business probably encompassed only home duties. But a surprising number were able to answer the call to serve the kingdom beyond their essential service to their families. Brigham Young had already informed the Saints that "everything that pertains to men [and women]—their feelings, their faith, their affections, their desires, and every act of their lives—belong [to the kingdom], that they may be ruled by it spiritually and temporally."[21] All things were thus integrated into one—all aspects of their lives had spiritual significance. And all willing hands were needed to build a temporal kingdom worthy to receive a spiritual king.

Women had learned in Kirtland and Nauvoo, when assisting to build the temples, that there was power in collective effort. And so they organized. There were committees and associations for saving grain, for managing the *Woman's Exponent*, for organizing and maintaining a hospital, for supervising the production of silk, for managing a woman's commission store, for retrenching in food and finery, and for gaining the vote. Women served in Relief Society, in Young Women and Primary presidencies for twenty, thirty, or more years, virtually a lifetime calling for some. They saved grain and then built the granaries in which to store it. They made clothing and household items and then built the stores in which to sell them. And they built their own halls for their Relief Society and other women's meetings. All they seemed to need was an invitation to move out of their homes and into the community—there seemed to be no limit to what they could do.

Isabella Horne took Eliza's counsel to heart. She didn't stop with one assignment or even two but extended her service to serving simultaneously in a number of important callings, not unlike many others of her peers. For thirty years she served as the first Salt Lake Stake Relief Society president, presiding over an area that for most of those years comprised the entire Salt Lake Valley. She also served for thirty-four years as President of the Retrenchment Association, an ad hoc group of women from throughout the city who met twice monthly on Saturday afternoons for instruction, planning, and inspiration.[22] Isabella was also treasurer of the central [general] board of the Relief Society for twenty-one years and served twelve years as a member of the Deseret Hospital Committee, which supervised the hospital founded by the Relief Society in 1882. For fifteen years she also presided over the Women's Cooperative Mercantile & Manufacturing Institute. She must have been a superlative organizer; she was also the mother of fifteen children, including three sets of twins.

Brigham Young encouraged women to attend the university and to train for the trades and professions, all with an eye to better serve the kingdom. Some happily wedded his call with their own private ambitions. Both Louisa Greene Richards, first editor of the *Woman's Exponent*, and Susa Young Gates, daughter of Brigham Young, found President Young's invitation irresistible and took classes at the university level. Both expressed a desire to make themselves "useful to the kingdom." And both served it very well. After her university training and a stint as editor of the *Exponent*, Louisa became a teacher, a writer, and member of the Primary General Board. After her training, Susa organized two departments at the Brigham Young Academy in Provo and founded the Genealogical Society. Others such as Ellis Shipp, Martha Hughes Cannon, and Romania Pratt Penrose found that their personal interests in health and medicine meshed perfectly with Brigham Young's call for women to study to become doctors. All served as important medical resources throughout the Church.

Not everyone found the path to achieving their goals as smooth as Susa Young Gates and Louisa Greene Richards, however. Like them, the teen-aged Martha Cragun Cox also longed for an education, but her road was full of rocky impediments. The new settlement of St. George, where she lived, didn't afford much opportunity for schooling, especially for girls. Martha decided to teach herself. Then one day, while walking along a St. George street, the teen-aged Martha had a remarkable epiphany. "I one day passed a group of boys who had stolen out of school to play marbles on the street," she remembered. "The poor old crone who was trying to teach them must have been glad they had played truant, for they were of the age and disposition to be most trying in school. And truly, the fact that a great many children were growing up on the streets of St. George without schooling or moral training even was truly alarming. I said to the boys mentioned, 'If I were your teacher I'd be sorry to have you out of school.' A big fellow answered, 'Oh the old woman's glad we're out.' I told the boys I was sorry to see them growing up without education. 'If you're sorry for us,' they said, 'why don't you teach us? We wouldn't stay out of school if you taught us.' 'I wish I knew enough to teach you,' I said, 'and I'd see whether you would.' One bright little fellow spoke up and said, 'I should think you'd teach us [whatever] you *do* know.' Here was a new thought. There were many children who knew less than I. Why not give the little I had, if I could not give much. The bantering words of these rude boys on the street aroused a feeling hard to resist, and I resolved that henceforth as far as it lay in my power to do so I would spread light into darkened chambers. I decided to become a teacher."[23]

From a pack of boys playing hooky, Martha learned the truth in the familiar lines: "I am only one, But still I am one. I cannot do everything, But still I can do something."[24] Like Eliza, Martha didn't wait for the strength—or the education—to begin her life's work. She began, and the education followed. "Why not give the little you have" is Martha's postcard to us.

As the blessings of the gospel were available to all, all were expected to serve. "It is the duty of each one of us to be a holy woman," Eliza R. Snow observed. "We shall have elevated aims, if we are holy women. We shall feel that we are called to perform important duties. No one is exempt from them. There is no sister so isolated, and her sphere so narrow, but what she can do a great deal towards establishing the kingdom of God upon the earth."[25] Surely a message for our time.

Lest we think that a uniform adherence to gospel principles and church practices will diminish individuality, let us look under the ubiquitous sunbonnets and observe the wide range of these early Saints' personalities. Any stereotypical image of the pioneer woman is a false reading of our fascinating pioneer foremothers. As much as anything else about them, they would want us to know that they were distinct individuals who brought spunk and humor as well as earnestness and sobriety to the Mormon community. Even the sedate Eliza R. Snow could easily turn clever and lighthearted among friends. In 1848, for instance, she wrote to Leonora Taylor (John's wife) a thank-you poem for a "medicinal" bundle of tea hidden in a bouquet from Leonora's garden:

With flow'rs from your garden, my toilet is grac'd.
Their unstudied selection does honor to taste.
They're a compliment too, to your patience & toil
And their growth is a proof of our newly tried soil.
. . . .
Dear Lady, I'm thankful indeed for the flow'rs.
They afford me *amusement* in my lonely hours;
But for *med'cine*, there's nothing more welcome to me,
Of the "vain things of earth," than *the bundle of Tea*.

. . . .
You were sly as a smuggler: I chanc'd to espy
Something hidden, just when you were bidding "good bye";
I might have expos'd it with thanks, but you know,
Good manners prevented.

Eliza R. Snow[26]

At that time eschewing tea and coffee had not yet become a hallmark of "the peculiar people." Scarcely twenty years later Eliza wrote the famous children's song, "In Our Lovely Deseret," with its equally famous line, "Tea and coffee and tobacco they despise."[27] Between these two women in 1848, however, a little shared tea denoted something other than a taste of "forbidden fruit." At that time tea evoked memories of shared tea times and a taste of the hidden treasures of friendship.

Louisa Barnes Pratt was another Mormon original. After her trauma in Nauvoo over leaving the home she had worked so hard to complete in her husband's absence and rallying to manage the trek west without him, she began to be more confident and comfortable as an independent woman and head of her family. While on the trail in Iowa, she decided to pursue an interest in horseback riding, being fortunate enough to own a horse. "I found great pleasure in riding horseback," she noted in her journal. "By that means I could render some assistance in driving the stock. There was, in the company, a fellow by the name of Ephraim Hanks. He had charge of the loose cattle, was a dashing rider, gave me some lessons in that art till I became expert. He assumed the title of Captain, gave to me that of Commodore."

Later she wrote about how the group with whom she was traveling set up a company organization. Louisa was not especially happy with the proceedings. "We soon camped near a creek," she wrote. "The brethren met by themselves, organized, and chose a president without the aid or counsel of the women. This evening the sisters proposed to organize themselves into a distinct body, to prove to the men that we are competent to govern ourselves. If they set the example of separate interests, we must help carry it out. . . . Several resolutions were adopted: 1st. Resolved: that when the brethren call on us to attend prayers, get engaged in conversation and forget what they called us for, that the sisters retire to some convenient place, pray by themselves and go about their business. 2nd. If the men wish to hold control over women, let them be on the alert. We believe in equal rights."[27] Her postcard message might read: Sisters, cooperate but don't kowtow.

Not only did women not act alike, they didn't always think alike, even on issues that affected them directly. For example, Eliza R. Snow and Emmeline B. Wells, two honored leaders of LDS women, held very different views on the women's rights movement of their time. Eliza was ever the stalwart Latter-day Saint, zealous in her commitment to the kingdom and grateful to be able to turn her back on "Babylon." She was repelled by "strong-minded" women "battling for their rights" and rationalized that Mormon women were given the vote (in 1870) only because God had put it into the hearts of the brethren to give them that privilege. Only through obedience to gospel principles, she preached, could equality be gained. She was insular to the point of removing herself from any close relationship with non-Mormons.

Emmeline B. Wells was also zealous in the cause of the gospel and devoted her adult life to defending gospel principles and serving the women of the Church. She, however, admired the "strong-minded" women who were willing to put their reputations at stake in order to advance women's position in all walks of life. She felt that she was herself a "strong-minded" woman, partly from necessity but also from choice. Representing LDS women in the national suffrage conventions and councils of women, she crossed the barriers between LDS and non-Mormon women. She was a skillful bridge builder who brought respect and recognition to her Mormon sisters where before, in Utah and elsewhere, there had been only denigration and ridicule.

Despite such major ideological differences, these two strong women worked side by side in the Relief Society and in many other undertakings in the Mormon community. Both were exemplars of faith and commitment, Eliza strengthening Mormon women from within the Church, and Emmeline from without. Both were zealous advocates for the Church and both were loved and respected by the Saints.

By accepting differences, like those exemplified by these two influential leaders, our foremothers were able to build a strong sense of community and sisterhood. Zina D. H. Young, a beloved midwife and Relief Society worker, carried into her administration as general president of the Relief Society the strong appeal for unity that had begun with Emma and Joseph Smith in Nauvoo. Among the thousands of women she addressed and visited in 1889, her first year as general president, she heard English, British, Welsh, Scottish, and Scandinavian languages and dialects. She saw women, single and married, in homespun as well as in silk. But she urged this diverse group of women of varied nationalities, economic and religious backgrounds, and family relationships to be "one grand phalanx and stand for the right."[28] Her appeal echoed that of her predecessor Eliza R. Snow who had earlier recognized the widely diverse religious backgrounds of that first generation of convert Saints: "We have not been taught alike," she told them, but "we want to raise a generation that will know and see alike."[29] Whatever religious differences existed in their pre-Mormon life, there was to be a unity of faith in the restored gospel.

The *Woman's Exponent*, begun in 1872, created a connecting network, a means whereby the women of Snowflake, Arizona, could relate to the women of Franklin, Idaho, as they shared their experiences and thoughts on its pages. The visits of Eliza and her co-workers to all the Mormon settlements connected even the most remote with those at the center in Salt Lake City. And within the individual towns, clusters of women found every kind of reason to come together. For the seventieth birthday of Mary Ann Maughan of Cache Valley, nearly seventy of her friends celebrated by performing temple ordinances for her deceased relatives. In Salt Lake City, a group of friends met annually on the anniversary of the death of one of their group, writing poems and tributes for the occasion and often socializing until late evening. Visiting, a common nineteenth-century female pastime, kept friends and families close and communities tight-knit and cohesive.

Years of shared service in the women's organizations cemented these friendships and created enduring bonds of sisterhood. Emmeline B. Wells spent her life in women's activities, more than thirty-five years as a general officer of the Relief Society. In her later years she reminisced about that time: "Sometimes I feel like 'the last leaf upon the tree,' when I think that scarcely any of the friends of my generation are left to recall with me the days that are gone." She continued: "The beloved friends with whom so many years I worked in the Relief Society: Sister Eliza, Aunt Zina, Sister Kimball, Aunt Bathsheba, Sister Richards, Sister Horne, and oh, so many others whose names I now recall, and whom I loved as much as if bound by kindred ties, closer, perhaps, because our faith and work were so in tune with our every day life."[30]

If such feelings of kinship, which bound these women together in love and sisterhood, brought unity and loyalty to the Mormon community, they also impressed many of the travelers who visited Utah. An 1869 visitor was unapologetic in voicing her wonder at this female bonding. "There is one feature among the Mormons that I will mention and do admire," she wrote in her travel reminiscence. "That is the true friendship that exists among them. It is not hypocrisy; it is genuine affection, no motive but honesty of purpose. See their women, how they treat one another. It is this devotion and real affection they possess which makes them in the eyes of strangers so beautiful. I have no motives of stating any facts but the honest expressions of one that cannot be false to the truth."[31] As a concluding postcard from the past, those brief words reveal the source of spiritual power that energized and inspired our Latter-day Saint progenitors. As their own words attest, it is within the matrix of shared experience and commitment that one can find the key to the unity and genuine sisterhood observed by that traveler.

Despite the brevity of these postcards from the past, they are conduits into the minds and spirits and experiences of a generation of Saints who accepted the tremendous responsibility of laying the foundation of God's kingdom on earth. If we could summarize the essence of the messages they have left us in their journals, letters, and reminiscences, I believe they would want us to know, first, the joy of their conversion and the strength of their testimonies. They would then want us to know the depth of their commitment to the gospel and the breadth of their service to the Church. Next, they would hope that we could see, and perhaps experience ourselves, the power of sisterhood as they knew it. But above all, I believe they would want us to know from their lives something about the endurance of their faith.

A few years ago, William Raspberry, a noted Washington journalist, addressed the graduating class of the University of Virginia. In his remarks he apologized to the young graduates for the failure of his generation to give them the things they really needed. "We have been so concerned to give you the things we never had," he said, "that we have neglected to give you what we did have."[32] Few of these pioneer women had it in their power to leave much of material value to their descendants, but, oh, what a legacy their lives and written words are for us. As Alma wrote of the value of the records left to his generation, I believe that the records left by our foremothers can enlarge our memories and bring us through their testimonies to the knowledge of their God unto the salvation of our souls (see Alma 37:8). Their lives admonish, indeed challenge, us to be true to the faith they cherished. May we do as well by our descendants.

NOTES

1. Mercy Fielding Thompson Papers, Daughters of Utah Pioneers Collection, LDS Church Archives, Salt Lake City, Utah.
2. *Hymns of The Church of Jesus Christ of Latter-day Saints* (Salt Lake City: The Church of Jesus Christ of Latter-day Saints, 1985), no. 254.
3. From "Life History of Nancy Naomi Alexander Tracy Written by Herself," typescript copy in Special Collections, Harold B. Lee Library, Brigham Young University, Provo, Utah, 51; see also "Life and Travels of Nancy M. Tracy," *Woman's Exponent* 38 (August 1909): 64.
4. Ellen Douglas to Fathers, & Mothers & Sisters & Brothers, Nauvoo, 14 April 1844; copy in LDS Church Archives.
5. Tracy, "Life History," 62.
6. "Saturday Evening Thoughts," from her Nauvoo Journal and Notebook, as quoted in Maureen U. Beecher, ed., *Personal Writings of Eliza Roxcy Snow* (Salt Lake City: University of Utah Press, 1995), 62.
7. See "The Mother of Mothers in Israel," *Relief Society Magazine* 3 (April 1916): 188.
8. Emmeline B. Wells, "L.D.S. Women of the Past, Personal Impressions," *Woman's Exponent* 36 (February 1908): 50.

9. Annual Meeting of the Nineteenth Ward Relief Society, 18 August 1875, *Woman's Exponent* 4 (1 October 1875): 67.

10. Eliza Cheney to Parents, Brothers & Sisters, January 1848, LDS Church Archives.

11. *Hymns*, no. 108.

12. Minutes of the Female Relief Society of Nauvoo, 28 April 1842, LDS Church Archives.

13. Emmeline B. Wells Diary, 7 January 1878, Special Collections, Harold B. Lee Library, Brigham Young University, Provo, Utah.

14. Emmeline B. Wells Diary, 30 March 1892.

15. Journal of Louisa Barnes Pratt, in Kate B. Carter, comp., *Heart Throbs of the West*, 13 vols. (Salt Lake City: Daughters of Utah Pioneers, 1947), 8:235.

16. Editorial, *Woman's Exponent* 5 (1 July 1876), 20.

17. Reminiscences of Sarah DeArmon Pea Rich (1885–93), typescript in possession of author.

18. Sarah Pippin Jolly, "Reminiscences," as quoted in Carol Cornwall Madsen, *In Their Own Words: Women and the Story of Nauvoo* (Salt Lake City: Deseret Book, 1994), 23.

19. Elizabeth Ann Whitney, "A Leaf from an Autobiography," *Woman's Exponent* 7 (15 February 1879): 191.

20. Eliza R. Snow, "An Address," *Woman's Exponent* 2 (15 September 1873): 63.

21. Brigham Young, *Journal of Discourses*, 26 vols. (London: Latter-day Saints' Book Depot, 1854–86), 10:329.

22. For details about this association, see "Retrenchment Association," *Encyclopedia of Mormonism*, 4 vols. (New York: Macmillan, 1992), 3:1223–25.

23. Biographical Record of Martha Cragun Cox, 1852–1932, typescript copy, LDS Church Archives, 119–20; punctuation standardized.

24. Edward Everett Hale, in John Bartlett, comp., *Familiar Quotations*, 15th ed. (Boston: Little, Brown and Co., 1980), 590.

25. Address, 14 August 1873, *Millennial Star* 36 (13 January 1874): 18–19.

26. John Taylor Collection, LDS Church Archives.

27. See *Hymns*, no. 307.

28. Journal of Louisa Barnes Pratt, in Carter, *Heart Throbs of the West*, 8:237–38.

29. "First General Conference of the Relief Society," *Woman's Exponent* 17 (15 April 1889): 172–73.

30. Smithfield Ward Relief Society Minutes, 1868–1891, 7 July 1879, LDS Church Archives.

31. "Mothers in Israel," *Relief Society Magazine* 3 (February 1916): 68.

32. Mrs. R. Frazier, *Reminiscences of Travel from 1855 to 1867 by a Lady* (San Francisco: n.p., 1869), 152.

33. Commencement Address, University of Virginia, May 1995; copy in possession of author.

Women's Voices:
Teamwork at Home and at Church

MARGARET D. NADAULD
AND STEPHEN D. NADAULD

Councils are the way of the Lord. We follow the pattern of heaven when we hold council together at home and at church. We are taught about the Council in Heaven, and we know of the Council of the Twelve Apostles. Other councils, which may affect us more personally because we participate in them, may include stake councils, ward councils, and family councils.

Elder M. Russell Ballard of the Quorum of the Twelve Apostles has given two conference addresses on the subject and has followed those teachings with a book entitled *Counseling with Our Councils*. His book reflects our Church leaders' concern that we recognize the importance of councils, at home and at church, and that we learn how to implement them. We want to focus, first, on the importance of women's voices at home and in councils, and second, on how best to make that feminine voice heard, in councils both at home and in other settings.

The voices of women have been heard through the ages as they've counseled with families and in Church. And they've made a difference.

Margaret D. Nadauld and Stephen D. Nadauld are the parents of seven sons and the grandparents of five. Margaret serves as the Young Women General President and is a member of the board of trustees of Brigham Young University. She has taught high school English and served as a member of the Relief Society General Board. Stephen, a former member of the Second Quorum of the Seventy, is a professor in the Marriott School of Management at Brigham Young University. He is an author, speaker, business consultant, and former president of Weber State University.

In the book of Moses, we learn that "many days" after the Fall (Moses 5:6), an angel appeared to Adam to teach him about the Savior and his atoning sacrifice. Adam spoke with gratitude of the future that a Redeemer had made possible for him. "Because of my transgression my eyes are opened, and in this life I shall have joy, and again in the flesh I shall see God" (Moses 5:10). Adam recognized that he would have joy in this life by living the commandments and that he would have joy in the hereafter through the atoning sacrifice of the Savior. In the next verse we learn that "Eve, his wife, heard all these things and was glad." Eve felt joy, as well, but note how her observation differs from Adam's: "Were it not for our transgression we never should have had seed, and never should have known good and evil, and the joy of our redemption, and the eternal life which God giveth unto all the obedient" (Moses 5:11). Eve processed information differently from Adam and came to some very interesting, different conclusions. Each understood separate parts of the plan of redemption. Together, they understood the whole, each adding individual threads to enrich the fabric of their understanding.

Consider Sariah, the mother of Nephi, who worried so much about her sons when they returned to Jerusalem for the brass plates. In one of those husband-and-wife council sessions, she expressed her honest concerns to Lehi, her husband. In fact, we are told Sariah, her anxiety for her children paramount in her heart, "complained against" Lehi (1 Nephi 5:3). Disagreements often occur in families, and effective family councils depend on open communication of feelings. The safe return of her sons proved a powerful witness, and Sariah affirmed her rekindled faith to her family, saying, "Now I know of a surety that the Lord hath commanded my husband to flee into the wilderness; yea, and I also know of a surety that the Lord hath protected my sons, and delivered them out of the hands of Laban, and given them power whereby they could accomplish the thing which the Lord hath commanded them" (1 Nephi 5:8). Councils that begin in disagreement can work through to deep loyalty and commitment as council members take part in resolving problems together.

In family leadership, a mother's contribution is invaluable. Children naturally sense the special insight, intuition, and faith of their mothers. May we share two examples from our own experience.

STEPHEN: One day I was about to leave for work when Margaret said, "You know, there aren't as many eggs in this carton as there were last night, and it's not because we've cooked them." She then added, "I'm a little nervous. I think you'd better go down to the junior high and see if our son might know anything about those unaccounted-for eggs." I had no idea why that would be necessary, but I drove to the junior high. I found our son, got him out of class, and said, "Son, your mother wonders if you know anything about some missing eggs." He turned a little pale and answered, "They're in my locker? How did you know?" Sensing an opportunity, I wanted to take full advantage of, I said, "Well, by now you should realize, wherever you are or whatever you do, your mother knows." I retrieved the eggs and saved a possibly embarrassing situation for the family.

The other example is a little more tender. I was sitting at home one night about ten o'clock contentedly reading the newspaper when the telephone rang. It was our missionary son calling from a foreign country. The first thing he said was, "Dad, I've received permission from the mission president to call you and tell you that everything is all right." I said, "Son, a moment ago I was sitting here, just reading the newspaper assuming that everything was all right, and now when you call and tell me that everything is all right, I'm suddenly very anxious." He told me that he had been involved in a serious incident with some dissidents in that country. "I knew Mom would be worried," he said. "I knew she would know that something wasn't right with me. And so I asked permission of the mission president to call and tell her that everything turned out all right."

These are just two personal examples that illustrate that mothers have a special spiritual insight and sensitivity, which children know about and rely on.

MARGARET: Children learn about this insight in family council situations, surely, but there are other times as well. For example, they learn about it in discussions as the family sits together at mealtime every day, or talking together while riding in the car, or whenever family members are just chatting, working, or playing together and something comes up so that the mother is able to express her faith to her children.

Book of Mormon mothers instilled great courage in their sons. The two thousand stripling warriors said of their mothers' unshakable faith, "We do not doubt our mothers knew it" (Alma 56:48).

The women of the early restored Church in Nauvoo counseled together to find ways to bless families and individuals. From this counseling together was born the Relief Society, the greatest, oldest, and largest women's organization on the face of the earth.

I think of Ruth, who spoke loving words in counseling with her mother-in-law, Naomi, when they were at a crossroads in their lives: "Intreat me not to leave thee, or to return from following after thee: for whither thou goest, I will go; and where thou lodgest, I will lodge: thy people shall be my people, and thy God my God" (Ruth 1:16).

Few of these councils have been recorded in the scriptures, but the final history of the world has yet to be written. Informal councils are held today between mothers and daughters and sisters and friends to find ways to bless families and strengthen one another. I like to call them kitchen councils.

STEPHEN: Our family spends time in Manti, often in the kitchen of the wonderful, old, restored family home. Margaret's mother gathers the family around her, her daughters and daughters-in-law, and now the granddaughters and wives of the married grandsons. There is no longer any room for men in the kitchen. These gifted, insightful women counsel with one another and talk about the truly important issues of life. We see the effects of those informal kitchen councils almost every day.

Elder Ballard reminds us that through the ages, women have contributed "the power of faith, through which 'the worlds were framed by the word of God' (Hebrews 11:3). They can bring the power of purity, through which 'we may be purified even as [the Lord] is pure' (Moroni 7:48). And they generally possess the power of love, that which the Apostle Paul called charity, the greatest of all the godly virtues (see 1 Corinthians 13:13)." Because women possess the power of faith, of purity, and of charity, they have much to contribute in councils. Elder Ballard continues, "It is a short-sighted priesthood leader who does not see the value of calling upon the sisters to share the understanding and inspiration they possess."[1]

MARGARET: An interesting exercise illustrates the importance of women's voices. In one version of this exercise, called the earthquake game, participants imagined they were trapped in a basement after an earthquake and would not be rescued for forty-eight hours. Fifteen items in their environment needed attention: a bleeding colleague, an egg-salad sandwich, a pitcher of water, a communication device, and eleven other similarly diverse items. The earthquake victims were to prioritize these things for survival.

The participants in the exercise were medical doctors who were in management training. To round out the numbers, the facilitator invited two female secretaries to participate. The participants filled out their forms, prioritizing the items from one to fifteen. Then the facilitator divided the group into teams of four. On one team were four doctors, all male. On another team were three male doctors and a female doctor. The last team had two male doctors and both female secretaries. The teams were to discuss their individual rankings and arrive at a team ranking of what they thought was most to the least important. Then the facilitator had them compare their answers with a survival expert's and score them, both as individuals and as teams.

What would you predict would be the outcome? Would you think, for example, that the team scores were higher than individual scores? The answer is yes. Almost without exception, judging by the survival expert's priority list, a team can do a better job of ranking these important items than can an individual. Keeping in mind that these were doctors, trained and experienced at handling emergency situations, which team do you think was the best—the all-male group of doctors, the team of three male doctors plus one female doctor, or the team of two male doctors and two female secretaries? Many of the group were surprised when it turned out to be the two-doctor, two-secretary team. What do secretaries know about emergencies?

It turns out that, even if she is inexperienced, a woman's perspective, her voice, and the way she processes things differently from men makes a significant difference. Add women's processing together with men's processing and the result is a superior outcome. Women's voices are important. Women's perspectives are necessary.

Why do councils have greater potential for good than one person acting alone? Because point of view matters. What you see depends on where you're coming from. And that's why councils are so useful. One person brings one point of view to the council; another person brings another point of view. When all perspectives are discussed in a council, the group can make a better decision.

STEPHEN: As a professor in the Marriott School of Management, I have had a special interest in this topic. It's incredibly valuable to have more than one processor, particularly in today's very complex society. One person cannot process all of the input. Corporations, universities, all run better if they have multiple processors and if the multiple processors have different ways of processing. It's just amazing how much better decisions are made in secular organizations that involve everyone in the process.

One of my vice-presidents at Weber State was a woman, and her voice in our decision making was invaluable. I became a great convert to the notion of diversity, especially in processing complicated issues and decisions. Women's voices are extraordinarily important.

Team processing always produces a better understanding of the problem, better formulation of recommendations, and better implementation. Good team processing and women's voices being involved produces superior performance, whether in the Church, a secular organization, or the family. So in any organization, especially in Church councils and in the home, women should help their husbands and their children process this complex environment that we live in. We'll all be much better off.

Now let us consider how women and men contribute in a council setting. First, you *contribute by listening*. Sometimes in council situations, it's easy to get so focused on your own agenda that you have difficulty hearing the other things that are going on around you. Don't let your own agenda drive you so hard that you disrupt the communication. In the process of giving your input, don't neglect listening to others.

Elder Rulon G. Craven served for several years as the secretary to the Quorum of the Twelve Apostles. He observed about their council meetings: "I have noticed that each of the Brethren is not so much concerned with expressing his own point of view as he is with listening to the point of view of others and striving to create a proper climate in the Council meetings. They are sensitive to one another's thoughts and rarely interrupt one another during their conversations. During discussion they do not push their own ideas but try to determine from the discussion what would be best for the kingdom."[2]

Second, you can contribute more as you *develop a cooperative style*. Each council member must be a considerate communicator who feels responsible to the whole group. Have you ever been in a council in which someone is a complainer? Or too verbose, or strident? Or too emotional, or stubborn and inflexible? These qualities are not helpful to a council. A voice of reason is what helps a council.

Third, each participant needs to *be succinct*.

MARGARET: Being succinct is not my natural inclination. I just love to talk to my sister because when she tells me about something, she tells me how it looked, how it felt, how it smelled, how it fit in with this and that and the other. I get every detail from her.

STEPHEN: That's way too much for me.

MARGARET: On the other hand, when I ask my husband, "How did it go today?" he answers, "Fine." I ask, "Well, tell me about it." He answers, "Oh, it was good." And that's that. From one extreme to the other. Succinct lies somewhere between my sister and my husband. In a council we need to learn to say enough but not too much—to be succinct.

STEPHEN: Bishops, stake presidents, and husbands will be grateful to hear just the theme, not the whole symphony.

MARGARET: In my new calling, I have attended various council meetings with general officers and general authorities of the Church. In the beginning I wanted to sit very quietly and just listen and learn. I did not want to say anything.

But the Brethren soon encouraged me, "Sister Nadauld, what is your opinion on this matter?" I'll never forget that moment. I had been Young Women General President three days and was in a meeting with nine women and a vast roomful of general authorities. As all eyes turned toward me, I did some quick thinking. And from then on, I came expecting to contribute.

A woman friend taught me how important it is to come to a council setting (if you're coming with a problem) and say, "We have three concerns in the Young Women. They are one, two, and three. We would like to counsel with you about those three concerns. We do have some recommendations, but we would like to hear what the council would recommend as a solution to our concerns." Make the problem very clear. Don't just dump the problems on the council but offer some possible recommendations and then be willing to accept suggestions.

On another occasion, Elder Dallin H. Oaks, who was presiding at a council meeting, said, "Now I'm going to go around the table and ask each one of you to express your point of view to help us understand this situation better." There was no decision that day. We were invited to take the ideas home, think about them, write some new ones, consult with our counselors and boards, and come back to the next council session to discuss the matter further.

Fourth, *be clear about who you represent*—both yourself with your own wealth of personal experience and then the organization or group you represent. For example, last week I was representing the Young Women. In the middle of our discussion I said, "I just have to say this as the mother of teenagers who are still at home" and then explained something that made a bit of a difference in the direction we were going. The insight was valuable in that circumstance, I believe. So remember, when you come to a council—whether you're single, married, married with children, or whatever the circumstances—you represent two points of view: the organization's and your own. Both can contribute to good decision making.

Fifth, *contribute with kindness and with dignity*. I've been greatly touched by the remarkable kindness of the Brethren I've served closely with and whom I've admired, followed, and loved my whole life. Their voices are so kind. They spoke with much more gentleness, sensitivity, and love unfeigned than I did in the beginning of my service. They are wonderful servants of our Father in Heaven, and they speak with great refinement, always. I have learned a great lesson from them about the expression we have in our voice. I've learned that my opinions should be voiced, but that if they are not always in complete agreement, I should express my point of view with great care, with the greatest kindness, the greatest refinement I am capable of. I would recommend that we use that kindness in our homes as well as in more formal settings. Sometimes we are so used to the people that we live around that we don't talk to them as kindly as we should.

Once when Steve was serving as a general authority, he rushed home to gather his materials and pack his bags to go for the weekend to a stake conference. With seven boys, there was a lot of hubbub at home, and I have to admit that I tend to be a little dramatic—I raised my voice to communicate a point. He said, "We have to stop. I have to tell you all that unless I can feel the Spirit of the Lord when I come home, I can't go do this work that I'm assigned to do. Please, let's have the Spirit of the Lord in our home all the time in the way we speak and in what we say." It was a great lesson to us all.

STEPHEN: My life has been blessed endlessly by this wonderful, wonderful woman. She has sustained me emotionally as well as in all other ways, never criticizing, never withdrawing support of decisions that we make, always being a voice of reason. From her I have learned about the spiritual nature of women, about your special gifts of insight and inspiration. I have learned about your special point of view, the unique way you process information. I have come to value that knowledge greatly. I believe strongly that women have much to offer in the home and much to offer in the councils of the Church. I pray that you will be willing to do so with reason, with humor, with kindness—but please, please make your voices heard. We'll all be much the better for it.

NOTES
1. M. Russell Ballard, *Counseling with Our Councils* (Salt Lake City: Deseret Book, 1997), 53.
2. Rulon G. Craven, *Called to the Work* (Salt Lake City: Bookcraft, 1985), 111–12.

Songs of My Heart

GLADYS KNIGHT

"Let the words of my mouth, and the meditation of my heart, be acceptable in thy sight, O Lord, my strength, and my redeemer" (Psalm 19:14). Song to me is symbolic of joy—the joy in my heart. That song is not "Heard It Through the Grapevine," or "Neither One of Us Wants to Be the First to Say Good-bye," or "You're the Best Thing that Ever Happened to Me," or my most popular song, "Midnight Train to Georgia" (though I love those songs—especially since they were hits). The song in my heart is of Jesus Christ and all the things in the restored gospel that I have learned and of the peace he has given me since I have joined this Church. He has blessed me with a wonderful family. My son Jimmy and my daughter-in-law Michelene set the example and led us to this Church. My daughter, Kenya, and son-in-law, Jimmy, followed them. They, too, were a great light to me, and along with them, my ten grandchildren.

Now I finally understand what my song is for. It is to be a part of my light, shining so that people may see and I can be a missionary for Heavenly Father. I'm so excited about all of this. I want to tell the world about it—shout it from the mountain tops! I've never been one for gossip, but I want to gossip about the Lord and what he has done by restoring his truths to the earth. I want to tell all about the blessings we can receive by following him. My friends have reminded me that because of my travels and singing I am in a position to share the

Gladys Knight, the Grammy-winning "queen of soul," is an internationally renowned recording artist. She has been singing in public since she was a young child, more than fifty years. She is the mother of three children and the grandmother of ten. Following the example of her children, she was baptized into The Church of Jesus Christ of Latter-day Saints in August 1997.

message of the Restoration all over the world. I accept that. I am so pleased that God has chosen me to be one of his disciples, and I am so ready to shine his light.

Music and the gospel go hand in hand. To Emma Smith, the Lord said: "For my soul delighteth in the song of the heart; yea, the song of the righteous is a prayer unto me, and it shall be answered with a blessing upon their heads" (D&C 25:12). To Brigham Young it was revealed: "If thou art merry, praise the Lord with singing, with music, with dancing, and with a prayer of praise and thanksgiving" (D&C 136:28). We also learn that the great latter-day events will be initiated with the "sound of a trump" (D&C 42:6) even up to the time when Michael the Archangel will sound his trumpet at the last resurrection. We don't hear that kind of music much in meetings. But we should get ready for the great band of trumpets that will accompany the Lord at his great second coming.

When it comes to bridging certain kinds of gaps, music is definitely one of our Heavenly Father's best tools. That's why music is considered the universal language. On a personal level, if you're down, you can put on good music that lifts you; or if you need to meditate, you can play something that helps you get deeper into the Spirit. Music is like being quickened; it gets you close to the Lord right away. Music does touch the heart. To liken joy in the Spirit to having a song in your heart is a perfect analogy because of the role music plays in our lives. We all should carry a song in our hearts.

During the time of slavery, we were calling upon the Lord in the spirituals we sang in the fields. We found a way to put into song the heavy load we carried as a people, even the joys we felt in the midst of pain. The Lord gave us the gift of music to get us through, and the old Negro spirituals were definitely a part of that. When you're troubled, you can sing your blues away. You can sing a lullaby to a little baby and soothe his tiny spirit. Song is a wonderful gift from the Lord.

The beauty of music is one side of the picture. Let me say a little about the other side if I may. The adversary is always working, trying to mess up Heavenly Father's great works. And music is no exception. Too much music plays into the power of the adversary and it's unfortunately making its mark. Music has power, so we must be very careful with the music we put into our spirits. If we choose the right music, we definitely experience a good power in our lives.

There are not words to express the power and joy I feel as the result of finally finding this Church. The Lord said, "Seek, and ye shall find; knock, and it shall be opened unto you" (Matthew 7:7). The Lord keeps all his promises; and after a long journey, the Lord kept that promise for me. He knew I was looking. He knew I was hurting. He knew I was confused. He knew I was diligently wanting to draw closer to him. But his way is like no other way. Now I know why Paul said, "Study to shew thyself approved unto God" (2 Timothy 2:15). We must learn to understand his language and to rise to his level of doing things.

This gospel was there all along, hidden in plain sight. Some people will see it, some won't. I'm so honored and happy that the Lord led me to find it. Coming to the fulness of the Lord's gospel has been life-changing. Without a doubt, this Church is "The Best Thing That Ever Happened to Me"—if I were to sing my own song. The difference between my life yesterday and today is that I'm a brand new me. Even my show when I perform is different. People tell me all the time, "There's something different about you. I see a light in you. What is it?" The gospel gives me hope. It gives me joy. And I know it will do the same for others. What a wonderful song Heavenly Father has placed in my heart!

The Lord's prophet today, President Gordon B. Hinckley, said, "I invite every one of you, wherever you may be as members of this church, to stand on your feet and with a song in your heart move forward, living the gospel, loving the Lord, and building the kingdom. Together we shall stay the course and keep the faith, the Almighty being our strength."[1] The best way to put a song in our hearts is by following the counsel and teachings of the Lord's prophet. I am so grateful that I know with a certainty that we have a real prophet of God on this earth, just like Peter was to the ancient church.

Last October I had the privilege of meeting President Hinckley. It was another dream come true—but I never dreamed I would be so nervous about its fulfillment. I was waiting with my family in a room in the Church Office Building in Salt Lake City. My first sight of the prophet was when he walked by our door to speak to someone else. He wasn't even in the room yet, and my heart began pounding. The moment was intense. He entered, and as we were introduced and shook hands, my mind went completely blank. We all stood there in a family receiving line, and I could not remember one single name of my grandchildren standing there with me. The prophet was very attentive to each of us. He started with my first grandchild, Sterling—whose name completely escaped me at the time. To help me out, the prophet suggested we all call my grandson "Bill" for the time being. "He kind of looks like a 'Bill,'" President Hinckley said. Finally, Sterling piped up and said, "My name is Sterling!" That broke the ice, and finally I was okay.

But later on I became flustered again when I remembered I was to sit at the table of President and Sister Hinckley the next afternoon at Sister Hinckley's birthday celebration, when I would be performing for them. The next day rolled around, I was escorted to the table of President and Sister Hinckley, and, sure enough, I was nervous all over again. But the Lord certainly knows how to choose his prophets. What a wonderful man! He kept me laughing and eased my spirit all afternoon. Sometimes we imagine that our Church leaders are always stern, but I learned first-hand that our prophet has a great sense of humor. He made me laugh, and he made me feel loved.

It's wonderful to know that Heavenly Father speaks once more to his chosen servants. He communicates. He has not turned away from us. I have always felt that, but now I know it with certainty—a certainty given to me and magnified by the power of the Book of Mormon. It is the blueprint and foundation of my testimony.

I seek the Spirit in everything I do now. I don't feel right if I don't take the sacrament. I attend church every Sunday, wherever I am. I'm better at it than the postman—rain, snow, sleet, or the dark of night can't keep me from my appointed sacrament meeting. In these meetings, I hear the testimonies of my wonderful and loving brothers and sisters. The foundation of their testimonies is the same as mine: Because of the Book of Mormon, we know our Lord is a gracious and merciful Savior. I am so grateful to be acquainted with his plan of salvation.

I'm blessed to have two earthly brothers right now, Bubba and David. So many times I have sought their help, and always they've bailed me out. But that eldest brother of ours—Jesus Christ—oh, will I ever be out there singing his praises! He has bailed us out of physical death and also spiritual death, if we love him enough to follow his teachings and example. Our eldest brother gave up his life for us. It's such an amazing gift to know that he loves us that much.

I am so grateful to Heavenly Father for my wonderful mother. I'm so glad she was still alive when I made that great conversion to this wonderful Church. She was not Mormon, but we were always coaxing her—knowing the very spiritual being that she was—to step into the waters and get into the true Church. And she would answer us by saying, "I'm more Mormon than any of you. Who tells you about general conference?" We'd answer, "You do, Gram." "Who tells you to do what the prophets tell you to do?" Again we would reply, "You do, Gram." I sincerely believe—though she never told me—that she was a believer in this Church. She was a great believer in God and in family. She knew that we are to nurture our children and help them find their way.

I attended a class in a ward other than my own a few Sundays ago. A class member who was new in the Church expressed concern about little children attending sacrament meetings. I raised my hand and said, "Look at our world today and what it's becoming. It's jet-set, it's microwave, but it's not spiritual. In the restored gospel, as soon as our babies are born and breathing, we have them in church. I think this is a wonderful thing." Church is the way we are exposed to his laws, his gospel, his word, his Spirit, and his light—by being taught from our very earliest years, when we are fresh from heaven. We should always be exposed to the truth and light found in his gospel, whether we are young or old.

In sacrament meeting, sometimes as my grandchildren are drawing pictures and coloring, I have the greatest sense that the word is getting through. Just the environment itself—being in church with their moms and dads—promotes spirituality. Another thing I love about our Church is that the mothers and fathers come together to nurture and raise their families. That is so important. That's why God gave us two parents. Even though we fall short of the mark sometimes, this is the way it was intended. I love it, even though sometimes I have to strain to hear over the children being a little noisy and wonder, *What did that speaker just say?* That's okay; our children need to be here; it's worth it.

In the world, there seems to be a pessimism about families and family relationships. But through the restored gospel, we know that we can have eternal families—something I did not know before. Just knowing that we can have our mates and our children eternally makes our life's journey worthwhile; it helps us keep the song in our hearts eternal. True sisterhood, true brotherhood, the sealing covenant, and eternal families are some of the unique gifts of love our Heavenly Father extended to us through the restored gospel.

Our Heavenly Father is so generous and kind to us. He also chastens his children sometimes. But to me that's the measure of a good parent, because then you know he really loves you. If we ever feel his chastening, we know that he is very mindful of us—that we have his attention—and that he wants us to qualify for all the wonderful gifts he has to bestow.

God deals with us on our level. He knows we can't comprehend certain things in a worldly environment, so he has a house right here among us. On weekdays, I like to find a nearby temple to attend. I'm addicted to the temple—it has been a journey unlike anything I've ever known. Just as the glory we will experience after this life is unimaginable, so also has been this experience for me in contrast to my life before I joined this Church. Like visiting a friend, I can go to the Lord's house to visit him. I feel his presence, and I know he is there. He welcomes me to his holy house, where I can feel his Spirit in great abundance.

I am so grateful for Jesus Christ. We're like fish swimming around in water. The water is a fish's lifeblood, just like the gospel is ours. It's everything! But the fish doesn't realize it until he chases that worm that's on a hook. When he's pulled out of the water, then he realizes, *Where's my water! I need my water! I miss my water!* At last he sees how precious the water was to him.

I know this is the Lord's true Church and kingdom here upon this earth. God is truly just and merciful. On the basis of how we use our agency, he gives us those things we are willing to receive. I am so grateful that in this dispensation of time Gladys Knight has been given the fulness of the everlasting gospel of Jesus Christ.

NOTE
1. Gordon B. Hinckley, *Ensign*, November 1995, 72.

What's Love Got to Do with It?
Conversations That Heal

LORRAINE M. WRIGHT

I relished my days at women's conference because I listened to many conversations—the conversations I was privy to while sitting at breakfast and the conversations I heard while waiting between sessions. Those conversations were healing.

One morning in the hotel at a breakfast table next to mine, four sisters were eating and talking about their children. I was anxiously checking my watch to be sure I'd get to the Marriott Center in time, but these sisters weren't rushing. I felt like tapping them on the shoulder to inform them that the opening session was going to start very soon, and if we didn't trek up there, we'd miss it. But they seemed oblivious to the time. They were talking over the difficulty two of them were having with their daughters, offering each other advice and counsel. I thought, *What a beautiful, healing conversation—right in front of me.*

Later that same day, as I waited for a session to start, I listened to many conversations about food. In all this listening, I've noted that Latter-day Saint sisters talk most about two things: relationships and food. I made some new friends at the conference talking about food. We compared notes about whether the mango yogurt was as good as the strawberry. We debated if the food line was so long that we had better leave someone to hold our place in line and go reserve seats with books

Lorraine M. Wright, an author of several books, is a professor of nursing and director of the Family Nursing Unit at the University of Calgary, Canada. She also maintains a part-time private practice in marriage and family therapy. A former president in both the Relief Society and the Young Women organizations, she is serving in her ward as a Relief Society teacher.

and sweaters in the next session. I heard of a wonderful soup served in a restaurant in Montana, but I didn't catch the name of the restaurant.

The most tender, sweet conversation I heard was when I was high up in the bleachers waiting for Gladys Knight to come in. I eavesdropped on three sisters sitting behind me. (My friends will tell you I eavesdrop even when I'm with them.) One sister said, "I was in a session this morning, and three sisters kept talking and giggling. Do you know, I became so irritated that I was going to turn around and tell them to stop talking." Then she said, "But I caught myself and thought, *What would that accomplish? I would probably hurt their feelings.* And then I thought about the times when I have done the same thing—talking while others were trying to listen. You know, I learned something from that. It was a great lesson to me." The younger-looking sister commented, "I just love sitting with you. You always teach me something."

That was a wonderful conversation: an opportunity to teach and an opportunity to respond in a positive way. These are examples of healing conversations, conversations that remind me of a fascinating Latin definition of the word *conversation:* "turning around together."

Why do we talk in the first place? When you think about it, talking gets us into a lot of trouble at times. Revealing our thoughts and feelings can be a risk. We often wonder what the person we are talking to is thinking. Our internal conversation might sound like this: *What is she thinking about me? Does she understand what I'm saying? Why is she interrupting?*

Sometimes I wonder why we bother talking at all. Maybe we should remain mute like other creatures. Why did Heavenly Father grant us this astonishing ability to talk?

There *are* some people who choose to talk very little, and some not at all. Certain religious groups, for instance, take an oath to refrain from talking. Some people are mute from birth. Teenagers can be masterful at not talking when they want to give you the silent treatment. Sometimes we just don't feel like talking, so we go to our rooms, for a walk, or for a hike in the mountains.

This year I worked with a remarkable Jewish family whose nine-year-old son, Yasha, is mute, but he was not born that way. I learned from his mother about some of the experiences that account for why Yasha doesn't speak. His father died two days before they left Russia for their new home in Israel. There, Yasha began to learn Hebrew. His mother, however, was very lonely, and things were not going well in Israel, so when a young Jewish man she had met wanted to emigrate to Canada, she decided to go, too. In Canada, Yasha had to learn yet another language: English. Because of these upheavals in his young life, Yasha now rarely speaks. I was able to get him to say yes or no. I tried to initiate a healing conversation with Yasha, a conversation in which he could know I cared about him. "It must be very difficult not to talk," I said to him, "because I'm sure you're talking in your head all the time." He nodded. "I hope I can hear some of those thoughts some day." He nodded his head again. When he left my office that day, I shook his hand and said, "Yasha, I look forward to the day I can hear you."

We are born with the ability to talk, but along the way some of us learn to fear what's going to happen when we open our mouths. Why do we talk? I offer you two ideas: We talk to exchange ourselves with each other—to share our thoughts and feelings, our deepest emotions—and we talk to render ourselves human. The ability to talk and to record our talk in writing distinguishes us from every other living creature. Talking identifies us as human beings, kin to our Heavenly Father. It's also the very thing that can make us most cruel and inhuman if we misuse it. If we characterize another person with negative labels, such as "You're evil," "You're ugly," "You're dumb," "You're lazy," we wound that person. On the other hand, if we affirm others with our words, we lift and heal them.

Let me relate two profound experiences of healing conversations in my life. I live in downtown Calgary where there are some lovely condominiums. As in most cities, however, downtown is also a place prostitutes frequent. One night on my way home from work at eleven o'clock, I stopped at the 7-Eleven. As I walked to the entrance, I saw ahead of me a young woman wearing high white boots and very abbreviated shorts—quite different attire from what I was wearing. We reached the front door at the same time, and she opened it for me. I walked through, turned to her, and said, "Thank you." She looked back at me with visible shock—for a simple thank you. Inside, I got my milk, and again we met at the checkout counter. Our eyes met and, in a way that truly was not ordinary, we connected. I felt something for that woman, and I know she felt something for me. What I saw in her at that moment was the divine in her, and simultaneously I knew she was seeing it in me. As I walked out to my car, I couldn't believe the internal conversation I was having: *I wonder what she would think about Relief Society?*

Can you imagine? As I puzzled about it, I knew that thought had come to me so I would think about her in a positive way, picturing her in a different setting. And that thought led to other thoughts about her being a Relief Society teacher and seeing her for what she was—a child of God.

My heart ached for her as I wondered how she ended up in her situation in life, and I grieved over how different our lives were. Not once did negative thoughts cloud my feelings for this young woman. In that one moment, the Spirit had connected us. A simple phrase—"thank you"—had opened a door. I have found that if we yield our hearts to the Spirit, even our briefest conversations can be occasions for enlightenment and healing.

Another conversation illustrates this same truth. I was visiting my mother before I flew to Provo for women's conference. I usually visit my mother before I go out of town because my mother is in the final stages of a very debilitating illness. I want to have had a good conversation with her in case that visit is the last time I see her. One thing I have learned from life is that the best conversations occur during suffering. On this particular night, as often happens, I was helping a nursing assistant with the bedtime care. My mother is a quadriplegic and is able to move only her head, so I was helping turn her in bed. The young assistant this evening was by chance one of my undergraduate nursing students. When she finished helping me care for my mother, she bent down and kissed her. In the bathroom, cleaning up my mother's bath things, this young student turned to me and said, "This must be very hard for you" and then hugged me. That one sentence was incredibly healing. One sentence from a young person I taught in class nurtured me in ways that were much more significant than anything I had taught her. Healing conversations can happen all the time in our lives if we will only let them, only be open to them.

These two conversations were affirmative and affectionate.

Unfortunately, we have other sorts of conversations with each other from time to time—conversations of accusation and recrimination.[1] When someone hasn't met our expectations, when we feel that someone has behaved badly towards us, we begin to criticize and accuse: "You never come home on time." "You're always late." "You never bring me flowers." "You don't care about my feelings."

Words do affect us. Conversations can be toxic. Scientific studies are being conducted in the field of psychoimmunology to track patterns within marriages. These breakthrough studies show that our conversations actually affect our health. At some level, we all know that already. When you've had lunch with a wonderful friend, you come away feeling good, exhilarated, happy. In contrast, other conversations have left you with a splitting headache, or a sore neck, or an upset stomach. Conversations can either build up our spirits or tear them down.

Here are some general dos and don'ts, starting with the don'ts. Please, never ever, ever, ever, *ever* say to anyone, "I do not love you anymore." Even if your love diminishes for a husband, a family member, a friend, withhold saying so because that is the commandment upon which all others hang: to love our neighbor as ourselves. If you are not able to love someone at that moment, pray that your love will return. Pray that it will increase. Never ever say, "I will never forgive you," no matter how much your heart is broken, no matter how much you feel betrayed in a relationship. And please don't say, "I can never be my true self with you." It leaves the other person feeling inadequate, helpless, and ashamed. Instead, try to find ways to describe how you would like to be in that person's presence. Please never say, "I will leave you or divorce you if . . ." Relationships cannot build, you cannot have the Spirit there with you, if you are threatening to leave. Please do not say, "If you say that again, I will tell your father," or "I'll tell your bishop," or "I'll tell your friend." Threats create enmity and prevent any real conversation in the sense of "turning around together."

By contrast, here are words I believe we can never say enough, words we are taught by our prophets and our Savior to say: "I am sorry; I ask for your forgiveness." You can never seek forgiveness or give forgiveness enough. When conflict or disagreements emerge, we need to offer hope for resolution. Recently, a friend said to me, "I know we are going through a difficult time, but I am confident we will work it out." What a beautiful, uplifting way to approach a conflict. What else can we never say enough? "Thank you. That was very kind, that was thoughtful, that was considerate." Or, "I appreciate you. I am grateful for you in my life." These sentences come from the Spirit. These words foster and invite love. You can never say enough, "I like being with you. I like spending time with you. I feel good when I'm with you." And finally we can never say or hear too often, "I love you—I *love* you, I love *you,* I love you." At what point will we have said it enough? I read the scriptures and find such answers as "a new commandment I give unto you, That ye love one another; as I have loved you, that ye also love one another" (John 13:34) and "bridle all your passions, that ye may be filled with love" (Alma 38:12). We can never say "I love you" enough.

Toxic conversations over a number of years with people we love, or people we had hoped loved us, can result in emotional suffering and illness. We must shield ourselves from such exchanges. After twenty-five years of marital interaction studies, University of Washington professor John Gottman has documented that politeness is the first thing that goes out of a relationship in difficulty.[2] Think of the many talks from our general authorities about kindness and politeness.

Professor Gottman also isolated four patterns of relating that characterize troubled marriages. One pattern is habitual criticism. (Criticism is even worse than complaining, which is also a less-than-wonderful trait to bring to a relationship.) Defensiveness and stonewalling are two other patterns that perpetuate trouble in a marriage. Fourth is contempt, which includes name calling, hostile humor, and sarcasm. Professor Gottman could actually predict the number of infectious diseases, such as colds and flu, that a spouse who had been treated with contempt would have over the next four years. The correlation is even stronger than the correlation between heart disease and cholesterol. Now, don't think that a phone call today that ended in a tiff with your husband will bring on colds for you both tomorrow. Long-standing patterns, patterns that characterize what *usually* happens in your interactions, are what define a relationship.

Perhaps the most useful finding from recent studies is that marital happiness depends on how we resolve conflict, not whether it is present or absent in a relationship.[3] Marriages that are happy and satisfying have a five-to-one ratio of positive to negative emotional interactions. What constitutes positive interactions? Smiling, touching, praising, commending—the healing conversations we have been talking about.

It is vital in life that we have with each other conversations of affirmation and affection, conversations in which we tell each other how much we care. I've been amazed at the conversations I observe among LDS women. I hear more conversations of affirmation and affection during church services on a Sunday than I hear all week, perhaps because church is a place where we express love, where we try to build each other up, and where we consciously invite the Spirit, the Holy Ghost.

The scriptures warn us against toxic conversations: "Keep thy tongue from evil, and thy lips from speaking guile" (Psalm 34:13). How do we do that? Keeping our lips from speaking guile and gossip can be a great challenge. In any intense relationship, differences will surface. Anytime we are close to someone, that person will have ideas that differ from ours. When we differ, how can we build up instead of tear down? How do we invite conversations of growth and change, of "turning around together"? How do we deal with our differences, disagreements, and conflicts?

One way is to be open. Anytime we are open in our relationships, our hearts may be comforted and "knit together in love" (Colossians 2:2). I truly believe that is what happens.

Another way is to invite the Spirit into our conversations. A young man with multiple sclerosis (MS) with whom I worked over several months came to see me again this fall. This young man is not a Latter-day Saint. He uses a lot of colorful language, at times more colorful than any language I've ever heard in movies. My students know my standards and often remark sympathetically after one of his visits, "Oh, Dr. Wright, listening to that language must have been so hard on you." But on one visit the coarse language disappeared. I had asked him a very simple question: "Do you have any spiritual or religious beliefs that are helping you cope with this illness?" He then told me a moving story of the death of his brother and the feeling he had had at the time that his brother's spirit had visited him. In telling this moving story, he did not once swear or use offensive language. Why? I believe it was because he was talking about things of the Spirit. The interview continued, and at the end of our conversation, I said to him, "You and I have something in common. My mother has MS. I can relate to many of the things you are talking about." In the gentlest, sweetest tone, he said to me, "If there's anything I can do to help you, let me know." Aren't those healing words? If you invite the Spirit to direct your conversation, wonderful connections will occur.

The final suggestion I want to offer about dealing with differences and disagreements comes from an experience with my mother. It has to do with struggling to understand another's point of view. A few weeks ago, my brother and I wanted my father to have some much-needed respite, but my mother didn't want him to leave town. I kept trying to understand why she was upset, but she didn't seem to be able to tell us. Finally, she said to me, "I don't want to die without your father here." My mother is not LDS, but she talks about dying and love more now than she ever has her entire life. I tried to reassure her, "We don't want you to die alone; we all want to be with you." I finally understood her feelings when she answered, "I don't know what's going to happen to me when I die. I just hope my family has enough love for me to make time for me now when I am so ill." These conversations—when we speak of our fears, loves, and hopes—can invite growth and change in us. These are the conversations I feel greatly privileged to have had with my mother.

My mother was a businesswoman before she had MS. A willingness to share deep feelings and express her love hasn't come easily to her. Yet now she tells me she loves me all the time. We express our love for each other frequently. We wouldn't have the relationship we now have without MS, so I am grateful for MS in our lives. I'm grateful for the change it created in my mother and in me. It has taught me to ask for, and to create opportunities for, healing conversations and expressions of love.

A sweet, young woman illustrated for me how to create opportunities for healing conversations. As our ward Relief Society education counselor, she phoned to tell me she wanted to drop off some teaching materials. "I could get those from you on Sunday," I kept saying. "You don't need to make a special trip." But she insisted, "No, no, I want to bring these to you," and she came. She didn't have any teaching materials for me. She had cookies. She also had a conversation of love and healing for me. "I'm moving from the ward," she explained, "and before I go, I just wanted to tell you how much I love you." That offered me an opportunity, didn't it? To tell her how much I loved her. I told her, "Since I have been in this ward, you have showered me with love." She's a twenty-seven-year-old young woman with some great heartaches over the health of one of her children, but she still had time enough and love for me. And as kindness invites kindness, love invites love.

Perhaps the most healing conversations are what we call prayer. Our sincere prayers are, without doubt, the most sacred, powerful conversations we can possibly have, and they will always provide healing, if we will only listen. These are the conversations that have brought me the greatest comfort in times of great struggle. I am grateful for such conversations.

Professionally, I have been astounded to learn how many research studies are looking at the effects of prayer on illness, although the term researchers use for prayer is "distant intentionality." Numerous studies are being conducted to see how prayer can influence the course of illness. What Latter-day Saints already know, but what astounds these researchers, is that when prayers are offered for individuals who are ill, even if they don't know that someone is praying for them, their condition usually improves.

Of course, the question always comes, What happens when our prayers are not answered in the way we would like? What happens when the illness isn't cured? What happens when the person dies anyway? What are we to think and do then? During my mother's long struggle with MS, I have wrestled with these questions. My recourse has been to go back to the Lord for more healing conversations. We must draw upon our faith to help us understand why sometimes our wonderful conversations with Heavenly Father don't produce the results we would like.

Clearly our calendar is sometimes not the same as Heavenly Father's. Many times in my prayers, especially when I'm suffering about my mother's condition, I wish I knew Heavenly Father's schedule. I wish I knew when the suffering would be over for my mother. To be honest, I think what I really want to know is when my own suffering will be over.

But while the suffering persists, I find I listen in conversation with my Heavenly Father more intently than I ever have before.

Many times our heavenly conversations are one-word prayers: "Help!" Do you ever pray like that? Sometimes it's even more ego-centric: "Help me!" We are taught that our prayers should include thank you, so I'm trying to be grateful to share my mother's suffering and be with her these final weeks or days of her life. I can learn something from this time, though some days I feel like I've done all the learning I can possibly do around this particular piece of suffering. But that isn't so, of course, and sometimes what we learn through our conversations with our Heavenly Father may not become clear until weeks, months, or even years later.

I'm grateful for my membership in this great Church and for those wonderful, healing conversations we call prayer. I'm grateful for the mistakes I have made in my conversations with others, for the humbling and learning that comes from mistakes. How I've had to grow and learn and change! I am striving to be more loving, for I know that in our loving conversations with each other, we truly draw closer to our Savior, who so often and in so many ways tells us, "Love one another as I have loved you."

NOTES

1. See Lorraine M. Wright, Wendy L. Watson, and Janice M. Bell, *Beliefs: The Heart of Healing in Families and Illness* (New York: Basic Books, 1996).

2. John Gottman, "Why Marriages Fail," *Family Therapy Networker* 18 (1994): 40–48.

3. See Howard Markman and Clifford I. Notarius, *We Can Work It Out: Making Sense of Marital Conflict* (New York: Putnam, 1993), 17. See also James M. Harper and Colleen Harper, "After the Honeymoon: Crazy Glue for Marriages," in *May Christ Lift Thee Up: Talks from the 1998 Women's Conference* (Salt Lake City: Deseret Book, 1999), 263–76.

Making Their Own Peace: Women of Jerusalem Today

ANN N. MADSEN

My hope is to let you into the lives of some of my closest friends in Jerusalem, women who are surrounded by a maelstrom of war and impending war and yet know peace. As you get to know them just a little, you will see the moments when they didn't know a thing could not be done, so they went ahead and did it; you will see the energy that carried them along—fueled by their beliefs; their common determination not to count the cost; and the extraordinary way they make their own peace or find it in their lives.

Speaking of their lives is a gateway into the concept of personal peacemaking—the principle Christ taught us and which we must struggle to implement in our own daily lives. "Blessed are the peacemakers," Jesus said on a mount overlooking the beautiful, sometimes tranquil Sea of Galilee (Matthew 5:9). But peace is a rare commodity on this globe as we approach the close of the most violent of all centuries since the world began. Many claim to seek it, but few ever claim to have found it. Why?

As we define *peace*, various words come to mind as its opposite. *Conflict*, *violence*, and *war*. These words are as current as today's headlines. *Noise* and *confusion*. Isn't peace what we have when noise and confusion cease? What ever happened to silence? Is peace and quiet only

Ann N. Madsen, Isaiah scholar and poet, has taught ancient scripture at Brigham Young University for more than twenty years. She lived and taught in Jerusalem from 1987 to 1993. She and her husband, Truman G. Madsen, are the parents of three children and a Navajo foster son, and the grandparents of sixteen.

158

to be found deep in the forest, high on a mountaintop, or in a holy temple? *Argument, anger,* and *abuse.* These sometime intrude in our own homes, together with *contention* and *fear.* So where, in this world, can we find peace, and if we can't find it, how do we make it?

"There is beauty all around / When there's [peace] at home."[1] That's the answer: home. I know the hymn says *love,* but I think *peace* and *love* are synonyms.

Not long ago I heard Jehan Sadat's address at a Brigham Young University commencement. She seemed to speak directly to me. She spoke of the bridges of peace, which are built with kindness and understanding. She taught us that the university of peace is the home. Mothers are the first professors, who demonstrate what they teach by gentle spirits and unselfish love, which wants for everyone else what they want for themselves. She said that ordinary people can change the world, people who begin just like us, and who reach beyond themselves when their situation demands it. Her examples included Gandhi, Mother Teresa, and her own husband, Anwar Sadat. She indicated that the path to peace is found through our hearts. We must search our hearts to find that path.

Jesus said, "Peace I leave with you, my peace I give unto you: not as the world giveth, give I unto you. Let not your heart be troubled, neither let it be afraid" (John 14:27). What a superlative gift! How do we discover this gift that has already been bestowed? First, his peace will be found in giving, not in getting. Second, his peace comes as we count the simple abundance of our lives. Third, his peace is grounded in love and in loving relationships, especially our relationship with him.

The remarkable women of Jerusalem whom I will cite as examples practice what Christ preached, though some of them would not define themselves as his disciples.

Bertha Spafford Vester

The first woman I met in Jerusalem who was a real resident of the city was Bertha Spafford Vester. She would want to be remembered as Christ's disciple. Her life embodied the three qualities of peace I listed. Giving was a natural response, bred in her by devout Christian parents who came to give their all in a lifetime mission to the Holy City and its people. They arrived in a time of peace, but it was not to last. Bertha spoke of her earliest memories of that peaceful time in these words:

"I can remember lying awake in the early morning, when the first glimmerings of light outlined my windows, and listening to the pit-a-pat, pit-a-pat of the unshod hooves of a donkey as it led a long caravan of camels through the street outside. Then came the soft shuffling footfalls of the camels and the rhythmic sighing of the ropes that fastened heavy loads to saddles, as the caravan plodded toward the market.

"That was [in 1881]. I was three years old, and my parents had just brought me to live in Jerusalem, the Holy City that was to become the only home I have ever known."

I first encountered Bertha in her little book of watercolors celebrating the wild flowers of the Holy Land. Her lovely face on the book jacket enthralled me. That she directed a hospital for children of all races inspired me. Some referred to her as "Mother of Jerusalem," a legend in her own time. When I realized that our trip in the summer of 1968 would include Jerusalem, I hoped to meet Mrs. Vester in person. On our arrival, I called and her daughter said, "Come." So we went. Happily, my husband, a friend, and I had her all to ourselves that lovely afternoon.

As I have studied her life since, how I wish I had asked her a long list of questions. But on that day I had barely arrived. The city seemed strange and a bit forbidding. One must study Jerusalem over time, not just glimpse it, to begin to sense its history. Over time one discovers the incredible warmth and hospitality of its citizens: Arab, Jew, and Christian. And here was Bertha Spafford Vester, whose life had spanned nearly nine decades of its recent stormy story, a veritable repository of that history and hospitality.

We had arrived on the day of the first anniversary of the Six-Day War. I knew only what the average first-time tourist would know. Most of what I knew had come from the Bible. She and I shared that legacy.

My abbreviated personal journal entry for Sunday, 9 June 1968, reads: "Next to visit Mrs. Bertha Spafford Vester, ninety-year-old American at the American Colony Hotel. Lovely lady. She said the reason she had gotten on so well with Jew and Arab and Turk and English was that she was a Christian. Eighty-seven years she has lived in Jerusalem. She said, 'I have seen history.'"

As the sun set that Sunday I wrote some lines about her effect on me:

Mrs. Vester in her garden at vespers,
Outshining her flowers.
A Christian, having little problem
With Turk or Arab or Jew,
A lethal love,
Alive and wise at ninety.
Lover of the little . . .
Flowers, babies.
So sensible
She found the small to prize.

My impressions of this gracious, strong, beautiful woman were that she had done what she perceived needed doing with all the resources at her disposal. She was obviously a woman of enormous talent, yet she seemed hardly conscious of herself.

She died within days of our visit. We read of her death as we toured Lebanon.

How I cherish our visit in her garden that day, on what she referred to as the "one small patch of lawn in all Jerusalem." I had the good sense to savor our brief time together, intuiting somehow who she really was. Her garden was one of the few spots of color in a newly united Jerusalem only one year after the dust and dirt of the Six-Day War. I don't recall seeing any other garden in the city on that trip. My first impression was that Jerusalem was a drab, dusty place. No wonder she chose to paint bright, lovely flowers!

Her mother, Anna, had pioneered the Colony's humanitarian causes in the ancient city. Bertha never saw herself apart from the tasks her parents had begun when they came to Jerusalem in 1881. Even her own marriage in 1904 to a young German businessman, who was also reared in the tradition of Christian service, was a continuation of her parents' covenant. Her determination to continue that service without stint was most unusual. It was a legacy inherited by her own daughter, Anna Grace Lind. Through peace and war these three generations of Jerusalem women served the needy of that city from 1881 to our own time. Their

161

lives touched the lives of other women, some of whom took up the tasks they had pioneered.

Bertha's book, *Our Jerusalem,* is filled with matter-of-fact accounts of superhuman efforts of which the following is but one example. It is taken from a letter written in 1917 before America had entered World War I. Conditions in Jerusalem were deteriorating daily, on account of the approaching war. That same winter, of 1917, Palestine had had the worst locust infestation in generations and therefore had produced little grain. A Mr. Loud had sent money, and this letter from Bertha's mother was to thank him for his help:

"If you could stand one day at our gate, and see the pleasure on the gaunt faces as they go away with their pails and saucepans filled with the nutritious soup, enough to satisfy their family, it would repay you for your trouble. When I last wrote we were giving soup to four hundred people daily. Since then, we have every day been obliged to increase the number, until Saturday (day before yesterday) there were eleven hundred and eighty-six souls who were fed. Working around the poor as we have, in and around Jerusalem for so many years, we get to know them all personally. Several of the sisters make it their duty to visit the homes and see exactly what they need. Some may think it wiser to limit the number of recipients and thus make the money last longer. This one could only advise from a distance where you do not see their [faces]. It is utterly impossible to refuse [when you do]."[2]

Bertha's vigor, vision, and virtues are apparent throughout her writing but not in a conscious effort to impress. She traced her mother's footsteps. Their lives were their message. As she describes life in the Colony she says: "The atmosphere of the Colony was happy, the aura reverential and devout. Need was the incentive that put every bit of accumulated knowledge to work and every talent to use."

Bertha loved Jerusalem, and Jerusalem returned that love, partly because of the Spafford Home for Children, which she founded in honor of her mother. One day almost thirty years after my visit with Bertha, as I walked up the hill to the Spafford Home with Bertha's daughter, Anna Grace Lind, who was then eighty-eight, a little Arab woman stopped her, calling her "Mother of Jerusalem" in Arabic. Afterwards I commented:

"Didn't she call you 'Mother of Jerusalem'?"

"Yes," she replied, "but I'm not."

"Isn't that what they called your mother?" I asked.

"Oh yes," she smiled, "but she was."

Jesus teaches us that we can capture peace in our own lives, regardless of the condition of the world around us. Bertha Spafford Vester lived that truth. She taught many others by her deeds. Seventy years later, Christmases at the American Colony were remembered fondly by my Palestinian friend, Hind Husseini.

Hind Husseini

Hind Husseini, age seventy-seven, a pale, sprightly Palestinian Muslim, took her leave of me after our first meeting with the following words: "You see why I am putting on a shawl? The other day I fell down. I fell down the staircase, because I have a refugee cat. I started to feed her and be very nice to her, and she started to be very nice to me. But as I was going down the staircase she screamed, so I didn't know where to put my feet and I fell down three steps. I landed on all fours like the way to pray. I got up to feel if my limbs were okay, and I feel that my hands and my feet are okay. Then at night I started to think that my shoulder is hurting me. I forgot that I fell down. Now I must keep it warm."

"I forgot that I fell down." Such a characteristic statement. Forgetting herself had been her lifelong habit. "I have a refugee cat." Another typical explanation of her concern for the homeless, the helpless.

All I knew of Hind Husseini was that she ran a girls' school for Arab orphans and displaced girls in Jerusalem. Only moments into the interview I was surprised to discover that Hind had known Bertha Spafford Vester very well. She had, in fact, grown up as part of the American Colony family. Such serendipity! Her present home and school are joined by a gate to the American Colony Hotel.

Hind was born in 1916 and was two years old when her father died of the plague. She had no memory of him. She described the circumstances of her birth: "I was born in Jerusalem, in the same house I'm living in. My mother used to come and give birth to us in her father's house. In the same room we're all born." She was born during the time of the Ottoman Empire, when the Turks occupied and governed Jerusalem.

She grew up with four boy cousins who had also lost their father. The venerable Husseinis had property north of the Old City. They had lived in this quarter for centuries. Part of their property had been leased and later sold to the American Colony. As she recalled her childhood she said: "We were very happy. We didn't feel at all that we are without fathers, playing and having nearby the American Colony and Mrs. Vester [Bertha Spafford Vester]. Her children and we play all together. So my best memories, my playing, is something ordinary.

"[But my very best memory is of] Christmas at the American Colony, and Mrs. Vester preparing a very nice Christmas party for all the children of the quarter, and going and sitting, waiting for Father Christmas to enter with his big, big, big basket to give us the presents. And to eat the Christmas cakes, and go home. She is like an auntie to me, Bertha Vester."

Curious about this little Muslim girl's reaction to Christmas, I asked, "What kind of gifts did Father Christmas bring you? Do you remember any of them?"

"Oh yes, I remember the beautiful dolls—once such a big doll they gave me! They were giving very nice Christmas gifts and sweets, all packed nicely in red paper. We had very good times. Easter was very exciting also . . . coloring the eggs was a happy memory."

By the time she was thirty-two years old she had known the occupation of the Turks and the British, and now she was experiencing the new state of Israel and Jewish sovereignty. She was trained at the Jerusalem College for Girls as a teacher and later as a social worker. She watched as Arabs left Jerusalem during the war with the Israelis in 1948. But she stayed.

Describing that period, she said: "One day when refugees were pouring into the Old City, they were stationing them in the schools, because there were no other places, and the acting mayor of Jerusalem, Anwar El Hatib, called us for a meeting, some men and women. . . . He was a very good man and the only one who could have called us together. He called me also. At that time I didn't know him, but it seems that he got my name.

"So I went. It was so difficult to jump and enter the Herod's Gate at that time from the Notre Dame de France. They were shooting.

"On my way to the meeting, passing by the Holy Sepulchre, I saw a strange picture—several little children. They were from two up to eleven or twelve years old, standing there. I couldn't see them without asking, 'What are you doing here? Don't you see bullets are coming? Go home.' I was in a hurry; I wanted to arrive on time to the meeting. I walked maybe two steps and then I came back. 'Why are you standing? Go home, I tell you!' Then this 'elderly lady,' eleven or twelve said, 'We are the Deri Yassin children. [The adults in their village had all been killed in the war.] We are the remnants. We were collected by the Jews, and they brought us to Damascus Gate [which is the entrance to the Arab Quarter of the Old City] and they said, "Go to your people, and they'll look after you." And here we are.'

"I became dizzy. I went to the meeting. I put up my hand. I said to them, 'Excuse me, but before you start with the agenda, I want to tell about some children.'

"Mayor Anwar El Hatib said, 'I'm sorry, Miss Husseini, but we are going to discuss the problem as a whole. We have so many refugees, we don't know how to deal with them all.' I said to them, 'All right, I have an idea,' because I had two rooms I had used as a day nursery. I said to them, 'You continue with your meeting, but I want to go and see what I can do with the children.'

"These two rooms were not far from the meeting place, but when I arrived they were closed. I knew the house of the nurse—she was living near the American baby home [the Spafford Children's Home] in the Old City.

"I went to the nurse. I said to her, 'Hana, I want to reopen the nursery, because of what I have been seeing. Are you ready to come and work, or shall I see somebody else?' She said, 'No, of course I work. I'm not better than you.' So, I took her. We opened the place. We tried to furnish it with these reddish Bedouin carpets, the handwoven kind. They were very cheap at that time—five dinars for every carpet, it was. We bought five of them.

"And we said, 'It is now warm. We can manage with the few blankets we have for the whole nursery.' [Note her making do with what was at hand.] As for the second day, I went collecting, and at the social worker department I collected a young man who was called Amin Tamini. He said to me, 'If you like, I can come with you.' Of course I like! Come! And we started collecting children. We collected within that week around fifty-five, as far as I remember.

"I have only a little bit of money. I had in my pocket 138 dinars, worth maybe 40 dollars. I said, 'I'm going to live with the children as long as we can, as long as the money lasts and then everybody goes home.' The headmistress of a school, which is now near us, was Basima Faris. She came running to me. She said, 'Do you like me to come and help you?' I said, 'Please, come.'"

For a time this was enough, but soon they started needing more help. Speaking of this she said: "One day, we had needs. And we said, let us go and see this acting mayor of Jerusalem. We went together, Miss Faris and myself. There were so many people, but the doorkeeper knew us from our work. When we enter we asked, 'Is he busy?' They said, 'He is meeting . . .' but then [they] opened the door for us. We found him standing up and speaking.

"I never forget that day. Me and Basima listening, and he was speaking. He did not notice us. He was telling them, 'Look here! If you want me to give you a license, you send a sack of potatoes to Hind Husseini at Dar Tefl.' They said to him, 'Where do I find this place, this Dar Tefl?' He said to them, 'In these two basement rooms . . . You send rice, you send sugar, or whatever . . .' Before we asked . . . when he noticed us he looked at us like this, [and she made a wonderful face!] he saw us standing at the door, he said, 'What can I do for you?' I said to him, 'Don't ask what we want, it is fulfilled. Thank you very much. Thank you very much and also your merchants.' And we went."

There they stood, listening to their shopping list being enumerated before they asked, like a prayer being answered even before you speak the word. Just as Isaiah 65:24 explains, "Before they call, I will answer; and while they are yet speaking, I will hear." This was obviously such a moment for Hind.

So, when she was about thirty-two, these motherless, homeless children became her children. I was touched when she said over and over, "And then I went to my children." I asked her, "Did you ever think to be married?" Her reply was quick and enthusiastic, full of energy, coming from that frail frame. She said, "No, no, no, how can I even think of marriage? I had my children. I was very busy."

The ravages of the war eventually made it necessary to leave the two rooms for a time. She explains: "One day I went to the children. I went alone. I found them sitting—I'll never forget that sight—making a circle, the little ones in the middle, sitting and crying and . . . becoming hysteric. 'Why do you make like this? What is the matter with you?' I asked. They said, 'We are very much afraid. At night we hear the shooting, and the shooting is now coming near us. We hear it.' What a frightening sound to orphan children. So I said to them, 'Don't worry. Now I go and fetch my things and come and sleep with you.'

"I went home crying to the nunnery where I stayed, but I started quickly packing some things to take with me. I took a small bag and as I was going, the Superior Mother met me and asked, 'Where are you going, Hind?' I said to her, 'I am going to my children. So, so, and so happened, and I can't leave them to sleep alone; I want to go and sleep with them.' She said, 'No, you don't go and sleep with them.' She was very kind, really. She was Spanish, a soft and nice woman. I never forget her. She said to me, 'Come with me, I go with you and you pick the place you like and bring the children to it.'"

What a moment as Hind was packing up her things to take her chances with the bullets and shells so that she could be there to be a comfort to "her children"! How her eyes lit up as she explained the spot she and the Mother Superior chose that morning:

"So I went, I said to them, '*Yelleh* [hurry], children, we are going to go to a very nice place where I am living.' And you should see how we were passing through the Old City streets and ruins, some of the children carrying things, and the very little ones each wanted to hold my hand. I cannot hold them all; I was with a pleated, gathered skirt. I said to them, 'Yes, you have my skirt.'"

I tried to picture this scene: children, crowded in a bunch, making their way through the narrow streets of the Old City carrying their few possessions and holding to Hind's gathered skirt. I asked, "How many were there at this time?" Her answer staggered me.

"At that time there were around fifty-five. As we passed the Old City streets, people were sometimes laughing, sometimes crying; same with us, 'til we arrived, and there we settled. We continued there for forty-five days exactly. It was very nice, really."

Her memories of the war were vivid. The details came rushing back as she lifted the lid of her Pandora's box of memory. She recalled: "The nuns were helping us. They did many things, and we do all the rest of the work. I was going sometimes to see about the children's food and for this and that, sometimes helping in other places as well. The Austrian hostel was turned into a hospital. I helped nursing the wounded people. There were plenty of wounded people without nurses. So we used to go and help. We cleaned, rolled bandages, sat beside the wounded people to feed them, to speak with them, and so on."

Notice how Hind didn't mention whether the people she helped were Jews or Arabs. It is an understatement to say that war tends to interrupt the normal flow of life. Yet, when Hind saw what needed to be done, she simply gave herself to the task. The little girl who had loved Christmas in the American Colony was now able to care for an impoverished, portable orphanage of fatherless children, just as she had been cared for and loved. These children did not lack a mother. She became their mother, in her ample, gathered skirt, as she took up as many hands as she could, by turn, and led them to safety. It was to be her life's work.

That was really how the school where she now presided had begun. She carried on until the 1948 Israeli War of Independence finally was over, leaving new boundaries and a new government. She remembered: "So, when things settled a little bit, we went back to our two rooms in the Old City. In time we grabbed some other rooms. And then before the end of 1948, the cease-fire took place, and I went quickly, repaired our house [the one next door to the American Colony, the one where she had been born]—it was damaged—and Musa Alami helped us with some money to repair it. Five hundred dinars, I think, or a thousand, I don't remember. We repaired the whole house where I am now living, my grandfather's house.

"So we settled here, in the house where I am now. We started having more children and more and more and more, and we came to what we are. And we are very, very happy."

On the day of our interview, as she prepared to leave, Hind pulled her shawl over her aching shoulder. I now knew her agenda. I knew this had been a time granted to me by sheer serendipity. Yet, I, the intruder in this wondrous life, didn't want her to go. But in a moment she was gone. In later interviews with those who knew her, I found that she was always addressed with great respect as *Set* Hind, "Lady" Hind. How appropriate!

Set Hind Husseini died in November 1994. She finished her last strenuous encounter, not with a government official but with cancer, a thing that seemed unthinkable on that lovely April morning when we met. How indestructible she had seemed as she walked away, rather briskly, to continue her many tasks.

Hind Husseini's life shows us in broad strokes how we give ourselves. Her life was her gift, her legacy, and it is still being given in a large school on her ancestors' land where hundreds of orphan girls are taught in peaceful surroundings, provided by a single woman (in both senses of the word), an orphan herself, whom many call "mother."

Jesus' peace is found in giving ourselves. The world, through the media, has us almost convinced that *getting* is the key. *If only I had more* _____. You fill in the blank: money, clothes, friends, room (which translates "bigger house"), time, education, talent, or maybe just "more stuff." *If only I had more, then I'd finally be at peace.* Is more really what you need?

When I asked a dear friend that very question, she answered, "Why would you want more? If you have more, you need to sweep it, mop it, or mow it!" And in the same vein, my daughter Mindy routinely remarks, "If you don't keep moving, it all stacks up around you." Simplify! Declutter.

A cross-stitch piece I embroidered for the wall of our first apartment tells it all: "It is in giving, not in seeking gifts the heart is blessed." Peace and joy follow the giving of oneself.

Jesus' peace comes as we count the simple abundance of our lives—count our blessings. Hind Husseini counted five inexpensive Arab rugs as abundance. Elder Richard G. Scott has taught us to concentrate on what we have rather than on what we don't have: "Do you find yourself often thinking of all of the things that you wish you had that you've not been blessed to have—maybe even very desirable ones like a husband or wife or children, good health, more personal attractiveness, more joy and happiness and peace of mind—while neglecting to recognize all that the Lord has blessed you with already? Do you ever pray to him when your heart is so filled with things to thank him for that you do not feel inclined to ask for anything else?"[3] As we calculate our lives, let us always add to the sum rather than subtract from it.

I fell in love with the words *simple abundance* even before I opened the book by that name given me by a dear friend. Sarah Ban Breathnach, the author, explains on the fourth page of her book that "you already possess all you need to be genuinely happy."[4] She goes on to suggest that we pray (I'm not sure she said "pray," but I would) "to open up the eyes of your awareness to the abundance that is already yours." That's the key. She suggests that the abundant living she describes "wraps us in inner peace" and begins with gratitude. I will always be grateful for her suggestion, one I acted upon: keep a gratitude journal. Choose an especially lovely, blank book, and record the gratitude part of your prayers. Even if it is the only journal you keep, it will be a legacy for your children and grandchildren. Here are two examples from mine: "I am thankful for the tender turning of my heart to kin, living and dead." "I am thankful for the blessing of forgiveness, both given and received."

It's easier to mention blessings to others when you've listed them. And mentioning blessings is contagious, just like mentioning violence. We need the mentioning of blessings to counteract the plague of violence around us. Peace also comes from counting our blessings and then sharing our bounty wisely.

Diodora Manachi

Diodora Manachi, nun, abbess of a monastery, is one of the most beautiful women I have ever met and a perfect example of counting our simple abundance.

Diodora Manachi explains her philosophy about consecrating ourselves to help others: "God gives us gifts and different talents, and we have to use them. Whether our help or what we do is needed by somebody, this is judged by God. We don't know. We have to do what we can all the time, at every moment. Whenever something comes up, we have to give everything. Now whether or not I believe that I can do something, I can. It is my obligation to give everything which I have been given."

Diodora was twenty-eight when I first met her. She had come with a handful of Greek Orthodox friends to a symposium at the Jerusalem Center to listen to one of the presenters, a Father Dionysios. I helped to host an informal luncheon during the proceedings. It was pure pleasure to sit with the participants at lunch, discussing the search for human nature and comparing ideologies. Struck by her beauty, I asked Sister Diodora if I might take her photograph and interview her for a book I was writing. With her eyes she asked Father Dionysios if it would be appropriate, and he nodded. I took her photo, and I knew that we would indeed meet again. She graciously offered to come for me, which she did.

She came to my office at the Jerusalem Center. Sweeping down the light, marble hallway in her long, black robes, she was making her own breeze as she came. I greeted her and gave her three Easter lilies that had graced my office—they suited her in her black habit. Sister Diodora, holding those lilies, is a picture I shall never forget. Her youthful features were beautiful without a touch of makeup. Her fair complexion was framed by her nun's veil, which hid her hair. The week before, when we had met for the first time, I had not noticed she was so young. I wondered if the clothing of the cloistered celibate is meant to eradicate age. Perhaps it is.

She drove me across the top of the Mount of Olives to the Greek Orthodox Monastery called Little Galilee, just two minutes away. The old, red car putted along, and I wondered if we might not have done better to walk. It was such a short distance, and she was certainly fit and able. We later walked that mount many times, talking together nonstop. She seemed completely at ease.

Only two Greek Orthodox women lived in this pleasant compound. Somehow I had expected many nuns to be housed there. It was a lovely, peaceful spot; I was captivated. Probably part of my fascination was having entered the gate I had so often passed, trying to picture what would be inside. Now I had been welcomed there. She showed me around a bit, and then we sat at a table in the sunlight, drank fresh lemonade, ate freshly made white, salty cheese and crackers, and began the planned interview. As I look back on that idyllic day, I cannot really set a boundary between our pleasant conversation and the probing interview. It was as if I had always known her.

She had been in Jerusalem nearly a year. When I asked her how she came to be in Jerusalem, she explained that it was a long story. I suggested she start at the beginning. So she did.

"I lived in Gottingen for the first ten years of my life. My family had six children and my father, who is a heart surgeon, was called to a university in Hamburg, close to Saarbrucken, where I lived the next six years. When I was sixteen I left my family because I had applied for an international college in England to do my two last years of high school there. I learned English and had my first experience far away from home with international students. It was a boarding school, and it was a very, very important experience for me."

I wondered how she had come from England to live thousands of miles away on the Mount of Olives in Jerusalem and how she had come to choose the life of a Greek Orthodox nun, a life of celibacy, when she had likely been born a Lutheran. I inquired if her family had been religious. She said not in the ordinary sense. "Instead," she said, "they created a search in me to look for more and to believe that there is something very high, deep, and everlasting." That search led her to Greece as an art student. There she unexpectedly found what she had sought upon meeting Father Dionysios and determined that the only way to demonstrate her newfound fervor and connection to God was a lifetime commitment of service and love.

Some of my favorite memories of Diodora Manachi are of our walks on the Mount of Olives. I also treasure our times working together, whether at her beautiful, walled compound, where we swept chapel floors and polished brass that had long been neglected, or in my packing at the Jerusalem Center or my home. How could I have known that my final days spent packing to leave Jerusalem would be lightened in every way by a Greek Orthodox nun? She was on hand to help me pack the books and files at my office and later, my favorite, precious things at my home, as my husband and I prepared to return to the United States. She was the personification of her words: "It is my obligation to give everything which I have been given."

During this process I put a few things aside to give away, feeling virtuous in preparing to give a few castoffs to the poor. She genuinely shared my joy as she told me that the happiest day of her life was the day she gave away everything she owned and became a nun. How foolish I felt, how selfish. I was sobered. The contrast in attitude was stunning. Yet now I see clearly my responsibility in living in the world and distributing whatever goods come to me—a continuing practice in consecration—while she accomplished another goal by giving all her possessions at once.

She labeled everything carefully. I should have been suspicious as I saw her writing on sticky labels at such length. She often said how she wished she might be with me to help me unpack because that would be a real task. Only upon unpacking did I realize what she had been doing. She was with me. Small notes in her unmistakable, artistic handwriting were tucked here and there or pressed onto carefully wrapped precious things in smaller boxes inside the larger crates. They were written in Greek, expressions simple enough that she knew I could decipher them. I remember especially "agape en Christos" which means roughly "love in Christ." It was as if she had come home with me to help me unpack.

Jesus' peace is grounded in love and loving relationships such as Diodora's and mine. Are *love* and *peace* synonyms? It seems so to me. Love is the motivation for peace. Peace is the fruit of love. "Perfect love casteth out fear" (1 John 4:18). "Charity is the pure love of Christ, and it endureth forever" (Moroni 7:47). "Charity . . . is not easily provoked" (Moroni 7:45). "Charity never faileth" (Moroni 7:46). Add to those, "Pray unto the Father with all the energy of heart, that ye may be filled with this love [charity], which he hath bestowed upon all who are true followers of his Son, Jesus Christ" (Moroni 7:48).

Listening once to Professor Terry Warner, I caught a much larger vision of what it means to be filled with Christ's love. He spoke of Satan as the great prototype of self-seeking or selfishness. Brother Warner asked, "How can we ever make things better in this world? In Jesus' way. He conquered the forcefulness of force. He defeated all the pressures that push humanity toward enmity and discord. He absorbed the terrible poison of vengeance into himself and metabolized it by his love."[5]

Does that mean we can metabolize hate and pain by love? Indeed it does. Our increasing capacity to love will bring increasing peace to us and the world. His love changes everything to another level. Love instead of resistance. Christ's love calls forth love.

Professor Warner asks us to "sacrifice all taking of offense, forswear vulgarity, abhor violence, renounce war, proclaim peace, do good to all. Let your sunshine and warmth fall on the just and the unjust."[6] He explained that Satan doesn't need to overpower us to win his eternal war. He only has to convince us to use his way to fight the war. We must reach out even to those who violate all these principles. The telling blows against evil are struck one act of love at a time. We must devote time and energy to each other. There are no time-outs. Everything makes a difference. A little casual sin collaborates with the enemy. We fight this war by means of love. Christ is the model of all peacemaking.

English statesman William Gladstone described this same formula for peace when he declared, "We look forward to the time when the power of love will replace the love of power."[7]

Betty Majaj

Like the other women of Jerusalem who exemplify love is another dear friend, Betty Majaj. I first met Betty in her official role as the director of the Center for Disabled Children on the Mount of Olives. I noticed immediately her kindness, her courtesy, her innate gentleness. She is a woman of peace in every sense of the word. The few lines in her face trace a lifetime of smiles. As I was to learn, she has not always had a tranquil life, but her native optimism has carried her along. Laughter comes easily to her, and the cultural differences between us disappeared in our joking together.

Betty was born in Sidon, Lebanon, a city surviving from antiquity and one of the main cities of ancient Phoenicia. She first came to Jerusalem as a nurse, assisting her doctor husband, Amin, in setting up an emergency hospital in the Austrian Hospice during the 1948 war. At the end of the war, they settled in East Jerusalem, where they reared their family and where Amin became one of the most beloved pediatricians in the city. When their children were grown, Betty became director of the Princess Basma Center for Disabled Children, where BYU students volunteer.

The following incident will let you into Betty's world: "When my son was nearly ten years old, a Jewish lady came to visit us. [An unusual event for an Arab family in today's take-sides world.] She was my sister's mother-in-law. I was afraid that my son might say something to hurt her or harm or embarrass her. So, I taught my son. I said, 'You know, we have a Jewish lady coming to spend a few days with us. She's Jewish [to him that translated "enemy"], but she is family.'

"It was summer. We were sitting outside on the patio, and the ground was covered with jasmine flowers. Saleh, my little son, went into the house and got a needle and thread. I didn't notice what he was doing. I was busy, you know, very anxious to meet her and talk to her and all that. She was a Cohen, one of the important tribes of Israel. Saleh sat at our feet threading those jasmines and making a necklace. We hardly noticed him. He didn't care. He didn't mind, Jew or not Jew, she was family. Immediately, when he finished it, he put it over her neck.

"As she was dying two years ago [1992] in Haifa, I went to see her. She reminded me of that story on her deathbed, how my son only cared that she was family, that it didn't matter what the Jews did to the Arabs."

When Betty Majaj told me this lovely story of her young son, she may have been thinking to explain to me how peace can come when we all think of each other as family. She might have been trying to tell me of her son's innocent reaction or to show me how long the "Jewish lady" remembered the olive branch that was presented to her as a jasmine necklace. Whatever she was trying to communicate, what I heard was how a mother teaches a child of peace and love, for *family* to Betty Majaj was synonymous with love. And with love in place, hatred automatically evaporates, as Betty explains: "Hatred will slowly, slowly disappear, naturally, spontaneously, because people are not born with it. And they are not taught to hate by their religion. No religion teaches hatred, not the Muslim, nor Christian, nor Jew."

That is the way Betty sees it, while others, among whom she lives, somehow learn to hate with a kind of everlasting hatred that predates their own experience. No one seems to remember just when the hatred began, but the venom continues from one generation to the next, and some individuals can be observed in Israeli and Arab camps collecting poisonous offenses day after month after year. It is a sordid task, but to some it seems essential. Betty's credo precludes such collecting. We can learn from her that love is the path we should take. Collecting grievances places stumbling blocks along that path.

Sharon Rosen

Another friend who also demonstrates love is Sharon Rosen, an Orthodox Jewish mother married to a rabbi. Some years ago she traveled to Russia on a dangerous mission of mercy, which she speaks of rather matter-of-factly: "We traveled into Russia in 1984 taking things for the Jewish Refuseniks: goods they could sell, kosher foods for prisoners, and literature, like prayer books. We also went to ask what they needed. It was secret work—a bit dangerous, as we could have been expelled. I knew one Jewish couple who were expelled from Russia the week before my visit for similar activities."

This brave young woman was born in London and schooled there until her father brought his family on *aliya,* or emigration, to Israel in 1970. There she attended college and met her future husband. She explains: "David and I met as a result of my mother's determined efforts to get us together. She didn't know him personally but had heard about him and his illustrious family and worked on common friends to drop tidbits about me in his and his mother's ears.

"I, of course, refused to meet a rabbi, but he phoned me one day while I was home visiting my parents in Tel Aviv. My mother immediately cottoned on to who was at the other end of the phone and confused me so much with her simultaneous persuasion to accept his offer to go out that I relented. He picked me up from the house, and it was love at first sight—my mother fell in love with him immediately and has remained his greatest fan ever since! It took David and me about two days more. We were engaged five weeks later and married four months after that, while he was still serving as an army chaplain and I was in the second and middle year of university. I was nineteen. He was twenty-one."

Many times Truman and I have been invited to join this fine couple and their children in their home for their Shabbat evening meal. They sing. The harmony is symbolic. Their voices blend like those of a quintet that has practiced hundreds of times, which of course they have. As we listen to song after song, I can almost hear in my mind their ancestors singing the familiar tunes. The most moving moment for me, however, is when Rabbi Rosen and Sharon take turns embracing each of their lovely daughters, intoning a mother's and a father's blessing in whispered

Hebrew phrases. It is a transcendently beautiful Sabbath connection repeated weekly. This woman tenderly enfolding her daughters in her arms while praying for them speaks to my soul.

Sharon's oldest daughter, Yakarah, has now been married under the canopy, and a new family has begun, one that will undoubtedly enfold each other in arms of love, in the pattern they have lived since birth.

Please remember this image, this pattern. Though most of us cannot whisper Hebrew prayers to our dear ones, we can hug them, enfolding them in the arms of our love—our husbands, our children, our parents, our friends. We can whisper our love and live it in Christ's perfect pattern.

These few women whose names are unfamiliar are ordinary women like you and me. But their lives thunder to us across time and space: "I can make a difference wherever I live." I was surprised to discover that not one of them felt powerless. Living on the edge had honed them, strengthened them in ways they might never have imagined possible. That can happen to us. There were chasms to be crossed, but they learned to be their own bridges. In their beleaguered city, whether at war or fighting for peace, they weren't waiting for anyone to solve their problems. They did not wait to see what would happen next. Each, in her own way, was working on the tiny interim miracles she could manage, and if the big miracle of political peace materialized, fine, but if it was longer in coming, surely more private miracles were possible.

Is this not the ultimate truth? We are the makers of peace. "Peace cannot be imposed," taught President Ezra Taft Benson. "It must come from the lives and hearts of men [and women]. There is no other way."[8] We pray for peace in Kosovo, Jerusalem, Pakistan, Ireland, Soweto, and Littleton, Colorado. St. Francis of Assisi teaches us the proper prayer for peace:

> Lord, make me an instrument of thy peace.
> Where there is hatred, let me sow love . . .
> Where there is despair, let me sow hope,
> Where there is darkness, let me sow light,
> Where there is sadness, let me sow joy.[9]

"Lord, make *me* an instrument of thy peace." I pray that we may find personal peace by giving ourselves, by acknowledging the simple abundance of our lives, and by letting Christ's charity fill us until we are purified, even as he is pure.

NOTES

1. *Hymns of The Church of Jesus Christ of Latter-day Saints* (Salt Lake City: The Church of Jesus Christ of Latter-day Saints, 1985), no. 294.
2. Bertha Spafford Vester, *Our Jerusalem: An American in the Holy City* (Jerusalem: The American Colony, 1988).
3. See Richard G. Scott, "Finding Happiness," *Brigham Young University Speeches, 1996–97* (Provo, Utah: Brigham Young University, 1997), 360; see also Richard G. Scott, *Ensign*, May 1995, 25.
4. Sarah Ban Breathnach, *Simple Abundance: A Daybook of Comfort and Joy* (New York: Warner Books, 1995), 4.
5. C. Terry Warner, "Honest, Simple, Solid, True," *BYU Magazine*, June 1996, 35; see also C. Terry Warner, "Scapegoating and Atonement," in *To Rejoice as Women*, ed. Susette Fletcher Green and Dawn Hall Anderson (Salt Lake City: Deseret Book, 1995), 125–44; or "Why We Forgive," in *Best of Women's Conference* (Salt Lake City: Deseret Book, 2000), 564–79.
6. Warner, "Honest, Simple, Solid, True," 35.
7. William Gladstone, quoted by John Longden, Conference Report, October 1963, 31.
8. Ezra Taft Benson, *The Teachings of Ezra Taft Benson* (Salt Lake City: Deseret Book, 1988), 703.
9. "A Prayer of St. Francis of Assisi," trans. F. Robert Wilson, in *Best-Loved Poems of the LDS People*, comp. Jack M. Lyon, Linda Ririe Gundry, Jay A. Parry, and Devan Jensen (Salt Lake City: Deseret Book, 1996), 271; emphasis added.

How Do I Develop
"Affirmative Gratitude"?

MARCI MCPHEE AND ROSALEA MCINTIRE

Keep an open mind. (Marci) President Gordon B. Hinckley taught that "we must cultivate a spirit of affirmative gratitude"—not mere tolerance or a patronizing pity, nor steamroller missionary spirit, but affirmative gratitude—"for those who do not see things quite as we see them. We do not in any way have to compromise our theology, our convictions, our knowledge of eternal truth as it has been revealed by the God of heaven. We can offer our own witness of the truth, quietly, sincerely, honestly, but never in a manner that will give offense to others."[1] Especially with those friends of other faiths who might be in your own family, cultivating a spirit of affirmative gratitude by keeping an open mind and an open heart might make an enormous difference.

Bear witness but "never in a manner that will give offense." (Marci) Perhaps a small thing, such as saying, "Oh, my goodness" instead of something profane or disrespectful will let others know you are a follower of the Lord Jesus Christ. Those young men and women with black name tags challenged me to bear my testimony to nonmember friends. I thought I was doing that, until I listened to myself.

Marci Gregory McPhee is the administrator at the International Center for Ethics, Justice, and Public Life at Brandeis University in Waltham, Massachusetts. She and her husband, George R. McPhee, have a combined family of six children. She serves as the Relief Society president in her ward.

Rosalea W. McIntire, an artist and homemaker, received her history degree from Brigham Young University. She and her husband, J. Rodney McIntire, are the parents of four daughters and the grandparents of twelve. She serves on the Relief Society homemaking committee in her ward.

While working on an e-mail message, I typed, "Well, Mormons believe . . ." I hit the backspace key and wrote instead, "I know." Talk about your religion or don't, as you are guided by the Spirit.

Appreciate the contribution other religious traditions can make to your spirituality. (Marci) My friend Ifty tells me about Muslim students who pray five times a day in the Muslim prayer room in the dorms. How much better our lives would be if we stopped for just a moment five times a day and refocused on the things that really matter! Did you know that if a Persian rug is perfect, it is not Persian? Persians deliberately put in a flaw as they weave a rug because only God can make perfect things, and they don't want to blaspheme the name of God by making a perfect rug and pretending to be perfect.

At Brandeis University, where I work, about two-thirds of the students are Jewish. For me, understanding Judaism better has been incredibly enriching. Though Judaism is an evolving, vibrant religion of today's world, its rituals feel like a time capsule of Old Testament history. And I believe in the Old Testament! I can study the miraculous exodus of Moses and the children of Israel, or I can go to a Passover seder and relive it through the ritual of the service and the symbolism of such different foods as the unleavened bread and the bitter herbs in the seder meal. I have watched a thirteen-year-old young man read from the Torah scrolls at his bar mitzvah and imagined Jesus reading from the sacred scrolls in the synagogue in his hometown of Nazareth.

Treat new friends as you would Latter-day Saints. (Marci) If a neighbor is sick or just home from the hospital with a new baby and you're thinking, *if I were her visiting teacher, I'd take her a meal*—then take her a meal! She may not expect it as a Latter-day Saint neighbor might, but she will be touched by it. Years ago, as a student at Brigham Young University, I worked off-campus with two older women, one LDS and one not. An event was being held at my ward that I thought they'd be interested in, so I invited them. The nonmember looked at me in astonishment. She replied, "In twenty years of living in Provo, no one has ever invited me to your church." Reach out—outside your comfort zone. You will bless others' lives, and they will bless yours. Reach out to them as friends—include them in your life, not just in your church. I promise that you will become a better Christian and a better Latter-day Saint.

Respect the spirituality of others. (Rosalea) For several years, my husband's work required us to live in the sultanate of Oman, an Islamic country located at the bottom of the Saudi Arabian peninsula. One cannot be in an Arab country very long without hearing the call to prayer. Five times a day, the muezzins, the men who deliver the call to prayer, will climb the tower, or minaret, of their mosque and, using amplified sound to reach their sometimes sleeping congregations, greet the neighborhood in song from the many mosques in each of the housing quarters. Their individual voices rise and fall independently of one another; there is no prearranged, cooperative musical plan. Although their songs differ, their message is always the same. Most men in Oman arrange to attend the mosque for prayer, but I have seen automobiles screech to a halt on major highways during the call to prayer and watched both the noble and the humble bow themselves at the side of the road facing the holy city of Mecca, in fervent prayer and thanksgiving to Allah. I loved hearing the call to prayer and felt it a privilege to be among people whose emphasis on prayerful communication with God is such an important part of their daily lives.

Admire the good works of others. (Rosalea) In Oman, Christians are tolerated, but they are strictly forbidden to proselyte. Lifelong missionaries from other Christian churches set a wonderful example for us while we lived there. One was an American doctor named Donald Bosch who had arrived in Oman in 1952 with his wife and three children. Sent by a Christian church in South Carolina to serve as humanitarian missionaries, they had chosen to stay and dedicate their lives to helping the people in a country with one of the highest infant mortality rates in the world, a country in which uncontrolled diseases such as malaria and leprosy were common. Dr. Bosch left the promise of a lucrative medical practice in the United States to serve in a country with only one small clinic and ten hospital beds, no schools, bad water, and no air conditioning in temperatures of 120 degrees Fahrenheit in some summer weeks. Oman is now modern and boasts one of the highest rates of newborn survival in the world. As I listened to stories of Dr. Bosch's experiences, I realized what an important part he and his wife had played in that transformation. I remarked to him that I thought it must have been very hard to be missionaries and yet not be allowed to carry scriptures. I will never forget his answer: "Rosalea, you are your scriptures."

Appreciate their culture. (Rosalea) Omanis have a sincere love for their fellowman. They experience great joy when meeting a relative or friend unexpectedly, and whether traveling by foot, animal, or vehicle, will stop in the middle of the road, greet each other with kisses, and take a moment out to sit and enjoy coffee together. The coffee pot is the symbol of graciousness in the desert. This custom became the first hurdle our family had to overcome, because to refuse the gift, as well as to fail to offer it, is considered ill-mannered. I asked an Arab friend how to explain in Arabic that God had forbidden something. Not understanding exactly what I was asking, he suggested I use the word *harram*, meaning literally "God forbids it." I used that word for seven and a half years each time I was offered coffee or tea. My hosts would always quickly withdraw the offer and replace it with another choice to avoid offending me. Just before I left the Middle East, a Lebanese friend gently corrected my Arabic and explained that the term *harram* was only used for behaviors universally known to be forbidden in the Old Testament or the Koran. The Omanis, being familiar with both, knew that the use of coffee and tea is not forbidden in either. *Harram* has a second meaning. The second meaning, and the one they thought I meant, is a refusal of the offering because it appeared to me to be filthy and disgusting. Thinking back on the many gracious hosts who chose not to take offense at my words, I am humbled. There was true charity, as described by Moroni and Paul: "Charity suffereth long, and . . . is not easily provoked" (Moroni 7:45; 1 Corinthians 13:4–5).

Encircle your friends of other faiths with love. (Rosalea) Some time ago I met a European woman who had not been able to overcome the effects of culture shock while her husband worked in Oman. She disliked all Arabs and warned me that no matter how much I might think of them as friends, they would never invite me into their homes. I chose not to tell her that we had already been invited into many Arab homes. We had held their babies, laughed at each other's language mistakes, sat on the ground eating with our fingers out of the same communal bowl, and mourned together the loss of a child. We felt each other's love for God, and as we grew to know each other, we grew to love each other.

NOTE
1. Gordon B. Hinckley, "Out of Your Experience Here," *BYU Today*, March 1991, 37.

How Can I "Comfort Those That Stand in Need of Comfort"?

BETH VAUGHAN COLE AND
RAE JEANNE MEMMOTT

Value the contribution you can make. (Beth) The summer after I joined The Church of Jesus Christ of Latter-day Saints, I left Ohio to study child psychiatric nursing at Boston University. I loved it. I loved learning about children, how they grew, and how people and events influenced their personalities and behaviors. One child I worked with for about six months was a seven-year-old boy I will call Bobby. Two years earlier, his older brother had died of leukemia. Although Bobby had often talked about dying, he seemed fearless. Bobby would jump off his garage "like Superman" and had terrified his parents with a variety of other daredevil activities. A few weeks after getting to know him, he told me that he was about to become the age his brother had been when he died. "When I am eight," he said, "it is my turn to die, like my brother." It took several months to convince him that his brother died of a disease, not because of his being eight, that the disease was something his brother had and Bobby did not. After the loss of their first son, his grieving parents had barely enough strength to get through each day. Bobby was making his own logic of the circumstances, nearly destroying

Beth Vaughan Cole, a professor of nursing at the University of Utah, where she also coordinates the doctoral program, is a mother, grandmother, and Relief Society teacher. She is also the director of Caring Connection: A Hope and Comfort in Grief.

Rae Jeanne Memmott, a single mother of four, is an associate professor of nursing at Brigham Young University with a special interest in international nursing. She serves as the Gospel Doctrine teacher in her ward.

himself in the process. That is one of several experiences that brought me to my work as a grief counselor.

The saying that "God has no hands but our hands" is a perfect description of our efforts to help others. So many people in this world are grieving. Like Bobby's parents, they need to know of our support in their trials. No one on earth has all the knowledge or all the skills to bring to a situation, but we all have hands to help. I need your hands to help me when I am discouraged and in sorrow, and let me offer my hands to help you in yours.

Remember why you serve. (Beth) I knew there would be many ramifications if I took the position to lead a grief program: it would take me away from my leadership position with the college, my salary would decrease, and my ability to influence decisions within the college would change. I remember the day I decided: Easter Sunday of 1997. The spirit of that day ran through Relief Society, Sunday School, and sacrament meeting. My children had passed the squirming-in-their-seat phase, so I could actually pay attention to the sacrament, the bright spring flowers, the excellent speakers. I didn't have any great epiphany; I just remembered why I was at church—this Church. "Now, as ye are desirous to come into the fold of God, and to be called his people, . . . and are willing to mourn with those that mourn; yea, and comfort those that stand in need of comfort, . . . that ye may be redeemed of God, and . . . that ye may have eternal life" (Mosiah 18:8–9). I knew that Easter Sunday I would serve in the new role. The job didn't come as a Church calling, but I knew that it was right, that with the Master's help, I would bear others' "burdens, that they may be light" (Mosiah 18:8).

Consider the parable of the talents. (Rae Jeanne) Eight years ago, my four children and I spent a summer in Guatemala doing volunteer work with mentally and physically handicapped children. At the time my daughters were eighteen, fourteen, and twelve, and my son was ten. I had been a single mother for more than nine years and the sole financial support for our family. When I knew from a clear, forceful answer to my prayers that my children and I should go to Guatemala, I had only my monthly salary, with no savings or other income. None of us spoke Spanish, and until the day we arrived in Guatemala, we didn't know where we would live or how much this journey was going to cost. Going with an established volunteer organization seemed an obvious solution, but that was not an option for us. Most cost too much, didn't take young children, or sponsored short, two-week projects. Driving was not safe, but I had nowhere near the funds for airfare for five. I tell these daunting circumstances not to demonstrate my ability to leap tall buildings in a single bound—frankly, at that point in my life just making it from day to day was challenging—I tell them to emphasize how utterly dependent my small family and I were on the Lord.

The parable of the talents suggests that our Lord expects us to use whatever gifts he has given us, no matter how minor or paltry they may appear. What we use will increase; what we choose not to use will be lost. I am convinced by our experiences in getting to Guatemala that the Lord is so eager to bless us when we seek to bless the lives of others that it is almost impossible to fail in our righteous endeavors.

Expect miracles when you serve. (Rae Jeanne) The Lord performs miracles in the lives of ordinary people: a junior high school Spanish teacher tutored us in some very basic Spanish and charged us next to nothing; a colleague at work handed me an envelope containing a hundred dollars; members of our ward gave us money and offered to take care of our home for the almost two months that we would be gone.

Less than a week before we were to leave, the hose on the car radiator broke and the engine overheated so badly that the first mechanic to look at it told me the engine was ruined. I left my car at a shop near where it had broken down and found a ride home. We were not a two-car family, despite our teenagers, so at home I called my bishop to see if I could use one of his vehicles for a few days. When he dropped off his truck, I told him that I guessed there was no way we could make it to Guatemala now that our car was ruined. He didn't console or sympathize. He simply said, "Well, the Lord hasn't told me to take my children to Guatemala, but he has told you to." My first thought was, *What, am I some kind of magician?* My second thought was, *He's right. I will find a way to do this.* The next day when I called the repair shop, the mechanic told me the engine was okay after all and gave me the day and time he'd have it repaired—amazingly, within hours of the latest possible time we had to leave to make our flight from Los Angeles. So with loaned cars, miraculous repairs, and family and friends going out of their way to help, we got on the road. That was the pattern—a continual trial of faith—but each time I took a step into the dark, the way would appear. Obstacle after obstacle appeared, but in response to exercising the faith to proceed, small and monumental miracles occurred, often through the hands of family, friends, and neighbors.

How Can I Feel Motivated
to Volunteer?

BILLIE B. EMERT

Realize the importance of community service. Humane, civilized behavior on the community level is affordable (both in money and in delivery of services) only through volunteerism. In Cache Valley, for instance, we care for the elderly, whether they can pay or not pay, through a community-owned facility called Sunshine Terrace. The backbone of Sunshine Terrace is its volunteers. The Food Pantry, providing food to the needy, is another organization totally staffed by volunteers. Essentially, volunteerism is an integral part of the conscience of a community. Given today's economic realities, many acts of humane, civilized behavior are possible only through the work of volunteers.

Don't be afraid of a bumpy start. I walked into the world of volunteerism backwards and with both eyes closed. The PTA president, a neighbor who had been especially kind to me when we moved to Kansas City, called one day to explain that she needed a mother to be in charge of refreshments for the PTA meetings. You would think that since I was running a technically challenging company, the thought of doing something as simple as refreshments for a PTA meeting would be a snap. Not so, not by miles. I found ridiculous ways to worry about how I could mess up and wondered if anything I could do would possibly be good enough. I know now that my concerns arose from leaving my comfort zone, but

Billie B. Emert is a full-time volunteer for Utah State University where her husband, George H. Emert, is president. After obtaining a degree in mathematics, she had a career in the computer world. She and her husband are the parents of four daughters. Now grandchildren, writing, and volunteer activities bring joy to her life.

then all I knew was that by the time I got table coverings, flowers, and food to the PTA meeting, I was obsessing. However trivial, it was my first venture into community service, and within a hair's breadth it nearly turned out to be my last.

At that first meeting, the PTA president, in an effort to help intro-duce me to my neighbors, asked me to give the invocation when the person assigned that task had not arrived. I came up with a prayer that I hoped would appeal to everyone. I have a memory of mentioning kids, who are my passion, and, for some long-forgotten reason, of mentioning peanut butter. Overall, it was not the grandest of prayers, but it sufficed. When I finished, the principal actually rolled off his chair, stone dead. He had died of a massive brain aneurysm, but I did not learn that until days later. While frantic women tried to resuscitate him and called for an ambulance, I stood lamely by, remembering that he had sampled some of my goodies from the table before the meeting began and that I had watched him listen attentively as I started to pray. I was convinced that either my food or my prayer had killed him. When I finally got home that night, I closed the front door and swore I had made my last trip into the outside world for anything but groceries.

But time soothes; eventually I did venture back out. One volunteer job led to another, and then two, and then I found myself "complexly multitasking." That is, I was keeping up with home, a job, and an expanded world of volunteer activities.

Evaluate the match before you volunteer. Volunteering has the best chance of succeeding when you approach the task in much the same way you would approach an organ transplant. From the onset, you should establish the expectations of the volunteer job and have some rough-draft notion of your talents, or lack thereof. How much time and energy do you have to give? Are they compatible with the job? That is exactly what blood and tissue matches are for in a transplant. If you do not eval-uate the match before you enter the volunteer world, you will, unless you are just plain lucky, experience rejection in some way. Either you or the organization will reject the graft, and rejection is painful.

Don't expect volunteer work to be all fun. Taking responsibility or leadership in an organization is not all fun nor always rewarding. For one thing, volunteers work with people, and people are not always perfect.

You may encounter some with less than altruistic agendas. I classify these people into three categories: the control freaks, those who come with a secular agenda, and the drama kings and queens who love gossip. Fortunately, in my experience, the vast majority of volunteers are people you will learn to love and admire and even come to revere.

Be realistic and selective in the jobs you volunteer for. No matter how important or altruistic a volunteer job is, you have to be realistic about the scope of the undertaking and the effort required to get the job done. In other words, be realistic about time management. Volunteer your valuable time only on those projects for which you feel a passion. To do otherwise is not to give your best.

Let God work through you. When you truly volunteer your time and talents with an open heart and open mind—with no selfish or egotistical agendas—when you open your mouth to speak or your eyes to look, what comes out is pure light or energy from God. I can say this after serving with and learning from some of God's most beautiful spirits. If any sort of leadership results, it is because others are choosing to follow not the person but the light. I absolutely believe that. Leadership results when an individual focuses on being as good an instrument of God's plan as is humanly possible. That word *humanly* admits to a lot of loopholes, it's true, but it is possible to do the best we can. One definition of a leader is a guide. In volunteer work, the guide is not the person, but God's plan coming through a person who has chosen to open her mind and heart to God's syllabus. In this way, the winding paths of volunteerism can lead to one of God's wonders: inspired and selfless community leadership.

How Do I Bring a Spiritual Dimension to Community Service?

CAROL NIXON

Recognize your divine predisposition to serve. It is in our divine nature to serve, given to us by a loving God who knows that if society is to stand against adversity, it must have its better angels. The great Utah writer Wallace Stegner tried to identify these complex feminine qualities in writing about his own mother, but he realized that so exquisite were they that it was impossible to make them credible on paper: "I felt always on the edge of the unbelievable, as if I were writing a saint's life. We are skeptical of kindness so unfailing, sympathy so instant and constant, trouble so patiently borne, forgiveness so whole-hearted."[1] Stegner identified the noble dimensions of our spiritual nature—those that incline us toward service and community.

Realize that societies are based on service. Our society is a place of infinite and exponential power when its spirit is the spirit of service—individuals giving more than they take, producing more than they consume, sacrificing short-term gain for long-term promise. Service is the essence of community when community is more than just a place on a map. To speak of community is to speak of a state of mind, a shared vision and destiny, a concern for the needs and welfare of others, a down payment on the promise of tomorrow.

Resist barriers to service. As a young Relief Society president, still in

Carol Nixon served as chief of staff to former Utah governor Norman Bangerter and was director of Utah's Community Development and the Utah Arts Council. She is now the director of This Is the Place Foundation. She serves as public relations director in her stake. She is the mother of six children and has seventeen grandchildren.

my twenties and pregnant, I was intimidated by the calling and overwhelmed by the conditions in my life. I expressed my inadequacies to the bishop. He gave me some counsel that I often find myself thinking about: "Carol, the willingness to serve is more important than the ability to serve." Just as each of us identifies the spirit of willingness that resides within us, we also are aware of the social threats and conflicts that try to undermine that predisposition. These include self-doubt and outright fear, lack of time, fatigue, and what I call midnight emotions—those long, dark hours that can often turn into anger when we believe our efforts are being misused, neglected, or unappreciated. The value of understanding such threats is that we are able to overcome them.

Feel the joy of serving. A year or so after I had been called to be the ward Relief Society president, I found myself working with a sister who was going through depression. The bishop and I prayerfully considered the course of action to take. She was withdrawing from the ward, even becoming ill from the emotional state she had fallen into. "How," I asked the bishop, " can we help her feel the joy she's entitled to? Isn't the promise that men are that they might have joy?" (see 2 Nephi 2:25). I'll never forget Bishop Stoddard looking at me as light flooded into his countenance. "Carol," he said, "this good sister needs to lose herself in service." Together we came up with a plan for this wonderful woman to help another sister in the ward. She accepted the assignment and within weeks was back on her feet, smiling, participating fully in the congregation. "Life," Tolstoy wrote, "is a place of service, and in that service one has to suffer a great deal that is hard to bear, but more often to experience a great deal of joy. But that joy can be real only if people look upon their life as a service, and have a definite object in life outside themselves and their personal happiness."[2]

Envision what your service is accomplishing. I recall the story of the mother who walked into her young son's bedroom. It was a mess. Pennies were strewn all over the bed and the floor. She demanded to know what he was doing. "I'm counting pennies for my mission," he replied innocently. What do we imagine we are doing in our efforts? When we volunteer for the PTA, do we see ourselves frantically making cupcakes to raise money at the Christmas carnival, frustrated that our busy lives are being complicated by such a mundane task? Or do we see our effort in the larger context of enriching future opportunities for our children? Our vision, like that of the young man counting pennies, must carry beyond the horizon. We need to see that being active participants in our communities results from God inspiring us to serve; our actions further his work. "When ye are in the service of your fellow beings ye are only in the service of your God" (Mosiah 2:17).

NOTES
1. Wallace Stegner, *Where the Bluebird Sings to the Lemonade Spring* (New York: Penguin, 1992), 24.
2. Leo Tolstoy, *A Confession and Other Religious Writings* (London: Penguin, 1987), 127–28.

How Do I Influence My World?

CATHY CHAMBERLAIN

Capture a vision of who you are. I have one brother who is younger than I am. Being the oldest, I appointed myself his conscience and boss early in his life. One day he invited a friend to spend the night. For some reason, our parents were out, and I, being the big sister, was in charge of my brother and his friend—which in my mind meant I was in complete control. The friend's mother later told my mother her son's comment about me when she asked, "So, what is your friend's older sister like?" Her son said, "Well, she's nice, I guess . . . she's kind of like a mother!"

Clearly he had noted my bossy personality. Now, as an adult, I try to tone down the bossiness, but I also find a very positive message in this assessment. Even as a single woman, I am a mother: we are all mothers, all nurturers of each other and of the children of this world. All of us have the power to influence, to affect, other people and ultimately the course of events in this world. That is our calling, the reason we are here. We nurture and influence in many different ways. As women selected in councils on high to possess the sacred knowledge of who our Father is and who we are, we are the very women responsible to bless, nurture, and bring our Father's children back home.

Accept and learn from your struggles. Sometimes our most profound blessings come tucked in the blankets of our greatest sorrows. It requires a little more effort to find them, but once discovered, they often become our greatest source of strength and security. My aunt shared a story about

Cathy Chamberlain served in the California Los Angeles Mission. She now resides in Arizona, where she is a senior research executive for an international company. She is also the executive director of an organization that designs and conducts conferences for women throughout the United States.

me as a small child. She said we were walking together in the grocery store to buy cookies. She was, of course, holding my hand, so as not to lose me. She heard sniffles, looked down, and saw tears running down my cheeks. When she asked what was wrong, I told her she was squeezing my hand too tight, and it hurt.

"Oh, I'm sorry," she apologized, "that's just a little love squeeze."

"It is?" I brightened up between sniffles. "Well, then, go ahead and do it!"

She had reframed my experience into something positive. Besides the power of reframing, two other powerful lessons can be drawn from this incident. First, love does hurt sometimes. And second, it's okay to acknowledge that it does hurt as long as we're willing to say, "Well, okay then, if it's love, you can go ahead and do it." The key for me was to realize that someone who really loved me was holding on to my hand very securely. I was not walking alone.

Half-full or half-empty? How we view it is our choice. Joy and even ease come with focusing on our "heart-joys" rather than our "heart-aches." Life provides plenty of both. When we hold a rose, is it the prick of the thorn or the silky curve of the petal that captures our attention? If our influence on others is to be positive, we must be positive.

Recognize your sphere of influence. In the histories of the pioneer days in the Salt Lake Valley are found such statements from the sisters as "standing as we do at the head of the women of the world" and "in our position as leaders of women of the world."[1] Utah pioneer women envisioned themselves as leaders and defenders of women in the world. Women everywhere are looking for the same things we are: to value themselves, to grow spiritually, to find a deeper purpose in life, to make a difference, and most importantly, to have healthy relationships with spouses, children, and friends. A look in any bookstore at the number of best-sellers about spirituality and relationships verifies that women are hungry for spiritual growth and meaningful relationships. These women and their families are your neighbors. You have an opportunity to nurture and influence them. Make your influence felt. They are your sisters.

NOTE
1. Belle S. Spafford, *A Woman's Reach* (Salt Lake City: Deseret Book, 1974), 95.

How Do I Become a True Friend?

SANDRA ROGERS

Recognize true friendship as a gospel principle. Friendship is such an important element of the restored gospel that Joseph Smith declared, "Friendship is one of the grand fundamental principles of 'Mormonism'; [it is designed to] revolutionize and civilize the world, and cause wars and contentions to cease and men to become friends and brothers. . . . Friendship is like Brother Turley in his blacksmith shop welding iron to iron; it unites the human family with its happy influence."[1]

Avoid counterfeits of friendship. Without Christ as the center of our friendly feelings, we may be led away from true friendship into destructive imitations. Our need for inclusion and acceptance is strong, and Satan employs counterfeits of friendship to delude and defraud us. Just as he hopes we will confuse lust for love, and unrestrained autonomy for agency and accountability, he would substitute false friends for true. Counterfeit friendships most often are gossipy, self-aggrandizing cliques that exclude and look down on others. At the worst, these counterfeit friendships are formed among those who are "friends in iniquity" as in the hideous secret combinations spoken of in the Book of Mormon (Mosiah 29:22; see 3 Nephi 6:27). In our century, these "friends in iniquity" range from the perpetrators of the Holocaust to the Trenchcoat Mafia at Columbine High School.

Strive for Christ's ideal of friendship. The basis of true friendship is being a friend of God. Christ's ideal of friendship requires that we be

Sandra Rogers is dean of the College of Nursing at Brigham Young University. She was a welfare services missionary in the Philippines and serves as a teacher in her ward Relief Society.

friends on a high moral and spiritual level. Under his divine guidance and discipline, if we are humble enough to accept it, our affection and friendship can mature into charity, the pure love of Christ, and we can be Zion, a people with one heart. Charity elevates friendship to a plane that will endure through the years and all eternity because such friendship is bound by ideals that are themselves eternal.

Follow the Beatitudes to fashion hearts capable of true friendship. The Beatitudes are truly the simple yet eternal guide to becoming closer to God and more like him—and to becoming Christlike friends. For instance, consider the beatitude, "Blessed are the meek" (Matthew 5:5). The meek have self-mastery and discipline. They are not easily provoked or irritated and forbear with patience injury or annoyance. Or consider "Blessed are all they who do hunger and thirst after righteousness" in our interactions with our friends (Matthew 5:6). Hungering and thirsting after righteousness may help us to be honest and helpful, open, candid, and supportive. False reassurances are not, after all, true friendships. An obligation of friendship, even at the risk of losing that friend, is to give wise counsel, even if the friend cannot take it in.

In relation to friendship, consider these three beatitudes: "Blessed arc the merciful" (Matthew 5:7). Sometimes it is easier to forgive those somewhat removed from our circle for large hurts and offenses than it is to forgive friends for tiny little infractions of things we think they should know and do better. Similarly, "Blessed are the peacemakers" (Matthew 5:9). Among other things, peacemaking means supporting our friends in forgiving those who have been hurtful to them. If we provoke and encourage feelings of victimization or retribution, we hurt our friends more seriously than has any previous offender. Consider, "Blessed are the pure in heart" (Matthew 5:8). The pure in heart see the spark of divinity in others. They are not critical but look for decency and goodness in others and practice it themselves. They do not easily believe ill of others and their motivations. The pure in heart have the Spirit of the Lord, which purifies their affections and lifts friendship to the level of charity.

NOTE
   1. *Scriptural Teachings of the Prophet Joseph Smith*, sel. Joseph Fielding Smith and annotated by Richard C. Galbraith (Salt Lake City: Deseret Book, 1993), 354–55.

Personal Purity and Intimacy

WENDY L. WATSON

As women of the latter days, we believe firmly in being honest, true, chaste, benevolent, and virtuous. As women who have made sacred covenants with the Lord, we seek only after those things that are virtuous, lovely, or of good report, or praiseworthy (see Article of Faith 13). We, as spirit daughters of heavenly parents and as women of Christ, know that it is only through such persistent seeking after virtue and purity that we will be able to endure the days ahead. And we, who are daughters of Eve, know that personal purity is the only way for us to bring life into this world—and to bring forth life and love in all our relationships.

I believe in the power of beliefs to focus our thoughts, to generate our feelings, and to influence our behaviors.[1] I believe that if the words of bedrock belief from the thirteenth Article of Faith were embroidered on sweatshirts, silk-screened on tote bags, cross-stitched on pillows, and most importantly, engraven upon our hearts—so that we were increasingly honest, true, chaste, benevolent, and virtuous—we would have enough and to spare of intimacy in our lives.

We need intimacy. Our souls are enlarged when we experience deep-core caring—interpersonal connections which are heart-, mind-, and strength-sustaining. All relationships—parent-child, husband-wife, grandparent-grandchild, sibling, friend—all have the potential to be intimate, in developing mutual feelings of trust, emotional closeness,

Wendy L. Watson holds a Ph.D. in family therapy and gerontology from the University of Calgary in Calgary, Alberta, Canada, and also holds degrees in nursing and psychology. She is a professor of marriage and family therapy in the School of Family Life at Brigham Young University and served as chair for the 1999 BYU Women's Conference.

and the sharing of thoughts and feelings. Exclusively, those in marriage relationships have the privilege of enjoying an additional kind of intimacy, that of physical intimacy. First, we will discuss the incredible intimacy that can be part of all friendships and family relationships. Then we will address physical intimacy, that unique and grand intimacy that is sanctioned only in marriage.

We, as women of faith, need true intimacy. No illusions of intimacy will do. I believe that true intimacy is impossible to achieve in the absence of personal purity. In fact, through my more than twenty-five years of working with individuals, couples, and families in counseling—many of whom have been affected by the devastations of impurity—I am more and more convinced that decreased personal purity leads to decreased intimacy. And conversely, I am more and more impressed that increased personal purity leads to increased intimacy.

What else have I come to believe?

That love is brought to us by the Spirit.

That lies about love are brought to us by Satan.

That love can be present only if the Spirit is present.

That love and the Spirit coexist. You cannot have one without the other.

I believe that personal purity increases intimacy. And it is clear that keeping the Lord's commandments with ever-increasing precision increases our personal purity. Thus it follows that keeping the Lord's commandments increases intimacy. What a marvelous and sure connection! We can increase the experiences of intimacy in our lives by doing what the Lord has asked us to do. It really is just that simple!

One major issue that affects relationships is the ability to show love to the other person in a way that means love to him or to her. The Savior has asked us to show love to him by keeping his commandments (see John 14:15). And as we are faithful and diligent in keeping his commandments, he promises to encircle us in the arms of his love (see D&C 6:20).

His showing his love to us in such an affectionate way—encircling us in the arms of his love—increases our desire to keep his commandments and increases our ability to show our love to him in the way that he has asked. And thus this virtuous cycle gyroscopically spins, drawing us, lifting us upward in our thoughts and feelings and actions, increasing our personal purity, and bringing us closer to the Savior. Our closeness to the Savior fills us with love, increasing our ability to love others and to feel love from others. Truman Madsen, in his *Four Essays on Love*, said: "You cannot love until you are loved. You cannot be loved until you are Beloved, Beloved of God."[2]

Not long ago in my office, a woman of great faith closed her eyes and described to her husband her feelings as she pictured herself being held by the Savior. "Brilliance!" she said. "More love than I've ever experienced in my life!" She instantly knew the feelings. Perhaps her soul was remembering.

Those light-filled, love-expanded feelings stood in stark contrast to feelings experienced for so many years in her relationship with her husband. She found his touch to be lustful. She felt like a thing, not a companion. Those feelings had been planted in her heart and mind when earlier in their marriage her husband had not kept the Lord's commandments and had broken sacred covenants. They were now facing the daunting, though not impossible, task of trying to achieve intimacy after significant exposures to impurity. Despite obstacles, the wife's closeness to the Savior filled her with love and a great desire to join with her husband in overcoming their past.

If you want to be filled with the love of the Lord, keep his commandments.

If you want to feel loved, keep the Lord's commandments.

If you truly love someone, keep the Lord's commandments.

If you truly want to experience intimacy, increase your personal purity—by keeping the Lord's commandments.

I believe our ability to experience true intimacy of any kind in any relationship is directly related to how intimate our interactions are with the Lord. The First Presidency message commencing the year 1999 was a plea from President James E. Faust to "not just . . . know about the Master, but to strive . . . to be one with Him (see John 17:21)" and to seek to "have a daily, personal relationship with [Him]."[3]

I believe that a personal relationship with the Savior is the only way to achieve true intimacy in our relationships with others. Without close and very personal interactions with our Savior Jesus Christ, any and all of our interactions with others will be found wanting. Without the Savior's influence, our relationships lack, and always will lack, the power to truly sustain our hearts and minds. Without the Savior's touch, there is no staying power to loving words and actions. Without the Savior's tutoring, there is no ability to see beyond the obvious, to look deeper into the soul of another, and to see the lovable, the redeemable, the possible.

Without the love of the Savior in our lives, no other love can fill the void of being out of his presence. We lived with him and with our heavenly parents before coming to this earth. What a gift it is to know that! What a heart-comforting thought it is to remember. No wonder we long for that feeling of deep-core love, of true intimacy.

We hunger to feel understood. We thirst for someone to really trust. We yearn to really commune. We long for an interweaving of our life with another's—mentally, emotionally, socially, physically, and spiritually.

As women who continually strive to honor covenants we've made, we will never find intimacy in relationships that do not honor those covenants. When we find ourselves in relationships that neither remember nor honor our covenants, we are left bereft—and we wonder what is wrong with us. Why can't we communicate better? Why doesn't he understand what I'm trying to say? Why doesn't she really care? Why do all our best relationship efforts, even those the world would applaud, fail to provide us with the palpable feelings we long for—of really being known by another, of being connected with another, of really mattering, of really being loved, even adored? Why? Because true intimacy of any kind in any relationship must involve the Savior.

As faithful Latter-day Saint women we will never find intimacy—not the true intimacy that sustains a spirit daughter of heavenly parents—within marital, family, or friend relationships that don't involve the Savior. Without the Savior, we may have loving and kind feelings for others. We may have our hearts drawn out to them. We may find great joy in sharing activities with them. We may experience moments of happiness because of their kindness to us. Yet the yearnings will always be there for more—more emotional connection, more trust, deeper sharing of thoughts and feelings.

A deep and abiding relationship with the Savior is indeed the only way to achieve true intimacy in our relationships with others. Because intimacy requires the involvement of both partners, each person in a truly intimate relationship must have a connection with the Savior, a connection that is strong and vibrant and growing. True intimacy requires that both parties' offerings of love be embedded within an intimate relationship with Him. All else will feel like a sorry substitute.

If you find yourself slipping into dark blue feelings as you reflect upon the present state of your relationships, that could be a very good sign—a sign that you are a seeker. If you are a seeker of everything that is virtuous, lovely, and of good report and praiseworthy, it means that you will be able to seek for—and find—everything that may be praiseworthy, lovely, virtuous, and of good report in those with whom you want to build a more intimate relationship, a relationship in which the Spirit is present.

As you strive and work with each of your loved ones for an increasingly intimate relationship, one that is blessed by the presence of the Spirit, the distinction between the Lord's truth about intimacy and the adversary's lies will become increasingly clear. For truly, the adversary promotes anything impure, defiling, of an illicit nature, or obscene and seeks to convince us that these things are normal, good, and part of intimacy. They are not!

Scholarly literature and research conclude that intimacy requires three things: reciprocal feelings of trust, emotional closeness, and the ability to openly communicate thoughts and feelings with another.[4] I believe that true intimacy also involves at least one more vital ingredient—vision. And when we approach the topic of physical intimacy, vision is even more crucial.

The following story is told of a famous ethologist, Konrad Lorenz: One day in his backyard he experimented with imprinting baby ducklings—that is, getting them to respond to him as though he were their mother. Crouching over, he walked in a figure-eight pattern, quacking steadily while he glanced repeatedly over his shoulder to signal that the ducklings were to follow. To his delight, the ducklings lined up and began waddling after him. Dr. Lorenz was congratulating himself on his spectacular feat of getting the baby ducklings to follow and attach themselves to him, an elderly man with a long white beard. At this moment of self-congratulation, he looked up—right into the faces of a group of passing tourists. They looked horrified. And Konrad Lorenz realized that from where they stood, the tourists could not see the baby ducklings. They were hidden in the tall grass. Consequently, what the onlookers saw was a demented old man walking in circles and quacking. Without the fuller picture—that is, the ducklings as well as the intent behind Konrad's behavior—a brilliant ethologist's imprinting experiment looked only like craziness.[5]

Truly we can never really understand a thing until the frame within which we are looking at it is enlarged to include all the relevant elements.

When we are seeking increased understanding about physical intimacy, which is so sacred, so powerful, we need wide-angle eternal vision and Spirit-enhanced depth perception. If our understanding of physical intimacy is based on a picture that is taken, developed, and framed by none other than the father of all lies himself, our experiences with physical intimacy will be deadly. We must mediate our understanding by the death-defying power in the Savior's atonement.

Satan's portrayal of physical intimacy is cunning, counterfeit, and contorting. His skewed view of physical intimacy comes to us through movies, magazines, and music—actually, through any and all publications and productions known to humankind—from stage plays to Internet chat rooms. When our vision clears and our frame is enlarged, we see the adversary's ploys for what they really are: elaborate and extensive maneuverings to capture our very souls. Lucifer covets our bodies and our spirits and those of our loved ones, and he is relentless in his sinister pursuit.

If you wonder how really old the adversary's craftiness is, and therefore how really good he is at his craft, just read Romans 1:24–31 and 2 Timothy 3:1–6. What Paul describes there is available for you to see in living color in your own home, with the assistance of your television, VCR, and computer. Paul's account of what the people were involved in—people who once knew God and yet turned away—sounds just like one night's worth of prime-time sitcoms (better, "sick coms").

Here is Paul's report: "[And they were] filled with all unrighteousness, fornication, wickedness, covetousness, maliciousness; full of envy, murder, debate, deceit, malignity . . . backbiters, haters of God, despiteful, proud, boasters, inventors of evil things, disobedient to parents, without understanding, covenantbreakers, without natural affection, implacable, unmerciful" (Romans 1:29–31).

Next, here is how Paul, writing to Timothy, describes the last days—our days. Think about where you may have seen these things before: "This know also, that in the last days perilous times shall come. For men shall be lovers of their own selves, covetous, boasters, proud, blasphemers, disobedient to parents, unthankful, unholy, without natural affection, trucebreakers, false accusers, incontinent, fierce, despisers of those that are good, traitors, heady, highminded, lovers of pleasures more than lovers of God" (2 Timothy 3:1–4).

And then the most chilling message of all. It's not bad enough that those horrible things are happening out there in the world. The worst part is that they come sneaking, creeping into our homes and influencing us.

Here is verse 6: "For of this sort are they which creep into houses, and lead captive silly women laden with sins, led away with divers lusts" (2 Timothy 3:6). Could Paul possibly be talking about afternoon soap operas and talk shows—and how, through them, all these offenses creep into our homes? And could he be describing those who watch them? Are we silly when we watch them? And is watching them leading us away into divers lusts?

Could Isaiah possibly be speaking to us, the Lord's women of the latter days, when he says: "Rise up, ye women that are at ease; hear my voice, ye careless daughters" (Isaiah 32:9). Have we been careless? Have we drifted far too much in the direction of the world's view, which is so saturated with Lucifer's lies about physical intimacy?

It is indeed time for Zion's daughters to rise up and be not careless but careful! Careful about everything that comes into our hearts, minds, and homes which pertains to physical intimacy. Could the words of the Prophet Joseph Smith apply to how we may at times have carelessly thought about, and talked about, physical intimacy? Joseph Smith said: "How vain and trifling have been our spirits, our conferences, our councils, our meetings, our private as well as public conversations—too low, too mean, too vulgar, too condescending."⁶ We must be very careful with our language and our conversations about everything that relates to this sacred physical endowment.

On the other hand, we need to be bold in exposing Lucifer and his lies. We need to rise up and with ever-increasing clarity point out his counterfeits, his deceptions, his trickery. I believe that all satanically influenced presentations about physical intimacy should be stamped "More Lies!" To protect our minds and hearts, our homes and families from the intrusions of the devil's devices, perhaps we need big, bold warning signs on every book, magazine, videotape, audiotape, TV sitcom, movie, or play which has been coproduced by the adversary himself—warning signs that would reveal his works for what they really are: angry protests against God and persistent, power-hungry efforts to obliterate the truth. When I think about all the individuals I have had the privilege to assist, whose lives in one way or another have been shattered and shackled as a result of moral transgressions, I want to post a warning on each and every satanically coproduced product about physical intimacy. The warning I would post is simple. It would read: "If you choose to open this, you will be giving the adversary more power over you."

I would also display six other, more explicit, warnings on Lucifer's contaminated and contaminating material. As you read, note which warnings, if heeded, might form a protective barrier, encircling our families and shutting the adversary out.

Warning 1. To be stamped on the cover of his magazines: "Contents highly addictive. Materials enclosed are extremely corrosive to the soul. Be prepared to have your mind twisted, your views of love ravaged, your spirit shrunk. Be aware that the Spirit of the Lord will not be with you during or after viewing. Be prepared to experience an initial rush and then prolonged feelings of depression, loneliness, despair, and guilt. With repeated exposures over time, however, you can numb those feelings and enter an almost total amnesia about who you really are and about truth itself."

Warning 2. For the beginning of Satan's coproduced movies: "The following scenes are brought to you in the hope that you will think of yourself as merely an animal. (Nevertheless, be advised that animal dung is actually more pure and would harm you less when taken into your system.) Extreme caution required. This movie will make you believe that lust is really love and that all that love really is, or can be, is lust. This movie will have its greatest effect if viewed when you are feeling misunderstood, alone, blue, or just that you don't fit in. If you are not in any of these moods, viewing the movie will assist in getting you there. If you are in one of these moods, your spirit will be more vulnerable and thus your ability to distinguish good from evil will be even more quickly extinguished."

Warning 3. For the devil's Internet connections: "Share the following with someone whose soul you would like to destroy. Complete success is ensured if you can offer it in the spirit of friendship and under the guise of love. By thinking and talking together about the content, all sweet, pure feelings will be distorted into grand perversions. Pick a perversion, any perversion. That may be one of the very last choices you will get to make. In fact, if you are tired of making choices, just view the following several times—or keep immersing yourself in similar material—and your freedom will be progressively diminished with each successive viewing. The irony is that you will be provided with a personalized illusion that your freedom is actually increasing. We've taken this effect far beyond the old smoke-and-mirrors tricks, and the illusions that will influence your heart and mind will be stunning. Virtual reality is here to replace virtuous living."

Warning 4. To announce the adversary's influence on prime-time viewing: "How many lies can you find in the following sitcom? If you can't find any . . . Gotcha! In the following time slot, we will offer you ideas that you have never before entertained. They may at first repel, but with repetition and humor, we will slowly dilute the initial recoiling of your spirit, and you will begin to forget that a time ever existed when you didn't believe these lies to be true."

Warning 5. A lie-busting warning for rented videos: "Fantasy only allowed here. Only erotic illusions contained. No empathic love depicted. No consequences noted. No effects on your body, your spirit, or your relationships with God, family, and friends are addressed. Please note that interactions will appear far more splendid than they really are. This is not real life, but it is a really great lie. We have left out the gory details that would only ruin the subtle appeal this movie will have for you."

Warning 6. For videos purchased: "Congratulations! You bought the movie this time instead of just renting it. In fact, you are buying this whole scheme—hook, line, and sinker. Let's just have this be our little secret. No one needs to know. No one will ever be able to tell. When people tell you that you are looking or talking differently, darker somehow, or that you are more difficult to get along with, just get angry at them and go buy another movie or magazine with similar content. Actually, you will soon be ready to advance to our total-destruction-of-the-senses line. You, too, will soon be past feeling."

What is the effect if those six warnings are not heeded? That would bring us to an intermission. Here is the announcement: "We will soon be taking a commercial break. You viewers, on the other hand, now a bit more dull in your thinking, a little more under the spell of adversary-induced amnesia—you are now primed for a different kind of break. How about breaking your covenants? Breaking your husband's heart? Breaking apart your marriage? Breaking your children's and parents' and siblings' and friends' hearts? All of these breaks that you never thought possible are now just a little more within your reach."

One client told me that after watching a certain popular movie she first started thinking about having an affair with the man who was building her family's new house. She had the affair. Her house was built. Her marriage was destroyed. Those involved now live in three separate houses: the builder (it seems strange to call him that) with his wife in one home, the woman with some of her children in another, and her former husband and the rest of the children in yet another. No one lives in the house the affair destroyed. Now, this was and is a good woman. She was not a woman without a sense of right or wrong. She understood gospel principles and had served as a Relief Society president before this very sad, destructive time in her life.

That's the horror. Lucifer hates good women and is poised and ready to intrude his lies into good women's lives. He's swift. He's very effective. He knows if he can take down a good woman, he can take down a whole family in one fell swoop. Talk about the economy of Lucifer. The devil's domino effect in action!

206

It's time to make certain that Satan does not have a grip on our hearts, minds, homes, and families. If we find any evidence of his blatantly obvious or even his covertly subtle presence, we need to cast him out. We need to do more than just loosen his grip; we need to cast him out so that the Spirit can teach us the grand eternal truths about physical intimacy, which we are to teach to our families.

The Lord has not left us alone. He has provided his truth about intimacy through his scriptures and his prophets. As you prayerfully seek his guidance, you will come to know what you can do right now to determine if the adversary's impure influence is in your life—and if so, to know how to remove it. It may just be time for some very serious spring cleaning. Only when our hearts and homes are cleansed from the adversary's filthy falsehoods can the Lord's words about physical intimacy lodge deep in our hearts and bring the sweet peace that truth always brings.

The Proclamation on the Family addresses physical intimacy, declaring that "God has commanded that the[se] sacred powers . . . are to be employed only between man and woman, lawfully wedded as husband and wife."[7] Could it be any clearer than that? This declaration means that any and all other physical intimacies are outside God's law. They're wrong. So, when I speak of physical intimacy, I am speaking about it only in the context sanctioned by God—within the marriage relationship. God intended physical intimacy for only husbands and wives to share. Doesn't that one truth speak volumes about its sacred importance?

Years ago at a BYU devotional, Elder Jeffrey R. Holland presented three eternal truths about physical intimacy in his landmark address "Of Souls, Symbols, and Sacraments."[8] He reaffirmed those same truths as an apostle of the Lord in October 1998 general conference.[9] Recognizing the truth about physical intimacy often invites a paradigm shift. I love to watch clients when they experience paradigm shifts about physical intimacy after reading Elder Holland's talk. Those with eyes to see, ears to hear, and hearts and minds to understand almost immediately take several giant steps forward in co-creating love, often for the very first time.

Elder Holland clearly sets forth three grand truths about marital intimacy. First, physical intimacy is a soulful experience, involving the body and the spirit. The body is indeed the "great prize of mortal life."[10] We, as members of the Lord's Church, are doctrinally distinct from other religions in understanding that the body and the spirit are the soul of man.[11] Physical intimacy should involve your soul—your body and your spirit, not just your body. One righteous and articulate woman who is a wife, mother, and grandmother expressed it beautifully when she said: "I believe that physical union is a completion of the temple sealing. It is the completion of the temple covenants—truly consummating the love that brought you to the temple. Physical love is like a seal upon a seal."

What would need to be different for you and your husband to experience physical intimacy as a more soulful experience?

The second grand truth offered by Elder Holland is that physical intimacy is a symbol of the total commitment and union a husband and wife should have for each other in all areas of their lives. If the only time a husband and wife unite is during physical union, they are probably experiencing "counterfeit intimacy," as Victor L. Brown Jr. describes it. "Counterfeit intimacy" occurs when we relate to each other in fragments—a fragment of a wife here connecting with a fragment of her husband there.[12] So how do you and your husband unite in ways other than physical union? What needs to change in your life, in your relationship with your spouse, so that there is more uniting, more intertwining of your lives, more demonstration of commitment to each other in many ways—talking with each other, working on problems together, learning to enjoy small moments and the joy of just being together? And how about learning to laugh—together, not at one another. One woman said pure laughter unites her heart with her husband's. In fact, she said, "I've learned that while anger kills my desire for physical intimacy, laughter gives life to it."

How united are you in your daily activities, such as teaching and loving your children, paying your bills? How united are you in your thoughts and feelings? I remember one couple who rarely overlapped in their activities or shared their thoughts or feelings. They continually bickered and disagreed about everything. In fact, the only thing they expressed similar opinions about was how very disagreeable the other was.

Could your physical uniting be enhanced as you and your husband do more things together? Your physical uniting is meant to be a symbol of your total union, not the total and only occurrence of union.

The third grand eternal truth is that physical intimacy is a kind of sacrament, a time to draw close to God, a time "when we quite literally unite our will with God's will, our spirit with His spirit, where communion through the veil becomes very real."[13] That is a profound truth. Sadly, however, it is the exact opposite, the antithesis, of what far too many people believe. Blinded by the adversary's lying lens, many suppose that they are never more distant from the Lord than when joining together in physical union. Nothing could be further from the truth. So now, consider the real truth: Physical intimacy is a sacramental moment.

Elder Holland states that at sacramental moments "we not only acknowledge [God's] divinity but we quite literally take something of that divinity to ourselves."[14] The Lord counsels us not to partake of the sacrament of the Lord's supper unworthily (3 Nephi 18:28–29) because his blessings will not be there (in fact, damnation will be there). I wonder if that counsel applies also to partaking unworthily of the sacred sharing of physical intimacy.

In my clinical practice, I have worked with couples who have broken covenants of marital fidelity and couples in which one spouse has approached this marital sacrament with unclean hands and an impure heart. The outcomes are tragic and sadly predictable. I salute the husband who, following disfellowshipment, chose on his own to wait for physical intimacy with his wife until he was more pure. Following this self-imposed period of abstinence, he read to his wife one evening from Doctrine and Covenants 46. Her heart was irresistibly drawn towards his. She experienced that moment as the most wonderfully effective prelude to physical intimacy they had ever shared in twenty-five years of marriage. Feeling spiritually more connected with her husband enhanced her desire to be connected with him physically.

In another instance, a woman spoke of times when her husband, ravaged by self-doubts and collisions with the brutal world, felt unworthy in almost every way. She then said tenderly, almost reverently, "In those moments, physical intimacy was the only way I could really help him feel loved—worthy of love, worthy to love." Probably there are many ways and many reasons why spouses can feel closer to the Lord as they unite in the marital sacrament.

When marital intimacy is embedded in personal purity, love is co-created—pure love, the kind of love Elder Parley P. Pratt describes. "I had loved before, but I knew not why. But now I loved—with a pureness—an intensity of elevated, exalted feeling, which would lift my soul from the transitory things of this grovelling sphere and expand it as the ocean. I felt that God was my heavenly Father indeed; that Jesus was my brother, and that the wife of my bosom was an immortal, eternal companion. . . . In short, I could now love with the spirit and with the understanding also."[15]

I believe that the Lord blesses spouses who love each other purely. I believe he blesses spouses whose passions and appetites have been influenced by the Holy Ghost. We were given the gift of the Holy Ghost for exactly such a time as this. Is it difficult to believe that the Holy Ghost will help you express your love physically? He will. Pray for it.

Listen to what the Holy Ghost will do for you, as written by the hand of Elder Parley P. Pratt: "The gift of the Holy Ghost . . . quickens all the intellectual faculties, increases, enlarges, expands, and purifies all the natural passions and affections, and adapts them, by the gift of wisdom, to their lawful use."[16] Isn't that wonderful? The Holy Ghost will make us smarter! That's a much-needed blessing for lots of us!

No matter what our IQ, when we embrace sin, even in the slightest way, the Holy Ghost departs, and our intellectual faculties are not as sharp. We are just not as bright as we could be. And we behave in increasingly stupid ways. We start acting as if we are the center of the universe, and we calculate everyone's mistreatment and cruelty to us. I don't know about you, but I believe sin makes me even more than selfish. I believe that sin makes me stupid! Conversely and happily, as we seek to become increasingly pure and therefore are increasingly open to the influence of the Holy Ghost, we can become brighter in every way and more benevolent, more empathic—all great advantages for spouses and spouses-to-be.

Now, back to Elder Pratt's words: "The Holy Ghost . . . increases, enlarges, expands, and purifies all the natural passions and affections, and adapts them, by the gift of wisdom, to their lawful use." So we need not worry that increased purity might decrease our God-given passions. Our natural passions (the operative word is *natural*) will be increased, purified, and adapted to their lawful use. Spirit-magnified and spirit-purified passion will always be greater than lust. The ability to have our passions magnified, purified, and adapted seems to be something very worthy of prayer or even of fasting. Whether married or unmarried, we need our natural passions and affections to be purified, and we need the wisdom to use them lawfully. And just think of the healing that could come to so many who struggle with the effects of their own moral sins or those of others. Think of the healing that is available as they seek to receive this blessing, this gift from the Holy Ghost. As we seek the increased influence of the Holy Ghost in our lives, we need to do all we can do to overcome the temptations that so easily beset us. Elder Holland's address is filled with striking truths that change our thinking and thus our behavior. I have offered clients the opportunity to reflect on some of those truths:

A woman who was perpetually tempted to behave in an illicit manner rehearsed in her mind a question when she felt herself weakening. The question that helped her was, "If I were to remember that by acting on these illicit impulses I am actually toying with that person's very soul—the body and the spirit, both of which are sacred—how would I quickly manage this situation?"

A man struggling with serious financial problems who also sought to loosen the bands of pornography from his heart and mind was assisted by the following question: "If I were to believe that by sinning morally, trivializing my own body and that of another's, I was both trivializing the Savior's atonement and also setting myself up for financial ruin, how would I manage these illicit impulses?"

Life is filled with unexpected events. "But if [we] are prepared [we] shall not fear" (D&C 38:30). And if we are prepared, we also will not be caught off guard and will not succumb to temptation. How would you respond if someone you like and admire approached you to engage in something illicit? Be prepared with something to say, such as, "I am so sorry that you don't know that this is wrong. I am so sorry that you believe that this is a loving request. It is not. It will ruin both our souls, and it trivializes all that the Savior did for us through the Atonement."

And what if the person asking you to engage in something defiling is your husband, whom you love? President Boyd K. Packer anticipated this attack on personal purity from within marriage. He counseled: "A married couple may be tempted to introduce things into their relationship that are unworthy. Do not, as the scriptures warn, 'change the natural use into that which is against nature' (Romans 1:26). If you do, the tempter will drive a wedge between you."[17] Anything that offends the Spirit or either spouse's spirit will allow the tempter to drive a wedge between husbands and wives.

"I was talked out of my feelings." Those haunting words are from a woman whose husband on their wedding night had convinced her to consummate their love in a manner that offended her spirit. For years afterwards they carried on the illusion of a marriage. That was the best they could do in a union where the woman felt numb and the man felt rejected.

One last word about Elder Holland's address. I believe our responses to truth reflect our present spiritual state. Thus, "Of Souls, Symbols, and Sacraments" can serve as a Rorschach test of our present spiritual growth and development. These truths, like the truths in the scriptures, speak to us differently at different times, depending on the light within us. Changes between how we respond to Elder Holland's apostolic offering today versus how we respond reading it a year later could measure changes in our personal purity. As we increase the light in our lives, more and more is illuminated about these three grand truths: physical intimacy is a soulful experience; physical intimacy is a symbol of total commitment and union; and physical intimacy is a sacrament. The more pure our hearts, minds, and hands, the clearer will be our understanding of these truths.

The Prophet Joseph Smith spoke of this process. He said, "We consider that God has created man with a mind capable of instruction, and a faculty which may be enlarged in proportion to the heed and diligence given to the light communicated from heaven to the intellect; and that the nearer man approaches perfection, the clearer are his views, and the greater his enjoyments, till he has overcome the evils of his life and lost every desire for sin."[18]

We need to be women who increase in our understanding of these three grand truths about physical intimacy. We need to live by them. These are lifesaving, eternal truths for each of us and our families.

As women of the latter days, we need to seek diligently to increase the purity in our lives by keeping the Lord's commandments with ever-increasing impeccability. As women who have made sacred covenants with the Lord, we need to draw closer to him and invite others to come unto him. We, as spirit daughters of heavenly parents, need to ensure that Satan is continually cast out of our hearts, minds, homes, and families. We, as women of Christ, need to forge intimate relationships with others that involve him. We, as daughters of Eve, need to distinguish good from evil and partake of physical intimacy only within the sacred ordinance of marriage. And as we do, we will co-create intimate relationships that are truly out of this world!

When our faith is tried, when we become weary and discouraged about our ability to do *all* we have been charged to do, perhaps remembering the sacred vision of Elder Melvin J. Ballard will help us never to waver: "I was taken into the most splendid room. . . . Seated on a raised platform was one of the most beautiful and exalted beings I had ever beheld, and I was informed that I might be introduced to him, and I came forward, and as I did so he arose and descended to meet me, and the smile he extended towards me I shall never forget through all the ages that are to come, and as he took me in his arms and kissed me and hugged me to his bosom and gave me a blessing that made the marrow in my bones to melt, and as I kissed his feet I saw the prints of the nails. The feeling that came to me then was one that I cannot describe other than to say that I felt unworthy of that privilege. I felt, oh, how little I have done to receive such distinguished privileges as these. If the day will ever come that I may have that privilege I would be willing to give all that I ever may and ever hope to be. If I can only obtain that which I have felt and know as the joy and the privilege of faithful Latter-day Saints. It is no myth. I know it as I live, and it is worth giving everything for. These days when your faith may be tried, waver not, be true and faithful towards the word of the Lord. I testify to you that it is true, and every promise and blessing that has been sealed upon your heads you will realize. When you do, it will be beyond anything you have contemplated in this life."[19]

"Wherefore, my beloved [sisters], pray unto the Father with all the energy of heart, that ye may be filled with this love, which he hath bestowed upon all who are true followers of his Son, Jesus Christ; that ye may become the [daughters] of God; that when he shall appear we shall be like him, for we shall see him as he is; that we may have this hope; that we may be purified even as he is pure" (Moroni 7:48).

NOTES

1. Lorraine M. Wright, Wendy L. Watson, and Janice M. Bell, *Beliefs: The Heart of Healing in Families and Illness* (New York: Basic Books, 1996).
2. Truman G. Madsen, *Four Essays on Love* (Salt Lake City: Bookcraft, 1971), 29.
3. James E. Faust, "That We Might Know Thee," *Ensign*, January 1999, 2, 4.
4. Kenneth R. Timmerman, *The Death Lobby: How the West Armed Iraq* (Boston: Houghton Mifflin, 1991).
5. Paul Watzlawick, Janet Helmick Beavin, and Don D. Jackson, *Pragmatics of Human Communication* (New York: Basic Books, 1967), 20.
6. Joseph Smith, *Teachings of the Prophet Joseph Smith*, sel. Joseph Fielding Smith (Salt Lake City: Deseret Book, 1976), 137.
7. First Presidency and Quorum of the Twelve Apostles of The Church of Jesus Christ of Latter-day Saints, "The Family: A Proclamation to the World," *Ensign*, November 1995, 102.
8. Jeffrey R. Holland and Patricia T. Holland, *On Earth As It Is in Heaven* (Salt Lake City: Deseret Book, 1989), 182–97.
9. Jeffrey R. Holland, *Ensign*, November 1998, 75–78.
10. Holland and Holland, *On Earth As It Is in Heaven*, 187.
11. James E. Talmage, Conference Report, October 1913, 117.
12. Victor L. Brown Jr., *Human Intimacy: Illusion and Reality* (Salt Lake City: Parliament Publishers, 1981), 5–6.
13. Holland, *Ensign*, November 1998, 77.
14. Holland, *Ensign*, November 1998, 77.
15. Parley P. Pratt, *Autobiography of Parley P. Pratt* (Salt Lake City: Deseret Book, 1979), 260.
16. Parley P. Pratt, *Key to the Science of Theology*, Classics in Mormon Literature Series (Salt Lake City: Deseret Book, 1978), 61.
17. Boyd K. Packer, *The Things of the Soul* (Salt Lake City: Bookcraft, 1996), 113.
18. Smith, *Teachings of the Prophet Joseph Smith*, 51.
19. Melvin J. Ballard, Conference Report, October 1917, 111–12.

Peace amidst Suffering

MARY ELLEN EDMUNDS

I'm convinced that we're not going to get through this life without suffering, but I'm also convinced that as we stay close to our Heavenly Father, our Savior, and the Holy Ghost, we will also not have to go through this life without *peace*.

What is suffering? Usually it's tied to our experiences that are painful or unpleasant. It seems to imply holding on, waiting patiently, and enduring. "To suffer" also means "to allow, to submit to." And most likely there isn't anyone reading this article who does not know about suffering firsthand.

What is peace? Peace is knowing that the One in charge of everything is our Father and that he not only knows everything but he understands, and his plan is called the great plan of happiness! Peace is a critical ingredient of happiness.

Let me share from the scriptures three of the many examples of times when Heavenly Father's children have experienced peace amidst suffering.

The first is at a time, recorded in Alma, when the people of God are being persecuted terribly. But they keep the commandments and establish a Zion society right in the midst of their adversity and suffering. "And thus they did establish the affairs of the church; and thus they began to have continual peace again, notwithstanding all their persecutions" (Alma 1:28). Hang on to that in your darkest, hardest hours—

Mary Ellen Edmunds, author, speaker, and MTC Relief Society teacher, earned a bachelor of science degree in nursing from Brigham Young University. She has been a member of the Relief Society General Board, served four missions in Asia and Africa, and was a director of training at the Provo Missionary Training Center.

hang on to the fact that they did it! They experienced peace and joy amidst suffering.

The next example is of Alma Senior, when he and the people whom he baptized at the waters of Mormon are in captivity. They were being persecuted by the priests of Noah, a group to which Alma had belonged before he came to his senses with the help of Abinadi. Alma had told the people of his sore repentance and conversion: "After much tribulation, the Lord did hear my cries, and did answer my prayers" (Mosiah 23:10). Then Alma and his people settled in the land of Helam, where they prospered exceedingly, but then "the Lord seeth fit to chasten his people; yea, he trieth their patience and their faith. Nevertheless— whosoever putteth his trust in him the same shall be lifted up at the last day" (Mosiah 23:21–22). (Do you ever wish it could be a day or two *before* the "last day"?)

The Lamanites stumble upon the people of Alma and put them into captivity, guarded by the former priests of King Noah. Life becomes extremely difficult. "It came to pass that so great were their afflictions that they began to cry mightily to God" (Mosiah 24:10). All this praying makes Amulon, who has authority over Alma and his people, mad. He tells the guards to kill anyone caught praying. So they "did not raise their voices to the Lord their God, but did pour out their hearts to him; and he did know the thoughts of their hearts" (Mosiah 24:12). Then the voice of the Lord came to the people of Alma in their afflictions. He told them to be comforted because he would deliver them out of bondage. And he shares a sweet, tender message with them. Put yourself in these verses—think about some of the difficult things you might be experiencing: "I will also ease the burdens which are put upon your shoulders, that even you cannot feel them upon your backs, even while you are in bondage [*before* they're delivered]; and this will I do that ye may stand as witnesses for me hereafter, and that ye may know of a surety that I, the Lord God, do visit my people in their afflictions" (Mosiah 24:14). "And now it came to pass that the burdens . . . were made light; yea, the Lord did strengthen them that they could bear up their burdens with ease, and they did submit cheerfully and with patience to all the will of the Lord" (Mosiah 24:15).

The last example is another familiar one. The Prophet Joseph Smith is languishing in Liberty Jail. He has poured out his heart and feelings to his Heavenly Father, beginning with, "O God, where art thou?" (D&C 121:1). "Where are you?" Joseph asks. Among many other comforting things, the Lord answers: "My son, peace be unto thy soul; thine adversity and thine afflictions shall be but a small moment; and then, if thou endure it well, God shall exalt thee on high" (D&C 121:7–8).

I think that's what God asks of us: "My daughter, peace be unto thy soul. I know what you're going through. Endure it well." Joseph Smith's experience and his teachings tell us that all the Saints, including prophets and apostles, have had to come up through great tribulation.[1] Does God expect too much of us? Has he asked too much of you? Elder Neal A. Maxwell tells us that we are not expected to like it, but we are expected to endure it.[2]

What bothers me most is the suffering of the innocent. I can't stand to see news reports about man's inhumanity to man. I can't stand to see helplessness and hopelessness reflected in the faces of children and the innocent of any age or circumstance. I really can't stand it.

I've always been deeply moved by the account of the death by fire of the believers whom Alma and Amulek had taught in Ammonihah. I think I'd have been like Amulek: "And when Amulek saw the pains of the women and children who were consuming in the fire, *he also was pained* [these were the people of his village]; and he said unto Alma: How can we witness this awful scene? Therefore let us stretch forth our hands, and exercise the power of God which is in us, and save them from the flames. [Let's get 'em!] But Alma said unto him: The Spirit constraineth me that I must not stretch forth mine hand; for behold the Lord receiveth them up unto himself, in glory; and he doth suffer that they may do this thing . . . that the judgments which he shall exercise upon them in his wrath may be just; and the blood of the innocent shall stand as a witness against them, yea, and cry mightily against them at the last day" (Alma 14:10–11).

Like Amulek, I would have wanted to save loved ones from the flames. Are there times when it's difficult for you to see the purpose in your suffering? Listen to the wisdom found in the words of this hymn:

When through the deep waters I call thee to go,
The rivers of sorrow shall not thee o'erflow,
For I will be with thee, thy troubles to bless,
And sanctify to thee thy deepest distress.

When through fiery trials thy pathway shall lie,
My grace, all sufficient, shall be thy supply.
The flame shall not hurt thee; I only design
Thy dross to consume and thy gold to refine.[3]

Can you see that to sanctify and purify us, our Heavenly Father designs experiences which will help us become more like him—more pure and holy, more "fit for the kingdom"?

As we respond with faith and patience to adversity and suffering, we become stronger, sweeter, more gentle and kind; our feelings about the Savior are deeper, our communication with our Heavenly Father is so much more meaningful and real. We can feel him and his Son and the Comforter helping us to endure. Elder Neal A. Maxwell teaches us: "When in situations of stress we wonder if there is any more in us to give, we can be comforted to know that God, who knows our capacity perfectly, placed us here to succeed. No one was foreordained to fail or to be wicked.

"When we feel overwhelmed, let us recall the assurance given through Joseph that God who knows we 'cannot bear all things now,' will not overprogram us; he will not press upon us more than we can bear (see D&C 50:40)."[4]

So much suffering is going on in this world, some close to us and some far away. You're already aware of the heavy burdens and pain of many of Heavenly Father's children, including your own. There is so much illness, injustice, insensitivity, poverty, loneliness, helplessness, being misrepresented, misquoted, misunderstood, estrangement from loved ones, physical and emotional abuse, loss of hope, disappointment, broken hearts and spirits.

All that suffering makes me a little uncomfortable to share my own experiences. I've not had many of the same experiences others have had. But some things have been difficult for me and I remember them as being times of some degree of suffering.

I thought for sure I would marry and have children, for example, and it's hard knowing that has not happened for me. One Sunday after sacrament meeting, as I was helping my mother into the car, she said something like, "One of these days *you'll* be old, and then you'll know how I feel." I responded (without really thinking about it), "I know. And when that day comes, oh, how I wish I could have a daughter like me." My spontaneous remark caught us both off guard, and we both cried. The pain was real.

I wish I could share *your* stories, that I could know something about your heavy burdens and trials. I doubt there is anyone who does not have some kind of adversity or suffering. Do you ever feel empty? Tired? Sometimes frightened? Inadequate? Does it sometimes catch you off guard that you feel so discouraged? Do you wonder why some of your prayers aren't answered in the way you had hoped? Has it been a long time since any of your fondest dreams have come true? Do you ever feel lonely? In despair? Do you have bad habits that you just can't seem to break? Is your battery low? Have you lost a child or another loved one? Have you been, or are you being, treated with unkindness or cruelty? Do the days go by too quickly . . . or too slowly? Has someone betrayed you—broken your heart and your trust? Are you overwhelmed? Deeply in debt? Deeply in doubt? Disappointed? Weary? All of the above?

Let me share one more personal experience. Have you ever been in a situation where you wanted to give all you had and yet you couldn't because of some personal limitations? That is what happened to me when I was in Nigeria, West Africa, to help with a child health project. (I was *not* a visual aid for good health.)

I had felt reluctant to say yes to this assignment because I know I don't do well in humid climates. (Think Nigeria . . . think African rain forest . . . think *humid*.) When my prayers about going to Africa were answered—"Yes, I want you to go"—I thought that meant I'd be well. I was wrong. I became sick almost immediately, and I was sick the whole time I was there. Asthma made it impossible for me to sleep or rest well. Those who have had it can identify with how frightening asthma is. There was never a day when I could breathe deeply and freely.

Somewhat because of asthma and other allergies, my resistance to disease was at zero. I've since said with a smile that "the people made me sick!" I'd hug and kiss the children, and within hours, it seemed, I'd get whatever they had.

I didn't like murmuring. I turned my distress inward. I never felt mad at God, but I was puzzled and curious. I'd had enough experiences in life to know that God hadn't planned this to get back at me for something. I also knew from my previous experience that something good could come of all of this, so while I was frustrated, it was mostly with myself for not having what it took to get well and stay well.

Keeping my spirits up was hard, especially in a situation where living was difficult. Whether it was purifying our water, washing our clothes or dishes, keeping the house clean, or doing what we had come to do—the child health project—it all was much harder for me because of my poor health. I had several very special priesthood blessings, but when I didn't improve, I got discouraged because I felt I lacked the faith to help them "come true." One day near Thanksgiving I wrote a short but revealing entry in my journal: "Sometimes I really wonder if I'll ever in my whole life feel strong and healthy again."

Then came Tuesday, January 8, 1985. My incredible companion, Ann, had gone to another village with the couple missionaries and was gone the whole day. It was an unusual, unforgettable day for me. I had a long, long talk with Heavenly Father. I cried a lot. I didn't want him to think that I was complaining, that I was mad at him or felt like he was the cause of everything I was going through. But I felt convinced that he had asked me to come, and I wondered why. The why question was not "Why do I have to suffer?" I didn't feel like a martyr, but I wondered what this experience meant—what I was supposed to do with it and about it.

That was one of the most sacred and important days of the whole experience. I was at a low ebb, but I wasn't bitter. If I'd been bitter or angry, what happened would not have happened. I know that. I just needed to talk to Heavenly Father. I needed him to let me know that he knew where I was and that *he* knew the why. I needed to know things that only he could tell me.

And so, on that day alone, I wasn't alone at all. I was closer to my Heavenly Father than I've been very many times in my life. I sat at the window in the living room, held onto the security bars over the opening, and wept. I asked, "What do you want from me?" That may sound like a sarcastic or biting question, but I asked it softly and humbly. I *knew* that he had not asked me to come to such a place for no reason. I didn't think he would laugh at me (he never has) or tell me, "Oh, it's really nothing, what you've been through, when compared to my Son, and Joseph Smith, and millions and billions of others." I have had a relatively trouble-free life, and this time in Africa was indeed a "small moment," so he *could* have said such things.

But he chose not to.

What he whispered to me was so completely comforting and personal that the feeling remains with me today. First, he put the following thought into my soul: "I will make it up to you." Those are my words, not his. I don't remember exactly what I "heard" inside me, but that's what it meant in my earthling language—"I will make it up to you." I told him that was not what I wanted or needed, but he wouldn't take it back. It was a definite, strong impression, and it wouldn't go away.

Then we had a long visit about what he wanted me to do. He asked if I had any idea how much I would have learned and understood if I had felt completely healthy over the several months I had been there. I told him I likely would have missed *much*. He agreed. He gave me an indication that some of my most important lessons might still be coming. I didn't ask how long he wanted me to stay in Africa. It wasn't one of those times I was in a hurry for anything. I wanted time to pass very slowly so that I could take in everything the best I could and *remember*. I wanted to *remember* this most significant day and time in my life. I wanted to have it sink deep into my soul and be there forever. I felt so personally and sweetly attended to during that time. It may be that others helped to comfort and teach me on that unusual day—"and my Spirit shall be in your [heart,] and mine angels round about you, to bear you up" (D&C 84:88).

I am not capable of adequately sharing with you all that I felt on that day, but it was so sweet amidst all the awfulness that I let him know I would go on and on if he asked me to—that I would stay as long as he wanted. I pray that I will never forget that day in Africa when he *visited* me.

Is it really possible for us to have peace amidst suffering? Hear the words of our Savior: "Peace I leave with you, my peace I give unto you: not as the world giveth, give I unto you. Let not your heart be troubled, neither let it be afraid" (John 14:27). The answer is yes! We can experience peace amidst suffering, because the Prince of Peace said so.

> Come, ye disconsolate, where'er ye languish;
> Come to the mercy seat, fervently kneel.
> Here bring your wounded hearts; here tell your anguish.
> Earth has no sorrow that heav'n cannot heal.
>
> Joy of the desolate, Light of the straying,
> Hope of the penitent, fadeless and pure!
> Here speaks the Comforter, tenderly saying,
> "Earth has no sorrow that heav'n cannot cure."
>
> Here see the Bread of Life; see waters flowing
> Forth from the throne of God, pure from above.
> Come to the feast of love; come, ever knowing
> Earth has no sorrow but heav'n can remove.[5]

Does it help to know there's One who understands? Jesus is described as a man of sorrows and acquainted with grief (see Isaiah 53:3). Having experienced our suffering, he says to us: "Come unto me, all ye that labour and are heavy laden, and I will give you rest. Take my yoke upon you, and learn of me; for I am meek and lowly in heart: and ye shall find rest unto your souls. For my yoke is easy, and my burden is light" (Matthew 11:28–30). He promises not a shortcut to heaven or a life free of adversity but rest—rest to our souls.

Does it help you to know that a prophet is praying for you? Listen to President Gordon B. Hinckley's words: "May you have health, strength, vitality to carry the heavy burden that is yours. May you have loving friends and associates to bear you up in your times of trial. You know the power of prayer as perhaps few others do. . . . Please know that we also pray for you."[6] President Hinckley was addressing single parents, but I know he prays for all and each of us.

Let me suggest some responses to suffering that could help you. Use humor, as best you can, to balance life's inconsistencies and surprises. Shortly after my father passed away, a very official letter came to our post office box addressed to "Friends and Family of Ella M. Edmunds": "We were recently notified of the death of Ella M. Edmunds. However, the exact date of death was not given. Please enter the date of death in the space provided below and return this letter to us. (An envelope which requires no postage is enclosed for your convenience.)"

In mock horror I said to Mom: "Why didn't you tell us?!" My brother Frank suggested a lottery: we would all put in some money and guess Mom's exact date of death. Whoever won would get all the money, and Mom could certainly enter too, if she wanted. It's not always possible to find anything humorous in tragedy and suffering, but when and if you can, it might make a marvelous difference.

Here's another trait you must have: *Don't give up*. Imagine if the pioneers had become weary and quit. A bulletin in the *Evening News* would read something like this: "This just in. The Mormon pioneers who were heading west after being driven from the city of Nauvoo have apparently changed their minds. They've halted their trek. In an exclusive interview, one member of the party reportedly said, 'This is much more difficult than we had imagined or anticipated. We're tired. There's too much dust some days and too much mud other days. We've had it. We're not going on. We've lost hope. This isn't fun. We've quit circling the wagons, and we've quit singing "Come, Come Ye Saints."'"

Of course, the pioneers met adversity, but they didn't give up! Sometimes it helps to know that others have been brave and strong and true. Learn to hang in and hang on—endure well. If we give up, it's almost like we're saying to Jesus, "You didn't do enough." Or as if we were saying to our Heavenly Father, "You haven't been listening to me, and I don't know if you're strong enough or care for me enough to help me." Ouch!

Prayer can help. I love the line from the hymn, "Oh, how praying rests the weary!"[7] Sometimes I have heard myself say, "Well, all I can do now is pray"—as if that's not very much. As Bishop H. Burke Peterson said, "Prayer is the preparation for miracles."[8] "I sought the Lord, and he heard me, and delivered me from all my fears" (Psalm 34:4).

I remember hearing Relief Society general president Elaine L. Jack tell of having seen this message posted above the sink in a friend's house: "At night I turn all my problems over to Heavenly Father—He's going to be up all night anyway." The critical message you must understand for prayer to work is that it takes complete trust in our Heavenly Father to be able to leave things in his loving hands. *Trust him.* Oh, isn't it hard sometimes to say and mean those words: "Thy will be done"? (Some mistakenly say, "For dumb! That cancels out your prayer!") One of my friends once admitted: "I gave the Lord at least six great options, A through F. He chose Q." Has that happened in your life? But have you ever realized, with the passing of time, that Q was *exactly* what you needed?

I'm probably not the only one who has wondered sometimes about all of this—about why things happen the way they do. How do we keep from becoming bitter or angry or separated from God if we feel that something that happens is unjust or unfair? I sit in meetings where testimonies are being shared about miracles, and I hurt for others sitting in the same chapel who are suffering because the miracle *they* had hoped for didn't happen.

One thing I do is turn to the scriptures again. In the Book of Mormon, Alma Senior had a son who was very wicked and anti-Church. He went about with his friends trying to destroy all that his father was doing. Alma Senior fasted and prayed long and hard for his son, Alma Junior. (So did his mother.) You know the story—Alma Junior and his friends were visited by an angel in an experience that changed their hearts and their lives. They became some of the most powerful missionaries in history. And Alma Junior became a great prophet and chief judge.

Contrast his story with that of Lehi's eldest son Laman. Laman was also anti-Church and anti-father. He even sought to murder his father and his brother Nephi. *His* visit from an angel doesn't seem to have had much lasting effect on him.

Both prophets prayed and fasted for their sons and did everything they could think of to persuade them to believe in Christ and follow Heavenly Father's plan. Was Alma Senior more faithful than Lehi? Was he more obedient, more worthy? Did God love him more? Did he pray with greater faith?

Remember what President Spencer W. Kimball taught: "Prayers are not always answered as we wish them to be. Even the Redeemer's prayer in Gethsemane was answered in the negative."⁹ Don't ever quit pouring out your heart to your Heavenly Father. When it seems others' prayers are being answered but yours are not, don't ever doubt his love for you. You *are* his child.

Other helps in times of suffering include attending the temple. The temple can be a place to find some measure of peace. Go to the temple, even if you can't go inside yet. Find solitude, read the scriptures, listen to music.

You might also review your life to see if you need to repent or to forgive. Sometimes suffering comes because we're angry, full of a desire for revenge, holding too tightly to a grudge. One of the most priceless gifts we can give to others is to forgive them (even if they don't ask us to, and even if they don't seem to have repented—Someone Else is in charge of judging all of that). You know what it has meant to you to forgive someone else—it is almost a surprise how much our own burdens are lifted, how much better *we* feel when we can freely forgive.

"Blessed are the merciful, for they shall obtain mercy" (3 Nephi 12:7). That scripture applies to extending our mercy to others who are suffering as well as to forgiving those who may have caused us to suffer. We are our sisters' keepers. We are covenant women, and we really are willing to bear one another's burdens, to mourn with each other, and to comfort each other (see Mosiah 18:8–11). We would never intentionally add to another's pain or suffering. We "rejoice with them that do rejoice, and weep with them that weep" (Romans 12:15). Often we truly suffer in learning of another's burdens. Sometimes the suffering that we feel when we seek to lift, to mourn with and comfort one another, is the most exquisite and painful. We wish we could solve all the problems of the world. But one person can't even solve all the problems in his own nation, village, neighborhood, or even in his own home or family. One person can, however, visit another person. One willing, covenant woman can reach out and lighten another's burden. One kind soul can call another, can write a note, can pray with all her heart, can share hope.

> Take my life, and let it be
> Consecrated, Lord, to thee.

225

Take my moments and my days;
Let them flow in ceaseless praise.

Take my hands, and let them move
At the impulse of thy love.
Take my feet, and let them be
Swift and beautiful for thee.

Take my voice, and let me sing,
Always, only, for my King.
Take my lips, and let them be
Filled with messages from thee.

. . . .

Take my will, and make it thine;
It shall be no longer mine.
Take my heart, it is thine own;
It shall be thy royal throne.

Take my love; my Lord, I pour
At thy feet its treasure-store.
Take myself, and I will be
Ever, only, all for thee.[10]

Are there some things that are not helpful when others are hurting? What things perhaps should we refrain from doing as we face adversity and suffering, or as we try to help others through their hard times? Let's not compare our suffering to see if we can "top" and "bottom" others because ours is so much more spectacular or difficult. "Oh, you think *that's* bad!" "My kidney stone was way bigger and uglier than yours!" "My tonsils were a *lot* worse than that!" "I was in labor for forty days and forty nights!" "My root canal went clear to my collarbone!"

Let's not discount anything that is heavy for anyone else to bear, just because it seems less awful than what we (or someone else we know) is experiencing. If we're ever tempted to try to top someone in their suffering, thinking it's not much compared to what we've been through, just remember that some day we will see the Savior again. And there will be no way we can even approach an adequate, accurate understanding of what he has suffered for us.

It is also rarely helpful to say something like "Oh, I know exactly how you feel," or, "I know exactly what you mean!" We probably don't. We need to be more honest. "I'm not sure I understand, but I'm so sorry." What did Paul mean when he taught us that if "one member suffer, all the members suffer with it"? (1 Corinthians 12:26). I think he meant that to lighten another's burdens, to mourn with those that mourn, you suffer with them—you *feel* with them. Weep with those who weep—and just *listen*.

Sometimes we try to talk people out of trials instead of helping them through them. We seem to want a quick cure from every single ounce of suffering or adversity that comes our way. Our greeting cards often say "Get well SOON." What other kinds of messages might we share with someone who's suffering? How about these:

"Hope the learning and growing aren't *too* painful."

"May your deep water and fiery trials not be more than you can handle."

"I hope you'll let me travel part of the journey with you."

"May you feel comforted in this time of learning and refining."

"Can I help in any way?"

"I know our Heavenly Father is aware of you, and I feel he is weeping with you."

Elder Marvin J. Ashton said, "Satan wants us to feel unequal to our worldly tasks. If we turn to God, He will . . . lead us through our darkest hours."[11] He will not remove us from them but lead us through them. Think of some experience you've been through that was extremely difficult, one of the hardest you've ever had to face. (Maybe you're going through it right now—maybe it's because you're wondering, "How much longer is Mary Ellen going to go on?") What have these experiences taught you?

Elder Levi Edgar Young said so beautifully: "When the darkness comes, let us remember that the night brings out the stars as sorrows show us the truth; and the insight that comes through pain and disappointment may be the insight into the value of what we are."[12]

And I'm sure you've heard this statement by Elder Orson F. Whitney: "No pain that we suffer, no trial that we experience, is wasted. It ministers to our education, to the development of such qualities as patience, faith, fortitude, and humility. All that we suffer and all that we endure, especially when we endure it patiently, builds up our characters, purifies our hearts, expands our souls, and makes us more tender and charitable, more worthy to be called the children of God . . . and it is through sorrow and suffering, toil and tribulation, that we gain the education that we come here to acquire and which will make us more like our Father and Mother in heaven."[13]

What have you learned from your suffering? Have you learned compassion? Is your heart more tender? Do you judge others less quickly, less harshly? President Spencer W. Kimball taught that if we close the doors upon sorrow, distress, and anguish in our lives, we might be "evicting our greatest friends and benefactors. Suffering can make saints of people as they learn patience, long-suffering, and self-mastery. The sufferings of our Savior were part of his education," as they are also a part of ours.[14] Our suffering does help to purify and sanctify us. Maybe we shouldn't try to get rid of everything so quickly, without or before the learning.

Remember, Jesus suffered as a part of his earthly experience. "Though he were a Son [the Son], yet learned he obedience by the things which he suffered; and being made perfect, he became the author of eternal salvation unto all them that obey him" (Hebrews 5:8–9). "The Father's plan for proving his children did not exempt the Savior himself," President Marion G. Romney reminds us. "The suffering he [endured] . . . equaled the combined suffering of all men."[15]

So many times when I think of Jesus, I think not just of the price he paid but of his parents, earthly and heavenly, who allowed him ("suffered" him) to experience incomprehensible agony so that we would not need to, if we would accept his atonement. "Eighteen hundred years after [Christ] had endured it, he spoke of it as being so intense that it 'caused myself, even God, the greatest of all, to tremble because of pain, and to bleed at every pore, and to suffer both body and spirit—and would that I might not drink the bitter cup, and shrink' . . . (D&C 19:18–19)."[16] And his father sent an angel to comfort him. So, too, God visits us in the midst of our suffering,

Maybe one of the most important lessons we learn from our own adversity, our own trials and suffering, is a deeper appreciation and love for our Savior. How can we not think of his infinite sacrifice and of the truth that he is our Redeemer and Savior, that he can heal us, make us whole, and bring us home? Through afflictions, we learn to trust the Lord completely, knowing that whatever happens, all, eventually, will be right. Everything will be sorted out, everything will be fair, wrongs will be made right, tears will be wiped away, no one will be hungry or thirsty or naked or sick or imprisoned or frightened or lonely or hurting.

God bless you in your own struggling and striving to come unto Christ and be perfected in him—to become healed and whole. Don't worry or doubt or fear—your Father loves you dearly and will never forget or forsake you. Through all that is difficult in life, the gospel of Jesus Christ offers peace and comfort.

I am convinced deep in my soul that Jesus really is our Prince of Peace and that he really will and *does* encircle us in the arms of his love. I am convinced that because of him we can be the happiest people on earth no matter what we encounter in our daily adventure. Suffering can be holy and sacred. Suffer well, knowing you are never alone. May we feel that peace and hope that he has made possible, even in the midst of our suffering.

NOTES

1. See Joseph Smith, *The Teachings of the Prophet Joseph Smith*, sel. Joseph Fielding Smith (Salt Lake City: Deseret Book, 1938), 260–61.
2. Neal A. Maxwell, *Ensign*, May 1985, 72.
3. See *Hymns of The Church of Jesus Christ of Latter-day Saints* (Salt Lake City: The Church of Jesus Christ of Latter-day Saints, 1985), no. 85.
4. Neal A. Maxwell, *But for a Small Moment* (Salt Lake City: Bookcraft, 1986), 102.
5. *Hymns*, no. 115.
6. Gordon B. Hinckley, *Ensign*, November 1996, 67–70.
7. *Hymns*, no. 140.
8. H. Burke Peterson, "Adversity and Prayer," in *Prayer* (Salt Lake City: Deseret Book, 1977), 108.
9. Spencer W. Kimball, *Teachings of Spencer W. Kimball*, ed. Edward L. Kimball (Salt Lake City: Bookcraft, 1982), 124.
10. Frances Ridley Havergal, "Take My Life, and Let It Be Consecrated," 1874.
11. Marvin J. Ashton, *Ensign*, November 1980, 60.
12. Levi Edgar Young, Conference Report, October 1932, 58–59.
13. Orson F. Whitney, quoted in Spencer W. Kimball, *Faith Precedes the Miracle* (Salt Lake City: Deseret Book, 1972), 98.
14. Kimball, *Teachings of Spencer W. Kimball*, 168.
15. Marion G. Romney, Conference Report, October 1969, 57.
16. Romney, Conference Report, October 1969, 57

Still Point in a Changing World

HEIDI S. SWINTON

Twenty-some years ago, my husband and I and our baby boy moved from our apartment in the center of Salt Lake City to a rented house high on a hill overlooking the city. We were planning to build our dream house just blocks from where we were renting. It would have shingles and shutters, dormer windows, and a family room just off the kitchen. For five years we had lived in a tiny apartment, and we were ready to put down roots. My husband was serving in the bishopric of our ward of newlyweds and nearly-deads, so when a call came for us to meet with the stake presidency, we weren't surprised. I thought we were being called in for a release; after all, we'd moved.

"But suppose they call you to do something else," I said to Jeff. "You wouldn't do it, would you?"

"They wouldn't," he said. "We've moved."

Uneasy, I pursued the issue. "But what if they did," I said. "You wouldn't do it, would you?"

"Of course I would," he said. Reminding me of our obligation to the Lord, he pointed to our eight-month-old miracle child, whose twin brother had died at birth and who had fought for his own life for months.

I got specific. "What if they asked you to serve on the high council? You wouldn't do that, would you? Isn't that just for old men?"

"We don't live there anymore," he replied.

Heidi S. Swinton, a graduate of the University of Utah, has written several books on Church subjects and contributed to many others. She and her husband, Jeffrey, are the parents of four sons. She serves as a member of the Melchizedek Priesthood–Relief Society curriculum writing committee

The next night we met with the stake president. He looked at my husband, smiled, and said, "We'd like to call you to the high council."

I was speechless. *But we've moved*, I thought.

The stake president looked at me. "I know you've moved," he said.

I nodded.

He said, "Move back."

For several days I wrestled with that call. I couldn't imagine going back, giving up my house. Finally Jeff said to me, "I'll call the president and tell him I can't do it."

But it wasn't that Jeff couldn't do it; it was that *I* couldn't do it. I walked out in the backyard, turned on the barbecue, and set the house plans on fire. We accepted the call.

Many times I have looked back on that experience, which drew us back to the neighborhood where we still live. Because of our decision, we went in a direction different from the one we had intended to take. At that singular moment the Lord reached into our lives and said, "This way." And we followed.

It was a still point of our lives, a point of commitment. It set a pattern that has drawn us close to the Lord and reminded us often, "Be still and know that I am God" (D&C 101:16).

The concept of a "still point of the turning world" comes from the poet T. S. Eliot. He speaks of it as being the place "where past and future are gathered."[1] For me the words *still point* capture what's happening when life suspends, when mortality shifts from center stage in our attention long enough for us to hear in our hearts, "Be still and know that I am God." Though the actual words Jeff and I heard were, "Move back," the invitation was to come to know God. And that's what happens when we commit to follow him.

Remember the counsel of the Lord to Mary and Martha. Martha was "cumbered about much serving." But Jesus said to her, "Martha, Martha, thou art careful and troubled about many things: but one thing is needful: and Mary hath chosen that good part, which shall not be taken away from her" (Luke 10:41–42).

What did the Savior mean when he said that Mary's choice of the "good part" could not be taken away? The scriptures give us the answer when they define what commitment is: "Thou shalt love the Lord thy

God with all thy heart, and with all thy soul, and with all thy strength, and with all thy mind" (Luke 10:27). No one can take away what is in your heart.

Brigham Young described it this way: "Seek unto the Lord for his Spirit, without any cessation in your efforts, until his Spirit dwells within you like eternal burnings. Let the candle of the Lord be lighted up within you, and all is right."[2]

In the Book of Mormon, Alma gives wise counsel to his son Helaman that explains how to cultivate such love and commitment: "Cry unto God for all thy support; yea, let all thy doings be unto the Lord, and whithersoever thou goest let it be in the Lord; yea, let all thy thoughts be directed unto the Lord; yea, let the affections of thy heart be placed upon the Lord forever. Counsel with the Lord in all thy doings, and he will direct thee for good; yea, when thou liest down at night lie down unto the Lord, that he may watch over you in your sleep; and when thou risest in the morning let thy heart be full of thanks unto God; and if ye do these things, ye shall be lifted up at the last day" (Alma 37:36–37).

There is no better description of commitment: placing the Lord at the center of our mortal experience. The scripture also clearly reminds us that that kind of commitment will lead to eternal life. What a promise! Looking at this scriptural counsel one measure of commitment at a time can help us weigh our own commitment on the spiritual scale. Please don't set aside the references to "all" as overstatements. In this era of high contrast between good and evil, our effort to be "always" on the Lord's side has eternal significance. We must give "all."

"Let All Thy Doings Be unto the Lord"

The Lord describes such commitment in the parable of the ten virgins (see Matthew 25:1–12). This parable is directed to all of us today, for the virgins represent the Saints, the members of the Church. The essence of the teaching is to center our lives on the Lord.

Ten virgins took their lamps and went forth to meet the bridegroom. The women, as was the custom, were to honor the bridegroom by holding lamps high in the air to light his path. At the beginning, their lamps were bright and glowing, but the wedding party was late, and the maidens fell asleep. Suddenly, in the middle of the night the call came to light the lamps. "The bridegroom cometh; go ye out to meet him."

That was the moment they had been anticipating. But the wait had been long, and some had let their lamps grow dim. Some might have become distracted by the lights of others or lost interest in the wait. Some might have taken to polishing their lamps, finding satisfaction not in the light but in the brilliance of the outside sheen. Then came the announcement, "Go ye out to meet him."

Five of the maidens had sufficient oil to light their lamps, but five did not. "Give us of your oil; for our lamps are gone out," the foolish said. The wise refused. The five with empty lamps ran off to buy oil. While they were gone, "the bridegroom came; and they that were ready went in with him to the marriage: and the door was shut."

When the other five returned, they cried, "Lord, Lord, open to us." But he answered, "I know you not."

What had happened to their original commitment? What can we learn from these women? And most important, how can we come to know Christ and sustain that attention? The answer is commitment.

The women grew weary, perhaps as did Martha, for she "was cum-bered about" (Luke 10:40), and they fell asleep, or in other words, they napped spiritually. And then he came, and they begged their visiting teachers to share. After all, isn't that what visiting teachers are supposed to do? And yet, how do you share the time you spend in the temple or the hours you study the scriptures or your preparation to discuss the Relief Society lesson? How do you share the relationships developed while reading with a son or daughter or conversing with your husband? How can someone reach in and draw from your store of patience or from fortitude forged on your knees? And isn't the oil of service pressed in the lowliest part of the vineyard rather than purchased at the store?

I remember the surprise I felt several years ago when I was called as Primary president in our ward; I had always worked in Relief Society or Young Women. I was suddenly struggling in this new vineyard of little people, not knowing just what to do. It was a rainy Friday afternoon, and I was so busy I barely had time to take my son to Scouts.

When we arrived, the Scouts were ready, pineapples in hand to make into turkeys for Thanksgiving. Jan, my counselor who was doing double duty as the Cub Scout leader, had set out the pipe cleaners for the necks and the feathers and felt and jiggly little eyes for the decorating. I raced in to check if she needed help. I didn't mean to do anything, really, just ask. "Well," she said, "Alan isn't here. Could you call his mother and see if we should wait?" I phoned and learned that Alan was absent because his mother's car wasn't working. "I was going to put his little brothers in the wagon and walk over with him," she said, "but it's just pouring, so I guess he isn't coming." I pictured my list of things to do, but it was a two-mile trek from her house to the Cub Scout meeting, so I grudgingly said, "I'll come and get him." All the way to her house I thought of all the important things I had to do. Then I turned the corner and saw a row of little faces looking out their front window. I had barely stopped the car when the front door flew open and Alan raced out to the car. He looked at me, his face still a little tear-stained, and said, "Look, Sister Swinton, I have my pineapple."

The lowliest part of the vineyard? Yes, but that day the Lord opened up my heart and poured in oil. It may seem like a little thing, a small experience, but remember that the Lord said, "a very large ship is benefited very much by a very small helm" (D&C 123:16). He does indeed part the Red Sea for his people, but more often he sends us to pick up little boys toting pineapples. And we are changed forever.

Commitment. Many small things.

"Whithersoever Thou Goest Let It Be in the Lord"

Two years ago I stood at the top of Rocky Ridge in Wyoming. It is the highest point on the Mormon Trail and the site of one of the greatest tragedies of the pioneer era. We were there late in the day, and it was cold, windy, and growing dark. Good sense said, "Get into the comfortable Suburban that has brought you this far." But I couldn't. I stood chilled to my bones looking down that incline. It was here the Willie Company met the first rescuers and sent them on to the Martin Company trapped farther back on the trail. The Willie people kept little of the provisions for themselves, certain the conditions behind them were even more desperate. As I looked down the mountainside, I couldn't imagine how they pulled handcarts up that steep slope in a freezing blizzard. How had they kept going when they had no boots, no jackets, no protection? How, when they were so tired and so hungry, had they found the strength to carry on?

For weeks they had buried their loved ones in shallow graves, and there would be more deaths in the next hours and days. I looked at the hill those women had to climb and tried to imagine their thoughts. Did they hear in their hearts, "All victory and glory is brought to pass unto you through your diligence, faithfulness, and prayers of faith"? (D&C 103:36).

In the company were mothers like the young women of today. I can imagine that they looked at the circumstances and then put their faith in God and walked on. As families they had set out for Zion, come what may—and it had come. They hadn't expected the road to be easy, but certainly they had assumed they would make it. And then the trail got steeper, and the temperature dropped, and the food ran out. But these were hearty Saints who understood "whithersoever thou goest let it be in the Lord" (Alma 37:36).

Commitment. Come what may.

"Let All Thy Thoughts Be Directed unto the Lord"

The thoughts we fill our heads with—what we read, what we watch on television, what we talk about with our friends, what we peruse on the Internet—either enhances our communication with the Lord or interrupts it. What we think about determines much of who we are. The Prophet Joseph Smith said, "Thy mind . . . if thou wilt lead a soul unto salvation, must stretch as high as the utmost heavens."[3]

Stretching our minds to heaven happens in moments of prayer, of study, of pondering. And when we share our thoughts in testimony, we lift other souls with us. When we bear testimony we are bearing witness of our dedication. At times like these we can't help but feel greater love for our Father in Heaven and his Son Jesus Christ. And that can lift us, heighten our understanding, and bring us peace.

A testimony meeting some years ago stirred my soul. A young boy got up to bear his testimony. His mother and younger brother sat by his side. They had come through a difficult divorce; for him it had been particularly hard. In a halting voice he began to talk of his troubles and his fears. He stopped a few minutes into his thoughts and stood there, the microphone dangling in his hand. He couldn't go on. In the silence, we all wondered what to do.

After a few seconds, his younger brother popped up and put his arm around his brother. Taking the microphone, the younger brother, a deacon, said with such conviction that I still remember his words: "I love my brother. He is about the best older brother on the face of the earth. He helps me so much. I am so grateful for him, and so is my mom. And we are trying really hard to be what Jesus Christ wants us to be." And then he sat down and pulled his brother with him.

I will never forget that still point. In every way, the moment was a testimony of faith in Jesus Christ. Recently the older brother returned from a mission, and when he stood to address the congregation, he spoke in confident tones of his love for the gospel and Jesus Christ.

Commitment. The power of testimony.

"Let the Affections of Thy Heart Be Placed upon the Lord Forever"

How much do we love the Lord? And how do we show it? President David O. McKay reminded us: "Too many men and women have other gods to which they give more thought than to the resurrected Lord—the god of pleasure, the god of wealth, the god of indulgence, the god of political power, the god of popularity, the god of race superiority—as varied and numerous as were the gods in ancient Athens and Rome.

" . . . It is therefore a blessing to the world that there are occasions . . . which say to mankind: *In your mad rush for pleasure, wealth, and fame, pause and think what is of most value in life.*"[4]

Where are our affections? What are we willing to sacrifice for? Sacrifice speaks of what we love and what we value. Hannah in the Bible is such an example of love for the Lord. Hannah desperately wanted a child, so she prayed for a son, promising that if the Lord would answer her petition, she would dedicate the child to his service. Hannah was indeed blessed with a son, and when he was three, she took him to the temple and gave him to the Lord. At their parting, we don't hear words of loneliness or anguish. We hear devotion to God: "For this child I prayed; and the Lord hath given me my petition which I asked of him: therefore also I have lent him to the Lord; as long as he liveth he shall be lent to the Lord" (1 Samuel 1:27–28). We cannot doubt that Hannah loved her only son, but above all she loved the Lord God of Israel. Her sacrifice revealed the depth of her commitment to him.

In the Book of Mormon we read that the people of Zarahemla "did fast and pray oft, and did wax stronger and stronger in their humility, and firmer and firmer in the faith of Christ, unto the filling of their souls with joy and consolation, yea, even to the purifying and the sanctification of their hearts, which sanctification cometh because of their yielding their hearts unto God" (Helaman 3:35).

Commitment. The sanctification of our hearts.

"Counsel with the Lord in All Thy Doings"

Five years ago I visited the Peter Whitmer farm on a Church history tour. It was a bright July day, and I was eager to see the farmhouse reconstructed where the Church had been organized. I took my place in line and then stepped into the log house. We stood in the roped-off area and looked at the hearth, the table, the chairs, the pots and jars, the folded quilts. What a simple setting for the beginning of this now worldwide Church.

We then filed out into the yard. I stepped away from the crowd clustered on the lawn to stand by the fence near the rows of shoulder-high corn. With seemingly hundreds of people milling about me, I found a spot to be alone. Some issues weighed heavily on my mind, and I wanted to talk them over with the Lord. Instead, I found myself thinking about what had happened at the farmhouse on 6 April 1830. I had the powerful impression that the Church indeed had been organized here. It had happened just as the guides had explained. That Joseph Smith was chosen by God to lead the Church of Jesus Christ. And then came this very direct thought: "There will come a time when you will need to know that."

I was startled. *Why would I need to know that? What does that mean?* I wondered. *For as long as I can remember I have had a testimony of Joseph Smith.*

Something important had just happened to me, something I wouldn't ever forget, but I just didn't know why.

I thought about that experience three years later when our family went on a similar Church history tour to upstate New York. There were no words for me outside the farmhouse that time, just the recollection of the former moment and its message. The question remained, *Why would I need to know that?*

I thought about that experience again more recently when I visited the farmhouse with a film crew. But this time that moment in the yard made sense. For the preceding year and a half I had been writing a video documentary and a book about Joseph Smith for a largely non-Mormon audience. I had not initiated the project; I was brought in to do the writing by a producer who had no knowledge of my curious tie to the Joseph Smith story and the farmhouse.

With this project, as you can well imagine, came tremendous pressure and adversity. In some ways I felt like Joseph, who described the religious revival and controversy among the various sects in upstate New York: there were "some crying, 'Lo, here!' and others, 'Lo, there!'" (Joseph Smith–History 1:5). Some would tell Joseph's story by veering to this side and others to that. Writing the Joseph Smith story has been my most difficult assignment; it has also been the most rewarding. I have felt a commitment in my heart to "stand by my servant Joseph, faithfully," as directed in Doctrine and Covenants 6:18. That commitment was forged at the fence on the Fayette farm.

Part of counseling with the Lord in all our doings is hearing his inspiration. The other part is acting upon it. The Lord counts on each of us to do our part. Sometimes our work is highly visible; sometimes it is tucked in the middle of other efforts and hardly anyone knows we were there. But the Lord knows. He is all that really matters.

The story of Joseph Knight is a good example of that in-the-middle, unrecognized service. He was a successful New York farmer who believed in Joseph Smith and "in whose heart" was "written [the] law," as described by Isaiah (2 Nephi 8:7). He had been touched by God, and he stepped up amid the persecutions to do all he could for Joseph Smith. It was his wagon Joseph borrowed to get the plates late on a September night in 1827. Months later, he wrote of going to visit Joseph in Harmony, Pennsylvania: "I bought a Barrel of Mackerel and some lined paper for writing . . . nine or ten Bushels of grain and five or six Bushels

[of] taters and a pound of tea, and I went Down to see him and they ware in want."[5]

A whole discourse on conviction and contribution is in that simple historical account. Joseph Knight had wakened in the morning and felt that Joseph and Emma needed supplies. I can just see him loading up the mackerel, the grain, and the potatoes to stock their cupboards. And then he added to his delivery some lined paper for writing. Joseph was in the process of translating the plates, and no doubt he had great need for lined paper. I want to pay tribute to Joseph Knight for his seemingly insignificant service that when looked at more closely was a contribution of great measure.

Commitment. Hearing and hearkening.

"Let Thy Heart Be Full of Thanks unto God"

It's easy to be thankful to God when life is easy, but cheerful gratitude in hard times is also part of commitment. Hosea Stout said when the pioneers reached the Valley, "Thus ends this long and tedious journey from the land of our enemies. And I feel free and happy that I have escaped from their midst. But there is many a desolate and sandy plain to cross. Many a ruged sage bed to break through. Many a hill and hollow to tug over and Many a mountain and Cañon to pass. and many frosty nights to endure in mid-summer."[6]

This year I have also tugged over the hills and passed the canyons only to endure the frosty nights in midsummer. It has been a year of change in our family. My father died. Our oldest son got married; our second son went on a mission; the third son graduated from high school; the youngest got his driver's license. Writing, Church callings, and family responsibilities seem to require additional time . . . and commitment.

Most of us look back on that era of pioneer courage and say, "I could never have done it." But each of us, not once but often, struggles up one hill only to find, as did the pioneers, that before us are more "hills piled on hills, and mountains in every direction."[7]

The Lord doesn't often reach down and move the mountains to clear our way. Usually he helps reorient our thinking and gives us added strength.

Hanging on my wall at home is a painting of Joseph Smith in Liberty Jail. Joseph exhibited tremendous commitment. He understood things so clearly, and yet he came to the point in Liberty Jail where he questioned the difficult time the Saints were having (see D&C 121:1–6). Joseph had been dragged off to jail; his future was uncertain. The people had been driven from Missouri, making a ragged retreat to Illinois. They had lost their homes, their farms; some had lost their lives. Emma wrote to Joseph: "I hope there [are] better days to come to us yet."[8]

They didn't come quickly. Through the winter, Joseph and a handful of others lived in that dark, dirty jail. The food was wretched; it was cold, and they had no blankets. How can your heart be full of thanks in circumstances like these? "O God, where art thou?" Joseph cried out to the Lord (D&C 121:1). Many of us have asked that question. I love the Lord's response: "My son, peace be unto thy soul; thine adversity and thine afflictions shall be but a small moment; and then, if thou endure it well, God shall exalt thee on high" (D&C 121:7–8).

"Peace be unto thy soul" is a significant answer. The Lord could have solved Joseph's problems, but He had confidence in this bold young prophet, and instead He said, "If the very jaws of hell shall gape open the mouth wide after thee, know thou, my son, that all these things shall give thee experience, and shall be for thy good" (D&C 122:7). I don't think that was what Joseph expected to hear. That answer has become very much a marker for all who are called to endure.

When the Lord speaks peace to the soul, he says something like this: "Therefore, dearly beloved . . . , let us cheerfully do all things that lie in our power; and then may we stand still, with the utmost assurance, to see the salvation of God, and for his arm to be revealed" (D&C 123:17). "Stand still," he says. Cut out the weeping and wailing and busyness that is crowding your sight so that you can see salvation and see his arm revealed—his arm that encircles us.

So, despite the circumstances or the changes and challenges, we must be filled with thanks to God for his Spirit that is with us and for his showing us the way, though often it is not the way we expected.

This past February, I was in the middle of revisions for the documentary and the book on Joseph Smith. It was a hard, soul-searching time because I felt the weight of the responsibility so intensely. I had only one desire and that was to tell the story the way Joseph would have wanted. But it wasn't getting there.

One morning, having just pleaded with the Lord for direction and help, I decided to read the scriptures. I felt directed to 2 Nephi 8. When I read the heading, I realized it was Isaiah, and I thought to myself, *Oh, great. I'll have to figure this out. This is going to be hard, and everything is hard already.* But I pressed on, and it was a still point in a changing world.

The words jumped off the page and into my heart. I was hearing and seeing and feeling all at once, and I wept as I read. I felt as if Isaiah wrote those words thousands of years ago just for me, that Nephi had put them in his account to make sure I wouldn't miss them.

"For the Lord shall comfort Zion, he will comfort all her waste places," said Isaiah. I was Zion, and I was wasted, exhausted, wrung out.

"Lift up your eyes to the heavens," he said. "Hearken unto me, ye that know righteousness." What a thought, to know righteousness. Here I was struggling over this word and that phrase, and yet I knew righteousness. He was reminding me of that. Righteousness is the accumulation of day-to-day living when we live by the words of the Lord.

"In whose heart I have written my law," he said. The Lord looks on the heart. Is he going to grade us on the words we didn't get just right, or is he going to judge the intent, the willingness, the conviction of the heart?

"Fear ye not the reproach of men, neither be ye afraid of their revilings." I could hear all the voices countering each other that the story should go this way or that. It was as in Joseph's day, "'Lo, here! and others, 'Lo, there!'" (Joseph Smith–History 1:5).

And then this charge, "Awake, awake! Put on strength . . . I have put my words in thy mouth, and have covered thee in the shadow of mine hand, . . . O captive daughter of Zion" (2 Nephi 8:3, 6–7, 9, 16, 25).

This insight was so much more than just a pick-me-up for the day. Like the moment outside the farmhouse, it was a moment I will never forget. "Ye that know righteousness . . . in whose heart I have written my law . . . put on strength." I wanted to call everyone I knew and read them those words of comfort and direction. I wanted to shout, "Listen to this!" And then I realized the Lord was saying, "Heidi! Listen to this." "Be still," he was saying, "and know that I am God."

Commitment. To him whose work this is.

I know that Jesus Christ lives. He counts on us to be strong, for we are his daughters and in each of us is divinity. May we be committed to fulfilling that destiny.

NOTES

1. T. S. Eliot, "Burnt Norton," line 139, in *The Complete Poems and Plays, 1909–1950* (New York: Harcourt, Brace, and World, 1958), 119.

2. Brigham Young, *Teachings of Brigham Young,* comp. Fred C. Collier (Salt Lake City: Collier's Publishing, 1987), 320; see also *Journal of Discourses,* 26 vols. (London: Latter-day Saints' Book Depot, 1854–86), 7:139.

3. Joseph Smith, *History of The Church of Jesus Christ of Latter-day Saints,* 2d ed. rev., ed. B. H. Roberts (Salt Lake City: The Church of Jesus Christ of Latter-day Saints, 1932–51), 3:295.

4. David O. McKay, *Man May Know for Himself,* comp. Clare Middlemiss (Salt Lake City: Deseret Book, 1967), 156.

5. Joseph Knight Sr., Joseph Knight Reminiscences [n.d.], Archives of The Church of Jesus Christ of Latter-day Saints, Salt Lake City, 6; or Heidi S. Swinton, *American Prophet: The Story of Joseph Smith* (Salt Lake City: Deseret Book, 1999), 57.

6. Juanita Brooks, *On the Mormon Frontier: The Diary of Hosea Stout* (Salt Lake City: University of Utah Press, 1964), 1:327; entry for 24 September 1848.

7. *Orson Pratt's Journal,* entry for 17 July 1847, in B. H. Roberts, *A Comprehensive History of The Church of Jesus Christ of Latter-day Saints,* 6 vols. (Salt Lake City: The Church of Jesus Christ of Latter-day Saints, 1932–51), 3:213.

8. Joseph Smith, *The Personal Writings of Joseph Smith,* comp. Dean C. Jessee (Salt Lake City: Deseret Book, 1984), 389.

The Savior, the Sacrament, and Self-Worth

TRUMAN G. MADSEN

In the legend of Babette's feast, two single sisters make a place in their small home in Denmark for a woman named Babette who seeks refuge from war in Paris. Together they live an austere life. One day Babette learns that she has won a prize of ten thousand francs. She ponders, she plans, and then she spends it all to import boatloads of the finest foods for one lavish feast. The guests from the neighborhood gather, not knowing a culinary genius is in the kitchen. Babette never appears at the table during the dinner but remains perspiring in the kitchen, performing her craft with meticulous skill and artistry. A young boy serves as her waiter and follows her instructions to the very letter. From the turtle soup to the succulent grapes for dessert, the meal is savored by the guests. Men and women who have been estranged begin impulsively to revel in mutual forgiveness and fellow feeling. In the spirit of a toast, a guest of honor stands. He is a uniformed general. He discourses on the glories of divine mercy and says, "This feast reminds me of a woman chef in Paris." Unbeknownst to him, she is standing only a few feet away. "She could," he says, "transform a dinner into a kind of love affair, an affair that makes no distinction between bodily appetite and spiritual appetite."

Truman G. Madsen, author and lecturer, is a professor emeritus of philosophy at Brigham Young University. He served as director of the BYU Jerusalem Center, as president of the New England Mission, and as a member of the Sunday School General Board. He and his wife, Ann, are the parents of three children and a Navajo foster son, and the grandparents of sixteen. He serves as president of the BYU Fifth Stake.

We watched this film years ago with Jeffrey R. Holland. He has written what for me is one of the clearest and most in-reaching talks ever given on the relationship of souls, symbols, and sacraments.[1] He helped me see this story as an elaborate metaphor of what the scriptures call the wedding supper, or the marriage supper, of the Lamb.

Jesus does indeed liken the kingdom of heaven to a wedding feast. He calls the Church his bride. And when she is adorned as a bride, he, as the Bridegroom, will appear in triumphal reunion. To this consummating feast the poor and the meek of the earth will be invited. It will be a feast of feasts. All this was envisioned by President John Taylor, who said that in the sacrament of the Lord's Supper, we "shadow forth the time when he will come again and when we shall meet and eat bread with him in the kingdom of God."[2]

Note the Master's sacramental promise in 3 Nephi: "He that eateth this bread eateth of my body to his soul; and he that drinketh of this wine drinketh of my blood to his soul; and his soul [which we know is both spirit and body] shall never hunger nor thirst, but shall be filled" (3 Nephi 20:8). The account continues, "Now, when the multitude had all eaten and drunk, behold, they were filled" (3 Nephi 20:9). The phrase "they were filled" is absent from accounts of the Last Supper, but it is present here. As President George Q. Cannon observed, "It seems from this that in partaking of this ordinance they satisfied their appetites—that is, they ate and drank until they were filled."[3] And in that moment they were likewise filled with the Spirit, and they cried out with one voice and gave glory to Jesus (see 3 Nephi 20:9).

We, almost alone in the Christian world, have been taught that when spirit and body are inseparably connected, they may receive a fulness of joy. But in this world, both body and spirit may be famished.

Some time ago, Ann and I stood in the Upper Room, the room in Jerusalem in which the Last Supper took place. Standing there with us, amidst the hollow echoes of ancient limestone walls, were Elder David B. Haight and his wife, Ruby. Not long before, after a serious medical emergency, this apostle of the Lord had been clinging to life, unconscious, in a hospital, where he was given a repeated dream-vision of Jesus' last week on earth. Now, gratefully, we listened to him, and he spoke, in a way that left us breathless, words like those he had spoken in general conference: "I heard no voices but was conscious of being in a holy presence and atmosphere. . . .

"The first scene was of the Savior and His Apostles in the upper chamber on the eve of His betrayal. Following the Passover supper, He instructed and prepared the sacrament of the Lord's Supper for His dearest friends as a remembrance of His coming sacrifice. It was so impressively portrayed to me—the overwhelming love of the Savior for each of them. I witnessed His thoughtful concern for significant details—the washing of the dusty feet of each Apostle, His breaking and blessing of the loaf of dark bread and blessing of the wine, then His dreadful disclosure that one would betray Him. . . .

"Then followed the Savior's solemn discourse when He said to the eleven: 'these things I have spoken unto you, that in me ye might have peace. In the world ye shall have tribulation: but be of good cheer; I have overcome the world' (John 16:33)."[4]

In the Upper Room, in Jerusalem, Elder Haight turned to me and said, "We do not appreciate the sacrament enough. It happened! It is real! It is our access to the Savior."[5] One does not forget such a moment nor the resolve to search deeper.

Then, as if to seal these impressions in me, another privilege came some time later. We were in a special meeting in the Salt Lake Temple. Elder David B. Haight was officiating at the sacrament table. At ninety years of age, he has weakened eyesight, but he has obviously memorized the prayer on the water. After the phrase "blood which was shed for them," and the phrase, "that they may have his Spirit to be with them," he paused. With our heads bowed, we thought to ourselves, *Surely he remembers the next word: Amen.* But he did not hurry. This is the man who has taught that every word in the sacrament prayers is vital. After a heavy pause, he added a word with apostolic dignity: "Always. Amen."[6] I looked up to see the face of the presiding apostle, President Gordon B. Hinckley, and he smiled through his tears.

If we do not come to the sacrament table with such inspired recognition, why don't we? Because sometimes, as Elder Marvin J. Ashton once put it, "we take it upon ourselves to pass self-judgment and simply declare, 'I am not worthy.'"[7] In some extreme cases, that is true, in which case there is no way back except repentance through Christ.

But in many more of us, something else may be amiss. We often con-sider ourselves more or less worthless and in some moods, even beyond help, and we approach the sacrament hesitantly and superficially. Worse still, we do not trust the good news. We do not trust the glad tidings. We do not trust the second opinion of the only Physician who will ever finally judge. That is Christ. That is he who pleads with us to approach boldly the throne of grace. He has called himself the Spirit of Truth, and that Spirit, which he has received in fulness, brings knowledge, we are taught, of things past, present, and future. Therefore, he, a Seer who transcends all seers, knows our past and our future and whatever our pre-sent soul sicknesses are; he knows who we were in the premortal spheres, and he envisions our future—what we are to become in the resurrection. In contrast to that, we live in the blur of amnesia about our past, and we are subject to fits of doubt and disbelief about our real potential. But hear these words of President George Q. Cannon: "Now," he says, "this is the truth. We humble people, we who feel ourselves sometimes so worthless, so good-for-nothing, we are not so worthless as we think. There is not one of us but what God's love has been expended upon. There is not one of us that He has not cared for and caressed. There is not one of us that He has not desired to save and that He has not devised means to save. There is not one of us that He has not given His angels charge concerning.

"We may be insignificant and contemptible in our own eyes and in the eyes of others, but the truth remains that we are children of God and that He has actually given his angels . . . charge concerning us, and they watch over us and have us in their keeping."[8]

In his sacrament, the Lord gives us glimpses of ourselves. And in self-examination we are most blessed when we see ourselves as we are seen by him and know ourselves as we are known by him; then, knowledge of the Savior and self-knowledge increase together. In this world, we do not really grasp who we are until we know whose we are. And week after week the Master invites us to take upon us his name so that we will never forget whose we are. We are his. Isaiah asks, "Can a woman forget her sucking child, that she should not have compassion on the son of her womb?" (Isaiah 49:15). Sadly, the answer is Yes. She may forget. But the Lord says, "Yet will I not forget thee. . . . I have graven thee upon the palms of my hands" (Isaiah 49:15–16). He will never forget us nor our real identity. It is in this spirit that President Harold B. Lee said again and again, "Begin now to show an increased self-respect and reverence for the temple of God, your human body, wherein dwells a heavenly spirit." Over and over he repeated: "Be loyal to the royal within you."[9] President David O. McKay used to say to his teenage daughters and granddaughters not "What an awkward girl you are!" but "What a queen you are becoming!"[10]

It is a truism among us that when we partake of the sacrament, we renew our covenants. That is sobering enough. As President McKay said: "Who can measure the responsibility of such a covenant? How far-reaching! How comprehensive! It excludes from [our] life profanity, vulgarity, idleness, enmity, jealousy, drunkenness, dishonesty, hatred, selfishness, and every form of vice. It obligates [us] to sobriety, to industry, to kindness, to the performance of every duty in church and state. [We bind ourselves] to respect [our] fellow men, to honor the priesthood, to pay [our] tithes and offerings, and to consecrate [our lives] to the service of humanity."[11]

No wonder we sometimes shrink. A little voice may say, "I'd rather not do that. I'm not sure I can carry it through." But that is the very nub of our stumbling block. Until we covenant—which is more than a casual New Year's resolution—he cannot bless us to keep our covenants. Without exception, the Lord appends a divine blessing to every covenant we make, guarantees a response from on high, and gives a promise and blessing. In the Church our duties expand into privileges, and our privileges expand into higher duties. The most inclusive attendant blessing of the sacrament is his Spirit. And his Spirit, like the Savior himself, is not sent into the world to condemn the world but to lift us. He is not interested in putting us down. The gifts and the fruits of the Spirit engulf all our deepest needs, whatever our present desires: insight, flashes of guidance, energy, all the virtues that center in Christ, and through them, all the fire that purifies our feelings and our aspirations. Yes, we come to the sacrament to renew covenants, but we also come to be renewed—to be renewed with a divine infusion—and then we increase in our strength to honor our covenants with him and with each other.

Why do we think we can do it alone? And why do we turn our back on him when we need him most?

The priest officiating at the sacrament table is told in the scriptures to kneel "with the church" (D&C 20:76). That can mean "in the presence of," but it can also mean that all of us kneel with him—and in spirit, we all can. When we do so, the Savior yearns for us to understand that he is kneeling, and when he kneels, he offers a prayer, which is in the Doctrine and Covenants and which may be the essence of what he said when he knelt in the Garden of Gethsemane and spoke to the Father: "Behold the sufferings and death of him who did no sin, in whom thou wast well pleased; behold the blood of thy Son which was shed, the blood of him whom thou gavest that thyself might be glorified; Wherefore, Father, spare these my brethren that believe on my name, that they may come unto me and have everlasting life" (D&C 45:4–5).

If souls are of value in direct proportion to the concern and sacrifice of our Redeemer, then we know that in the eyes of the Father and the Son, your soul—even yours—and mine—even mine—is of infinite worth. Who of us really wants to deny that or throw it away?

But where does the Spirit come from that heals and redeems? I suggest that the residues of divine light are already locked within us; our glory-laden spirits are covered with the lamp shade of the body. Nevertheless, they are still directly subject to the light and life of God, "as though," Joseph Smith wrote, "we had no bodies at all."[12] I take literally the sayings of the Savior that this light, which is in us from birth, cannot be extinguished, no matter how we neglect or abuse it. He says, "I am the light which shineth in darkness, and the darkness comprehendeth it not" (D&C 6:21; see also John 1:5). The Greek word translated here as *comprehendeth* suggests "cannot lessen or diminish it." The full-bodied flame is his, and when that flame meets the flame within us, as two candles blend, so the light becomes one; this is the process by which old things pass away and all things become new.

Sometimes, when I am interviewing young people for a temple recommend or renewal, I hand them a card on which is written this statement: "Being born again, comes by the Spirit of God through ordinances."[13]

"Have you ever seen that before?" I ask.

Very few have.

"Do you know where it comes from?"

They usually don't.

"It comes from the Prophet Joseph Smith in instructions to the Twelve before they went to England. Do you know what it means?"

"I'm not sure."

Then I say, "It means, as I understand it, that the fullest flow of the Spirit of God comes to us through his appointed channels or ordinances. The sacrament is the central and oft-repeated ordinance that transmits that power to us. Indeed, it is the ordinance that gives focus to all other ordinances. And that is what President David O. McKay meant, I believe, when he said he loved the phrase of Peter: 'We may be partakers of the divine nature' (2 Peter 1:4)."[14] Eventually, through a lifetime, His spirit can sanctify the very elements of our bodies until we become capable of celestial resurrection.

In baptism we are born once—born of the water and of the Spirit. In the sacrament we are reborn, over and over, of the bread and of the wine or water, and we are truly what we eat. But not all at once. Can we eat one meal that will last us a lifetime? Some of us occasionally try. Do we not need daily nourishment? In fact, the phrase in the Lord's prayer, the model prayer, which is "Give us this day our daily bread" (Matthew 6:11) may mean "Give us today a foretaste of the meal we will eat with you when you return to us."

We need it often, and thus on the Sabbath we gather together, having been told that we are to be together, so that our communication may become communion. And though we come from every degree on the emotional compass, each of us is more or less empty and more or less in need.

We have a faith in unity, and the Prophet Joseph Smith made it clear in a remark to the Relief Society that it is by "union of feeling that we obtain power in God."[15] We may have different beliefs and temperaments and backgrounds, but we can all feel as one when we are taking the sacrament together. Indeed, it is by union of feeling that we obtain power.

A repeated statement of the Lord is that we must be in a particular condition to participate fully in the sacramental meal. It is in his revelation on the Sabbath: "Thou shalt offer a sacrifice unto the Lord thy God in righteousness, even that of a broken heart and a contrite spirit" (D&C 59:8).

What is a broken heart? In common parlance it usually means, on one level at least, that a hope has been thwarted or blasted, or romantic love has been met with apathy. It is as if something outside us has broken our heart. But clearly the Lord is saying we can offer a broken heart to him. *Broken* now does not mean distressed or tormented; it means an open heart—it means a heart that is susceptible to the Spirit and willing to keep its covenants. A broken heart is an open heart, and he can fill it.

The full reach of a broken heart is this: that we put ourselves on the altar. A saying flourished among the ancients: Only he who brings himself to the Lord as an offering may be called man (see Leviticus 1:2).

The one thing that can most readily prevent that openness and that sacrifice is unforgiveness. All of us need—and often refuse to give—three kinds of forgiveness. We sometimes cannot forgive ourselves. We sometimes bear a catalog of grievances against others that still binds us. And we sometimes need to forgive even God and his Son, for there are resentments in us for such things as his calendar, which never quite corresponds to ours. We pray and we know when we want an answer, but the Lord's timetable and our watches are not always synchronized.

After such forgiveness can come the flow of which I speak.

As I have pondered the seeming contradiction between the Lord's justice and the Lord's mercy, it has become clear to me that when we offer a broken heart to him, then it is perfectly just that he should have mercy on us, for such a heart is now willing to change, to honor his will, and to draw closer to him. Then the outpouring follows. He, I also believe, can justly and mercifully ask for our hearts thus, because he gave us his whole heart and because he put himself on the altar. He chose to be humble and, indeed, chose even to be humiliated.

In Chaim Potok's novel *The Chosen* are some lines that are his version of the great parable of the prodigal son. A person leaves home, rejects, rebels, and finally says to a friend, "I can't go back."

The friend says, "Go back. You must go back."

He replies, "I cannot."

The friend says, "Go back as far as you can, and he will come the rest of the way."[16]

Yes, that is divine grace, and yes, that is what Christ holds for us.

Can we imagine that? I am thinking of Gethsemane and Golgotha. I thought I could imagine those scenes because I have lived in the Holy Land for five years, but recently I was totally shaken by an experience at a movie studio crowded with actors and staff. They were preparing a film that focuses on the life of Christ and upon his coming as a resurrected being to the Nephite multitude. A convert to the Church, an actor named Thomas who was portraying Jesus, was trying to simulate that moment most significant in eternity when Jesus is nailed to the cross. We watched from a short distance a monitor that framed the scene. We saw them force him down on the transverse beam. We saw them stretch his arm. We saw them place the spike and pick up a huge mallet. Then the camera focused on the profile of his face. When we heard the horrifying "thwack" and the repeat of the mallet, his face and body twisted in contortion. "Cut!" said the director. They readjusted the lights, and they sprayed his body with red paint to simulate lines of scourging and cuts in his forehead. And then again. And then again. After the fifth take, he sat up, compulsively weeping. The director, at first mildly concerned and then really anxious, reached over to the actor and said, "Are you all right?" He couldn't answer, but he finally said, "It is so real . . . so real."

Our scriptures combined with ancient scripture are absolutely clear on this: as surely as Christ was secured to his cross, we must be secured to him. And if we are commanded (and we are) to take up our own cross, then the witness of Moroni clarifies that our cross is to deny ourselves of all ungodliness (see Moroni 10:32). But beyond that denial, which he exemplifies, there is great joy.

We cannot make it alone. We cannot make it without his encircling arms. We cannot make it without help any more than he could in the Garden of Gethsemane, without help. For he, even he, while praying most earnestly was visited by an angel who came to strengthen him (see Luke 22:43–44). Christ did not tell the Nephite multitude, "Think of me once in a while, and my Spirit will be with you." He said the sacrament would be "a testimony unto the Father that ye do always remember me. And if ye do always remember me ye shall have my Spirit to be with you" (3 Nephi 18:7). There is that word again: *always*.

After my first mission I asked my father several times, "Is there anyone in our history, in the whole history of man, who has had the Spirit of the Lord with him always?" He thought hard and then said, "Some have come pretty close." If so, then it was through Christ.

It is possible to have Christ in our undergirding consciousness, if you will, at the bottom of our heart, even if something else is, at the moment, at the top of our mind. That is, I believe, the meaning of the words: "Look unto me in every thought" (D&C 6:36). Then, knowing that we tend to shrink and say, "Oh, not these thoughts. These are unworthy thoughts," he says, "Doubt not, fear not" (D&C 6:36).

The Savior has the power to change us even when circumstances remain the same. Indeed, he promises that change, even in the midst of soul-searing afflictions. Think, for example, of the women in the Lehi colony, struggling, wading through sands mile after mile each day. They are forbidden to build fires, so instead of providing cooked meat, the Lord promises he will make wild and raw meat taste sweet. These are expectant mothers. These are nursing mothers. These are aged mothers (see 1 Nephi 17:2).

Think of the people, men and women, enslaved by vicious taskmasters who were commissioned to kill them if they were found praying. Instead of delivering them immediately, the Lord said, "I will . . . ease the burdens which are put upon your shoulders, that even you cannot feel them upon your backs, even while you are in bondage; and this will I do that ye may stand as witnesses for me hereafter, and that ye may know of a surety that I, the Lord God, do visit my people in their afflictions" (Mosiah 24:13–14).

Think of the three sons of Mosiah, away from their families, charged with an impossible mission, namely, to teach and convert people who have sworn eternal hatred to them and have murdered their friends. Instead of lessening the task, the Lord said, "Be comforted." I have marveled at that. "The Lord did visit them with his Spirit, and said unto them: Be comforted. And they were comforted" (Alma 17:10). No explanations. No attempt to talk them out of their feelings. Can it be so? Alma recorded that though they waded through afflictions of every kind, yet those afflictions were "swallowed up in the joy of Christ" (Alma 31:38).

The Savior said, "Be of good cheer" (John 16:33). Can it be that in tribulation, which he promises, he can say, "Be of good cheer" and we are of good cheer? Yes, even if the only thing to be of good cheer about is our relationship with him. And in the very depths and fibers of our being it can be so. I testify that may be his mightiest miracle. Someday we may even say to him, "Master, through all my life and all my prayers, most of the time all you really changed was me." He will smile and say, "Ah, yes. And what a glorious change."

I close with an entry from my journal. We were in Amman, Jordan, some years ago having just come from a parched visit to Egypt, where even the native Bedouin can survive at most three hours without water. We had said to some of our friends, "This should remind you of the two words spoken from the cross, his only self-regarding words, which are a sure sign of the loss of blood: Jesus said, 'I thirst' (John 19:28)."

That night I had a dream. I was beaten down to my hands and knees and was conscious of a burning thirst. In the illogic of dreams there was somehow a small cup filled with liquid—an unearthly liquid. It was radiant. It was delicious. It was cool. But as I lifted it to my lips, it was as if two hands were placed behind me, not touching me but close to my head, and from them came a kind of throb, a comfort, a warm feeling, and then the miracle. As I drank in relief, the cup filled again and again. The more I sought to quench my thirst, the more the liquid flowed. A wave of gratitude came over me to the Christ—for in the dream it was Christ. My impulse was to turn around, stop drinking, and thank him. But then came the sweet assurance that my drinking was his thanks, that this was what he most wanted, that this was his reward, even his glory— like a gracious host, who takes delight in seeing family and guests eat heartily. I knew, and I knew he knew, so I drank and drank until I was full. Only then was he gone.

Sometime later, these words in the Doctrine and Covenants leaped off the page: "For unto him that receiveth it shall be given more abundantly, even power" (D&C 71:6). And elsewhere these words, "Yea, even more abundantly, which abundance is multiplied unto them through the manifestations of the Spirit" (D&C 70:13).

My wife, Ann, has written a poem that she titled "The Sacrament Prayer," which we give to our grandsons when they become old enough to be ordained to the Aaronic Priesthood, an event that is for us a joy to behold and participate in with them.

> The words are repeated once again
> this sacred Sabbath time;
> words I can trace
> through the week,
> but this time unique,
> spoken,
> quietly,
> in youthful intonation
> and the nourishment
> is proffered me
> by a boy's hand
> in exchange for my changing.

I grew up in a single-parent home—a father and two brothers. My mother was gone when I was two. I have no memory of her, and I had no sister. What I am about to say I have learned from a queenly wife and from daughters and daughters-in-law.

You faithful sisters, married or unmarried, who move daily (and with hardly a break) from the garden plot to the crucial minutiae of food labels to the cups and measures of cookery; you, who struggle and preside in the kitchen and keep vigil; you, who reach out to the perennial needs of your family and loved ones; you, who with artistry gather flowers and turn an ordinary table into an altar that summons prayer and thanksgiving; you, who by your very presence, turn eating into a feast—into dining in the name of the Lord, and who, therefore, bring a bountiful measure of grace to your table—lend your faith to boys and sometimes inept men who officiate at the sacrament table. Let the tables turn on your serving. Lend your faith to our trying to act, as you do, in Christlike dignity, for this is as close as we may ever come to your divine calling to give and to nurture life itself.

Come to a foretaste of the marriage supper of the Lamb.

I bear witness with a cloud of witnesses that in the midst of affliction, yes, even and especially in the midst of affliction, his table is spread and that with blessings unmeasured, his cup runneth o'er.[17]

NOTES

1. Jeffrey R. Holland, "Of Souls, Symbols, and Sacraments," *Brigham Young University 1987–1988 Devotional and Fireside Speeches* (Provo, Utah: Brigham Young University, 1988), 73–85; also in Jeffrey R. Holland and Patricia T. Holland, *On Earth As It Is in Heaven* (Salt Lake City: Deseret Book, 1989), 182–97.

2. John Taylor, *Journal of Discourses*, 26 vols. (London: Latter-day Saints' Book Depot, 1854–86), 14:185, 20 March 1870.

3. George Q. Cannon, *Gospel Truth*, comp. Jerreld L. Newquist, 2 vols. (Salt Lake City: Deseret Book, 1974), 2:159.

4. David B. Haight, *Ensign*, November 1989, 60.

5. Personal conversation; used by permission.

6. Used by permission; see David B. Haight, *Ensign*, May 1983, 13.

7. Marvin J. Ashton, *The Measure of Our Hearts* (Salt Lake City: Deseret Book, 1991), 8.

8. Cannon, *Gospel Truth*, 1:2.

9. Harold B. Lee, *Stand Ye in Holy Places* (Salt Lake City: Deseret Book, 1974), 15.

10. Personal conversation.

11. David O. McKay, *Gospel Ideals* (Salt Lake City: Improvement Era, 1954), 73.

12. Joseph Smith, *Teachings of the Prophet Joseph Smith*, sel. Joseph Fielding Smith (Salt Lake City: Deseret Book, 1976), 355.

13. Smith, *Teachings of the Prophet Joseph Smith*, 162.

14. See David O. McKay, *Improvement Era*, June 1957, 452.

15. Relief Society Minutes, 9 June 1842, Archives of The Church of Jesus Christ of Latter-day Saints, Salt Lake City, Utah; see also Smith, *Teachings of the Prophet Joseph Smith*, 91.

16. See Chaim Potok, *The Chosen* (New York: Simon and Schuster, 1967).

17. See *Hymns of The Church of Jesus Christ of Latter-day Saints* (Salt Lake City: Church of Jesus Christ of Latter-day Saints, 1985), no. 108.

How Do I Balance
What's Important?

Heidi H. Clark,
Rosemary M. Wixom, and Jane F. Hinckley

Use your agency wisely. (Heidi) Every day brings choices, so the balance is up to us. At any given time, I may make a choice that upsets the balance in my life—or one that restores it. Sit back and think for a minute. Do you have realistic expectations of what you can do? In the last week, when did you feel the most at peace? Do you have such high expectations that you'll never find a peaceful, rewarding balance in your life? Too often we compare ourselves to others and make choices based not on our own needs and circumstances but on a desire to be like someone we admire. That can put our life totally out of balance.

Avoid making comparisons. (Rosemary) I think it's a woman thing to compare ourselves to others. We even compare our children to other children. Have you ever felt defeated by a Christmas letter? My husband,

Heidi H. Clark has taught high school and now coordinates programs for the Salt Lake City School District. She and her husband, Robert S. Clark, are the parents of six children. She teaches Relief Society and is the education specialist for the Inner City Project in Salt Lake.

Rosemary M. Wixom received her bachelor's degree in elementary education. She is a high school PTA president and teaches English to refugees as part of the Literacy Volunteers of America. She and her husband, B. Jackson Wixom, are the parents of six children. She has served in her ward's Young Women organization.

Jane Freed Hinckley earned her degree in mathematics from the University of Utah. She taught math in California and Utah in both junior and senior high schools. She and her husband, Richard G. Hinckley, are the parents of four children. She tutors math and teaches guitar in her home. She serves as a Relief Society teacher in her ward.

Jack, and I were at a wedding reception a few years back. It was May, and our oldest son was graduating from high school. He was a good student, and he was planning to continue his education. As we stood in line conversing with friends and neighbors about their seniors, the topic of "after high school" plans surfaced. From proud parents numerous announcements poured forth of accolades and scholarships. I was astonished to hear of all the awards that were available. Later that evening on the way home, the car was quiet. Jack asked me, "What are you thinking about?"

"Did every senior in Utah receive a scholarship except our son?"

He laughed. He always helps me when I am in the comparing mode. He encourages me to step back, count my blessings, and get my thinking in perspective.

Simplify your life. (Jane) Stephen Covey believes that most of us neglect our own priorities because we suffer from "the Urgency Addiction": we live from crisis to crisis and feel energized and excited by the resulting "high."[1] How can we simplify so that we are not racing from one "fire" to the next? Several years ago, a few days after Christmas, an old friend called me. "How was your Christmas?" she said. "Fine," I said, "but it was such a busy month. I felt overwhelmed. There I was buying gifts for my children, trying to create such a fun Christmas for them, while they were at home making a mess of the house. To tell you the truth, I'm glad it's over. I'm exhausted."

"You know," she observed, "that's how it used to be at our house. But it was different this year."

"Tell me what you did," I said. I liked her ideas and decided to try them. On Thanksgiving Day, I called the family in to a meeting. "Let's make a list of the things you like doing during the month of December," I said. "I love to buy a Christmas tree and decorate it," said one child. I wrote that down. Another child said, "I love to have the lights outside our house so when we drive up we see them." Another one said, "I think it's fun to do the Twelve Days of Christmas where we secretly leave gifts for some neighbor," and so the list went.

When the list was completed, I said, "Okay, let's start at the beginning. Who would like to buy the Christmas tree?" Not one hand went up. So I crossed that off the list. I said, "Okay, who wants to put up the lights outside?" Not one hand went up, so I crossed that off the list. In no time at all I'd crossed off every single thing on the whole list.

My children looked at me like I was crazy and said, "But Mom, then we're not going to have Christmas this year."

"Well, it will be a peaceful December, won't it."

"But we really want to do all of those things."

"Then I need help," I explained. "I can't do them all alone."

"Oh please, start again," they pleaded.

So I said, "Okay, who will buy the Christmas tree?"

My husband raised his hand. He said, "I will do it providing you don't criticize the tree I get." He likes tall, slender ones, and I like short, bushy ones.

"Okay," I said, "I'll agree not to criticize the tree you buy, if you'll just buy it and bring it home one night without my help. That would be terrific."

We went next to the outside lights. One of my sons raised his hand. "I'll do the lights outside if someone will help me." Someone volunteered to help.

When we got to the bottom of the list every single person had volunteered to help. And that was one of the best Decembers we have ever had.

Cultivate humor and good friends. (Heidi) Having a positive attitude and a sense of humor are keys to maintaining balance. Sister Marjorie P. Hinckley says, "You either have to laugh or cry. I prefer to laugh. Crying gives me a headache."[2] Friends who are uplifting and loyal help give us balance throughout our lives. We must make a conscious choice to nurture friendships and sustain our friends.

Serve others and let others serve you. (Jane) Service, both given and received, creates balance in our lives. Think each day, *Is there someone out there who needs my help?* Schedule ten minutes to do something nice for somebody else—a thank-you note, a phone call, an errand for an elderly neighbor. We need to be able to ask for help, too. When my husband and I were first married, we moved to North Hollywood, and I taught school there. Relief Society was in the middle of the week then, so I wasn't able to attend. Consequently, I didn't really know the Relief Society presidency. While we were there, I had our first baby.

When Dick drove the baby and me home from the hospital, who was waiting on my porch but the Relief Society presidency.

"What can we do for you?" they said. "How can we help?"

I didn't know what to say; I'd never had a baby before. I declined their help, thinking my husband and I could manage. After Dick got us settled in the house, he went back to work, and the baby started to cry.

Oh, oh, I thought, *now what do I do? Well, I can make it through this. Mom's coming tomorrow.*

Mom stayed for a week, which should have been enough, but after she left, medical complications kept me in bed. Day after day after day I lay there with just my baby. I could not even make it into the kitchen to fix myself something to eat. I got so hungry at lunchtime. At night Dick fixed dinner, tried to clean up, shop, launder (this was before disposable diapers), and do whatever he could to prepare for the next day. There was a lot to do.

When I look back on those days, I wish I had called that Relief Society president and said, "Please help me. If someone could just get me lunch, if someone would dust this room, I'm so desperate." Just to have somebody come over and say that they cared would have helped. Often when we think of service, we think of big projects. But service doesn't have to be time consuming.

Plan time for yourself. (Rosemary) In all of your giving, give yourself some space. Take time for exercise. Sign up for a class that you've always wanted to take. Develop hobbies. Read a magazine, poetry, a novel. My dad counseled, "You have to have something to think about while you're washing out the diapers." Those were in the cloth diaper days, but the idea still applies. And above all, don't feel guilty. A lot of us grew up with the idea that if you sit down, you're not being productive. I remember tapping my toe as I was nursing a baby, thinking, "And when I'm through here, then I'll do this and then I'll do that."

We allow life to move way too fast. Writer Richard Carlson says, "The purpose of life *isn't* to get it all done but to enjoy each step along the way."[3] Discover your passion, something that you really love to do. Do you know individuals who have a passion—perhaps a love for photography, running, quilting, genealogy, reading, gardening. They make time for the things they love. That passion enriches their lives, and they are still great mothers, wives, sisters, and grandmothers. In fact, maybe better. That's true balance.

Increase your faith. (Heidi) When the unexpected knocks us off our feet, we need faith to restore us to balance. Several years ago, I was sitting in a doctor's office listening to him tell me that I had cancer, that they would operate, but that the prognosis was bad. In fact, the odds were that I wasn't going to live. What I had just been told seemed unreal, a terrible dream. I kept expecting to wake up. Thoughts flew through my mind: *Not me. I'm way too young. I have too much that I want to do. I have two grandchildren about to be born. They need to know me. Yesterday I was fine; today I'm staring death straight in the eye. How could that be?*

As my husband and I walked out of the office, my shock turned suddenly to anger. I turned and told the doctor I knew that some people had come through this, and I planned on being one of them. Yet deep within, I also knew that what was going to happen was going to happen. I would face my surgery, however, with faith and my strong convictions of the power of prayer and of priesthood blessings.

As the days passed, I had to keep reminding myself that if I didn't make it through, I would be with my family throughout eternity. My faith took me to that point. But it still seemed so unfair. The night before I was admitted to the hospital, my husband, sons-in-law, and family members—the people who meant the very most to me in this world—joined together to pray with me and bless me. Afterwards, I knew that the Lord was not going to let me die, not just yet. Six weeks later, incredibly restored in health and renewed in my faith, I returned to work full time and began an arduous year of chemotherapy. Five weeks after my surgery, my husband and I were called into the stake president's office. I was sure that the stake leaders were going to thank me for my five years of service as a stake Young Women's president and extend a release. Wrong. They called my husband to be the bishop of our ward. How could he turn down a chance to repay the Lord for sparing the life of his wife? How could I hope for a better way to express my own gratitude? A morning doesn't pass without my thanking my Father in Heaven for the ability to wake up with my earthly family, to feel well, and to know that I have another day of mortal life to serve him.

Expect the unexpected. (Jane) There will be times in our lives when our circumstances may completely throw our lives out of balance, requiring all of our energy and attention for a time. That unexpected circumstance might be a terminal or chronic health problem. Or it could be a straying child, financial challenges, a job loss, or a crisis in our marriage. At times we may find our lives so stressed that it is utterly impossible for us to maintain our balance. In those cases, there is only one source of help—the Savior. We cannot do it alone. We need to lay our burdens at the Lord's feet and move on. When we have done all we can and know it is not enough to meet the day's requirements, we must trust the Lord. We must rely on him for strength. He will not fail us.

NOTES

1. Stephen R. Covey, *First Things First* (New York: Simon and Schuster, 1994), 33.
2. Virginia H. Pearce, ed., *Glimpses into the Life and Heart of Marjorie Pay Hinckley* (Salt Lake City: Deseret Book, 1999), 107.
3. Richard Carlson, *Don't Sweat the Small Stuff . . . and It's All Small Stuff* (New York: Hyperion, 1997), 20.

How Do I Teach from the New Relief Society Manuals?

MARGARET SMOOT,
IRENE STOUT, AND DIANNE J. EGGETT

Recognize the challenge of change. (Margaret) The recent change in Relief Society curriculum has been not just a minor course correction but a rather large blasting of a brand-new road. In contemplating the challenges of change, I am reminded of this reflection by Elder Marion G. Romney some years ago: "It is a great task to change direction, even a little, in a great organization, and many people suffer greatly from it. You can tell a man's [or woman's] age by the amount he suffers when he hears a new idea. I hope you people do not suffer too much, that you find joy in keeping current and helping us in this development."[1]

Understand the purposes and context of the lessons. (Margaret) We should look at this new curriculum not as an overwhelming mountain to climb but as steps which, if followed, ascend to greater gospel understanding, a more generous outpouring of the Spirit, and a renewed desire to feast on the words of God. We are being given an unparalleled opportunity to be more conversant with the inspired words and teachings of

Margaret Smoot, a writer and producer, has served as a spokesperson for Brigham Young University. She has also been a member of the Relief Society General Board and the Church's Pioneer Sesquicentennial Committee. She serves as a Relief Society teacher in her ward.

Irene Stout, mother and wife, is a long-time teacher of youth and Relief Society sisters in her ward. She loves the scriptures, the prophets, and life.

Dianne L. Eggett is a homemaker and has been an all-around teacher in Relief Society, Primary, and a private preschool. She serves as a Webelos leader in her ward Scouting program.

our prophets and thereby led to a scriptural feast upon the words of God. The curriculum surpasses in depth and complexity anything we have studied in the past. I don't believe we should be embarrassed that it's taking time for us to see what the Brethren had in mind when they crafted the curriculum. And I certainly don't believe we should be discouraged if we are not at the place of perfection in our understanding of how to teach it. We are all learning "line upon line," or in this case, "sentence upon sentence."

Realize the lesson material is modern scripture. (Margaret) "Whether by mine own voice or by the voice of my servants, it is the same" (D&C 1:38)—not merely similar or very close, but the same. It took me three months of teaching before I understood what that means. I had a personal epiphany that totally changed my approach and perspective on the lessons. I realized I must compare the lesson material to scripture. How would I study the scriptures? Would I be reluctant to delve into the material or to mark my lesson manual in the same way I do my scriptures? Of course not. Then I should do the same for these lessons. I determined that at the end of the two years of study I would have a good knowledge of the teachings of Brigham Young and that my manual would look much like my scriptures—well-marked and cross-referenced to other books of scripture.

Be a relentless seeker of truth. (Irene) I want to be able to stand before my Heavenly Father and say, "Yes, I tried to make the best of my time on earth. I tried to learn and gain knowledge. I tried to understand the commandments and the gospel. I tried to understand and know Thee." Our desire, our craving to learn, needs to be insatiable. Brigham Young said, "When we embraced the Gospel, the spirit opened up to our minds . . . the wisdom, the knowledge, and the power of God."[2] The familiar scripture in Moroni 10:4–5, which concludes, "by the power of the Holy Ghost ye may know the truth of all things," applies to more than just gaining a testimony of the Book of Mormon. It applies to our becoming gospel scholars.

Don't be intimidated by others. (Irene) You probably know more about the gospel than you think you do. Consider these questions: Do women lack the confidence to admit scholarship? Are we intimidated by the men? Some brilliant women in my ward make wise, perceptive comments in Relief Society, but in Sunday School they become very quiet. Do women have an equal opportunity to be scholars? Of course we do. Does our Church society expect us to be quiet in the presence of the brethren? On the contrary: speaking to men and women, Brigham Young said we are "endowed with the science, power, excellency, brightness and glory. . . . The more [we] learn the more [we] discern an eternity of knowledge to improve upon."[3] We can expand in every direction while we're here on earth, and we're expected to do so.

Plan time for personal study. (Irene) Look at the practical realities of gaining gospel scholarship and consider your time constraints. You cannot lock yourself in a closet, become monastic, and neglect daily duties, but you can make study time a priority that fits into every day. Consider these tips to help you become a gospel scholar: attend the temple frequently, include daily scripture reading, pray and listen to the Spirit, read good books and learn from other scholars, absorb information in every area, talk less, listen and think more, and thank Heavenly Father for the gifts of knowledge you receive.

Seek a testimony of what you are to teach. (Dianne) Begin study with a prayer expressing faith and asking for guidance—revelation from the Holy Ghost. That is the first step. To teach by the Spirit, we must also ponder what we have read. I often ponder the lesson as I go about my daily chores. Quotations from the lesson, words of the prophets, scriptures, and any other material I have read in preparation, as well as past learning and experiences, will come into my mind as my thoughts focus on specific teachings that I am preparing. Gradually, what I am learning sinks into my heart, and my understanding begins to expand. The seed, or the word, begins to take root and grows into a testimony (see Alma 32:27–34). Does our soul hunger to understand further the truths we are to teach and to be worthy to receive direction by the Spirit? This hunger takes us back to our Heavenly Father in prayer time and again.

Pray for those under your stewardship. (Dianne) Those we teach must also be diligent in their efforts. They must keep the commandments, read the words of the prophets and the scriptures, and come prepared with the Spirit to receive the blessings to which they are entitled. The choice is theirs. We prepare to teach with the Spirit and pray that

they will come ready to comprehend and lend their spirits and understandings.

Develop a lesson preparation strategy that works for you. (Dianne)
I skim the lesson over first for the general topic. Then I read the
quotations. I find I can never truly understand a quotation with one
reading. I reread it several times, stopping to ponder a different phrase
each time until I feel I understand its meaning. I next work with the
lesson by sections, trying to see how the quotations fit together to teach
the section topic. Then I consider the questions at the end and try to
find which quotations fit each question. I try to find as many quotations
as I can to teach or to stimulate thought and discussion about each question. Throughout this process, I think about and jot down experiences
I've had that illustrate the quotations. The last thing I do is answer the
questions on paper. Writing is another way for me to internalize the
truths I have studied.

NOTES

1. Marion G. Romney, "Church Correlation," address to seminary and institute of religion faculty at Brigham Young University, Provo, Utah, 22 June 1964, Historical
Library of The Church of Jesus Christ of Latter-day Saints, Salt Lake City, 10.
2. Brigham Young, *Discourses of Brigham Young,* sel. John A. Widtsoe (Salt Lake City:
Deseret Book, 1941), 247.
3. Young, *Discourses,* 249, 250.

How Do I Learn
"by the Way of the Body"?

LaNae Valentine

Reject society's standard of beauty. Probably one of the greatest burdens we women carry is our negative feelings about our own bodies. We base our feelings of worth and value on body size, shape, and beauty, and we engage in a never-ending struggle to change how we look. Most of us can find something about our body that we wish could be different—smoother skin, smaller thighs, a flatter stomach, a thinner body. Moreover, our beauty ideal is becoming more and more unnatural. The ideal American woman is five feet, seven inches and weighs 110 pounds; the real American woman is five feet, four inches and weighs 144 pounds. Research shows that virtually all females are ashamed of their bodies—even ten- and eleven-year-olds. Our quest for beauty—for physical perfection and control—and our alarm over the natural processes of aging lead us to feel trapped and frustrated by our bodies. Those feelings block us from the lessons we are to learn "by the way of the body."[1]

Realize that having a body is a great gift. Joseph Smith taught that having a body is essential to our growth and learning and that "all beings who have bodies have power over those who have not."[2] So important is the body that virtually every one of us will be better off for having come to earth simply because we will forever after have a body. Unfortunately, we Latter-day Saints are as prone as anyone else to act as if the body

LaNae Valentine is a clinical practitioner specializing in women's issues and eating disorders. She is coordinator of Women's Services and Resources at Brigham Young University. She serves in her ward Sunday School as the in-service leader.

were more of a nuisance than a blessing. We may do a little better job of avoiding things that harm the body than others do, but we are just as likely to ignore the body's needs, to distrust its appetites and passions, to feel ashamed of its appearance, and to disregard its teachings. We may blame the body for our sinful dispositions and may feel imprisoned by its fleshly inclinations. We think, *If I could just get rid of this body and its problems, its distractions, I could truly soar. I could be far more spiritual.* Yet, we are taught that only the reuniting of spirit and body, never again to be divided, makes a fulness of joy (see D&C 93:33–35). Our bodies are the next step in our spiritual progression, not a hindrance we discard at death. The purpose of our bodies, as psychologist Wendy Ulrich has said, is "much, much more than to simply carry our heads around. Embodiment is a sacred gift. The body is our gift, our tutor, our holy edifice, our eternal home, our freedom, our joy. We need to experience the joy and wonderment of our bodies. Our bodies are the room we heal in. They hold the keys to the lessons we must learn and to the doors of healing. They are the pearls of great price that we search for in our dreams."[3]

Don't disconnect your body from the Spirit. Author Blaine Yorgason said, "Because our spirits are housed in physical bodies, the effect of the Holy Ghost influencing our spirits and minds is almost always accompanied by at least some physical reaction; our bodies feel the workings of the Spirit."[4] If our bodies are dulled by addictions or abuse, we cannot feel or hear our spirit, nor can we feel the influence of the Holy Ghost. The opportunity to feel the influence of the Holy Ghost is a compelling reason to reverence our body and allow it to be as sensitive to the Spirit as possible. Satan wants us to dislike and abuse our bodies, because when we disconnect from our bodies, he has his greatest influence over us. In effect, he tries to turn our greatest ally into our chief enemy. We become a house divided.

Trust your body to help you become like God. Those who are not like God cannot live with him. When our spirit unites with our body, we become more like our heavenly parents, who have bodies of flesh and bones. Elder Rex D. Pinegar asserts: "We can learn truths by way of the spirit, *but by the way of the body we learn to be like Heavenly Father. The body constantly reinforces truth and is a constant testimony of truth;*

truly when kept pure, the body is filled with the Light of Christ. The body is a source of fulness for the spirit because *through the body the spirit learns how to feel.*[5] Elder Pinegar's words state a powerful truth: our feelings are vital tools in our journey to becoming like Heavenly Father. Yet, how often do we disregard and discount our feelings? How often do we stuff and ignore them? We regularly tell ourselves and others, "Oh, you shouldn't feel that way." "Don't be silly." "You're being petty." "You're overreacting." Life constantly presents us with experiences that stir up our feelings. It is crucial to our growth to be open to what our feelings are trying to teach us and to turn to Heavenly Father for guidance and wisdom.

NOTES

1. Rex D. Pinegar, quoted in Connie Blakemore, "Our Spiritual Eyeglasses: What You See Is What You Get," *Brigham Young University Speeches, 1997–98* (Provo, Utah: Brigham Young University, 1998), 329.

2. Joseph Smith, *Teachings of the Prophet Joseph Smith*, sel. Joseph Fielding Smith (Salt Lake City: Deseret Book, 1938), 181.

3. Wendy Ulrich, speech delivered at Brigham Young University, 2 April 1998, personal notes.

4. Blaine Yorgason, *Spiritual Progression in the Last Days* (Salt Lake City: Deseret Book, 1994), 184.

5. Pinegar, in Blakemore, "Our Spiritual Eyeglasses," 329; emphasis added.

How Do I Experience the Joy of Movement?

SARA LEE GIBB, SUSANNE J. DAVIS, AND REBECCA WRIGHT PHILLIPS

Recognize the language of movement. (Sara) Historical and archeological evidence shows that from the beginning of life on this planet, people have danced their sorrows, fears, pleasures, and ecstasy. Dancing lets us rediscover our body as a sacred instrument of expression. Pain, frustration, anxiety, exhilaration, curiosity, joy—virtually every thought we think or feeling we have manifests itself physically in some way within or through the body. Movement is a universal language of those statements, understood from friend to friend and culture to culture without translation. In many cultures, people dance the stories of their lives, learning to sing and dance from childhood. Some tribes in Kenya, instead of asking who or how are you, ask, "What do you dance?"

Take care of and rejoice in the sacred gift of a body. (Sara) I have a

---

Sara Lee Gibb, dancer and choreographer, is chair of the dance department at Brigham Young University. She has served as president of her ward's Relief Society and Young Women organizations and now serves as the Gospel Doctrine teacher in Sunday School.

Susanne Johnson Davis is a dance professor and folk dance division administrator at Brigham Young University. She is the mother of three children and grandmother of one. She has danced, researched, or visited in more than thirty countries. She serves as a Primary teacher and Young Women camp director in her ward.

Rebecca Wright Phillips is an assistant professor at Brigham Young University. She teaches modern dance and also teaches in the interdisciplinary music, dance, theater program. She choreographs for the Young Ambassadors. The mother of two young children, she serves as a Relief Society teacher and as Activities Committee co-chair in her ward.

beautiful friend in a wheelchair, her legs paralyzed after a car accident in her early life. She tells me she is a dancer. Her spirit soars; her face is animated; her eyes dance. Vicariously she participates in dance on many levels. Like her, we are grateful for the sacred gift of the physical body, with whatever capacity it has. It is the means of our understanding, expressing, and navigating life in this sphere. In Ecclesiastes we read that there is "a time to every purpose under the heaven," including "a time to dance" (Ecclesiastes 3:1, 4). When is that time? Anytime! I believe every human being has a right to move in ways that are primal, expressive, and transformational. I have even been known to dance in my private backyard in the moonlight . . . in my nightgown.

Appreciate our Latter-day Saint heritage of dance. (Susanne) During Joseph Smith's time, dancing, especially to the fiddle, was viewed at best as being a frivolous and perhaps immoral pastime and at worst as being of the devil. The Prophet Joseph disagreed. He was active by nature and was a skillful dancer who hosted dances in his home. He enjoyed and encouraged others to join in dancing, sports, and other joyful physical activities, endorsing the principle that "men are, that they might have joy" (2 Nephi 2:25).[1] Neither Joseph Smith nor Brigham Young were of the solemn, long-faced caste of religious leaders. Brigham Young said of dancing, "If you wish to dance, dance; and you are just as much prepared for a prayer meeting after dancing as ever you were."[2] King David honored God "with all his might . . . leaping and dancing before the Lord" (2 Samuel 6:14, 16). Brigham Young, however, did not suggest that dancing be part of a religious service. "I want it distinctly understood, that fiddling and dancing are no part of our worship. The question may be asked, What are they for, then? I answer, that my body may keep pace with my mind. My mind labors like a man logging, all the time; and this is the reason why I am fond of these pastimes—they give me a privilege to throw everything off, and shake myself, that my body may exercise, and my mind rest."[3] On the way west, the Saints danced waltzes, polkas, minuets, and quadrilles around the campfires. We as Saints have a legacy to follow by enjoying the many recreational dance forms that are possible today. Let us continue our heritage of dance.

Apply principles of dance to spiritual progression. (Rebecca)

Balance. For the dancer, balance is vital. Regardless of the complexity of the dance, as we work at finding balance in the dance studio, we find that the lessons the body teaches us are profound. Alignment must be correct—things must be stacked up just right to achieve the sense of control that brings freedom.

Upward focus. As the students were doing a series of leaps across the floor towards the end of technique class, I noticed that many of them had their eyes fixed on the floor and as a result their leaps seemed heavy, earthbound, and weighted. When I asked them to try focusing upwards and outwards, the results were amazing. Their leaps were higher, legs appeared longer, and the distance covered expanded. We too must look up if we are to make our own dances beautiful, and if we are to leap higher, cover more distance, or develop grace in our lives. In Doctrine and Covenants 88:67 we read, "If your eye be single to my glory, your whole bodies shall be filled with light." In nothing do I find this principle more manifest than in the dance.

Centeredness. We've all seen fabulous, vivacious dancers who can kick high, spin fast, or do all the latest steps. These can be great skills to acquire, but over the years I have come to value a different kind of dancer, not necessarily one who knows the latest trendy step, or one who can perform all the tricks, but one who possesses something that takes years to master. This is the dancer that moves from the core of her body. She engages the torso and dances from a deep, strong connection to the center of the body. This ability to be centered gives the dance life, meaning, and power. It draws people in and speaks to souls.

Joy. Dance and movement can truly bring joy. To experience these moments of joy the dancer must risk, let go, open up the body, and allow it to feel. A student of mine, Jen Ballif, wrote: "I truly believe that . . . once you learn to tap into the joy that is inherent in dance, it is possible to infuse that joy into all aspects of life." That is true. Movement can bring you to moments of joy, whether you are a trained dancer or not. As a former dance teacher told me, "Your spirit dances. It's not for you to decide." My sister Elaine Wright Christensen captured this idea in a poem:

271

Inside
me
there is a dancer.
Inside this middle-aged body
of a housewife
there is a dancer.
Don't laugh.

I have danced with sunflowers
in sandy September fields

   with fruit trees each spring,
   blossoms in my hair

      at the lake's edge in winter
      where tall grass
      and thin reeds
      wobble on pointed toes
      in the wind

         and in summer
         with the sea
where anyone can find the dancer
inside.
Don't laugh.
Barefoot,
arms outstretched,
palms raised to the sky, to the birds,
to the clouds, to God,
who choreographed it all, I danced.
I knew every step
and the waves stood up and bowed.[4]

NOTES

1. Leona Holbrook, "Dancing as an Aspect of Early Mormon and Utah Culture," *Focus on Dance* 8 (1977): 7–8.
2. Brigham Young, *Discourses of Brigham Young*, sel. John A. Widtsoe (Salt Lake City: Deseret Book, 1954), 243.
3. Young, *Discourses*, 242.
4. Elaine Wright Christensen, *I Have Learned Five Things* (Deerfield, Ill.: Lake Shore Publishing, 1996), 57; used by permission.

How Can I Feel Motivated to Do Family History Work?

JERI NELSON AND JILL CRANDELL

Claim your family heroes. (Jeri) When I was a child, my family tried out several different congregations. The result of this church-hopping was a feeling of being disconnected. I never knew my father's parents; they had both died before I was born. We occasionally visited my mother's LDS parents, but they lived far away in Wyoming. My friends took me along with them to Bible school or church youth activities through the years, but I was always a visitor. I was loved and I was happy, but I yearned to find that something that was missing in my life. I wanted to be anchored to something solid and lasting.

Something in our home helped to fulfill that desire. That something was a little red book entitled *The Life of Archibald Gardner*. That book became my treasure and my connection to something lasting. From the time I was small, Mother had read me stories of the adventures of my great-grandfather Gardner. They were wonderful stories about Grandfather's escaping persecution in Scotland; emigrating to Canada as a child and helping to clear the wilderness; walking sixty miles

Jeri Nelson, a graduate of the University of Utah, has taught early-morning seminary and served as a stake Young Women president and ward Relief Society president. An avid family historian, she serves as a ward family history consultant. She and her husband, Morris H. Nelson, are the parents of four children and the grandparents of fourteen.

Jill N. Crandell is an accredited genealogist in midwestern United States research. She received her bachelor's degree in family and local history studies from Brigham Young University and has served as a ward family history consultant. She and her husband, William K. Crandell, are the parents of five children. She serves as a Gospel Doctrine teacher in her ward.

through knee-deep snow as a young man intent on courting a young woman, only to find that he really didn't like her when he got there; joining the Church and then having to flee on horseback from his enemies; the miracle of crossing the St. Clair River on huge chunks of ice that were breaking up under his feet; trekking to Nauvoo, Winter Quarters, and then across the plains to the Salt Lake Valley in 1847. He was my hero, and he was also my grandpa. I could claim him for my own. I especially wanted to understand why he would sacrifice so much for his religion. In time, my questions were answered. His *Life* prepared me to hear, to understand, and to accept and live the gospel.

Look forward to a reunion in heaven. (Jeri) Brigham Young tells us that "we have more friends behind the veil than on this side, and they will hail us more joyfully than you were ever welcomed by your parents and friends in this world; and you will rejoice more when you meet them than you ever rejoiced to see a friend in this life."[1] Those on the other side love us and will help in our family history work when we have done all we can do. According to S. Michael Wilcox: "We often wonder if our ancestors will accept the gospel. Ironically, in many instances, they accepted it before we did. Their prayers and faithfulness have brought the gospel into our lives instead of the other way around."[2] I am convinced that the riches in heaven I have stored up are the people whose work I have been able to do here on earth. Someday, there will be a wonderful reunion.

Come to know your ancestors as real people. (Jill) The mission of Elijah is more than appreciating history; it is more than sealing ordinances. I believe the mission of Elijah is a binding of our hearts in love. What truly motivates us to continue searching, writing, documenting, and performing temple ordinances for our ancestors? We search out of love for our family. As Michael Wilcox urges: "We must never forget that we do the work for real people who had joys and sorrows just as we do. They faced the challenges of their lives with courage and dignity. They loved their families and made sacrifices for their God. We do not do the work for names but for lives, and in doing it our souls are bound to them and theirs to ours. That is why it is so glorious."[3]

A few months ago, I was proxy for the endowment of my second great-grandmother Susan Helton. I went to the temple that day with love in my heart for a grandmother who had raised thirteen children on a farm in southern Illinois in the mid-1800s. As I sat in that session, my thoughts changed, and I realized that they were not my own. One thought that came into my mind was that I had never worn anything so beautiful. Of course, that was a little strange—I was wearing temple clothing that I had worn many times before—but, I suddenly realized, my grandmother must have worn very rough clothing, probably dirty much of the time, and to her the shiny, soft, fine-woven temple clothes would have been made of the most beautiful fabric she had ever seen. As the endowment progressed, I shared other thoughts and experiences with my grandmother. I treasure the closeness of that sacred moment, the Spirit that we shared together. "'The spirits of the just,' Joseph Smith taught, 'are . . . enveloped in flaming fire, . . . *are not far from us,* and know and understand our thoughts, feelings, and motions.' (*Teachings of the Prophet Joseph Smith,* p. 326; emphasis added.) In the temple, where the veil is thinnest, the welding link of love is forged."[4]

Experience the binding of hearts through service. (Jill) We come to love those whom we serve, and family history research is many times a long, hard-fought search. After the time and effort expended in the search, our joy in the temple is indescribable. There is a binding, a closeness, that I have felt in no other way. The veil is very thin in the temple, and there is a connection between the sides that I have not found anywhere else.

NOTES
1. Brigham Young, *Discourses of Brigham Young,* sel. John A. Widtsoe (Salt Lake City: Deseret Book, 1954), 379.
2. S. Michael Wilcox, *House of Glory* (Salt Lake City: Deseret Book, 1995), 106.
3. Wilcox, *House of Glory,* 99.
4. Wilcox, *House of Glory,* 99.

How Do I Enter the Circle of God's Love?

JANETTE HALES BECKHAM

Step out of your smaller circles. Circles represent boundaries for our experiences. We have family circles, circles of friends, sewing circles, political circles, even prayer circles, but Heavenly Father's love encircles all of our circles. When something happens to one of your circles, there is that bigger circle to hold you together. When my husband died, I felt that my whole world had cracked open. I had lost the person most loved and dear to me. Yet I had the unexpected blessing of being encircled in love, feeling less fearful, more secure, and more loved than I had ever felt. For a moment I had stepped out of my circle and into His. In times of devastation, when what has seemed a secure circle has been broken, we are humbled and perhaps more receptive to love.

Keep your circles open. Although I was reared in a small Latter-day Saint community, my father was not a member of the Church and my mother was not active. When I went to Primary, I usually went with friends, but when I considered attending on Sunday, I expected to be alone. Some of my friends' families were so big that I knew seeing them would accentuate that feeling of loneliness. Even though I went expecting the worst, I soon learned that someone would always notice me and invite me to join them. As a result I have never been afraid of being alone or going places alone, and I am so appreciative of those who

Janette Hales Beckham, a former general president of the Young Women organization and a Utah state legislator, received her bachelor's degree in clothing and textiles from Brigham Young University. She and her late husband, Robert H. Hales, are the parents of five children. She married Raymond E. Beckham in 1995.

have open circles. The year after my husband died I practiced saying the words, "May I join you?"

The year I started junior high, my family moved to a different neighborhood. Although all the elementary schools in town funneled into the same junior high school, seventh grade was a time of changing circles and I experienced the anxiety of wanting friends and acceptance in my new neighborhood. Early in the school year, one of my new neighbors asked if I would like to be in her crowd. It sounded great to me! All of us had names that started with "J." JoAnn, Joanne, Jeannine, Jean, June, Jolene, and Janette. Perhaps that is why I was invited. I shall never forget being in the locker room a few days later when one of the "J's" asked one of my friends from elementary school, "How many do you have in your crowd? We have seven in ours." I was heartsick. I knew my old friend didn't have a crowd. I can still feel the tightness in my chest as I looked at her. I didn't ever want to feel that way again. Wonderful circles can come in all sizes, but I am still uncomfortable with closed ones. Perhaps keeping open circles will make us more receptive to being encircled in the arms of his love (see 2 Nephi 1:15).

Make space for God's love in your life. Our fast-paced world makes it easy to feel encumbered rather than encompassed. Failing to feel love does not mean, however, that love is unavailable. Think of the story of Mary and Martha, when Jesus said, "One thing is needful: and Mary hath chosen that good part" (Luke 10:42). Could that needful thing be the Savior's love that would encircle us if we took time to seek it? Knowing it is available, I am convinced that we must make space for "that good part" in our lives. Busy-ness can simply make us less receptive to the love that surrounds us.

Look for God's love in His surroundings. If we are bound up in our small, closed circles of busy self-absorption, we may lose the ability to take pleasure in the many small ways our Father surrounds us with love and beauty. Many years ago I was invited to play tennis on Robert Redford's tennis court. I felt privileged to be invited. It was a beautiful fall day, crisp clean air, and a pleasant ride up Provo Canyon. We were a bit awestruck as we walked around the Redford home and onto the court. Then I looked up to see Mt. Timpanogos ablaze with autumn colors, and I realized that the best part of what we were experiencing

277

didn't belong to Robert Redford. It belongs to all of us. I had only to step from my small circle into Heavenly Father's circle to recognize it. We are surrounded by his love, by his creations.

Expand the circle of God's love. One day last year I had been cumbered about through most of the day, preparing supper to take to my daughter and her family. Her husband had to work that night, and I had offered to tend her children while she got some much-needed sleep. As I loaded spaghetti and cinnamon rolls in the car, a neighbor asked if I had been listening to the news of the Littleton, Colorado, tragedy. I was shocked to hear of shootings in the school there. I quickly turned on the car radio and listened with anxiety and grief while driving slowly through heavy traffic to Salt Lake City.

When I arrived at Jane's, her five-year-old met me with a smile. After dinner, Dan went to work and Jane went to bed. The children and I did dishes, built playhouses out of sofa cushions, read stories, and had snacks. After prayers and I love you's, I tucked two contented children into bed. The house was quiet. I felt enfolded by God's love. Perhaps the contrast between what I was feeling in that little home and what I had felt earlier while listening to the news heightened my awareness of God's love encompassing us and of the love that greeted me at the door and that we helped create by being there. As I partook of their love and gave it back, it was multiplied, and the circle seemed larger. My thoughts again turned to Colorado. Suddenly, I felt more connected to those families, and I knew that Heavenly Father's love was there to encompass them.

I believe that we are encircled in his love when we are filled with his love. Our Heavenly Father's course is one eternal round that will lead us back to him. We must be partakers of the love of God; we must have it within us to be truly encompassed in his love. The process will surely take time, but we must *know* that the love is available to us. We must *seek* it. We must *identify* it and know that it comes from God. And most of all, as we partake of that love and have it within us, I believe that we will quite naturally *give* it to others in all we do.

How Do I Learn in His Holy House?

Barbara G. Workman

Open your hearts to learning. For more than forty years, I often felt a certain unrest about what I did not understand when I attended the temple. I was sure it was my fault. I was convinced that if I prayed harder, lived better, and was more attentive in the temple, the Lord would reveal to me the deep meanings of each symbolic representation. Despite my efforts and desire, I often came away disappointed, sure that I was not getting the answers that were essential to my spiritual progress. I wondered if I would ever be fully acceptable to the Lord. And yet, too frequently I was passive, almost mindlessly repeating a familiar experience with no effort to be spiritually stretched.

Then a few years ago, my husband was called to the presidency of the Mount Timpanogos Utah Temple, and we embarked on full-time temple service and many, many hours of study about temples and temple work. I began to understand that the gentle comfort—the cleansing, healing feelings that come so easily in the temple—are the essence of temple learning. The temple is meant to teach us, but even more it is meant to touch us. When these feelings envelop us, our minds and spirits become ready reservoirs for all else the Lord wants us to learn. I don't think there is a sadder verse in all scripture than 1 Nephi 17:45: "Ye have seen an

Barbara Gibbons Workman, homemaker, mother of nine, and grandmother of thirty-one, received her bachelor's degree in elementary education from Utah State University. She served with her husband, Dan J. Workman, when he was called as a mission president in New Jersey and on a Church Educational System mission in Europe. She has served as assistant matron of the Mount Timpanogos Utah Temple and as matron of the Vernal Utah Temple.

angel, and he spake unto you; yea, . . . he hath spoken unto you in a still small voice, but ye were past feeling, that ye could not feel his words." Even an angel of God could not teach Laman and Lemuel, because they could not feel. The temple can open us to a fulness of feeling and thus a fulness of learning.

Refine your nature. President Joseph F. Smith taught: "All those salient truths which come home so forcibly to the head and heart seem but the awakening of the memories of the spirit. Can we know anything here that we did not know before we came? . . . If Christ knew beforehand, so did we. But in coming here, we forgot all, that our agency might be free. . . . But by the power of the Spirit, . . . through obedience, we often catch a spark from the awakened memories of the immortal soul, which lights up our whole being as with the glory of our former home."[1] Sanctification, or spiritual learning, such as that which happens in the temple, is not "to discover" but "to awaken again." It is not the result of your endless struggle to find, grasp, and hang onto spiritual enlightenment. The promise is within you. Your spirit already knows everything you are trying to understand when you come to the temple. You did know it all before you came. It is not so much a process of learning as it is a process of rebecoming—letting in enough light so that the Lord can awaken your heart and illuminate your mind to match the memories of your celestial spirit. As you use your agency wisely, your celestial spirit unfolds within.

Realize your ultimate destiny. The Saints of Vernal, Utah, know now that the Uinta Tabernacle was always meant to be a temple. Physical characteristics foreshadowed and prophecies foretold of its unique destiny. The building was used for ninety years as a tabernacle until the time was right for its transformation. We ourselves are like that. We are living in a tabernacle of flesh, but our destiny has always been to become temples of holiness. "Know ye not that ye are the temple of God, and that the Spirit of God dwelleth in you?" (1 Corinthians 3:16). The last page of the children's book *The Stones of the Temple* reads: "This temple will stand a thousand years. But you are His forever."[2] Within physical temple walls, sacred ordinances are administered to the sons and daughters of God that they might become spirit temples. The eternal temple is you.

Wait for the Lord's fulness. If there is one word synonymous with temple, for me it is *fulness*. Consider these scriptural references to *fulness*: "That they may grow up in thee, and receive a fulness of the Holy Ghost" (D&C 109:15, the dedicatory prayer of the Kirtland Temple). "Build a house unto my name . . . for there is not a place found on earth that he may . . . restore . . . the fulness of the priesthood" (D&C 124:27–28). "They shall pass by the angels, and the gods, which are set there, to their exaltation and glory in all things . . . which glory shall be a fulness" (D&C 132:19). The fulness of the priesthood, the fulness of the Holy Ghost, a fulness of glory, the fulness of God are all temple promises. The Kirtland Temple dedication describes our Father "enthroned with glory, honor, power, majesty, might, dominion, truth, justice, judgment, mercy, and an infinity of fulness, from everlasting to everlasting" (D&C 109:77). If we can hope to ultimately be filled with that fulness, should we be worried about how it will happen? How do we learn majesty? How do we learn glory or fulness? We cannot. We become majestic and glorious and fulfilled. That is exactly the promise of the endowment. The temple is to bring us to Christ, and then he will bring us to that fulness: "Yea, come unto Christ, and be perfected in him" (Moroni 10:32).

NOTES

1. Joseph F. Smith, *Gospel Doctrine* (1919; Salt Lake City: Deseret Book, 1986), 13–14.
2. J. Frederic Voros Jr., *The Stones of the Temple* (Salt Lake City: Deseret Book, 1993), [27].

Planting Seeds of Testimony in Our Children

PATRICIA P. PINEGAR

Powerful scriptures and worrisome, even horrific, news reports remind us that life is not going to get easier on this earth. Although advancing technology brings wonderful blessings into our lives, Satan uses this same technology to ensnare our children. How can we protect them from the scum and filth of the evil one that washes up all around us, often seeping into our homes on the vast information highway? If children are taught the gospel of Jesus Christ with patience and with love, they have opportunities to feel and respond to the Spirit—the promptings of the Holy Ghost. If they hear over and over again our tender expression of testimony and faith, they will gain a foundation of strength that will protect them in this difficult world.

As we bear testimony of our love for our Heavenly Father and the Savior, our very young children will gain language to express the spiritual feelings that are so evident in their young lives. Being able to recognize and identify those feelings and then being able to verbalize their love for Heavenly Father and the Savior will give them power to make righteous choices.

Susan L. Warner, second counselor in the Primary General Presidency, said: "In a society of unstable values and confusing voices, testimony can be the means by which parents give children an anchor for their faith. . . .

Patricia P. Pinegar is a homemaker and former general president of the Primary. She and her husband, Ed J. Pinegar, are the parents of eight children. They have served missions together in England and at the Provo Missionary Training Center.

" . . . Who can measure the influence of simple, sacred words of testimony? Who can calculate the impact of the Spirit that confirms those words? The seeds of testimony that are planted in the hearts of children when they are young are nourished throughout their lives by hearing the testimonies of those who love them enough to bear witness of the truth."[1] "Love them enough to bear witness of the truth"—that is a profound message for all parents.

May I share a beautiful example, a story that comes from the *Friend*, March 1997. "Even before Mom got sick a few years ago, she took every opportunity to teach us about the Savior. She would say, 'Now, here's a little testimony for you,' then tell us how she could tell that Jesus Christ loved us. Dad says that's how we can tell that Mom loved us so much: She wanted to share the things that she loved most with us.

"On days when Mom felt good, we did fun things together. Sometimes we went to the park and flew our kites. She sat on the blanket while Dad helped us get the kites started. She cheered us on until all the kites were sailing high in the breeze. She looked happy, waving to us, her hair blowing in the breeze. 'Now, here's a little testimony for you,' she told us. 'The wind is a little like the Holy Ghost. You can't see it, but you can sure feel it! And you can see the things it does all around us.'

"On other days, we went to the mall to shop. When she didn't feel well enough to walk, we'd take turns pushing her in her wheelchair. She looked at everything we wanted to show her. At least once during the shopping trip, Mom said something like, 'Now, here's a little testimony for you. The pair of pants you needed is marked down! That's an answer to prayer, isn't it!'

" . . . When Mom wasn't feeling good, . . . she liked to rest near us when we practiced our music lessons and did our homework. 'Now, here's a little testimony for you. I have always wanted to hear you play that song so well.' 'Here's a little testimony for you. I can still remember how to do those math problems, so I can help you with your homework!'

"One day Dad woke us up very early. Mom had had a bad night, and she was very, very ill. She wanted to talk to us because she knew that it was almost time for her to go back to live with Heavenly Father.

"When we went into her bedroom, she reached out and touched each of us and told us how much she loved us. 'Now, here's a little testimony for you,' she said. 'Even though I'll be leaving you very soon, it's part of Heavenly Father's plan.'

"We all wept. . . . We loved her [so much].

"'Sweetheart,' she said to Dad, 'would you bring me the special book I have been keeping, please?'

"Dad handed her a pretty journal.

"'This journal is filled with lots of little things for you to remember when I am not here to talk to you anymore. It's full of little testimonies for you. I want you to remember how much I love the Savior. I want you to love Him that much, too, so that we can always be together.'

" . . . Mom has been gone for quite a while now. We still miss her, and we think of her a lot. . . .

"Dad got each of us a journal so that we [could] write down all of our own little testimonies. I have written a lot about the times I remember with Mom, but I am writing new little testimonies too.

"And you know what? Mom's journal of little testimonies is really one great big strong testimony about the plan of salvation, about the Savior's love for us."[2]

Love your children enough to bear testimony to them of the truth.

Children do have spiritual insights when they are very young, but they need parents and family members and loved ones to give them language to express the feelings and love that they have for the Savior. In a recent regional meeting, a temple president shared his feelings of concern as a bishop when parents brought their young children to the podium on Fast Sundays and whispered into their ears word for word what they should say in their testimony. One Fast Sunday, this bishop was especially struggling with his feelings as the parents came forward, dragging their children to the stand. As he prayed for patience, the Spirit communicated with him in a powerful way. He heard, "Everything great you ever learned was whispered to you."

The Holy Ghost whispers to us words of our Heavenly Father and Savior. We in turn whisper those words to our children, words of love and testimony. As Sister Warner said, "When we share our feelings with our little ones and bear record of Him, we open the door for [the children] to share their experiences and to give words to their own spiritual insights and feelings. And when we help children identify the divine source of those feelings, their understanding and love for the Savior will grow line upon line, precept upon precept."[3]

Several years ago, as I walked in the morning, I noticed a little plant growing out of a crack in the sidewalk. As the summer went on, the plant grew bigger and bigger, and I marveled at its tenacity and courage. Finally, toward the end of the summer, it bloomed. It was a sunflower with a lovely yellow blossom. And an incredible thing happened. As I walked by in the morning and looked at that little sunflower, its face was turned towards the rising sun. When I happened to walk by in the evening, that little sunflower's face had turned towards the setting sun. Each day it followed the sun from daybreak to sunset.

I wanted to share that story with my grandchildren, so I invited all of our families to a picnic. (They'll always come if I have food.) After we ate, I gathered my grandchildren around me, and we talked about what it meant to be tenacious like that sunflower. And then I asked them, "Who is the light that you follow?" Children all over the world know the answer to that question. They always say, "It's the Son of God. It's Jesus Christ." They know that he is the light that they should follow.

Years ago when I shared that experience with my grandchildren, I gave them each a little hat with a sunflower on it to remind them. I recently received a letter from my granddaughter Brooke, who is serving in the Washington Tacoma Mission. She said, "Dear Grandma, I used your sunflower analogy in my talk that I gave, and told them of the fall afternoon that you took us aside and taught us a simple lesson of following the Son. Thank you for taking moments to teach us the gospel. Every time I see a sunflower I think, *Am I following the Savior at this moment?* I need all the reminders I can get."

We must love children enough to bear testimony of the truth. Our actions and our words bear record of the Savior and his gospel. As we study the scriptures together, pray together, share family home evenings, enjoy music, and develop traditions, we create legacies of testimony for our families. It is important to identify for our children what is happening, whether we are joining in family prayer, bearing testimony, or feeling the Spirit through a song. Help your children identify their feelings. Help them understand that they are bearing testimony as they sing and talk about their love for the Savior.

NOTES

1. Susan L. Warner, *Ensign*, November 1998, 66–67.
2. Naomi L. Kohrman, "Little Testimonies," *Friend*, March 1997, 16–18; © by Intellectual Reserve, Inc.; used by permission.
3. Warner, *Ensign*, November 1998, 67.

Building an Eternal Family Even When It Appears You Don't Have One

SHIRLEY M. JOHNSON

Although I am a never-been-married single woman, I have had the opportunity to experience, other than the actual birth process, just about everything else a mother would. I have several hundred children, and they're all boys! I work in the football office at Brigham Young University, and although my boys range in age from seventeen to twenty-five, I've gone through the terrible twos, the terrifying teens, and the raging hormones with them. I pester them about their homework, tell them to get their feet off the furniture, yell at them to wipe their shoes so they don't track dirt, make them stop fighting before they break something, and gently chide them about their bizarre hair or clothes.

I also know the absolute joys. I get to witness baptisms, missions, weddings and sealings, births of their children, graduations, acceptances to medical or law or graduate school, and the hard but sweet road through repentance some of them travel to turn their lives around. The joy far outweighs the trials. In fact, I was once even mother of the week on a local radio station and got some lovely prizes.

When I was a teenager, it never crossed my mind that I wouldn't marry and have children. Everyone did. I remember feeling bad for those

Shirley M. Johnson holds a degree in English from Brigham Young University and is a counselor in her ward Relief Society presidency. Although single, she has had the opportunity to mother more than a hundred young men each year in the BYU football program, where she has served as executive assistant to Coach LaVell Edwards since 1980.

old spinsters in our ward and family—you know, the ones who were maybe twenty-nine or thirty and not married. I also remember thinking that men must be crazy because I admired those women tremendously.

Like many young women, I didn't date a lot, but I had my share of opportunities. I mainly participated in lots of group activities with wonderful friends. I enjoyed life. It wasn't until I hit thirty that I realized I *might* not get married, but I never did panic. A wise leader in one of my singles wards had cautioned us not to be obsessed with being unmarried but to move forward and make ourselves better people. Then if the opportunity came, we would have even more to offer. I took that advice to heart, and I have taken classes, read voraciously, kept up on what's happening in the world, strengthened myself spiritually, worked to develop new skills and talents, and learned from an ever-growing circle of friends.

What can women in situations like mine do to build our eternal families? I believe the single most important thing we must do is *to stay close to the Lord*. Having a spouse on this earth doesn't automatically qualify us for exaltation. We still have to be accountable for who we are as individuals. Elder Richard G. Scott has said: "You are here on earth for a divine purpose. . . . You are here to be tried, to prove yourself so that you can receive the additional blessings God has for you. . . . The Lord is intent on your personal growth and development."[1]

Second, *stay involved in your ward*. We get out of Church activity what we put into it. Many times I have heard someone bear testimony of the strong spirit in a particular meeting, and I wondered, where was I? The Spirit was there; I just wasn't in tune. Activities seemed dumb or boring, but it was because I wasn't putting forth any effort. In some cases single people "hate their ward" because they haven't let themselves become involved, even though they may have a calling. Feeling left out, they have perhaps pouted and allowed themselves some self-pity. I must admit that at times the emphasis on families in lessons or talks has bothered me. But let's face it: the Church is family oriented. I decided to accept that and not let it get me down. As both a teacher and a class participant, I let people know how the principles being presented apply to me, a single person.

Next, *maintain a close relationship with families*. I grew up knowing well not only my aunts, uncles, and cousins but also my great-aunts and great-uncles and second and third cousins. They still include me in everything—farewells, homecomings, weddings, and other special occasions. Of course, I'm also their conduit to the inside scoop on the BYU football team, so they have to be nice to me.

Be sure to *develop a circle of friends*. I have not one big circle of friends but a number of smaller circles that sometimes intersect. They also span many age groups and interests, which helps keep me on my toes. My ward is also my family and a good testing ground for my eternal family skills and worthiness.

Keep progressing. We must not let life pass us by while we sit around waiting for our knight in shining armor. We need to move forward constantly—stimulate our brains, our senses, and our hearts. "While traveling the sometimes difficult path toward eternal life, may we try to remember that our Heavenly Father wants us to find joy in the journey. The earth is full of beauty, and life offers many opportunities to develop rewarding relationships with others. . . . The gospel of Jesus Christ teaches us what we must know and do to live life fully and joyfully as we prepare for eternity."[2]

Recognize the eternal families we already belong to. Maria Cristina Santana wrote an article in the *Ensign* entitled "God Setteth the Solitary in Families." Though her viewpoint was that of being the only Church member in her family, she made a few comments that struck me forcefully as a single person: "Many of us . . . look to a future time when . . . we will be able to claim our eternal family relationships. Those seal-ings may be far off, but in the meantime we are entitled to rely upon . . . another kind of eternal family. . . . [which is] the kingdom, the Church, and the eternal family of God. By joining the Church, we are sealed into nothing less than a spiritual family."[3]

Last of all, *we can use the priesthood in our home*. The power of the priesthood is essential to preparing ourselves for an eternal family. If right now we don't have someone in our home who holds the priest-hood, that doesn't mean it can't be part of our life. It's a mistake to become so self-sufficient that we forget to call upon grandfathers, uncles, home teachers, or friends when we need a blessing. I had cancer last year, and I received some amazing blessings from men who honored their priesthood. It's a mistake to become so self-sufficient that we forget to call on worthy priesthood bearers for help.

We can enjoy the spirit of baptisms, confirmations, settings apart, ordinations, and healings. We can surround ourselves with the spirit of the priesthood. A couple of years ago, one of our graduate assistants found out he had inoperable cancer. Coach LaVell Edwards invited him into his office. All the assistant coaches gathered around and laid their hands on his head, and LaVell gave him a blessing. It was a very tender moment, and it brought home to me again the power of the priesthood.

Most important, as I was reminded in Marie K. Hafen's article in the March 1987 *Ensign*, the Savior is the source of the priesthood. We have been promised that if we are striving to live his commandments, his Spirit will be with us. If we invite the Savior into our home through our prayers, thoughts, and actions, we will have the power of the priesthood there.

I most assuredly want an eternal companion and children. And I have faith and peace of heart that if I live and progress the way the Lord wants, I will receive that opportunity. When? Only the Lord knows. I just want to be ready.

Until that happens, however, I will continue to feel great joy at the huge eternal family I will have along with husband and children. I have a loving immediate family as well as a wonderful extended family and ancestors to whom I am sealed. I have numerous circles of friends I adore. I have almost twenty years' worth of young men from the BYU football family whom I have nurtured, mothered, loved, and, as any parent does, prayed for; I want to be part of their lives for the eternities. My ward is also my family; they bring me joy, and I hope they will be part of my eternal family. And I am already a member of an eternal family as a child of God. If I live worthily to be part of the Lord's family, then I will be worthy to have my own eternal family. I have faith that the Savior will encircle me in the arms of his love, and he will grant me that blessing.

I pray that all of us who are waiting for an eternal marriage will have faith, that we will recognize and cherish the eternal families of which we are already a part, particularly our Heavenly Father's, and that we will strive each day to be worthy, as he has asked. If we do, we will receive not only the blessing of our own eternal family but also joy in such abundance that it will be hard to comprehend. We must never forget that the Lord knows our hearts, and he will bless us for our righteous desires.

NOTES

1. Richard G. Scott, *Ensign*, May 1996, 25.
2. "The Visiting Teacher: Live Fully and Prepare for Eternity," *Ensign*, March 1999, 65; or Richard G. Scott, *Ensign*, May 1996, 25.
3. Maria Cristina Santana, *Ensign*, December 1998, 22, 24–26.

Single Parenting: Doubt Not, Fear Not

SUZANNE TRUBA

I'll begin with the facts. Divorce happens, and unfortunately it happens in the Church. I was born in Cardston, Alberta, Canada, to very loving, ethical, hard-working parents. They were, however, not active in the Church. I don't remember going to Sunday School often. Because Cardston was a Mormon community, I did attend Primary. After school, we walked two by two right up the middle of Main Street and into the social center to Primary. From sixth grade on, our family lived in various Alberta towns with no Mormon church, so I didn't get to go to Mutual or seminary. As I grew older, a temple marriage was not a priority for me. In my twenties, I married outside the Church. My marriage lasted eight years. I thought I did not want children, a fact that haunts me to this day. Looking back, I realize I was probably selfish and a little caught up in the world.

In 1974 my father died. Six months later, I found myself pregnant and devastated. Why? Because my marriage was rocky, and I still didn't want children. I decided unhappily to go through with the pregnancy (don't judge me too harshly for thinking I had an option; I didn't know any better), and three weeks before I delivered, the doctor told me that I was having not one but two. Then I *really* cried. Just barely having adjusted to the idea of dealing with one child, I was overwrought wondering how

Suzanne Truba is a single mother of twins. She serves as a stake missionary and a volunteer institute instructor in the Calgary West Stake. She has been a self-employed businesswoman for many years after a brief career as a registered nurse.

I could ever cope with two. Those precious babies were born in June 1975. One month later, my husband and I separated and subsequently divorced. There I was at age thirty-two, a single parent with two brand-new babies.

Let me just say this on my behalf. When those babies were placed in my arms, my love for them was volcanic. It erupted in me like nothing I had ever experienced before. They were mine, and I loved them. But this was a "me" I was not familiar with. I had gone from a marriage to no marriage. I had gone from no children to two children. I had gone from working full time, running my own business, to not going to work at all for the first three months after giving birth. To my amazement, my only focus was sleep. All I wanted was a couple of back-to-back hours of sleep. This was all brand-new and overwhelming. Finally it all caved in on me: parenting, singleness, change, fear, loneliness, the world, the Church, pride, humility—all of it.

Twenty-four years later, I'm alive, well, reasonably sane, still very much single but gratefully very active in the gospel of Jesus Christ. I am so thankful to a loving Heavenly Father who knew my needs better than I did.

Because I have been single the better part of my life, my relationships with women have been a particularly meaningful source of joy and well-being. I have reflected often in gratitude to the Lord for womanhood and for motherhood. Often I have wished that there was more about women in the scriptures. Yet perhaps there is enough. In a conference address, Elder Jeffrey R. Holland mentioned two widows—the widow of Zarephath and the widow who gave her mite.[1]

The widow of Zarephath lived at the time of Elijah during a severe famine. The Lord told her that a prophet would visit her simple home and she should sustain him. When Elijah came, he asked her to fetch him some water and a morsel of bread to eat as well. She responded, "All I have is a little meal and a little oil in a cruse which I plan to make into a cake for me and my son to eat before we die." The famine was that severe. But Elijah said to her, "If you will just bring me a little something to eat first, I promise that you will find meal and oil remaining." This good widow did exactly what Elijah asked of her, and, of course, the Lord blessed her with meal and oil for many weeks to come (see 1 Kings 17:9–15).

In the story of the widow's mite, the Savior was watching people throw money into the temple treasury. The rich threw in much money. Then a poor widow tossed in two mites, which are equal to a farthing. Jesus called his disciples aside and said, "She has given more than any of them." He then explained, "The rich gave of their abundance; she gave all that she had" (see Mark 12:41–44).

What women do I know in our modern day world with that kind of faith and trust? There are many. Then I thought, is their faith and trust any greater than that of single mothers who send their wee children off for the very first time to spend a weekend or a week with their father, perhaps with their other mother or even with a girlfriend? I will forever remember the first time my curly-headed twins drove off with their dad, both of them sitting on his girlfriend's knee. I waved and said good-bye with a big smile on my face and then went into the house and fell apart.

The Lord says in Proverbs: "Trust in the Lord with all thine heart; and lean not unto thine own understanding. In all thy ways acknowledge him, and he shall direct thy paths" (Proverbs 3:5–6). The Lord does direct our paths if we choose to be directed. It is crucial for those of us who are single mothers to strive to honor the father of our children. It is not always easy, not always possible, but it's what we really need to do. To honor our fathers and our mothers is a commandment. In times of severe hurt and anger, we may want to criticize, to judge, and we may even feel justified in doing so, but that's not our place. In extreme situations, it may be impossible for a father to be honored, but as one good sister said to me, "What I encourage my children to do is to live their own lives so as not to discredit the family name. That is a form of honoring."

We find in Romans 15:1: "We then that are strong ought to bear the infirmities of the weak, and not to please ourselves." In most cases, it is possible to honor the father of our children. We can't betray the love that the children and their father have for one another anymore than we want to betray the love and trust that they have for us. Divorce takes forgiveness. We have to forgive our spouse (and ourselves, usually). If and when it comes time for our children to forgive us, perhaps our example will guide them.

Being a single parent is a daunting task. Many who, unlike me, have married a returned missionary in the temple, have been faithful all their lives, and kept their covenants would say, "How did I get here? Why me?" I don't have the answer for those questions, but I do know the questions that should follow: "Why not me?" or "What is required of me?" The sooner we see "things as they really are . . . [and] really will be," at least for now, the better our homes and the easier our lives will be (Jacob 4:13).

When the sons of Mosiah were doing missionary work with the Lamanites, conditions were extremely difficult. Ammon was preparing to visit King Lamoni's father, but the Lord told him to go instead to the land of Middoni because his brothers were imprisoned there. Ammon went directly, and "he was exceedingly sorrowful, for behold they were naked, and their skins were worn exceedingly because of being bound with strong cords. And they also had suffered hunger, thirst, and all kinds of afflictions; nevertheless they were patient in all their sufferings." Now this is the verse that speaks to me: "And, as it happened, it was their lot to have fallen into the hands of a more hardened and a more stiff-necked people" (Alma 20:29–30).

For some reason, that scripture brings me comfort. Maybe it is just part of my customized life plan that I was meant for a more hardened way. I'm not sure about that, but it makes sense to me. Difficulties contribute to our refinement in the eternal scheme of things. As we strive to be patient in our sufferings and continue to follow the Lord, he will bless us.

Children in single-parent homes might feel the way is more hardened for them; however, as I've told my children, perhaps their difficulties are for their refinement as well. To help them, we must teach our children who they really are. They need to know that the Lord is there for us. Many times, especially when our children are small, we don't have a priesthood bearer in our home, so the Lord is that for us. And home teachers bring the blessings of the priesthood into our family life once a month. We can welcome them and teach our children to revere that visit. They can learn to recognize and rely on the Spirit that accompanies a worthy priesthood holder acting in his calling.

If possible, take advantage of supportive immediate family. My brother has given my children a blessing before school each year. My mother has been such a help to me, more than an exceptional grandparent, almost like another parent. All through the years, she has been there to help me.

Find what you need. It's not always easy. My son told me he felt like a loser every time I had to phone a priesthood bearer to say, "Don't forget to pick up my son" for whatever the priesthood or fathers-and-sons event was. I was uncomfortable, too. It's easy to get a little proud and say, "Oh, I don't want to do that." But we have to. We must humble ourselves before the Lord, step outside our comfort zone, and ask priesthood leaders and our immediate family for the help that we need. Otherwise we neglect those blessings that are meant for our children, blessings that our children need and deserve.

The Lord is the most important person in our lives and in the lives of our children. The Lord, however, is a little less tangible to our children than we are, so it's important that they develop faith in their mother first. When they're little, mother is who they look to. "See this face?" I tell my children, pointing to my face. "Best thing that ever happened to you." When they were little, they used to laugh at me. Now that they're older, they're starting to think I might just be right.

"Look unto me in every thought; doubt not, fear not," we read in Doctrine and Covenants 6:36. This scripture is for single mothers. Doubt not, fear not. I repeat, we can reinforce faith in our children by our example and by the example of others.

One of my favorite heart-wrenching stories is about Amanda Smith at the Haun's Mill massacre. After the fighting, she found her husband and one son dead. The shock must have been overwhelming. Then she found her little boy, Alma, lying wounded, his whole hip shot off by a musket ball. Devastated and not knowing what to do, she knelt and begged the Lord to show her how to treat this terrible wound. She was guided in what to do. When she had finished praying, she turned to this little boy and asked, "Alma, do you believe that the Lord made your hip?" He said, "Yes, Mother." She went on, "Do you believe that the

Lord can make you a new hip in place of this one?" Her little son answered, "Do you believe he can, Mother?"[2]

Faith in a mother. Faith in God. They are so closely related. Our children do have faith in us, closely related to faith in the Lord. No wonder President George Q. Cannon said, "The effect of woman's influence cannot be over-estimated."[3] And that means us.

When my son Josh was sixteen, his father asked him to baptize his eight-year-old half-brother. Yes, my former husband remarried another LDS woman, and they have four children. He has still not joined the Church. Anyway, Josh was excited to perform his first baptism. He was sixteen and held the authority to do it, and he wanted to do it. Naturally, Josh wanted me to go along. Our small family traveled a couple of hours from Calgary to join in this baptism with the other Truba family. I get along well with my former husband and his wife, and I thought the baptism wouldn't be a difficult situation. It proved much more difficult than I had anticipated. I chose to sit off by myself because, after all, I didn't want the ex-wife being front and center. The Trubas, including my two children, were all lined up on the front row of the room where the baptismal font was. I immediately started to get lonely and feel a little self-pity. Later, when we were standing at the baptismal font, the most wonderful thing happened. My sixteen-year-old son stood with his little half-brother in that baptismal font, ready to perform his first baptism, both in their white clothing. When Josh raised his hand to the square, I started to cry. "Just think, Mom," whispered my daughter, "he's sixteen and he's worthy."

A scripture came into my mind: "The worth of souls is great in the sight of God" (D&C 18:10). Think about that. We were bought with a price. We are not our own. And I knew right then that I have to do whatever it righteously takes to see that others get there. Quite sincerely, that was a moment of revelation for me. It was a teaching moment in my life, and I hope in the lives of my children.

When Eliza R. Snow said, "It's no trifling thing to be a Saint,"[4] she was so right. And I would add that it's no trifling thing to be a Latter-day Saint woman, and even beyond that, a Latter-day Saint single mother. Rest assured, the Lord is aware of us in all that we do.

About four or five years ago, a young woman bounced into my shop.

Young, vivacious, spontaneous, and enthusiastic, she drew me to her with her opening hello. As we chatted, she said that she was divorced; so was I. Then she told me that she had kids; so did I. And then she told me she had a wonderful boyfriend; I could not respond with "So did I" to that one. We continued to chat. Suddenly she said, "I'm in the city to buy a gift for my daughter's baptism." She paused, "We do things differently in our church. We baptize children when they're eight."

"Hmm," I said, "you must be LDS."

"Yes," she said, and then looked at me, obviously shocked, and asked, "Are you?"

From what she had told me about her boyfriend, I knew that her standards were not Church standards. So when she said to me, "Are you?" I said to her, "Full blown," and then I asked her gently, very gently, "Have they changed the rules lately?"

This darling young sister, with tears in her eyes, said to me, "No, but I can't live that way. I won't live that way—it's too hard, it's too difficult, I'm too young. I won't do it, I can't."

I answered, "I understand the pain." But then I told her, or tried to in the best way I could, of the peace that comes, the strength that comes, when at all costs we strive to live our lives within the standards of the gospel. As we looked at one another with tears in our eyes, I knew that she knew.

This woman is my sister in the gospel, and I love her and care about her. I know that the Lord loves her and cares deeply about her. But I can't give her my testimony. I can't give her my commitment. No one can. She has to be the one who takes the Holy Spirit as her guide. She has to be the one who commits to that path daily.

After she left, I pondered about that experience the rest of the afternoon. When I got home that night, my two children and I knelt around our table, and before we said family prayer, my son took off his cap. Just a simple, small act of taking off his cap, which he didn't often do, reminded me that he loved and respected his Father in Heaven. For those few minutes of prayer, I knew that all was in order in my life and in my home, and I gave thanks.

I tell you this story for this reason. It is to declare to you sisters that loneliness is real. And loneliness is painful. The devil works on us incessantly when he knows that we feel our loneliest. He is right there to strut into our lives. Every day we have to renew for ourselves that we will make the choice to take the Holy Spirit for our guide. That's just the way it has to be, no matter what. In the scriptures we read, "For they that are wise and have received the truth, and have taken the Holy Spirit for their guide, and have not been deceived, . . . they shall not be hewn down and cast into the fire, but shall abide the day" (D&C 45:57).

Think of the parable of the ten virgins. Its message is that we cannot be prepared for someone else. We can only prepare ourselves for the day of Christ's coming. We can encourage, we can pray, but we cannot actually receive the truth for others. We each make our own commitment to Christ. We are each responsible for our own level of spirituality. Light cannot be borrowed, and we do not want to turn our backs on our own light. When we do, we reject who we really are and suppress our divine nature.

That is why we have to pray without ceasing to resist temptation. The devil's parade is very colorful, and life on the world's terms can be engaging and gratifying, even satisfying and entertaining. Why else would people sin? But this I know to be true: The adversary's parade leads down a one-way street to transitory pleasure and ultimate sorrow. We are not here to keep pace with the world. We are here to say no to the adversary, and yes to life, yes to eternal life.

Our children need to be aware that we as single mothers keep exactly the same standards we want them to keep. Why? Because they are the Lord's standards. We are in this together. President Spencer W. Kimball said, "The family is the basic unit of the kingdom of God here on earth. . . . Wise parents will see to it that their teaching is orthodox, character-building, and faith-promoting."[5] Personal experience tells me, in fact, that it's easy to be so intense in trying to keep our children centered on the straight and narrow path that we can become too rigid. A little lightheartedness around the home is necessary, and I still have to learn how to do that better. I have some good friends, four young adults raised by a single father, whom they adored, who said he'd come home sometimes, sit on the couch, put his feet up on the coffee table, blast the radio up, and say, "Look kids, no parents." They loved it. I wish I could be more like that.

Contrast that story with this one. One day my son and I were going to sacrament meeting. He was maybe two or three minutes slow getting ready—but, as we're driving along, his dear perfectionist mother here was yattering at him about how we're going to be late and how embarrassed I am walking in late and on and on. I could see that he was tiring of my tirade, and I could even understand why. But when I saw the look on his face, I thought, *Hey, you could do a lot worse than me*, and I said, "You should have *some* mothers." He kindly and politely turned to me and replied, "And you should have *some* sons." If I could have fallen on my knees right then to beg forgiveness, I would have. He taught me in such a nice, kind way that we're all imperfect. By the time I leave this journey of mortality, I hope that I have learned to have more charity regarding other people's agency, especially the agency of my children.

Children need to know above everything that we love them, no matter what choices they make. They will always have their mother's love and, hopefully, that love will be reciprocated.

Last year my grandmother died. She was 103. She had been in my life forever. I hoped that she would never leave. I asked her just a few weeks before she died, "Grandma, do you ever think of your mother?" Her answer shocked me. "Not a day goes by that I don't think of my mother." I think that to be loved by your children each and every day is joy at its best. We need to record our moments of joy. You might be thinking, *Let me see. When last did I have a moment of joy?* But I know that you have them, simple and small though they might seem to be. For instance, one sister told us in Relief Society that she sometimes gets carried away and yells a bit. One day her teenage daughter asked her, "Hey, Mom, when you act like that, what do you want me to do? Do you want me to hug you? Do you want me to leave the room? Leave you alone? What do you want me to do?" Wouldn't that teenager's compassion and insight add a moment of joy in a mother's life?

When my daughter was ten, we were driving up the alley to our modest bungalow in Calgary. Out of the clear blue she said, "I love my life." I gave thanks. We want our children to love coming home. We want our children to know that nothing compares with a family's love for them and the love of the Lord in their life.

We also need to teach our children that they share in the responsibility of bringing the Spirit into our home. They need to know that we rely on them to help us do that. We need their help no matter how little they are or how cool they think they are. We need their support. We need and desire those blessings that come from having the Spirit abiding within the walls of our home. We want to do those things that unite us as a family in mortality and again in the eternities.

So we need to try to record our moments of joy: the first time our son passes the sacrament or our daughter speaks in Primary, perhaps when one of our teenagers puts his arms around us and tells us he loves us, or when we look in the mirror and can simply say, "It's great to be me."

My daughter, Ashley, recently returned from a mission in Romania. She had a wonderful experience there, and her letters taught me about the gospel. She was influential in baptizing a sister who had six children and was married to an abusive, nonmember husband. For three weeks this sister did not attend church, and Ashley was concerned. On the fourth week, the sister was there. Ashley wrote: "When I saw her, it was a moment of pure joy, when nothing else can touch you, and all I could do was offer a prayer of thanksgiving to my Father in Heaven for blessing me far more than I deserved."

Moments of pure joy, I thought as I read her letter. We can cling to those moments. We have them. Maybe they don't come as often as we'd like, but they do come. Even one moment of recorded joy can heal our heart and comfort us amidst the frenzy of life as a single mother. By the time we get our meals together, the lunches and kids off to school or to lessons, our church duties completed, and work, we are exhausted. Exhaustion makes us vulnerable, unable to see clearly. We become irritable, impatient, less able to make good decisions. We start getting down on ourselves. Discouragement sets in. Sometimes we feel defeat. Sometimes we feel "lesser-than." Sometimes we even submit to both being and feeling inferior.

I can remember feeling all of those feelings. When I first started back to church at the age of thirty-two, I probably was one of two women in the whole stake who was divorced, and I felt horrible. I felt so lesser-than and inferior to other women who had seemingly done their life right, and I wondered how mine had gone so wrong. Satan loves for us to have these

301

feelings. He knows what will happen. Seek balance. Use memories of joy to fight discouragement and depression.

Finances can be an immense burden. I have gone to bed many nights worrying about the mortgage and the expenses and fretting over how to keep this caught up and that caught up. Had it not been for a fervent testimony of tithing, and a pleading prayer in my heart for the Lord to rescue me, often I would have despaired. Reading the scriptures does not pay the bills, but it does lessen the trauma by restoring faith and renewing hope. At one particularly difficult time in my life, I was abysmally low. I felt I could not do anything right, and I berated myself for everything that I wasn't. My brother took me aside and taught me from the book of Job. Job lost his wealth and his family, his friends turned on him, and he had boils and plagues. He was really, really burdened. To his friends who had turned on him, he said, "I am not inferior unto you" (Job 13:2). I love that: "I am not inferior unto you." We are not inferior to anyone. I repeat, we are not inferior to anyone.

Job goes on, "For I know that my redeemer liveth, and that he shall stand at the latter day upon the earth" (Job 19:25). Each and every day that we yield our hearts to God, we are becoming women of Christ. Women who are dealing with disappointment and despair are not inferior. In my opinion, they are the heroes of the world, the most courageous women I know.

In 2 Timothy 1:7 the Lord has promised us, "God hath not given us the spirit of fear; but of power, and of love, and of a sound mind." Heavenly Father knows that life can be lonely and tough and that sometimes we long for someone to take over for a day. Please know that joy comes after weeping. The Lord has promised that he will not leave us comfortless. He will fight our battles. Faith in the Lord Jesus Christ must be paramount in our lives. When all else fails, when reason no longer works and you're saying to yourself, *This is really it this time. I can't do it any longer*, when you want to be spread-eagled on the highway waiting for the Mack truck, faith in Jesus Christ will make a difference. I know that when we are saying, "Here I am; take me, for I can no longer carry on," he does deliver us from the pain.

Let these words of Elder James E. Talmage reverberate in your hearts: "Then shall woman be recompensed in rich measure for all the injustice that womanhood has endured in mortality. . . . Mortal eye cannot see nor mind comprehend the beauty, glory, and majesty of a righteous woman made perfect in the celestial kingdom of God."[6]

Let us take the Holy Spirit for our guide. Let us not be deceived. Let us not give in. Instead, let us validate for one another that we are precious daughters of our Father in Heaven, that we are co-creators with him, that we came equipped to succeed, and with his help, succeed we will.

NOTES

1. See Jeffrey R. Holland, Ensign, May 1996, 29–31.
2. Our Heritage: A Brief History of The Church of Jesus Christ of Latter-day Saints (Salt Lake City: The Church of Jesus Christ of Latter-day Saints, 1996), 47–48.
3. George Q. Cannon, Collected Discourses, ed. Brian H. Stuy, 5 vols. (Burbank, Calif., and Woodland Hills, Utah: B.H.S. Publishing, 1987–92), 2:339 (17 December 1891).
4. Quoted in Jill Mulvay Derr, Janath Russell Cannon, and Maureen Ursenbach Beecher, Women of Covenant: The Story of Relief Society (Salt Lake City: Deseret Book, 1992), 177–78.
5. Spencer W. Kimball, Teachings of Spencer W. Kimball, ed. Edward L. Kimball (Salt Lake City: Bookcraft, 1982), 331–32.
6. James E. Talmage, "The Eternity of Sex," Young Woman's Journal 25 (October 1914): 602–3.

Sisterhood Has No Boundary

CAROL CLARK OTTESEN

The Great Wall of China, nearly two thousand miles long, was built on the proposition that unbridgeable differences exist between peoples, differences so deep they can be dealt with only by physical separation. Originally built to keep out so-called inferior cultures, the wall is crumbling now in places; peasants have carried stones away to build houses, symbolic of change in China. In 1997, I was part of a group of English teachers sent by Brigham Young University to Shandong Medical University with a firm warning from the Chinese government never to speak of religion to any Chinese national. We went with our own set of preconceptions, with some caution about communism, and some latent concerns generated by the media's depiction of China as an enemy. I thought I was free of stereotyping after teaching university students of diverse cultures in California for several years, but I learned from the Chinese about the nature of true relatedness, about the meaning of erasable walls.

The suffering of the Chinese people, especially the women, is beyond belief; but it has made them, for the most part, humble and warm-hearted. Or perhaps that is their general nature. On one of our first days in China, we were walking in a park when an older Chinese woman dressed in the simple clothes of a country peasant hesitated in front of me, speaking in Chinese. Her son, who spoke English, stepped forward and said his mother wanted to know how old I was. (This is not an

Carol Clark Ottesen taught English at California State University–Dominguez Hills and in the honors program at Brigham Young University. She and her husband, Sterling E. Ottesen, are the parents of five children. They recently returned from China, where they taught English with the BYU Kennedy Center. She teaches in her ward Relief Society.

impolite question in China, where age is revered.) Her son told me she was seventy-six, and by her age I knew something of her life. I could see her feet had been bound when she was a child, and I knew she had experienced famine and the chaos of the Cultural Revolution and had lived in a country without freedom. She spoke to me in Chinese, and I replied to her in English. We smiled and nodded a lot as if we could understand each other. Amazingly, she took my face in her hands as we talked. And I felt her words were something like this: *I am Chinese, you are American, and yet we are sisters. We are both gray and have experienced much of life. We know what it is to be women.* We embraced and parted. When there are no common words, the body must say so much. We had been total strangers, but she had taken me in.

As I have reflected on the meaning of sisterhood, I have tried to discern what happened with this woman. First, the Chinese place little value on privacy and personal space. I have an image of my students crowded on the floor of our small apartment, overlapping, necessarily touching, entirely without self-consciousness. Their communal sense seems healthy to me. Students frequently took my arm or hand closely and firmly—I could hardly get away. So this woman's actions were not unusual.

Second, common experiences bind women. Even though we may not have biological children, we are, by biology and instinct, mothers. Many of my students in China wrote about their mothers and the poverty of their childhood. Here is one: "On my birthday, my mother bought a fish, a rare occasion. She portioned it out and put the head on her plate. I always wondered why my mother liked the head of the fish so much. But when I got older I realized she gave all the meat to us children and had only the head for herself."[1] Western women are not so different—my own sister says she always eats the burned piece of toast. Chinese women, like many women across the world who have been what one writer calls the "mule[s] of the world,"[2] have known sacrifice. Another Chinese student wrote unsentimentally of her childhood. "Everyone suffered from poverty in those days. I often picked out pieces of broken glass in the garbage to get a little money. To save bus fare, I volunteered at age four to pick up my sister from nursery school and carry her home on my back. I did that for several years."[3]

305

Yes, we are sisters. And another commonality binds us—the recognition of the light of Christ in each other. One day in China I woke up with a bad cold and an even worse attitude. I was tired of washing clothes by hand in the bathtub and drinking bad-tasting water out of a thermos. Besides, I was late and had a run in my hose. I grudgingly threw everything together in my briefcase and ran off to class, wondering why I had ever decided to go to China. Yet, as I walked down the hallway, I recognized I couldn't face fifty students with that kind of attitude. So I said a quick, desperate prayer that I'd be able to give the students what they needed. The class went all right, and as I was gathering my books, four girls came up to my desk. "May we ask you a question? We have been talking, and we just want to know what it is that happens when you come into the room. It's like light or sunshine, and we want to know what it is." I felt as though I had been physically struck. My small prayer had been so quickly answered. I fought a huge lump in my throat—I so very much wanted to tell them about the *real* source of that light, to tell them that in my weakness I had been encircled about by the Savior, the Father of Light. The light of Christ planted in every created thing lures us toward God and binds us together in this small room we call a world. No group or person has a corner on this light.

One day a graduate student demonstrated in class how her grandmother had woven fabric by hand. She brought the sturdy cotton fabric to show us, and many of the students recognized the pattern as the kind they had worn as children. After she spoke, she turned to me and said, "I would like you to have this fabric. It is not made in Shandong province anymore."

I protested, "I can't take this precious material. Your grandmother made it, and you should keep it as a treasure."

Her face became serious as I tried to put it back in her hands. She was adamant. "You must take it."

I still protested, but I could see in her eyes she was offended.

"Take it as a memory of the women of China. Show it to the American women as a sample of what we Chinese women do. Perhaps you can tell them we want to be their sisters."

Often on Sundays we went to the central park of the university for what the Chinese called an English corner. Usually within sixty seconds of our arrival, a crowd of fifty to a hundred gathered to ask questions. On our last Sunday in China, a man spoke up aggressively about religion: "We understand that 80 percent of Americans believe in God. How can these smart people be so deceived and believe in something that is simply not true?" I replied that some of the people, including a number of great scientists, deduced from the nature of the universe that there had to be a superior mind to create this kind of order—that even Shandong Medical School had a master builder. The man retorted, "But you can't prove these things!" I agreed and added that perhaps there are other ways of knowing.

A little skittery and also late for our Sunday meeting with fellow BYU teachers, we closed the meeting and began to walk away. While another student detained my husband, the man ran after me and said quietly so others couldn't hear, "I want you to know I don't necessarily believe that there is *not* a God, I just wanted to know how *you* know. *How do you know?*" (Another question arises here, and that is, How did he know I knew?) We were walking quickly toward the gate where a taxi waited for us with the door open. I had no time. What could I say to him? I was torn, as I often am, between expediency and attending to that which is most important. But something filled me. I put my hands on his shoulders. "Dear brother, I want you to know I don't just believe; I *know* there is a living God. He is aware of you personally and loves you. I know this from my mind and from intuition—something in *here*."

To my surprise, his eyes began to fill and he couldn't speak, so I said, "I sense your seeking heart, and I want you to know I love you too." I was startled at my temerity but was very sure of the consummate grace of that moment. He hastily took my phone number and address. "I must know more," he said, and my husband and I climbed into the taxi. That day at our sacrament meeting of ten people, I felt the aptness of the words "for I will go before your face. I will be on your right hand and on your left, and my Spirit shall be in your hearts, and mine angels round about you, to bear you up" (D&C 84:88). The more I pushed at the boundaries of my human limitations, the more amazing were the ways opened to extend His influence.

It is often easier, however, to love a passing brother or sister of another culture than it is to live day after day with some*one*—just as it's easier to love everyone than it is to love someone in particular. We see boundaries in our own culture, even in our own families, or in our own marriages. I have found there are no perfect relationships, no perfect families, only great moments that sustain us, like stepping stones across the ocean of ordinaries.

The day before our eldest son left for a mission to Germany, we assembled as a family to celebrate our twenty-second anniversary, planned by our children. We knew this would be our last evening together for a long time. The children blindfolded my husband and me, and we submitted as they took us in separate cars to an unknown destination. After a wild ride, they removed the blindfolds, and we found ourselves at a local park where a card table was set with a lace cloth, china, crystal, and candles. The children served us an elegant meal, and then all five of them, along with our Native American daughter, climbed up on a wooden platform to entertain us. The last number was eight-year-old Robin playing on her violin what has become our family song: "Edelweiss." As the wavery notes sounded out in the night, my son began to sing in German. By that time, my husband and I were on the platform too, and at the end of the song we became one hugging, teary mass of people—one of those moments where differences are forgotten and there is real love and wholeness. Even in families, polarities are with us, but there are moments of coming together, and memories of those occasions give us hope that they'll happen again.

We know, however, that overcoming the barriers of difference is not possible for any human without the Savior's grace. I can't just go around faking love and niceness or give condescendingly to those less fortunate. I have to have a real change of heart, possible only through making space for him who can teach us how to love even when we have been wronged, betrayed, or disappointed. The greatest conflicts in the world today are about those who believe their ideas, or race, or religion are superior to all others. To bring about change, we can only begin with ourselves—by completely ridding ourselves of competitive feelings and any hint of cultural self-righteousness. Can we ever, as God does, appreciate our very differences and learn to love without the desire to remodel anyone but ourselves?

Russell Schweickart, one of the Apollo 7 astronauts, says about gazing down at the fragile earth: "You look down there and you can't imagine how many borders and boundaries you cross, again and again and again and you don't even see them. . . . Hundreds of people in the Mideast killing each other over some imaginary line that you're not even aware of. . . . And from where you see it, the thing is a *whole*, and it's so beautiful."[4] Because of this new picture of a world with no boundaries, only a dark blue and white circle turning serenely in its orbit, we know even more strongly that boundaries are of our own making and that if we are to truly become brothers and sisters, it will be only because we allow Christ's encircling arms to move us beyond the walls that separate us. Only then may we understand how to love not only 1.2 billion Chinese but all our relatives on this small planet.

NOTES

1. Student paper; used by permission.
2. Jean Toomer, in Alice M. Walker, *In Search of Our Mothers' Gardens: Womanist Prose* (San Diego: Harcourt Brace Jovanovich, 1983), 232.
3. Student paper; used by permission.
4. Russell Schweickart, in Rollo May, *The Cry for Myth* (New York: W. W. Norton, 1991), 299.

Families—It's about Time

VIRGINIA U. JENSEN

A woman who had a magnificent garden was asked, "What is your gardening secret?"

Her answer was simple. "I stay close to the garden," she replied. "I go into my garden every day, even when it isn't convenient. And while I'm there, I look for little signs of possible problems, things like weeds and insects and soil conditions that are simple to correct if caught in time, but that can become overwhelming if left unchecked."

It takes time to grow a beautiful garden. It also takes time to grow a celestial family. It is through the family that the Lord's purposes are fulfilled. What happens in families can affect an entire nation.

President Gordon B. Hinckley has said, "The strength of the nations lies in the homes of the people. God is the designer of the family. He intended that the greatest of happiness, the most satisfying aspects of life, the deepest joys should come in our associations together and our concerns one for another as fathers and mothers and children."[1]

Think of the significance of this: In a world where everyone is seeking after fulfillment and happiness, our prophet says the greatest happiness, the deepest joys, come in our families. By our Father's design, the family is a sacred institution. The relationships within the family should be the most important relationships we have on earth. As women, we can

Virginia U. Jensen is first counselor in the Relief Society General Presidency. A homemaker, she and her husband, J. Rees Jensen, are the parents of four children and grandparents of seven. She has served in numerous volunteer and Church service missionary assignments and enjoys gardening, grandchildren, and family activities.

spend our energy and time in many worthwhile pursuits, but in only one of these pursuits is our influence irreplaceable.

Sisters, I congratulate you for all you do to strengthen your families. I know it is difficult, even in the best of circumstances. I know it takes sacrifice and dedication and total commitment. I compliment you for the time you invest in each family member.

President Thomas S. Monson tells us, "Time is the raw material of life. Every day unwraps itself like a gift, bringing us the opportunity to . . . evolve into something better than we are at its beginning. Success is contingent upon our effective use of the time given us."[2] As President Monson suggests, our success and our use of time closely correlate. Creating a celestial family takes time.

In Cradles and Kitchens

What are we doing with our time for heaven's sake? That question has never been more significant than it is in these last days when time is in short supply in more ways than one. Elder Neal A. Maxwell said: "When the real history of mankind is fully disclosed, . . . will what happened in cradles and kitchens prove to be more controlling than what happened in congresses? When the surf of the centuries has made the great pyramids so much sand, the everlasting family will still be standing, because it is a celestial institution, formed outside telestial time."[3]

I remember the time I spent as a young girl every fall working in the kitchen with my mother canning peaches. I would sit for hours peeling that fuzzy, sticky fruit. As I sat at my peeling station working away, the juice ran down my arms in little streams right to my elbows. I can remember to this day how miserable that felt.

But every once in a while, I would pop one of those beautiful, reddish-orange, perfectly ripe beauties into my mouth. I figured it was my pay for the sticky elbows. Knowing that when we were finished, we would have to clean the entire kitchen—the floors, counters, sinks, dishes, everything—I sometimes wondered why we didn't just bag the whole mess and buy canned peaches from the store.

But every fall, despite knowing the awful mess we would have to clean up, my mother and I canned peaches. And as we did, we talked, my mother and I. And I would watch her. She moved about the kitchen with such skill, filling the bottles so carefully that each one looked worthy of a prize at the state fair. She would pour the sweet syrup over the peaches, put on the lids, and lower the bottles into the canning kettle for processing.

As Mom and I canned those wonderful fruits on warm, autumn days, I would imagine a cold, snowy January. Even though it was hard, messy work in September, I knew that in January we wouldn't regret all the hours, mess, and trouble of canning those peaches. We would be glad we had spent the time.

Everyone in our family loved peaches. We loved the fruit, but we also loved what it represented: the many ways Mother took care of us. Over those bottles of peaches and in a thousand other ways, I learned from my mother as she and I spent time together. I learned basic and meaningful lessons, such as the importance of family and stories of my ancestors. From her I learned about Jesus Christ and other lessons of faith too numerous to mention but which have stayed with me to this day. What happens at home never leaves us.

Those bushels of peaches my mother and I labored over year after year are one type of fruit—a telestial kind. Our time together and all I learned during it represent another fruit—a fruit of celestial connections, and that fruit is delicious forever.

A wonderful line from Proverbs reads, "My fruit is better than gold" (Proverbs 8:19). How true when it comes to time spent with our families. President Ezra Taft Benson told us that "a child needs a mother more than all the things money can buy. Spending time with your children is the greatest gift of all."[4] The fruits of your time spent with and for your families are indeed better than gold.

The Savior taught, "By their fruits ye shall know them" (3 Nephi 14:20). I think that means in part that we as wives, mothers, grandmothers, aunts, sisters, daughters, and cousins bear a sacred responsibility to invest our time in our families so that our family members will be and will bear good fruit.

In the Time You Have

You who work so diligently to create an environment of righteousness in your home are performing a service that cannot be bought. No one can do what you do in your family. My son was only two years old and not yet talking perfectly when he said to me one day, "Do you know why mudders is so important?" I said, "No. Tell me why." He replied, "Because their boys luvses dem so much." As you can imagine, that is a memory I will always treasure. These moments are rare and precious. I know that most days it's not easy. In fact, it's a thankless job at times. For all of us there are days when family life can be very trying. But please know that you are making the best use of your time when you take time to put your families first.

As mothers we are often in a position where the needs of others come first. Often we find ourselves barely able to keep up with the diverse needs of various family members with no time left to address our own. President Gordon B. Hinckley reminds us, "Sacrifice is and always has been of the very essence of motherhood."[5] You can expect that not all that sacrifice, in fact, perhaps very little of it, will be fully appreciated. You can expect the world to look past or not value your accomplishments. But you can feel peace in knowing that when you use your time to help your loved ones, it is well spent.

The Proclamation on the Family can be a marvelous resource. Sometimes, on a particularly busy day, I have paused to read the sentence, "Mothers are primarily responsible for the nurture of their children."[6] Good mothering—nurturing—involves body, mind, and spirit, and as President Ezra Taft Benson reminded us, "Motherly teaching takes time—lots of time."[7]

Each of us must choose how to spend our time wisely in fulfilling this eternal responsibility. We are warned, "Do not run faster . . . than you have strength" (D&C 10:4). Focus on what you can do as a mother in the time that you have. You can't do everything. So, prayerfully consider your family's needs and personalities. Prioritize your tasks according to your circumstances. Then, attend to those needs as best you can in the time you have. If you've honestly done your best, then don't feel guilty. Be grateful for your family and thank Heavenly Father for your opportunity to serve, nurture, enjoy, and teach them.

To spend your time on what matters most, you may have to let go of some tasks. Here are a few verses of homespun advice from anonymous sources. You may have heard them before, but they are worth repeating.

> Cleaning and scrubbing can wait till tomorrow,
> For babies grow up, we've learned to our sorrow;
> So quiet down, cobwebs; dust, go to sleep.
> I'm rocking my baby—and babies don't keep.

And this:

> Cleaning the house
> While the children are growing
> Is like shoveling snow
> While it's still snowing.

The Glue That Holds the Family Together

Not every woman will marry. Not every woman who marries will bear children. It is my sincere and heartfelt desire that those nurturers of family life who are among that number do not feel hurt or excluded in discussions of mothering and families. Mothering is not synonymous with giving birth. Mothering can and must also be done by aunts, sisters, cousins, and so on. We can strengthen families without being the mother.

I saved a Christmas card I received from a friend whose elderly aunt died during the year. My friend wrote, "We lost our dear Aunt Alice, who was ninety-six years old. A great deal of fun, love, loyalty, and testimony went with her. She was the glue that held the family together. An avid genealogist, she never neglected any of her living relatives, either. Single all her life, she extended her interest to all the family members and was the main source of interfamily news."

What a tribute. Look at how Aunt Alice nurtured her family. She was fun, she gave love, and she helped others grow in testimony as she shared her faith and devotion to her Father in Heaven and the gospel with family members. Perhaps the most impressive statement from this Christmas letter is "she was the glue that held the family together." Aunt Alice understood that her roles in the family were sacred and that her contributions made a difference.

I salute all of you who work hard at your family relationships, who make them sacred relationships. As wives, mothers, grandmothers, aunts, sisters, daughters, and cousins we can do so much for our family members. We can give them the best of our time. Let's talk about ways to do that.

Dinner Jackets and Fancy Glasses

I had my first date with my husband, Rees, in June. We were engaged in October and married the next April. During our courtship, I enjoyed long, intellectual talks with him. We would sit in front of my parents' fireplace and talk about politics and the Church. I thought that was how our life would be. So, the Christmas before we were married, I gave Rees a dinner jacket and two beautiful glasses with hollow stems. I imagined he would come home from work, and we would share a delicious, gourmet dinner prepared, of course, by my hands. We would retire to the living room and sip grape juice. He would wear his handsome dinner jacket. I would look beautiful. We would discuss very important subjects.

Well, we married, and reality hit. Just before we celebrated our first anniversary, we welcomed our first child into our family. During the pregnancy, I experienced severe morning sickness. I did not look beautiful.

The only time the hollow-stemmed glasses were used was much later when our children discovered them in the cupboard and filled them with red Kool-Aid. The dinner jacket was used once—as part of a Halloween costume. The dinners I made were not that delicious. And the most stimulating things we discussed had to do with how many ways we could eat hamburger, which was the only thing we could afford.

I have learned that marriage and family life have little to do with dinner jackets and fancy glasses. Life is much more about smiling as we dine on hamburger casseroles and loving one another even when we are not dressed in fancy clothes or looking beautiful. If you are married, *take time* to strengthen your relationship with your husband. The love you and your spouse have for each other creates harmony in the home and is the all-important base of family stability.

Time for What's Timeless

Family relationships and eternal values are two of the very few things of this world that are timeless. Think about that. Houses, jobs, cars, and so much of what composes our busy days are only part of this mortal world. They will not be with us eternally. But our family members and the glorious truths of the gospel of Jesus Christ endure eternally.

The question we must ask ourselves is, "How can we make our family a truly celestial institution?" even though some days the most immediate question is, "How can I find enough time to do the laundry?" When so many demands yank at us, family life and celestial life may seem to have little in common. But the home is a celestial workshop. The timeless values of the gospel—like peach juice—stick everywhere. And in this case, sticky is not all that bad. If we live the gospel values we teach, they will permeate everything in a home. They will stick with us, and they will help us stick together as family members.

In the Church's *Family Guidebook,* we find this promise from the First Presidency: "We promise you great blessings if you will follow the Lord's counsel and hold regular family home evenings. We pray constantly that parents in the Church will accept their responsibility to teach and exemplify gospel principles to their children. May God bless you to be diligent in this most important responsibility."[8] Gospel reality reminds us that families, like gospel values themselves, are timeless and therefore worthy of constant monitoring. The fruit of timeless, celestial lessons learned is delicious forever.

President Ezra Taft Benson challenged us: "Mothers, teach your children the gospel in your own home. . . . This is the most effective teaching that your children will ever receive. This is the Lord's way of teaching. The Church cannot teach like you can. The school cannot. The day-care center cannot. But you can, and the Lord will sustain you."[9]

Take time to tell your children how much the gospel means to you. Take time to explain to them why we spend so much of our time in church activity and why these things are important in our lives and theirs. Take time to teach them about the Savior and what he did for them and for all of us. Take time to build a foundation of timeless values.

You never know when your teaching of these values might make a crucial difference in the life of a child. For instance, in the early days of the Southern States Mission, there was much persecution of missionaries. Elder Frank Croft was a missionary in the state of Alabama. One day a mob of armed and vicious men abducted Elder Croft and took him to a secluded spot in the backwoods to be whipped. They ordered him to strip to the waist. After he had removed his coat, shirt, and folded down his garments, they tied him, standing, to a nearby tree to prevent him flinching away from the blows while being lashed. While disrobing, there fell from his pocket a letter. A fearful Elder Croft, a short time before, had written his parents a letter denouncing mobs and condemning mob violence. The letter that had fallen from his coat was his mother's reply. In her letter she counseled, "My beloved son, you must remember the words of the Savior when He said, 'Blessed are they which are persecuted for righteousness' sake: for theirs is the kingdom of Heaven'; also 'Blessed are ye, when men shall revile you and persecute you and shall say all manner of evil against you falsely for my name's sake. Rejoice and be exceedingly glad for you will have your reward in Heaven for so persecuted they the prophets which were before you.' Also remember the Savior upon the cross suffering for the sins of the world when He uttered these immortal words, 'Father, forgive them; for they know not what they do.' Surely, my boy, they who are mistreating you Elders know not what they do or they would not do it. Sometime, somewhere, they will understand and then they will regret their action and they will honor you for the glorious work you are doing. So be patient, my son; love those who mistreat you and say all manner of evil against you and the Lord will bless you and magnify you in their eyes and your mission will be gloriously successful. Remember also, my son, that day and night, your mother is praying for you always."

Elder Croft, tied to the tree, saw the leader of the mob pick up the fallen letter and decide to read it before giving the word to his men to start the lashing. The elder's heart sank as he observed the hardness of his features, the cruelty in his eyes. No sympathy could be expected from him. Elder Croft closed his eyes in resignation and awaited the moment when the beating would begin. Thinking of home and loved ones and particularly of his beloved mother, he silently offered a prayer in her behalf.

A moment or two later, feeling that the leader had surely had time to finish reading the letter, he opened his eyes. He was amazed to see a change in the man's countenance. The hardness and cruelty in his face were ebbing away; his eyes brimmed slightly with tears. His whole demeanor appeared changed.

To Elder Croft, it seemed an awfully long time before the man roused from his reverie and walked over to the helpless elder. "You must have a wonderful mother," he said. "You see, I once had one, too." Then, addressing the other members of the mob, he said, "Men, after reading this letter from this Mormon's mother, I just can't go ahead with the job. Maybe we had better let him go." Elder Croft was released, his heart full of gratitude for the influence of a loving mother. How very near she seemed at that moment.[10]

Swell Bathrooms or Great Memories?

Recreation is such an important part of the time we share with family members. Children should be able to look back at the time spent in the family home as a time of great adventure, laughter, and joy in each other's company.

A father tells that every year his family saved money to have the bathroom done over. They lived in a house with an old-fashioned bathroom, with legs on the tub, separate hot and cold faucets, slow drains—that sort of thing. But every winter they would take the money out of the bank and go on a couple of family skiing trips. The father reports that the oldest boy, when he went away from home, always mentioned in his letters what a great time he had on those skiing trips. The father says, "I can't imagine his writing home, 'Boy, we really have a swell bathroom, haven't we?'"[11]

Vacations can be wonderful memories, but so can daily events—if we take time for fun. Play ball together as a family. Take walks. Take hikes. Eat banana splits. Rake leaves. Have races in the backyard. Find ways to laugh more often and enjoy one another. It is the way we prove, "I love you"—probably the most significant way. Elder Marvin J. Ashton told the story of a father who said to his young son, "I love you." Unimpressed by the verbiage, one day the boy replied, "I don't want you to love me. I want you to play football with me."[12] Mothers, often even more than fathers, have a hard time setting aside time merely to play with and enjoy being just one of the family. Time spent with others makes a tremendous difference in our influence on them. We must spend time with them.

The Lord counseled Joseph Smith, Oliver Cowdery, and David Whitmer, "Let your time be devoted to the studying of the scriptures, and to preaching, . . . and to performing your labors on the land" (D&C 26:1). These were the tasks assigned to them in building the Lord's kingdom. Sisters, let our time be devoted to the tasks the Lord has assigned to us as well. Let it be devoted to loving our family members, serving them, teaching them, and performing our labors as wives and mothers, aunts and sisters. Let us take time to stay close to our family garden. Let us examine it every day, even when it isn't convenient. Let us look for signs of possible problems and correct them in time so that they won't be overwhelming. And let's stop our tending and weeding every so often to just sit and enjoy what's growing in our lively, flourishing gardens.

My oldest child, a daughter, married just three weeks before her husband started medical school. Thirteen years later, he finished his medical training. In those long years of hard work, there were some deficiencies in their life. One was the amount of time they as a family had with Dad. Soon after my son-in-law began his work as a neuroradiologist, he was asked to lecture to an auditorium full of doctors at a noon seminar. It happened to fall on a much-needed day off. In response to the request, my son-in-law said, "I have promised my four-year-old daughter, Elizabeth, that I will spend the day with her. If I can bring her along to the lecture, I will do it." The agreement was made; Mom fixed a lunch for Elizabeth to eat while Dad spoke. With Dad at the podium, Elizabeth sat on the front row between a couple of doctors and ate her lunch. As Dad left the podium to return to his seat at the conclusion of his presentation, Elizabeth exclaimed in a voice that could be heard on the back row, "Good job, Dad!" The audience exploded in laughter.

I'm thankful for devoted children who take time to bless the lives of my grandchildren by their timeless and time-filled parenting.

For Heaven's Sake

In 1994 as my birthday was approaching, I told my children that I did not want them to buy me a gift. Instead, I asked if they would take the time to write me a letter. The letter could contain anything they wanted to say. I don't need to tell you that those letters, most too sacred to be shared, are a priceless treasure to me now. I can't imagine any gift purchased at any store at any price that would be of such value as these letters are to me. I particularly enjoyed an illustration in the letter from my daughter Suzanne that I feel I can share. Suzanne thanked me for being her defender and supporter, and then she said: "I am reminded of a day I went to lunch with a group of friends at the park a few years ago. A young duck was having a hard time getting the bread we tossed to him because a loud obnoxious seagull kept swooping down and snatching it before the duck caught it. Suddenly, from at least fifty yards away, the mother duck came cruising down the grass hill above the pond at a velocity exceeding sixty miles per hour. She pounced on that seagull with such force that he skipped across the top of the water like a small stone and flew away squawking like a scared bully, pursued at close range by that angry mother duck. We all cheered for her, and someone yelled: 'I am woman, hear me roar!' There have been many times when I've witnessed your love for all of us and thought of that duck. It's awesome."

I am also awed by Heavenly Father's plan. Mothering and nurturing are deep instincts and an integral part of our Heavenly Father's family design. I, in turn, am thankful for a devoted mother who took time to defend me and teach me and love me. I'm thankful for all of you devoted mothers and women who take time to do the much-needed nurturing of families.

There is nothing better you could do with your time for heaven's sake. It may be sticky and it may be messy, but in those cold January days, when your children and other family members exhibit the fruits of your labors, when the ripeness of your teachings and love is sweet to the taste, no matter how messy or sticky it has been, you will be glad you canned those peaches. And you will know the answer to Elder Maxwell's question, because, sisters, what happens in cradles and kitchens far surpasses and even changes what happens in congresses.

God, our Heavenly Father, wants you to return home to him. He wants you to bring all your family members with you, ripe and full of gospel knowledge and good works, and blossoming with a happy heart. I

know he will bless you if you will take the time, because with families—
it's about time.

NOTES

1. Gordon B. Hinckley, Ensign, May 1991, 74.
2. Thomas S. Monson, Pathways to Perfection (Salt Lake City: Deseret Book, 1973), 109–10.
3. Neal A. Maxwell, Ensign, May 1978, 10–11.
4. Ezra Taft Benson, Come, Listen to a Prophet's Voice (Salt Lake City: Deseret Book, 1990), 32.
5. Gordon B. Hinckley, Motherhood, a Heritage of Faith [pamphlet] (Salt Lake City: Deseret Book, 1995), 4.
6. First Presidency and Quorum of the Twelve Apostles of The Church of Jesus Christ of Latter-day Saints, "The Family: A Proclamation to the World," Ensign, November 1995, 102.
7. Benson, Come, Listen to a Prophet's Voice, 35.
8. "Message from the First Presidency," Family Home Evening Resource Book (Salt Lake City: The Church of Jesus Christ of Latter-day Saints, 1983), iv.
9. Ezra Taft Benson, Elect Women of God [pamphlet] (Salt Lake City: Bookcraft, 1992), 10.
10. Bryant S. Hinckley, The Faith of Our Pioneer Fathers (Salt Lake City: Bookcraft, 1956), 257–59.
11. Marion D. Hanks, Conference Report, April 1968, 57.
12. Marvin J. Ashton, Ensign, November 1975, 108.

How Do We Keep the Spark Alive?

DONNA B. HOMER, SABRA W. ANDERSEN, AND JAMES M. HARPER

Keep the home fires burning. (Donna) When you first get married, the spark is like vigorously burning pine that shoots sparks all over. Your love is young and new, and you're in the flame of it. As you get older, the sparks and flame fade down until the fire becomes a glowing ember. This glowing ember gives off continual warmth; it glows with a steady love and charity. Your love's bright ember keeps on glowing, and you can pack it up in your heart—and away you can go on a mission.

Nourish love with "consoling words." (Sabra) The Lord told Emma to be a comfort to her husband "with consoling words, in the spirit of meekness" (D&C 25:5). I think that means not to take exception to everything our husbands say, not to want to hurt, correct, or compete with them but instead to build and strengthen with our words. Out

Donna Brown Homer is a homemaker, wife, mother, grandmother, and great-grandmother. She graduated from California State University–Sacramento as a teacher. She and her husband, Don A. Homer, served a mission in Richmond, Virginia. They serve as ordinance workers in the Oakland California Temple.

Sabra Whittle Andersen and her husband, Dan Wayne Andersen, served missions for the Church Educational System in Western Samoa, the South Pacific, and the special needs seminary in Provo, Utah. They have a combined family of nine children, thirty grandchildren, and three great-grandchildren. Sabra serves as a supervisor in the Provo Utah Temple and works with the young single adults in her stake.

James M. Harper, chair of the Department of Family Sciences at Brigham Young University, is a licensed marriage and family therapist and psychologist and a fellow in the American Association for Marriage and Family Therapy. He has served as president of the Korea Pusan Mission and as a counselor in the BYU Fifth Stake presidency. He and his wife, Colleen, have five children.

walking with me one morning, Dan commented, "This yard really has a problem" and then explained what ought to have been done differently. I immediately thought, *Yes, and we have morning glory in our raspberries*. But I bit my tongue and didn't say anything at all. My husband, knowing me very well, understood what I was thinking, because he burst out laughing and threw his arms around me. Back home when he said the morning prayer, he thanked the Lord for our companionship in a way that reminded me of these lines:

> Oh the comfort—the inexpressible comfort
> of feeling safe with a person,
> Having neither to weigh thoughts
> Nor measure words—but pouring them
> All right out—just as they are—
> Chaff and grain together—
> Certain that a faithful hand will
> Take and sift them—
> Keep what is worth keeping—
> And with the breath of kindness
> Blow the rest away.[1]

Develop positive characteristics. (James) Older women and men who work daily to develop the following qualities report great joy in life and satisfaction in their marriages:

Zest, an attitude to live life to its fullest and to cherish all experience, good and bad.

Fortitude, the ability never to give up, to be hopeful always.

Completion, having done some of the things you wanted to do in life.

Transcending, recognizing that your being is as important as your doing, that your self-worth comes from who you are, not necessarily from what you can do.

Positive outlook, searching for the good even when there's bad, such as declining health or unexpected disappointments.

Accept aging. (Donna) One of the biggest challenges of change is to accept aging. President James E. Faust shared this observation at general conference: "In youth, time marches on; in middle age, time flies; and in old age, time runs out."[2] Perhaps that is why as we get older, we start to think back and wish we were young. We want more time. But wishing for the past diminishes the present. We need to accept the physical limitations that come as we get older. Sometimes we have big plans for when we retire, but when that time arrives, our health isn't such that we can realize those plans. We can't see so well; we can't hear so well; we can't walk as far; we can't work as hard. We can't do many things that we had planned for retirement. The aging process begins when we are born, and it continues until we die. We must accept what we cannot do, and go ahead and do the many things that we can.

Move on to new interests. (Donna) We should abandon plans that no longer match our interests and enthusiasms. A friend of mine took all of her bags of fabrics—not just scraps but good fabric pieces that she had been coordinating and collecting to make quilts—and gave them to Deseret Industries. "You'll never know what a great burden was lifted from my shoulders," she said. She knew that those quilts would be made and given to somebody who really needed them. The burden lifted also gave her more time to serve at the temple, her present calling. Look forward from here, because you will get stuck living in the past if you don't.

Nourish love with physical affection. (Sabra) As wives we can say I love you with acts as well as with words. Paul counseled husbands and wives to "depart ye not one from the other, except it be with consent for a time, that ye may give yourselves to fasting and prayer; and come together again, that Satan tempt you not" (JST 1 Corinthians 7:5). In modern times, Joseph F. Smith counseled: "Sexual union is lawful in wedlock, and if participated in with right intent is honorable and sanctifying."[3] That is a beautiful and strong statement. How marvelous it is to me that God made us as men and as women, as husbands and wives, perfectly able to provide that form of comfort and ultimate security for one another. Dan and I enjoy being affectionate. For me, there's something romantic about escalators. He's standing there, I'm standing there, we're not doing anything else, and we're so close to each other—I like to kiss him. I just can't help myself. As we kiss, I can see his eyes peering over my head, surveying the room to see if anyone is watching. But he's never yet pushed me off the escalator.

Enjoy being intimate and affectionate. (James) In many research studies, most older couples report that their sexual relationship is better at this stage of life than at earlier stages. It is a myth that once you reach a certain age you stop having a sexual relationship in marriage. It can be one source of bonding and one of the ways love is shared. In my four-year study of six hundred couples between the ages of fifty-five and ninety-six, the couples in their nineties said that they still have a sexual relationship and that touch and physical affection are extremely important to them. At any age, intimacy and affection nourish love.

Be quick to forgive. (Sabra) There's nothing the Lord wants more than to see our marriages not merely succeed but be glorious, be joyful. He will help us discover the answers we prayerfully seek. President David O. McKay said, "No other success can compensate for failure in the home."[4] Some families either love or hate that quotation, depending on how their teenagers are doing. The truth is that we love life when we love those around us. We fail when our arms are not stretched out still, when we aren't forgiving. We fail when we get hurt and build walls, when we keep the hurt in and the healing out. At Christmas we have a big dinner for our family. Last year I had everything timed to the minute. The chowder was done, the tree lights were on, the tables were set, the rolls were in the oven, and I was about to get myself ready when my darling husband appeared. "Honey," he announced, "I've done something that I think you will really like." I had compiled big, wonderful life history books to give to the children for Christmas. He, being the sweetheart he is, realized our little grandchildren were not going to be thrilled with a large book about a grandfather they had never known (they were getting one anyway), so he had spent hours shopping for each one of them individually. Fifteen presents. "All I need is for you to wrap them," he said. Without a word of thanks and not at all cheerfully, I grabbed tape and paper from upstairs, flew back down the stairs, wrapped them all—no one has ever wrapped so fast—and I almost threw them at him where he sat writing the name tags.

We got finished, and since the doorbell hadn't rung, I ran up the stairs to get dressed and then felt suddenly ashamed and weary. Over the years I've discovered that contention of any kind always leaves me feeling drained and dispirited. Back down the stairs I ran. "Oh honey, I need a hug." And the dear man said, "Oh good, because I sure need one, too."

He could have said, "Too little, too late. That won't work; it isn't good enough." But he didn't. What a good man I married.

What nourishes love? Being quick to forgive.

Don't dwell on the past. (Donna) As we age, one bad habit we may fall into is dwelling on the past. This habit is detrimental to our growth because a fixation on the past keeps us from moving forward. Consider this excellent commonsense advice: "The past is to learn from, not to live in." In what ways do we live in the past? We hang on to our old clothes, even though they may never fit again or be stylish or useful. We hang on to old plans to add an addition to the house, even though the children are all gone and we don't need extra rooms anymore. We hang on to holiday traditions that may need to be changed. We mull over past events, bad as well as good. We hang on to family feuds and grudges, resentments that should have no place in our life. Bad memories and grudges are like bulky coats and too-tight pants: if you get rid of your old garb and garbage, you might find fresh air and closet room you'd forgotten you had.

Keep growing. (James) Every stage of life is a growth stage, including the so-called retirement years. Three developmental tasks at this stage of life are important.

The first is *generativity:* supporting and nurturing younger generations, particularly our own children and grandchildren. Having a sense of our great potential influence on upcoming generations is important as we age.

The second task is *integrity,* particularly in reviewing the past. In this review, our task as a couple is to see that our lives have meaning because of what we have done and who we are. We should accept the negative and appreciate the positive, without dwelling exclusively on one or the other. Out of an honest, balanced review of life arises a sense of meaningful wholeness, or integrity.

The third developmental task is *transcendence.* This task concerns our attitude toward our physical body. We realize we are persons of great worth because of who we are, not what we can do or how we look. Neither our accomplishments nor our physical appearance determines our worth. To arrive at this realization is an accomplishment at any age, but it is essential to happiness in our later years.

NOTES

1. Dinah Maria Mulock Craik, "Friendship," in *Best-Loved Poems of the LDS People*, ed. Jack M. Lyon, Linda Ririe Gundry, Jay A. Parry, and Devan Jensen (Salt Lake City: Deseret Book, 1996), 102.
2. Quoted by James E. Faust, *Ensign*, May 1999, 17–18.
3. Joseph F. Smith, *Gospel Doctrine* (1919; Salt Lake City: Deseret Book, 1986), 309.
4. David O. McKay, Conference Report, April 1964, 5.

How Do We Help the Folks?

Marilyn Richardson

Do what you can, not what you can't. Everyone's experience with caring for a loved one is different. Don't feel that you should be doing what your cousin did with her mother, or what someone else in your ward is doing. You must consider your own family's needs, your own personality, your own nature. You do what you can, not what you can't. Note how different the following two experiences are.

My two aunts cared for their mother, my grandmother. These two sisters, Elaine and Penny, lived in the same town and agreed to take alternate twenty-four hour shifts caring for their mother. They had significant hurdles to overcome; one sister needed major surgery, and the other was a stake Relief Society president. Somehow they worked things out. Their experience was not unpleasant because their mother always kept up her spirits. "Mother . . . was such a good friend, a great listener," these sister-caretakers wrote. "Even up to a few hours before she died, if Mother was sleeping, we could rouse her and she would answer our questions. Her mind was clear right to the end. This definitely made it easier to care for her."[1] Both sisters said they had no regrets for the years of caring they gave to their mother.

Another woman cared for her mother for five years. She said, "I think I was wrong [to care for my mother at home for so long.] She took over our home, our lives, the lives of our children. . . . My children stopped bringing their friends home. They never knew what she might do or say.

Marilyn Richardson, mother of three and grandmother of six, lives in St. George, Utah. She has written a book about the problems and the rewards of caring for the elderly.

And it was almost impossible to keep her clean. My teenage daughter was a big help in giving her a shower, but it was hard."[2]

Taking care of aged parents is a difficult chore to face, even with family support and harmony. You get tired. You get angry. You feel terrible at times—mean and selfish when you meant to be, wanted to be, generous and loving.

Don't forget they are struggling too. Despite all the problems involved with caring for our elderly parents, we must not lose sight of their humanity. Don't let them simply devolve into a burden to be borne. They are still the people who loved and reared us. We owe them consideration, dignity, and love. When my mother-in-law, Velma, came to live with us, she probably had Alzheimer's disease. It was difficult to see her so changed, to have her not know or trust me. She had always said to my husband, "Now you be nice to Marilyn." And she was a good grandmother. Our two daughters had been enthusiastic, "Yes. Yes. Have Grandma come live with us!" The changes in her—her forgetfulness, her lack of interest in hygiene, her trouble communicating—were hard on us. Once I heard her speaking and stopped by her bedroom door. I heard her say, "Dear Heavenly Father, this is Velma A. Richardson. I want to die. That is the thing I really want. I am not crazy. This is Velma A. Richardson." It was like she was saying, "Get it straight." My heart ached for her.

Watch out for sibling stress. An aspect of human nature that may come to the fore when parents age is jealousy or rivalry between siblings. Unresolved feelings emerge, feelings the children didn't even know they had. These feelings seem to come out more noticeably when it is time to take care of parents' property. Heirs try to figure out an equitable way to do it, but someone almost always feels offended. For instance, I know of one sibling who was taking items and hiding them in the garage. He had a larger family than his brothers and sisters and felt he could make better use of certain items by sharing them with his six adult children. His wife encouraged him to do so, because she felt his siblings were better off and didn't need as much. They had worked out their own idea of what was fair based on how they perceived things. Other family members didn't have the same views. Trouble ensued. In addition to the family stresses involved in deciding what to do with parents' belongings—either at the time they move into a nursing home or when they die—a family also struggles with dividing up the workload of caring for elderly parents.

Be their advocate. Older people need an advocate, just as children do. They need someone who speaks up for their rights, someone who questions the doctor or coordinates their care. When illness or medication makes an elderly person unable to think or act clearly in his or her own best interest, someone must intercede, question procedures, challenge routines.

Accept that life won't stand still. Seeing your parents begin to change is stressful. I used to phone my mother and say things like, "Oh, my gosh, the wrinkles! I had no idea they'd come so fast." My mother would answer, "It doesn't get any better." Or I'd whine about being tired, lacking energy. Her answer would be, "You're talking to the wrong person." Accepting the natural aspects of aging, or the sudden problems caused by heart attack or stroke, is very difficult. You want your parents to go on being your parents forever. It's hard to think about going on without them. Sometimes people don't change for the worse, however; they may change for the better. When I was growing up, my father was a stranger, he was so seldom home; when he was home, he was grumpy, abrupt, and cross. I had said to my sister, years before, "When Dad gets old, who's going to take care of him?" meaning I wasn't. She answered, "Well, I guess I will." You can't believe how my dad has changed. He is so pleasant, so social, so grateful, so undemanding. He hasn't given up on life, even though many of his body parts are wearing out. His aging has changed our relationship for the better, and I'm grateful.

NOTES
1. Marilyn Richardson with J. Ryan Richardson, *We've Got to Do Something about Mother* (Orem, Utah: Empowering People, 1990), 86.
2. Richardson, *We've Got to Do Something*, 53–54.

How Do We Manage a Crisis as an Extended Family?

SUSAN ASHTON, ALLYSON CHARD,
WENDY CHRISTIANSEN, MARGED KIRKPATRICK,
AND ELLEN VAN ORMAN

The family. (Marged) Thirty-six years ago, our mother, Marian Ashton, died of cancer at age forty-three. She left behind her husband, Wendell J. Ashton; four daughters, ages twelve to twenty-one; and two sons, ages ten and six. The year after Mom's death, our father married Belva Barlow, nicknamed BB. A year after their marriage, our youngest sister, Allyson, was born.

The crisis. (Susan) It was a gorgeous Sunday evening on 14 September 1997. The Wendell Ashton family, spouses, and friends had

---

Susan Ashton recently retired after teaching elementary school for more than thirty-one years. She works with the Valiant 12 girls in her ward's Primary organization.

Allyson Ashton Chard has taught part-time at a business college and served on the Minnesota Board of Psychology. She and her husband, Daniel R. Chard, are the parents of three daughters. She serves in her ward as a Sunday School teacher.

Wendy Ashton Christiansen is a former stake missionary, Young Women president, and Relief Society president. She and her husband, Neil Christiansen, have a combined family of nine children and twenty-eight grandchildren. They serve as ward family history workshop coordinators.

Marged Ashton Kirkpatrick is a buyer at O. C. Tanner Company. She is married to Michael K. Kirkpatrick and is the stepmother of two children and the stepgrandmother of four. She serves on the Relief Society General Board.

Ellen Ashton Van Orman has taught second graders for nine years. She and her husband, James Robert Van Orman, are the parents of six children and the grandparents of four. She serves as the Relief Society literacy specialist in her ward.

gathered at my sister Marged's home for an adult family fireside. We had been meeting monthly for years—a tradition BB, our second mother of thirty-six years, had begun. BB was quite late without notifying anyone—not her usual style. After phoning her home several times without getting an answer, we began the meeting without her. But I couldn't concentrate. Where was BB? Finally, I whispered to my good friend Janet, "I am getting worried about BB. Would you come with me?" and Janet and I left. We found BB outside her home on the roughly paved family basketball court. It was a crisp autumn night, and she was dressed in her lightweight morning housecoat. We assumed from her swollen and distorted face that she had suffered a blow to the head. Janet stayed with BB, who was semiconcious, while I went inside to phone 911 and then the family at Marged's.

At the hospital we were told BB had had a stroke. Our father had died of a stroke just three years before. Several of us seven children spent an anxious, frightful night and several days at the hospital as BB seesawed between life and death. Allyson, the youngest (the daughter of Dad and BB), flew in from Minnesota, and Owen came from Chicago. We were pretty shaken. BB was relatively young and had been so well and active. Her unexpected stroke had crushed a bright and vibrant woman. When I returned to my classroom of fourth graders a few days later with BB still in the hospital, I remained unsettled. I explained to my understanding students where I had been for a few days. One student bravely raised her hand and said, "Miss Ashton, look at your shoes!" When I looked down at my feet, I didn't know whether to laugh or cry—I was wearing mismatched shoes! "At least they're both black," I smiled weakly and tried to laugh a little. From time to time all of us face life crises that shake us up. We're thrown off balance. Disoriented and numb, we are likely to set off in our world wearing unmatched shoes. Often with a crisis, there's also a hurdle to jump at a time when we feel the most unsure of our footing. That's what happened to the Ashton family.

Have faith that God will see you through. (Allyson) I was living in Minnesota at the time of my mother's stroke. After I received that unnerving call at midnight from my sister Sue, I immediately flew to Salt Lake City to be with my mother. When I realized that her situation was not one that could be solved in a week-long visit, I had my three daughters join me in Salt Lake, where we lived for the next four months while I helped care for my mother. This meant enrolling my first-grader in a new school, explaining to my four-year-old that she wouldn't be able to begin preschool this year, and wondering how I was going to entertain in a hospital room a one-year-old who was just learning to walk—not to mention abruptly leaving all the activities I was involved in. One morning as I was driving my first-grader to her new school, she broke down and cried, "I hate school. I hate school." I was under so much emotional stress myself that I couldn't deal effectively with this small but very important crisis in my daughter's life. My husband, Dan, supported me from a distance in Minnesota, where he had just started a new job. He visited us once a month. I saw how much my girls missed their father and how lonely Dan was with all of us gone. At times I wondered if helping Mom would destroy my own family. But Heavenly Father heard my prayers and gave me and my family what we needed to get through this challenging time. We made it, and all of us are stronger people because of it.

Make seasonal adjustments. (Wendy) Sometimes in the middle of spring, a freeze will come unexpectedly. Such unfavorable weather can stunt our growth, or it can become a season of strengthening and growth. How do we balance things during the winter storms of our lives so that we do not neglect husband, children, grandchildren, employment, and Church callings? It can become a real juggling act. BB had her stroke not long after my son had begun a series of reconstructive surgeries after a terrible auto accident that his wife and fourteen-month-old son had not survived. Many nights while driving home from the hospital or from BB's care center, I sobbed. I felt guilt for neglecting my husband and daughter at home. I was not fulfilling my Church calling as I wanted to, I was not doing compassionate service in my ward, and other family members were being neglected. Our youngest daughter was engaged to be married, and I did not want to let our family cares eclipse what should have been a season of rejoicing in her young life.

It was "a time to weep, and a time to laugh; a time to mourn, and a time to dance" (Ecclesiastes 3:4)—all at once! What were my priorities, where did I belong, and in what order? What in my life could be set aside for a time, and what must be attended to now? My family and I needed to make "seasonal" adjustments. I had to sit down and make a list of things that could go and things that could not. Decisions took prayer. Some things, like quitting employment, took a lot of faith. These are some of the "seasonal" adjustments my family and I made: I quit work and found other ways to provide health insurance for us. I did only what I could with my Church calling, and other stake missionaries took on some of our responsibilities. I was doing plenty of family compassionate service; ward service could come later, and it has. My husband learned how to bake potatoes and cook pasta; he learned how to run the dishwasher, and he made more beds than I did. My son hired a housekeeper. My daughter did a lot of her own wedding arrangements. The plan worked, the winter season is passing, and in the light of our Savior's love, the spring bulbs have bloomed and I have grown.

Hold family councils. (Wendy) I have learned through these challenges that it takes a lot of prayer, planning, encircling, and family teamwork to survive. Each time our family has been faced with tragedy, we have had family councils to plan and schedule carefully so that every person and thing is properly cared for. For instance, while BB was still in the hospital, we worked out a calendar with someone scheduled to be with BB every noon and every evening. Family councils weave a family and extended family together. Through encircling our stricken mother and other family members, we have become an even closer family, bound together with cords of love. These wonderful sisters are also my best friends. We meet and talk often, comparing ideas and finding solutions that best meet family members' needs.

Be financially and legally prepared. (Marged) Belva was a dynamic, intelligent woman who had served on the Relief Society General Board for sixteen years as well as having been a member of numerous boards of directors. She was a friend and a giver to many. After her stroke, she was suddenly unable to do much of anything, even for herself. Her left side was totally paralyzed. She spoke in a whisper and could barely swallow. She also struggled with short-term memory loss. As her children, we had lots of critical decisions to make. Luckily, BB had prepared well. She had arranged all her legal concerns, such as power of attorney, a will that included a living will, and so on. Her finances and documents were in order. Charles E. Gerrard in a *Deseret News* article warns, "The ability to care for our own personal needs is something most of us take for granted. . . .

"One out of 4 individuals will need some form of long-term care.

"Long-term care assistance is expensive. The average cost of a nursing home stay is more than $37,000 per year in Utah and varies across the United States to $100,000 per year in New York. . . . The average length of a nursing-home stay is about 2.8 years. . . .

"Staying home to receive care is preferable to most. Yet, the daily cost for home health care and community-based care can equal or exceed that of a nursing home."[1]

Listen to others' advice but look to the Lord for direction. (Susan) Many well-meaning and loving people with differing opinions gave us advice. Most of their comments brought comfort, but some prompted guilt and hurt. We knew our decisions had to be based on what was best for BB and our family, so we petitioned the Lord and moved ahead.

We don't know why BB remains earthbound and struggling, but from many experiences we do know that the Lord is at the helm. For instance, from 1985 to 1987, while they were in England presiding over the England London Mission, my parents asked me to take care of their financial affairs. I was nervous but naively committed myself to do the job. BB loved the stock market. She had always been a whiz at setting up financial plans for friends and family members. Plain and simply, she was an astute financial planner and director. From London, BB directed me step-by-step in how to deal with their finances and investment portfolio. When BB had her stroke in 1997, I knew where her financial records were. I knew generally how she liked things handled. I had the knowledge I needed to help manage BB's money matters. In this, as in so much else, I felt a sweet assurance that the Lord was aware of our family situation.

Be tough-skinned. (Marged) We have learned to be very thick-skinned. Well-meaning people concerned about BB's welfare have voiced opinions. Some demand, "How could you put your mother in a care center?" Others ask, "How could you think of taking your mother away from the care center?" To make these important decisions, we have relied on gathering information, holding family councils, and seeking the Lord's guidance. We have received answers to our prayers.

Anticipate a few bumps. (Ellen) Nearly forty years ago, when the family was young and my mother was dying of cancer, Dad assigned each of us household duties—Sue cooked, I cleaned, and Marged, still in elementary school, did all the laundry, including ironing. And that was before permanent press! Our younger brothers did outside jobs, such as raking, clipping, and weeding.

After our mother died, Dad asked our permission to look for a wife and mother. When he married BB, I was excited. Despite my desire to welcome BB into our family, however, the first couple of years of their marriage proved to be a very difficult adjustment for all of us. In my case, after running the house for a year, it was difficult to have someone else take over and tell me what to do. (I'm sure it was even harder for BB because, in all honesty, I was obnoxious at that age.) In many ways, BB was very different from my mother. They had different strengths and different personalities. It took time for us to understand each other's ways. I know Jesus Christ and his teachings are what helped us all hang on through this bumpy time of adjustment.

Expect stages of acceptance. (Ellen) BB has gone through different stages of mourning since she lost her good health so suddenly. The first several days after her stroke, BB thought she was not going to survive. In those first days, she seemed to be preparing to die. She constantly expressed great love and appreciation for all of us children. She also talked a lot about my mother dying and how we must have cared for her when her health failed. She often spoke of my Aunt Betsy, my mother's sister, and how much she loved her. I think she was preparing herself to meet our mother.

The second stage followed her realization that she was going to live, maybe for a long time, trapped in a body that didn't work very well. She experienced anguish and anger. It was difficult for us to see someone who had always been such a spiritual strength be so upset with the Lord. During this time, I just listened to her, but I remember thinking, *What are we going to do to help her through this?* I asked BB what helped her most when she was feeling the worst. She said that it was remembering her mother's strength through many trials. Alone, her mother faced her trials with faith and courage. BB said that she wanted to be like her mother.

The third stage has been acceptance of her circumstances. This ongoing stage has been the longest. She loves the Lord and is grateful for her many blessings, including a circle of friends and family who help her endure. She is facing her pain and other trials with courage and faith just as she had hoped—as her mother did. She is receiving love and care, and she is giving love and care.

Recognize that families don't need to be perfect to be unified. (Allyson) I did not grow up in a traditional family setting. I grew up in a blended family, the only child born to my mother. I had six half-siblings. The child closest to my age was nine years older; Wendy, the eldest child, was married and had three children before I was even born.

Although we were a supportive family who cared for one another, blending two families always causes dynamic issues. My mother as the stepmother and I as a half-sister did not always experience feelings of complete unity in my family. At times, I felt lonely and sad. I prayed often for a closer relationship with my brothers and sisters.

When Mother had her stroke, I stayed in Utah four months to care for her. That stay was one of the most emotionally trying times I have yet experienced. When I returned home, I felt trapped in Minnesota when I felt I needed to be with my mother in Salt Lake City. While I was in Minnesota, however, my siblings in Salt Lake encircled their stepmother with love. Each day one of them would visit Mother to spend either lunchtime or dinnertime with her. They spent hours rubbing her aching feet and legs, heating her chilled body with a blow dryer, and reading to her. Stepchild bonded to stepmother. My siblings' love and daily care for Mother made me feel bonded with them in a way I never had before.

No family is perfect. Some of you may be thinking, *My family can never be unified.* Or, *my family members are all too different.* Or, *I don't know if I want to be eternally linked with my older sister or my mother-in-law.* Heavenly Father is aware of our individual family situations. He knows that in some families individuals may be unfairly hurt by other family members. We are promised, however, that if we remain faithful to Jesus Christ, no blessing will be held from us in the eternities, even that blessing of a loving family unit. I now affectionately refer to my family as the "chain gang." Although we may not have perfect links on our chain, through this trial we have become a stronger family. I look forward to an eternal reunion with our father, our two mothers, and all of us children.

NOTE

1. Charles E. Gerrard, "Long-Term Care—Act Now," *Deseret News*, 18 April 1999, M-1.

How Do We Face Challenges as a Couple?

MARGARETH COSTA,
DORALEE MADSEN, AND MARILYN S. BATEMAN

Marry someone who values both you and your goals. (Margareth) I joined the Church in Brazil when I was fourteen years old, and everything changed in my life—my lifestyle, my habits, my friends, and my way of thinking. From that time on, I began to plan a future and work toward goals. The most important goal was to marry a faithful priesthood holder, firm in the Church and in the gospel. Elder James E. Faust served in Brazil at that time, and at our firesides I truly loved to hear him talk about his wife, Ruth. Afterwards, I would think, *I want to marry someone who will say that I am wonderful—someone who will respect and love me in the same way Elder Faust speaks about his wife.* I want you to know that this happened. Although I am not perfect, my husband says I am, and I almost believe him.

Accept the comfort of the Lord. (Margareth) In 1990 my husband was called to preside over a newly created mission in the vast Amazon

Margareth Costa and her husband, Claudio R. M. Costa, a member of the Second Quorum of Seventy, are the parents of four children. Formerly a ward and stake Primary president, she serves with her husband, who is a member of the Brazil North Area presidency.

Doralee D. Madsen and her husband, Richard H. Madsen, have ten children and twenty-one grandchildren. She is a graduate of the University of Utah, teaches private violin lessons, and serves as a Relief Society teacher in her ward.

Marilyn S. Bateman, wife of Brigham Young University president Merrill J. Bateman, is a mother and grandmother. She has served in leadership and teaching positions in ward and stake auxiliaries. The Batemans are the parents of seven children and the grandparents of twenty.

region. I was only thirty-four and had four small children—Moroni was ten; Moses, eight; Camille, seven; and Marianna, one year. My husband was forty, full of joy and a great energy for the work. He was constantly traveling by airplane because there were no roads. I had to stay home to receive calls from the missionaries and tend our children. It was hard to be without my husband. We have always been good friends, talking a lot and enjoying each other's company. But when he traveled, an interesting thing happened. I would tuck the children in bed and go to my bedroom to study the scriptures, read, and write letters. At some point, I would get up and walk to the balcony to look at the sky and the stars and listen to the sounds of the night coming from a small grove nearby. I truly thought the Amazon was a paradise on earth and that the Lord had kept his generous hand over that place while creating it. Without thinking, I started to talk out loud to the Lord, pouring out my inner feelings and my joy for living in such an amazing place. I was alone, but I never felt lonely or left behind. I felt the power of the Holy Ghost guiding and directing my life and my mission. Whenever my husband came back home, we were happy to be with each other again. Each temporary separation always drew us closer together.

Expect challenges. (Margareth) Sometimes we pay a high price for doing the right things. I never worked so much in my life as I did during our mission in the Amazon. It was full-dedication work, and we learned so much from the people we came to love so dearly. Our children were very happy there. They also learned to love and respect the people of that land. It was hard to finish the mission and come back home. I missed it terribly.

Then my husband was called into the Second Quorum of the Seventy, and we were transferred to Argentina. He spoke some Spanish, but our children and I spoke only Portuguese. Their high school classes were taught in Spanish in the morning and English in the afternoon. Our children spoke neither. Our oldest son returned to Brazil to live with my parents to complete school. Our life was turned upside down. The children never complained, but they missed their friends. We prayed together and asked the Lord to bless us, because the challenges have seemed overwhelming. Accompanying my husband in all his assignments has not been an easy task. I have felt inadequate many times, facing other people who seem more qualified and prepared than I. On the other hand, I know the Lord qualifies whom he calls.[1] I love my Savior and even in difficult times, I feel the comfort and the assurance that come only from his love.

Commit yourself to the Lord. (Doralee) During the springtime of my life, I went on Tuesday evenings to what was called MIA, and during opening exercises we would stand and repeat a theme or a scripture for the month. One scripture stood out in my mind: "Choose you this day whom ye will serve; . . . but as for me and my house, we will serve the Lord" (Joshua 24:15). When Richard and I married, that scripture stood as a guiding principle for our family. Problems arose, but our principles remained constant. We were committed. We were going to serve the Lord and look to him for strength in whatever we needed to face. We have felt confident, knowing that through trial and error, since we've already chosen whom to serve, we will accomplish what the Lord has in store for us.

Agree to disagree. (Doralee) The summertime of life was not always sunny. Sudden storms blew in, and rain clouds hung heavy over the house at times. We lost a much-wanted baby before its due date, and we were blessed with a lot of teenagers and their problems. Not unusual, is it? These were growing years for us as a couple. We did not always agree on which course to take, and yet we loved each other enough to agree to disagree, as we hammered out our parenting skills. I remember living with a knot in my chest many days during those summer years. We found comfort in knowing that we were not alone in our struggles. Others had passed through similar circumstances and survived, and we would, too.

Make time for each other. (Doralee) Richard and I had been married for eternity, but it seemed as if we were being separated for time. Busy schedules and more children arriving in our home meant we had less time to spend with each other. It's strange to look back and realize that during this season of our lives, some of our younger children actually thought their father's name was "Bishop." Richard and I connected by talking on the telephone at least once a day. I looked forward to those brief phone calls because with a family that eventually included ten children, sometimes that was the only private time we had together. Now

341

that we are older, Richard and I still schedule our calendars together every week. Sometimes I keep the midnight oil burning quite a bit longer than he does, and when I go to bed, I will find Post-it notes to me, or newspaper articles he thinks I will be interested in. It's another way of communicating. One night a newly returned missionary son stopped by at dinnertime and found only the two of us having dinner together. He had been used to the table being surrounded. "Well," he said, "this is certainly strange!" That's true, but I'm glad that Richard and I in these autumn years aren't looking across the table saying, "Who are you? You look strange!"

Realize that marriage is not easy. (Marilyn) The marriage relationship is never static. It is constantly changing and, hopefully, growing as two people—a man and a woman—strive to fit all facets of their beings together. I must add that the blending of lives together is not an easy or instant process. A passage from my journal written after twenty-eight years of marriage reads: "Today is our anniversary. I am really grateful for Merrill. We have both grown a lot in the years we have been together. I guess a good marriage does not come about overnight. It takes years of maturing and a lot of give and take. Each year seems better than the last. Merrill is very good to me. He tries hard to be a good companion—in his way. One of the challenges of married life is in not expecting one's own way of thinking and doing to be the same as that of your spouse— even after twenty-eight years of marriage."

Commit and recommit yourselves to each other. (Marilyn) Husbands need the support of their wives, and wives need the support of their husbands—especially in spiritual matters. In fact, according to Elder Boyd K. Packer, man and woman receive the fulness of the blessings of the priesthood together or not at all.[2] An incident recorded in the diary of Wilford Woodruff illustrates how in an eternal marriage the spirits of husband and wife are interdependent. During his wife's serious illness after the birth of their baby, Wilford "spent the day in taking care of her" but to no avail. Phoebe "seemed to be sinking gradually, and in the evening the spirit apparently left her body. . . . The sisters gathered around, weeping, while I stood looking at her in sorrow," President Woodruff said. And then unexpectedly, "for the first time during her sickness, faith filled my soul. . . . I then bowed down before the Lord, prayed for the life of my companion, . . . anointed her body with [consecrated] oil" and "rebuked the power of death." Miraculously, Phoebe's "spirit returned to her body, and from that hour she was made whole."

As she afterwards related to him, her spirit had left her body, and she saw her body "lying upon the bed and the sisters there weeping. She looked at them and at me and upon her babe; while gazing upon this scene, two persons came into the room carrying a coffin and told her they had come for her body. One of these messengers said to her that she might have her choice—she might go to rest in the spirit world, or, upon one condition, she might have the privilege of returning to her tabernacle and continuing her labors upon the earth. The condition was that if she felt she could stand by her husband, and with him pass through all the cares, trials, tribulations and afflictions of life which he would be called upon to pass through for the gospel's sake until the end she might return." Gazing upon the plight of her husband and child, she made her decision: "Yes, I will do it." That was the moment President Woodruff felt the power of faith fill his soul. Her decision to recommit to be his companion led and empowered him to rebuke the power of death. "When I administered to her, her spirit re-entered her tabernacle, and she saw the messengers carry the coffin out the door."[3] Marriage is a holy and sacred covenant that we have made together. We need each other, and we need to be committed to each other. No man or woman can reach perfection and exaltation in God's eternal kingdom alone.

Value your marriage. (Marilyn) A marriage does not succeed automatically. As I reflect on my own marriage of forty years, I realize that no matter how successful our relationships might be, there will always be challenges. Happy, secure, and successful marriages reflect the price paid to make them so. Unfortunately, marriage is under attack in America. As an institution, it means different things to different people until both the definition of marriage and the price required for its success are being obscured. To counter these trends, The Church of Jesus Christ of Latter-day Saints issued a proclamation to the world regarding marriage and families. That proclamation "affirm[s] the sanctity of life. . . . Husband and wife have a solemn responsibility to love and care for each other and for their children." Moreover, "children are entitled to birth within the bonds of matrimony, and to be reared by a father and a mother who honor marital vows with complete fidelity."[4] Marriage is the critical relationship in a family. Generally, as the marriage goes, so goes the family. President Gordon B. Hinckley has said, "If husbands and wives would only give great emphasis to the virtues that are to be found in one another and less to the faults, there would be fewer broken hearts, fewer tears, fewer divorces, and much more happiness in the homes of our people."[5]

NOTES

1. See Thomas S. Monson, *Ensign*, May 1988, 43.
2. See Boyd K. Packer, "A Tribute to Women," *Ensign*, July 1989, 74–75.
3. *Wilford Woodruff, History of His Life and Labors*, comp. Matthias F. Cowley (1909; Salt Lake City: Bookcraft, 1964), 97–98.
4. First Presidency and Quorum of the Twelve Apostles of The Church of Jesus Christ of Latter-day Saints, "The Family: A Proclamation to the World," *Ensign*, November 1995, 102.
5. *Teachings of Gordon B. Hinckley* (Salt Lake City: Deseret Book, 1997), 322.

How Do We Nurture Marriage in Adversity?

SHAUNA EWING

Understand that without adversity there is no joy. Had Adam and Eve not transgressed by partaking of the forbidden fruit, they would have remained in the Garden of Eden and they would have had "no misery" (2 Nephi 2:23). And yet, remaining in the garden would have also meant that Adam and Eve would have known no joy. Without trials— without sorrow, unfulfilled dreams, and pain—we cannot experience joy.

On 25 June 1987, when Terrell and I were sealed in the Manti Temple, I was happy beyond my dreams. After a sweet courtship, I knew I had married a prince. Terrell had been sick with mononucleosis before we met, but I didn't realize how sick he still was until after we were married. As a student at Brigham Young University in our first years of marriage, Terrell struggled with chronic fatigue syndrome, back-to-back respiratory infections, headaches, and horrible fatigue. By the time he graduated, he had begun to feel better, even though potentially more serious symptoms had appeared: short-term memory loss, slurred speech, and involuntary movements that made walking and balance difficult. In 1992 after we had been married only five years, Terrell was finally diagnosed with Huntington's Chorea, a hereditary, degenerative brain disease. There is no cure, and the condition is fatal. In one moment of terrible revelation, our dreams turned to dust, and our lives were in

Shauna Ewing is a software quality control engineer. She is also a mother, wife, homemaker, and full-time caretaker for her husband, Terrell Ewing, who has special needs. She serves as a Primary teacher in her ward.

turmoil. The knowledge that our two children were at risk of inheriting this disease greatly increased our feelings of helplessness and fear. Difficult decisions had to be made. I had to turn my job into a career, and Terrell had to give up his hopes of a law profession and become the house daddy. There were a lot of adjustments, tears, and anger, but we held on to hope and Christ's atonement.

Four years later, we learned of an experimental procedure that had some potential for patients with Huntington's Chorea. We decided we must take the risk of the brain surgery. Though the doctors pronounced Terrell fine after the three-hour operation, he would not wake up. An MRI revealed a hemorrhage deep in the left side of his brain. I can't put into words the pain and fear I felt as I waited another three hours for the surgeons to go back in and stop the bleeding. He had a will to live, or we would have lost him. The hemorrhage resulted in major damage to his speech center and right-side mobility. Together we spent the next seven months getting him well enough to come back home. It was a long, hard journey back. It took a huge emotional and physical toll on our family, but with the help of medical personnel, family, friends, and a loving Heavenly Father, the journey was possible and even joyous.

Build and maintain trust. Our marriage took a beating after Terrell's diagnosis. To the world he was Mister Positive, but with me he started becoming reclusive. The more I pushed, the quieter he got. We began seeing traits in each other that we didn't like. After some intense conversations, we learned that we were dealing with our pain in very different ways. We realized we had to allow for the ugly times and provide for each other a safe place to hurt and to heal. That was a conscious choice, and following through on it was not easy; however, working through that experience with trust and love made us one. We have never questioned the validity of our marriage since.

Learn to communicate. Because of the damage to Terrell's speech center, the art of communication has become a key part of our marriage. In fact, we've mastered charades. One day Terrell was pointing to a picture of the Manti Temple and then pointed to me and then to himself. I tried to understand, but it wasn't until I prayed later, while I was doing dishes, that the answer came. As soon as I said, "Heavenly Father, I need help with this," I immediately knew that Terrell had forgotten some important things having to do with the temple ceremony. I thanked the Lord and then went to Terrell and asked if the things that came to my mind were what he was trying to tell me. Terrell gave me the big thumbs up, obviously excited that I had finally figured it out. When Terrell and I were first married, we very quickly realized that we expressed ourselves differently. He had to process information before speaking, and I attacked it with the ramming speed of speech. Sometimes I would misunderstand something, and he would say, "Shauna, you took that totally wrong; that is not what I meant. If you knew my heart, you would know that." Now I have no choice but to do what I should have done better while he had the ability to speak, and that is to continually pray to understand exactly what he is saying. How many problems can be avoided when we seek to understand the heart.

How Do I Teach Children to Search, Ponder, and Pray?

Myra Tollestrup

Search the scriptures. One cardinal rule of good teaching is never to tell a child what he can be led to discover for himself. That rule comple-ments the often repeated admonition of prophets, apostles, and indeed our Savior himself, to search the scriptures. Searching implies that you are looking for something—an attractive idea to children—and also an expectation that you will find it—another exciting concept. Searching requires investing something of yourself in the endeavor, and that invest-ment creates a link to the task. The child who has sought after an answer and found it will value his discovery above any truth told to him by another person, however wise or well meaning that person may be. In our homes, then, we might decide to search the scriptures as a family instead of reading the scriptures as a family. The important first step to valuing the scriptures is to establish the searching approach to them.

Ponder the scriptures. When I was a child, my family lived on a farm in southern Alberta. We had no television; we didn't even have a tele-phone. Cars and roads being what they were then, we did not make many trips into town. My mother was not always going somewhere. She taught me to embroider, knit, and crochet, and we did it together as we talked. She taught me to bake and cook and can, and we did it together as we talked. When I was a preschooler, German prisoners of war worked

Myra J. Tollestrup has taught in a private school for children with learning disabilities and served as chair of the Okanagan University College Board in Kelowna, British Columbia, Canada. She is the mother of seven children and works with the BYU–Public School Partnership. She serves as the Primary chorister in her ward.

on our farm. One of them spent his lunch hours making dandelion necklaces for me because he said I reminded him of his own little girl in Germany. I found it difficult to understand why he was there when his family was in Germany. Mom took time to talk to me and tried to explain war in four-year-old terms. I thought about what she said. We had neighbors who were Japanese, and we talked about why their food was different from ours, and I thought about differences. One summer all the farmers around joined in coyote hunts, and we talked about why anyone would want to kill baby coyotes. We read Bible stories, and we talked about how someone as small as David could kill a giant.

What has all that to do with pondering? Pondering is the ability to think deeply about things. The ability to reflect must be carefully nurtured in children and young people; it involves measuring and sifting ideas and requires comparing new concepts to personal standards and ideas. One of the best ways to encourage pondering is to take the time to help your child develop a store of beliefs and ideas against which to examine new thoughts he may encounter. My mother took my questions and concerns not as opportunities to tell me what to think but as an opportunity to present beliefs and ideas to challenge my thinking and stimulate my mind. The best way to stimulate thinking is simply to take time to talk. Conversation is, without doubt, the most tragic sacrifice we have laid on the altars of the television god. As mothers we need to encourage our children's propensity to ponder and reflect by ensuring that our time and theirs is available for meaningful conversation. Conversations, not lectures from us nor lessons in school, lead children to become reflective.

Pray about the scriptures. Prayer, the companion of pondering, invites the presence of the Holy Spirit, which adds light to our ponderings. Elder Boyd K. Packer described the process of receiving answers to prayer: "I have come to know that inspiration comes more as a feeling than as a sound. . . . The Lord has a way of pouring pure intelligence into our minds to prompt us, to guide us, to teach us, to warn us. You can know the things you need to know *instantly*. Learn to receive inspiration."[1]

NOTE

1 Boyd K. Packer, *Ensign*, November 1979, 20; also in Boyd K. Packer, *That All May Be Edified* (Salt Lake City: Bookcraft, 1982), 11–12.

How Do I Keep and Teach Sacred Values?

SYDNEY SMITH REYNOLDS

Getting caught, getting taught. A friend of mine was about five years old when she went with her family to the store to buy little packs of treats because cousins were coming over. She said, "I remember thinking to myself, *I could just slip this package into my coat and we wouldn't have to pay for it. That would save my mom some money.* I thought I was being clever. When we got to the parking lot, I pulled out the cookies and said, 'Look!' I will never forget the look of horror on my mom's face. She grabbed the cookies, ran back into the store, and returned them. I wanted never to do anything that would make her feel that way again." Be grateful when you catch a situation early and can seize the teaching moment—whatever it costs in time, energy, or embarrassment. It is the children who don't get caught early or who don't have to face up to the moral consequence who really should be pitied.

The responsibility to teach is ours. As President Gordon B. Hinckley said, "I believe our problems, almost every one, arise out of the homes of the people. If there is to be reformation, if there is to be a change, if there is to be a return to old and sacred values, it must begin in the home. It is here that truth is learned, that integrity is cultivated, that self-discipline is instilled, and that love is nurtured."[1]

Sydney Smith Reynolds, who has served as a counselor in the Primary General Presidency, received her bachelor's degree from Brigham Young University and did graduate studies in history and educational psychology. She has written the Sharing Time page for the Friend *and is a member of the Timpanogos Storytelling Festival Board. She and her husband, Noel B. Reynolds, are the parents of eleven children.*

Instill self-imposed monitors. In these days when the problems and perversions of the whole world can enter our homes at the click of a button, we must find ways to ensure our children develop internal, or self-imposed, monitors. We cannot always be there, nor would we want to be. In addition to teaching by precept and example, we must allow children to make decisions appropriate to their age and help them invite and identify the Spirit in their own lives. In front of me in a check-out line was a mother with her little boy. She said, "You've been so good—you can pick any treat you want." He reached for one, and she said, "Oh, no, that's too messy." He chose another; she said, "Oh, no, you didn't like that one last time." Once more he reached out, and she said, "Don't you think it's too warm a day for chocolate?" Finally, he stood there with his hands hanging down while she chose a treat for him. How can we teach children to be responsible for their own decisions if we won't let them make decisions to be responsible for?

Model honorable behavior. An important component of our integrity is what we do when we are confronted with the need to repent. In *Hamlet*, King Claudius recognizes that his offense against heaven is rank, but he cannot pray "forgive me my foul murder" because he realizes that he still wants the ill-gotten gains of the murder, namely, "my crown, mine own ambition, and my queen," more than he wants forgiveness. He attempts to pray but ultimately admits, "My words fly up, my thoughts remain below; / Words without thoughts never to heaven go."[2] In other words, I don't really mean what I am saying; I don't really want to repent. Note the contrast when the father of King Lamoni realizes that he is a murderer and a sinner. He prays, "O God, . . . if there is a God, . . . I will give away all my sins to know thee" (Alma 22:18). In other words, I will repent, whatever the cost.[3] How do parents teach values? By example. We are the examples most closely observed by our children, and children are amazingly observant of cutting corners.

Notes
1. Gordon B. Hinckley, *Ensign*, November 1998, 99.
2. William Shakespeare, *Hamlet*, act III, scene iii, lines 52, 55, 97–98.
3. This comparison was pointed out by BYU English professor John Tanner.

The Great Power of Small Things

MARY ELLEN SMOOT

I wonder if sometimes we underestimate how much influence we are having and how much difference each one of us can make in our homes, our families, our wards, our communities, and even the world. Important work is being done—often one on one—by sisters just like you and me, for "by small and simple things are great things brought to pass" (Alma 37:6). It is critical that we never forget the one. As President Gordon B. Hinckley has said, "We are becoming a great global society. But our interest and concern must always be with the individual. Every member of this church is an individual man or woman, boy or girl."[1]

I learned this principle of the importance of the one as a mother. I spent many spring and summer afternoons on the sidelines with other mothers visiting my way through baseball games. But whenever it was my son's turn at bat, I stopped visiting and paid close attention. It was his turn to shine, his opportunity to make a play, and in that moment the team depended on him. Sometimes he walked to first base, sometimes he struck out, sometimes he made a base hit, and once in a while he hit a home run. Each turn gave him a new chance to make a difference in the game. His individual contribution mattered, and his participation helped him grow. But each time he took his turn at bat, I held my breath and hoped for the best.

Sisters, spiritually speaking, in the game of life it is our turn at bat.

Mary Ellen Wood Smoot has served as Relief Society General President since April 1997. She loves family history and research and has written histories of parents, grandparents, and their local community. She served with her husband, Stanley M. Smoot, when he was called as a mission president in Ohio, and they later served together as directors of Church Hosting. They are the parents of seven children and grandparents of forty-seven.

How we approach the plate, swing the bat, and follow the coach's instructions will make all the difference in this final inning of the world. But this is more than a game—it's a battle, and we must build and stretch our spiritual muscles if we are to further the Lord's cause. To contribute we must increase our faith in Jesus Christ through repentance, obedience, and sacrifice; we can also learn to pray powerfully many times during the day; and we can recognize revelation and act on the impressions that come from the Holy Ghost. The Lord wants all of us to understand his word, which requires us to ponder the scriptures each day.

We can do better in how we treat each other. As members of an organization with a mission, we cannot afford to criticize, tear down, or complain about any other sister. If you have issues with someone, work them out. Ask for the Lord's help to recognize your part and repent; then forgive and forget. Each person's unique spiritual gifts and abilities are needed. In other words, the time to practice is over, the game has begun, and we are each a vital member of the team, sent to this time in history with a specific job to do. The work of Relief Society moves forward one sister at a time. In our 1998 general Relief Society meeting, President Gordon B. Hinckley gave prophetic counsel to the women of the Church: "Each of you is a part of this vast enterprise, the Relief Society, a great family of sisters, more than four million strong. In your worldwide membership lies the power to accomplish incalculable good." He issued this challenge: "Rise up, O women of Zion, rise to the great challenge which faces you."[2]

Those words struck deep in my heart. I had the profound feeling that our prophet was asking us, the women of the Church, to magnify our role in a way we have never considered. As sure as Moroni waved the title of liberty to unite his people in battle (Alma 46:12–13), our prophet has called each individual sister in Relief Society to take her place in the battlefield of the twenty-first century, realizing that women of covenant must be different from the women of the world. We can be crucial to preserving the family, and we must make a difference in the world. He is confident that we will.

Perhaps you felt as I did—thrilled at the confidence he placed in us, yet frightened by the responsibility. I reflected on my paternal great-great-grandmother Sarah Stoddard, who years ago made her own decision to be a woman of covenant. From her history, I learned that the call to leave Nauvoo and travel west came just one month after she had given birth to her sixth child. She was in no physical condition for a difficult journey. The baby was new, and she had yet to regain her health and strength. I can see her in my mind, trying to decide between staying, for a while longer at least, in her familiar and comfortable surroundings or once again walking away from a home and most of their belongings to travel with her husband and young children to a place the Prophet Joseph, who was no longer there to lead them, had seen only in vision.

It could not have been an easy decision, but decide she did. She packed their things and with her family began the first leg of the trek west. I imagine her emotions as she turned for one last look at her home in Nauvoo and saw it in flames.

Her journey west did not last long. She died along the way. Five weeks later the baby died. And a short time after that, her husband died as well. The three are buried in a small gravesite in Montrose, Illinois. The five orphaned children alone continued to Salt Lake. My great-grandfather, Charles Henry Stoddard, was the eldest of the five remaining children.

Women of the world might say that my grandmother made the wrong decision. But women of covenant know she made the right one. She probably gave no thought to the power of her faithful example, but she laid the foundation of her testimony in my great-grandfather, who passed it to my grandmother, who passed it to my father, who then passed it to me. I only hope that I have been able to carry on the tradition and pass these seeds of faith to our children, who, we hope, will pass them on to theirs. Many blessings have flowed from Grandmother Stoddard's decision to follow a prophet.

So, what about you and me, we who are the pioneers of the next century? What will be written about us? Do we understand our role and mission as Latter-day Saint women? I can almost hear you say, "Can I really make a difference? I am only one, and my contribution isn't great." In Romans we are told, "For as by one man's [or woman's] disobedience many were made sinners, so by the obedience of one shall many be made righteous" (Romans 5:19).

I testify that each of us is part of the great work that President

Hinckley envisioned. As each faithful sister quietly surrenders her will to the Lord, she becomes a pure vessel he can work through. Critical events in the world turn on very tiny hinges. Actions that may seem small and insignificant at the moment will change the outcome of the battle. In Alma we are taught, "Now ye may suppose that this is foolishness in me; but behold I say unto you, that by small and simple things are great things brought to pass; and small means in many instances doth confound the wise" (Alma 37:6).

Let me give you an example. Ammon was sent to the Lamanites to teach them the gospel. He became a servant to the king and was blessed by the Lord to earn the king's confidence. Ammon taught King Lamoni the plan of salvation and redemption. The king believed all his words and cried, "O Lord, have mercy; according to thy abundant mercy which thou hast had upon the people of Nephi" (Alma 18:41). As he said these words, he fell to the ground as if dead. Servants carried his body to the queen, who was baffled by his condition.

When he did not revive after two days, the queen, hearing that Ammon was "a prophet of a holy God," sent for him to tell her what to do. Ammon reassured her that her husband was not dead but was caught up in the Spirit: "He sleepeth in God" (Alma 19:4, 8). The queen immediately believed in his words, and Ammon exclaimed, "Blessed art thou because of thy exceeding faith; I say unto thee, woman, there has not been such great faith among all the people of the Nephites." When King Lamoni awoke the next day and saw his queen, he stretched forth his hand and said, "Blessed be the name of God, and blessed art thou." After he told her of his vision of the Redeemer, she too fell to the ground "overpowered with joy," as again did the king, and then also Ammon and the servants who had witnessed these events (Alma 19:10, 12, 14).

Imagine the scene: the rulers of a nation perceived dead, a man rumored to be a powerful prophet also stricken. What would you think?

In walked Abish, a woman, a humble servant, "having been converted unto the Lord for many years . . . , and never having made it known, therefore, when she saw that all the servants of Lamoni had fallen to the earth, and also her mistress, the queen, and the king, . . . she *knew* that it was the power of God" (Alma 19:16–17; emphasis added).

She was prompted to do a simple thing. She ran from house to house, telling the people what had happened. She knew that a miracle was in the making. A multitude soon arrived and witnessed a scene that changed their destiny. When contention arose among the onlookers over what looked to be a calamity, Abish took the queen by the hand that perhaps she might wake her; as soon as she touched the queen's hand, the queen arose and stood upon her feet. After speaking of her experience but not being understood, the queen then took her husband by the hand. He arose with a new heart and a message for his people. Because of this experience, an entire nation became converted to the gospel (see Alma 19:29–30).

Abish, our sister, in the right place, at the right time, listening and acting on the promptings of the Spirit, did incalculable good. And so can you and I.

I am grateful for the scriptures and the powerful influence they can have in our lives. Have you ever thought where we would be without them? Are we taking the time to feast upon the words of Christ? President Gordon B. Hinckley has said: "I love our scriptures. I love these wonderful volumes, which set forth the word of the Lord—given personally or through prophets—for the guidance of our Father's sons and daughters. I love to read the scriptures, and I try to do so consistently and repeatedly. I like to quote from them, for they give the voice of authority to that which I say. I do not claim distinction as a scholar of the scriptures. For me, the reading of the scriptures is not the pursuit of scholarship. Rather, it is a love affair with the word of the Lord and that of his prophets. They contain so much for each of us."[3]

Think of your favorite passage of scripture. Perhaps it is Lehi's message of the tree of life; perhaps it is Enos and his experience with prayer. Maybe you love to read about the birth of the Savior or his Sermon on the Mount. We are highly favored to have this instruction at our fingertips. I testify that we will draw closer to the Lord as we seek it. Along with reading ourselves, we can each encourage others in gospel literacy and learning.

There are many ways to study. Each of us has probably read 1 Nephi a hundred times. You know what happens: we resolve to read, and then we stop, so we start over again. We don't need to start over. We can pick up right where we left off; or we might want to change tactics and study by topic or principle. If we need encouragement, we can find a friend and study together, or even share thoughts over the phone or by e-mail. Let's share our feelings about what we read and make our talks and walks full of the gospel of Jesus Christ.

Scripture study will bless our lives as we gain understanding of God's laws. Through our obedience to his commandments, we will increase in personal righteousness, which opens the door to the blessings of heaven. President Joseph F. Smith said: "God will honor those who honor him, and will remember those who remember him. He will uphold and sustain all those who sustain truth and are faithful to it. God help us, therefore, to be faithful to the truth, now and forever."[4] Obedience to gospel principles is essential if we are to lead the women of the world to Jesus Christ. Our good example will make a critical difference in the lives of everyone we know. The Lord needs each one of us, and he is waiting for us to give ourselves to him. We do that by being obedient and submissive to his will.

C. S. Lewis suggests, "Christ says, 'Give me All. I don't want so much of your time and so much of your money and so much of your work: I want You. I have not come to torment your natural self, but to kill it. No half-measures are any good. I don't want to cut off a branch here and a branch there, I want to have the whole tree down. I don't want to drill the tooth, or crown it, or stop it, but to have it out. Hand over the whole natural self, all the desires which you think innocent as well as the ones you think wicked—the whole outfit. I will give you a new self instead. In fact, I will give you Myself: my own will shall become yours.'"[5]

We are the women President Kimball was referring to when he said: "To be a righteous woman is a glorious thing in any age. To be a righteous woman during the winding up scenes on this earth, before the second coming of our Savior, is an especially noble calling. The righteous woman's strength and influence today can be tenfold what it might be in more tranquil times. She has been placed here to help to enrich, to protect, and to guard the home—which is society's basic and most noble institution."[6]

We need to look frequently at the Proclamation on the Family. Our leaders have asked us to read and understand and speak out in defense of the family, as outlined by the First Presidency. Ponder the significant role you play in the success of your marriage, home, and even your extended family. Make your family an example of what the Lord intended families to be.

It isn't always easy to keep an eternal perspective as we run from the grocery store to ball games. It's hard to feel close to husbands when we divide just to conquer a Saturday full of activities. Some of us are single parents trying to fill both roles. Some of us are single and yearn for the problems I am speaking about. I am aware of the problems and difficulties that you face, and so is your Heavenly Father. I know how you feel because I've been there. But the more we focus on our problems, the bigger they will seem. Several years ago I was buried in laundry, dishes, and housework. I had six children in eight years. My husband was involved in demanding Church callings, and he was also building a business. Those were the days of empty bank accounts and hand-me-down clothes. It was easy to get discouraged and feel that life was passing me by. I often wondered, "What about me? When is it my turn?" I felt a lot like a cartoon I recently saw in the newspaper: a mother was standing over a sink full of dishes and talking on the phone while trying to fix a bottle for a crying baby who was hanging on one of her legs. A little child was holding a book, coaxing her for a story, while pulling on her mother's other leg. Another child had climbed a stool and with a glass in hand was begging for a drink. Another little girl was standing at the doorway of the kitchen pleading, "Can Emily come and stay with us? Her mommy works!"

One day I was visiting my mother, who was dying of cancer. I was feeling overwhelmed. I was torn between supporting my husband, caring for my young family, and spending time with my mother. My mother lifted my spirits as she said, "Aren't you blessed to have such beautiful children? Look at how healthy and strong they are. Aren't you blessed to have a husband who loves the Lord and serves him?"

Through her counsel, I recognized the need to appreciate what I had and even to repent. My focus shifted quickly as she quietly taught me that an attitude of gratitude can make the difference in how we feel about life. It is up to us to adjust to our situations and focus on blessings and solutions, not just on our problems.

I have found that a feeling of sincere gratitude invites peace. And one of the best ways I know to invite a spirit of gratitude into our hearts is to kneel in sincere prayer. Every one of us can find something that we can be grateful for. The prophet Alma urged, "Counsel with the Lord in all thy doings, and he will direct thee for good; yea, and when thou liest down at night lie down unto the Lord, that he may watch over you in your sleep; and when thou risest in the morning let thy heart be full of thanks unto God; and if ye do these things, ye shall be lifted up at the last day" (Alma 37:37). Practicing an attitude of gratitude has lightened my burdens many times.

I learned another significant lesson during this time in my life. One night, after a long, discouraging day, I knelt in prayer and poured out my heart to my Heavenly Father. After I had rehearsed my plight, I closed my prayer and opened my mind and heart. I will never forget the clear message the Spirit sent me that night: "Forget yourself, and think of others."

The principle of service burned bright in my heart. I thought of the example of service the Savior set, and I had a desire to follow him. I had been taught an important lesson. There is always someone who is suffering more than we are, if we will just take a minute to think about it.

Mother Teresa tells this story: "One night a man came to our house and told me, 'There is a family with eight children. They have not eaten for days.' I took some food with me and went.

"When I came to that family, I saw the faces of those little children disfigured by hunger. There was no sorrow or sadness in their faces, just the deep pain of hunger.

"I gave the rice to the mother. She divided the rice in two, and went out, carrying half the rice. When she came back, I asked her, 'Where did you go?' She gave me this simple answer, 'To my neighbors—they are hungry also!'

" . . . I was not surprised that she gave, because poor people are really very generous. But I was surprised that she knew they were hungry. As a rule, when we are suffering, we are so focused on ourselves we have no time for others. This woman showed something of the truly generous love of Christ."[7]

All the women of the Relief Society can set important examples of devoted service. I recently spoke at a meeting after which I met and visited with a lovely woman. She said, "Sister Smoot, I am here because of a wonderful Relief Society president who played an essential role in the lives of my family. My mother had a nervous breakdown and spent my growing-up years in a hospital. My father was trying to raise us and provide for us at the same time, and it was not easy. This dear Relief Society president always sent a loaf of bread across the street every time she baked. When she bottled fruit, she would send ten quarts to us. She often came over while we were away and cleaned our house. We were not members of the Church. None of us joined the Church while she was alive. I hope she knows that through her example all four of us children are now active members of the Church because of her example and service."

That Relief Society sister never saw the fruits of her labor in this life, just as my great-great-grandmother did not. But charity never faileth, and its influence can span generations. Think of the good that will pass from one generation to the next because a Relief Society sister cared about a family in need. And we can follow her example.

You may be thinking to yourself, *How can I know what the Lord would have me do for him?* Elder Henry B. Eyring said, "You could, this moment, begin to think of those for whom you bear responsibility. If you do, and do it with the intent to serve them, a face or name will come to you. If you do something today and make some attempt to help that person come unto Christ, I cannot promise you a miracle, but I can promise you this: you will feel the influence of the Holy Ghost helping you; and you will feel approval. You will know that, for at least those minutes, the power of the Holy Ghost was with you."[8]

I invite you to take a few moments, no matter where you are, and offer a prayer. Think for a moment who in your neighborhood the Lord would be the first to visit. I imagine it would be one who has suffered a setback, a disappointment, or a physical struggle. Think about who you could help.

Now, if you saw a face or thought of a name, would you offer another prayer and ask our Heavenly Father what he specifically wants you to do for that person? Write it down. Would you be willing in the next week to act upon your promptings?

Can you see the acts of charity begin to flow? One act will follow another, and then another, until we will be unable to count them.

This is my relief and my society. This is welfare and compassionate service. It is visiting teaching and fellowshipping. It is retention and attention. It's becoming involved in a cause larger than ourselves. Our hearts will change, as did those of King Lamoni and his queen, because the Holy Ghost will lead us to higher ground. We will be united in our efforts to lift and lead and love others into the fold of Jesus Christ. It is taking our turn at bat and hitting a home run.

Not long ago I received a letter from a sister who shared this experience with me: "One of the most difficult times in my life came shortly after my husband and I were married. Our little family had been blessed with three beautiful and healthy children, but I struggled to regain my health. I experienced many days of discomfort and discouragement. It was on one such day that my doorbell rang early in the morning, and there stood the small, round, elderly woman who lived across the street. She was a convert from Kentucky and was living in a basement with her daughter. Although her own health wasn't good and she had received no specific assignment, she stood on my doorstep that morning and simply said, 'I've come to rock the baby.' She took my tiny new son from my arms and told me to go back to bed. She assured me that all would be well with my little ones. I protested for about thirty seconds and then crawled back in bed and slept like a baby myself. Her simple help was a powerful blessing to a young mother. Her quiet service made a lasting impression on me."

Several years later, this woman moved into another area. She said, "One day my phone rang, and it was one of the sisters in my neighborhood. She explained that she had just received word that her father was in the hospital. It was serious. Could I come and tend her children? It was in the middle of my busy life, but I placed my tasks aside and went to her home. I rang her doorbell, and as she placed her new little son in my arms, I thought, *I came to rock the baby.* It felt wonderful, and I was grateful to be entrusted with the care of her children as a loving grand-father passed from this life to the next."

Simple things have the potential to give power to our lives. As we serve others, we are serving our Savior, for "inasmuch as ye have done it unto one of the least of these my brethren, ye have done it unto me" (Matthew 25:40). As we move into a new millennial era, I, like President Gordon B. Hinckley, have a vision of the incalculable good we can do:

I see us as excellent visiting teachers, lifting our sisters through word and example.

I see sisters enjoying Home, Family, and Personal Enrichment meet-ings as they build friendships and learn gospel principles and practical skills.

I see sisters on Sunday with scriptures and hearts open to the good word of the gospel, sisters who are willing to obey, repent, and improve.

I see sisters fasting and praying for each other.

I see sisters who center their lives on firm testimonies of Jesus Christ and his restored gospel.

I see sisters who receive guidance from the Holy Ghost.

I see sisters learning and teaching the gospel literacy program, instilling in many the desire to read and study and learn.

I see sisters in homes that have become havens where prayer is prac-ticed, scriptures are read, kindness is expected, and unity prevails.

I see sisters involved in family history and genealogy.

I see sisters dressed in white, walking the peaceful halls of sacred, holy temples.

I see sisters working in unity in presidencies and with the priesthood—sisters who remember the Savior's warning against con-tention: "If ye are not one ye are not mine" (D&C 38:27).

I see sisters setting family values and creating homes of wondrous upbringing—families reclaiming family home evening, enjoying every-thing from simple activities to teaching moments.

I see sisters having fun together, laughing at their own mistakes, taking time for friendships, and enjoying life.

I see sisters flooding the earth with quiet acts of charity as they write notes of encouragement, check on neighbors, and listen to children.

I see sisters with an "eye single to the glory of God" (D&C 4:5).

I see sisters daily serving their family, immediate and extended, knowing that the routine things they do each day are essential.

I see sisters focusing as leaders on bringing women and their families to Christ.

In other words, I see you!

We don't need to worry about what history will write about us. We will let our quiet works speak for themselves. But I promise you there will be those whose lives you touch in simple moments who will tell others about you. And they will wonder, "How did she ever do it? How did her faith become so strong? I wonder what I would have done if her challenge had been mine?" Those who follow our generation will testify that we took the torch of obedience and brought it flaming brightly to them. We made the most of our turn at bat!

Elder Boyd K. Packer has urged us to "rally to the cause of Relief Society! Strengthen it! Attend it! Devote yourselves to it! Enlist the inactive in it, and bring the nonmember sisters under the influence of it. It is time now to unite in this worldwide circle of sisters. A strong, well-organized Relief Society is crucial to the future, to the safety of this Church.

"We now move cautiously into the darkening mists of the future. We hear the ominous rumbling of the gathering storm. The narrow places of the past have been a preliminary and a preparatory testing. The issue of this dispensation now is revealed before us. It touches the life of every sister. We do not tremble in fear—for you hold in your gentle hands the light of righteousness. It blesses the brethren and nourishes our children."[9]

I pray that we may catch the vision that President Hinckley and President Packer have for the women of Relief Society. I testify that each one of us, each of our individual roles, is essential to accomplish the work that lies before us. May you feel the love that our Heavenly Father and Jesus Christ have for each of you. I testify that they live and that they love us. And as we catch the vision of our essential role today, by small and simple means great things will be brought to pass.

NOTES

1. Gordon B. Hinckley, *Ensign*, May 1995, 52.
2. Gordon B. Hinckley, *Ensign*, November 1998, 97, 99.
3. Gordon B. Hinckley, "Feasting upon the Scriptures," *Ensign*, December 1985, 44.
4. Joseph F. Smith, Conference Report, April 1900, 50.
5. C. S. Lewis, *Mere Christianity* (New York: Macmillan, 1952), 167.
6. Spencer W. Kimball, *Ensign*, November 1978, 103.
7. LaVonne Neff, comp., *A Life for God: The Mother Teresa Reader*, (Ann Arbor, Mich.: Servant Publications, 1995), 82.
8. Henry B. Eyring, *To Draw Closer to God* (Salt Lake City: Deseret Book, 1997), 50.
9. Boyd K. Packer, *Ensign*, November 1980, 111.

God's Covenant of Peace

PATRICIA T. HOLLAND

This is the voice of Helaman to his sons Nephi and Lehi: "Remember, remember that it is upon the rock of our Redeemer, who is Christ, the Son of God, that ye must build your foundation; that when the devil shall send forth his mighty winds, yea, his shafts in the whirlwind, yea, when all his hail and his mighty storm shall beat upon you, it shall have no power over you to drag you down to the gulf of misery and endless wo, because of the rock upon which ye are built" (Helaman 5:12).

That is the same message the psalmist gave in another time but for the same purpose—to calm the fears of those who find themselves assailed by troubles, as a ship caught in a storm. In the rising wind and the perilous waves of life, the psalmist says, "they mount up to the heaven, they go down again to the depths: their soul is melted because of trouble. They reel to and fro, and stagger like a drunken man, and are at their wits' end. Then they cry unto the Lord in their trouble, and he bringeth them out of their distresses. He maketh the storm a calm, so that the waves thereof are still. Then are they glad because they be quiet; so he bringeth them unto their desired haven" (Psalm 107:26–30).

On some long days and even longer nights, we may have wondered why that guidance into a desired haven is not a little more evident—or at least evident a little sooner. That reminds me of an incident related by Mother Teresa of Calcutta: "I was consoling a little girl who was sick and

Patricia Terry Holland, a native of southern Utah, attended Dixie College and studied voice and piano in New York City. A homemaker and educator, she has served in the Young Women General Presidency and on the boards of Deseret Book Company and Primary Children's Medical Center. She and her husband, Jeffrey R. Holland, a member of the Quorum of the Twelve Apostles, are the parents of three children and the grandparents of two.

had much pain," said Mother Teresa. "I told her, 'You should be happy that God sends you suffering, because your sufferings are a proof that God loves you much. Your sufferings are kisses from Jesus.' 'Then, Mother,' answered the little girl, 'please ask Jesus not to kiss me so much.'"[1]

We all face storm-filled, tempestuous moments in life—moments when, for a time, we feel utterly alone and experience genuine despair. Nevertheless, whatever challenges we have faced and may be facing still, I know that God is caring for us, guiding us, and bringing us to his "desired haven." I know that because I know him.

So, near the end of an outgoing millennium and the exciting dawn of another, it is a good time to inventory spiritually the many changes, choices, and challenges we face individually and collectively as our missions continue to unfold. This year's turning is a good time to ask ourselves if we are truly built upon the rock of our Redeemer, that sure foundation upon which, if we build, we cannot fall. It is a good time to ask whether we are living in such a way that God can bring us into his "desired haven."

The most obvious external symbol of such refuge, of such safety, is the holy temple. Are we true to the covenants we have made there? Is our faith in God and in his promises such that when we enter his holy house it truly can be a sanctuary from the storm? And when we cannot be in a temple, do we keep our covenants in that other holy place, our own home, the other great sanctuary God has given to the faithful? Because of covenants made and kept, we have the blessing of taking our sanctuaries with us, much as the children of Israel did on their winding way toward the promised land. And given the storms that can come up in the Sinais of our life, it is a wonderful thing that God goes with us.

When the winds blow and the sea is storm tossed, we must not give in to self-pity. God is with us; Christ is our sure foundation; there is a safe haven ahead. We simply have to remember that in this mortal journey, all learning, all personal growth, all spiritual refinement carry with them the possibility of a little motion sickness. No one—not even the Saints, maybe especially not the Saints—are immune from such challenges. Remember the little girl and the kisses from Jesus. No one escapes God's refining fire. Our trials offer a training ground for godhood. Without some moments in darkness, would we ever cherish the light? Without confronting some doubt, would we ever recognize and cling to faith?

I dare say there is not a woman in this Church who has not been directly affected by any number of things—disease or death, loneliness or discouragement, divorce, or family or financial challenges—any of a wide variety of disappointments or seemingly unyielding tribulations. Many of these challenges have come not from personal choice but from God's divine timetable, a timetable that for obvious reasons is usually not put into our hands for prior review and approval. The loss of a spouse, concern for a child, a significant change in health or temporal circumstance—these can occur to any one of us at any time. So many things can unexpectedly play havoc with our hopes and darken our view of the future.

And if these burdens do not fall upon us directly, they can come to those we love. Such burdens are no less painful to us. In fact, as one friend of mine, a doctor, once said, "It's like asking a mother not to breathe" to ask her to remain a bystander when her children are in pain, even if there is little she can do to help. That's true whether the affliction is physical or spiritual. We may have seen children or grandchildren make choices so inconsistent with our own that their lives as well as ours have been changed forever. At least that is how it seems in the heat and the pain of the moment.

At those times our emotions can be out of control. As the psalmist says, "They mount up to the heaven, they go down again to the depths" (Psalm 107:26). Or, as another observer put it, we "go up to Heaven and down to Hell a dozen times a day."[2] And some days, particularly difficult days, days when the adversary seems to have an absolutely crushing upper hand, the spiral downward may appear more frequent than the reach upward.

Consider the following passage from a letter of John Winthrop to his wife, Margaret. After learning that their wildest and most irresponsible son had married a young woman against their wishes, John Winthrop, who discovered the news while on business in London, wrote to his wife back in New England, asking her to take in their son and his new wife until they could get the means to settle on their own. Then he encouraged her to take hope with these words:

"I know thou lookest for troubles here [meaning life here on earth] and when one affliction is over, to meet with another. But remember what our Savior tells us: Be of good comfort, I have overcome the world. See his goodness, he hath conquered our enemies before hand, and by Faith in him, we shall assuredly prevail over them all. Therefore my sweet wife, raise up thy heart, and be not dismayed at the crosses thou meetest with in family affairs, or otherwise, but still fly to him, who will take up thy burden for thee, go thou on cheerfully in obedience to his holy will, in the course he hath set thee, peace shall come, thou shalt rest as in thy bed and in the mean time he will not fail nor forsake thee."[3]

I don't pretend to have any prepackaged solutions to individual sorrows, but I can share my love and a message that I know to be true. No matter how terrible the current challenge may seem, if, as Mr. Winthrop said, we can go on cheerfully in obedience to God's holy will, peace shall come, we shall "rest in our beds," and God will not fail nor forsake us. God can mend our broken hearts. Indeed, I believe it is through the cracks of a broken heart that God sheds his purest and most illuminating light to the soul.

THE WELL OF GRIEF

Those who will not slip beneath
   the still surface on the well of grief

turning downward through its black water
   to a place we cannot breathe

will never know the source from which we drink,
   the secret water, cold and clear,

nor find in the darkness glimmering
   the small round coins
      thrown by those who wished for something else.[4]

My entire message is simply this: Please trust lovingly in the goodness of God. He will honor the covenants we have made with him!

Glorious and glimmering promises await us if we but trust in him. Illuminating secrets, clearly revealed, are awaiting us—the wonder of rewards found in "small round coins / thrown by those who wished for something else." We are God's children. He loves us—and he will never stop loving us. We are still being formed and transformed at his tender hand. Though his molding requires that we walk through the valley of the shadow of death, he has provided for us a pathway of peace. Even through the darkest of shadows, we can walk in comfort and consolation if we lovingly trust God.

Remember your baptism. Remember the sacrament table. Remember the temple. Remember an entire theology built upon covenants. Well did de Chardin write, "Not everything is immediately good to those who seek God; but everything is capable of becoming good."[5] Things are made good through the power of covenants.

I don't know exactly how old I was, maybe fifteen, when I learned that truth. I remember only being old enough to think I had made too many mistakes in my life to be of any use to anybody. I was not a rebellious teenager (one couldn't get into much trouble in Enterprise, Utah; population 350), but I was very curious and active and asked my parents a lot of questions. I suppose I just had all the fears and frustrations of an average teenager. I especially remember fearing that maybe my life would be lived more with a whimper than with a bang, to paraphrase T. S. Eliot.[6]

It was at that age—maybe fifteen—that I read for the first time Romans 8:28: "And we know that all things work together for good to them that love God." I was struck dumb for a minute. Speechless! I remember that moment as if it were locked in time. I was reclining on my white Martha Washington bedspread, surrounded by sea-blue walls, my head resting on a red velvet pillow. With my hands gripping the scriptures, I remember looking up, away from the page, and saying, "Heavenly Father, do you mean that everything that I have ever done, silly or not, good or bad, happy or sad, will come together for my good if I . . . just love you?" I was incredulous. I can't describe the joy that filled my heart.

At fifteen I hadn't had many such moments with what really was pure and beautiful revelation. It was wonderful. I already knew that I loved God; I just didn't know how deeply until that moment. And at that very moment, at that very instant, I knew that God loved me. I didn't know everything I needed to be forgiven of, but I felt forgiven. There on that Martha Washington bedspread with the red pillow, I truly knew for the first time that I could and would be helped, and if life was a whimper instead of a bang—well, that would be my fault and certainly not God's. If I could document the moments when I moved from a youthful view of God to a more mature one, to some beginning of what it means to love him with a more mature heart and mind, one key moment would be that day with Romans 8:28.

That moment in my life convinced me I could rise above sorrows or disappointments or mistakes or despair. I felt that day that God was an artist. He would use the very stone of my plain little life and refashion it, redeem it, producing something far more arresting and substantial. I knew even in that short span of life in Enterprise, Utah, that I might have to endure sometimes painful shaping, as with a hammer or chisel, if something precious were to be sculpted from this stone. To use a gentler metaphor, I believe we need to be as malleable as clay and from time to time feel the loving touch of his hand, if we wish him to form more exquisite lines and tones. At that moment, I trusted God perfectly, as perhaps only a fifteen-year-old can trust him.

It is easier to have that kind of faith in our youth, long before we have suffered through some of life's later challenges, such as having no opportunity to marry, or losing a loved one, or facing a debilitating disease, or any of the desperations of the mind that can come. But I think sometimes we too easily dismiss the faith of youth and the importance of youthful experiences in forming our testimony. Those youthful moments of revelation must be among the reasons that Christ said, "Except ye . . . become as little children" (Matthew 18:3). Let us be like children. Let us love God and trust God and keep our eye single to his glory, especially in time of stress and difficulty. I do know that all things will work together for our good. I promise you that on good authority. I promise it on the authority of God's own word.

May I share with you another witness of God's comfort for the natural and expected turbulence of our lives? "At times we may feel that we do not need God, but on the day when the storms of disappointment rage, the winds of disaster blow, and the tidal waves of grief beat against our lives, if we do not have a deep and patient faith our emotional lives will be ripped to shreds. There is so much frustration in the world because we have relied on gods rather than God. We have genuflected before the god of science only to find that it has given us the atomic bomb, producing fears and anxieties that science can never mitigate. We have worshiped the god of pleasure only to discover that thrills play out and sensations are short-lived. We have bowed before the god of money only to learn that there are such things as love and friendship that money cannot buy and that in a world of possible depressions, stock market crashes, and bad business investments, money is a rather uncertain deity. These transitory gods are not able to save us or bring happiness to the human heart.

"Only God is able. It is faith in him that we must rediscover. With this faith we can transform bleak and desolate valleys into sunlit paths of joy and bring new light into the dark caverns of pessimism. Is someone here moving toward the twilight of life and fearful of that which we call death? Why be afraid? God is able. Is someone here on the brink of despair because of the death of a loved one, the breaking of a marriage, or the waywardness of a child? Why despair? God is able to give you the power to endure that which cannot be changed. Is someone here anxious because of bad health? Why be anxious? Come what may, God is able."[7]

So how do we do this? How do we make the transition from being together in a cozy conference cocoon, or buoyed by a Gospel Doctrine class, hearing powerful testimonies from the scriptures, only to go out into that world of woe that confronts us from time to time? My answer is not new, and it has to do with covenants—the promise that if we will remember something as fundamental as our baptismal, sacramental, and temple covenants, we will carry an inner peace that God is with us. Knowing precisely the doubts and difficult moments all of us would face, the great Jehovah said to the children of Israel, "For I know the things that come into your mind, every one of them. . . . Yet will I be to [you] as a little sanctuary. . . . I will put a new spirit within you" (Ezekiel 11:5, 16, 19).

Having gone into the waters of baptism, or to sacrament meeting, or to the temple to make our covenants, we cannot (much as we would like to) always remain in those wonderfully safe settings. We know that. Soon enough we have to shoulder our backpack and take up the journey again. But that wonderful promise from the Lord recorded in the book of Ezekiel is that if we cannot always be in God's sanctuary, we can always have God's sanctuary be in us. "I will be [your] sanctuary," he promises. "I will put a new spirit within you." When difficult times come, when we realize things are not good the way they are, we trust in God who can provide a new spirit. That is the power of covenant making and covenant keeping.

Our covenants with God are the topic of many lessons and talks and conference addresses, and well they should be. Those promises and convictions, this way of faithful living, as someone recently said, "is our ticket home." But sometimes we feel inadequate to the challenge of those covenants.

What we too often fail to realize is that at the same time we covenant with God, *he is covenanting with us*—promising blessings, privileges, and pleasures our eyes have not yet seen and our ears have not yet heard. Though we may see our part in the matter of faithfulness going by fits and starts, by bumps and bursts, our progress erratic at best, God's part is sure and steady and supreme. We may stumble, but he never does. We may falter, but he never will. We may feel out of control, but he never is. The reason the keeping of covenants is so important to us is at least partly because it makes the contract so binding to God. Covenants forge a link between our telestial, mortal struggles and God's celestial, immortal powers.

We bring all we can to the agreement, even if that doesn't seem like much. Our heart, our devotion, our integrity—we bring as much as we can, but he brings eternity to it: he brings himself, priesthood and principalities, power and majesty beyond our wildest imagination. Just listen to the sure language of God's covenantal promise to us in 3 Nephi: "For the mountains shall depart and the hills be removed, but my kindness shall not depart from thee, neither shall the covenant of my peace be removed, saith the Lord that hath mercy on thee" (3 Nephi 22:10). God is saying, in effect, Think of the most unlikely things in the world, impossible things like the mountains departing and the hills being removed—think of the most preposterous events you can imagine, but still, even if they do, even then my kindness shall not depart from thee, neither shall the covenant of my peace be removed.

He goes on after that to enumerate lovely promises of temporal blessings and then this tender promise: "And all thy children shall be taught of the Lord; and great shall be the peace of thy children" (3 Nephi 22:13). I simply cannot imagine a more powerful nor hopeful promise.

The danger, of course, is that in times of pain or sorrow, times when the obedience and the sacrifice seem too great (or at least too immediate), we hesitate, we pull back from this divine relationship. How often when we have been asked to give our hearts, or give something from our heart, or give that latter-day sacrifice of a broken heart and a contrite spirit—how often when there is a difficult time or a bruising of our soul, do we shy away or openly retreat from a total and uncompromising trust in the One who knows exactly how to accept our gift and return it tenfold? God knows how to receive a broken heart, bless it, and give it back healed and renewed. He knows how to weep with love over such an offered gift, immediately bless it, mend it, and return it.

With God, whatever has become broken can be fixed. God doesn't just pull out the tiny spikes that life's tribulations have driven into us. He doesn't simply pull out what one writer has called the nails of our own guilt, leaving us bleeding and scarred forever. No, when we can finally trust our lives, our hearts, our whole souls to the Great Physician, then he not only heals what was but goes one better and makes all things new. We must remember, as my doctor son-in-law would say, "We are up against a surgeon here whose only determination is to heal us— and he knows exactly how to do that." He gives us a new strength of soul, a new birth, a new heart—holier and happier, healthier than it ever was before.

I know that just saying all of this doesn't necessarily make it easy to do. We sing that "sacrifice brings forth the blessings of heaven,"[8] but I know from experience that sacrifice is not a trivial thing, that it can bring sorrow with a very personal price tag attached. We can sometimes be terrified at what may be asked of us. I think of Sister Marjorie Hinckley's response when someone asked her how she felt about being the wife of the newly ordained prophet. With all four feet, eight inches of height and with her big, brown eyes opened wide, she said, "Oh, I just want my mama!" I think Sister Hinckley and I would agree with Paul the apostle when he wrote, "It is a fearful thing to fall into the hands of the living God" (Hebrews 10:31). "What?" we ask. "Paul, who seemed the very essence of courage and faith, talked about being fearful about falling into the hands of God?" Yes, that very same Paul. And those "afflictions," as he calls them, come "after ye were illuminated" (v. 32), after those moments of having received light, knowledge, power, and revelation. We make our covenant, we step forward with our offering, and then we stand absolutely speechless, more than a little terrified, sometimes sobbing with consternation when that offering is accepted.

To be honest, I must confess that this is a familiar pattern in my life. I have been afraid enough times that I am embarrassed to try to count them all. The most embarrassing part is that I will sometimes get lost in the self-preoccupation and self-pity that a little fright and anxiety can arouse in me. I forget too easily what price must be paid for God's precious gift of faith. I forget how many times God will ask us to practice our virtues, embrace our fears, and reiterate our covenants until they are truly established, strengthened, and settled in our souls forever (see 1 Peter 5:10). Sadly, what we all may forget in the heat of battle is that after these tests and tribulations, when God really is satisfied that we are settled firmly in the faith, then come the blessings that are too glorious for mere words. I stand as a witness that my most precious blessings, miracles, and the realization of God's covenantal promises have come after my fears have been aroused, my faith has been tried, and my heart truly broken in humility and supplication.

Paul, knowing these fears and frustrations, these fluctuating feelings, pleads with us to "cast not away therefore your confidence, which hath great recompense of reward. For ye have need of patience, that, after ye have done the will of God, ye might receive the promise" (Hebrews 10:35–36). What follows in Hebrews is one of the greatest chapters on faith in all the Holy Bible. For the next forty verses of Hebrews 11, Paul describes the faith that preceded the sacrifices and afflictions of Abel, Enoch, Noah, Abraham, Isaac, Jacob, Sarah, Joseph, Moses, Joshua, Samson, David, and Samuel—to name a few. He recounts there the examples of women who saw their dead raised to life again, accounts of the quenching of fire, escaping the edge of the sword, stopping the mouths of lions, and a host of weaknesses being made strong.

When I think of this kind of faith in the face of adversity and understandable fear, I think of a very current example. Shortly after Elder Neal A. Maxwell's leukemia was diagnosed and he began chemotherapy, my husband and I went to the hospital to visit with him. He was so sick and fragile and frail. I'll never forget the sweet look on his face and his tear-filled eyes as he said softly, "I just hope that I do not shrink from this cup which has been given me."

That was more than two years, one book, dozens of regional conferences, and four general conferences ago. And he is still serving without shrinking—walking by faith, knowing that he still has leukemia, and never knowing for sure what the Lord may have in store for the next leg of the race. The treatments go on, the nausea returns, the hair comes and goes, but there is Neal Maxwell with his shoulder to the wheel. Elder and Sister Maxwell are perfect modern examples of faith overcoming fear, of hope tinged with sadness, of light shining in otherwise dark moments, of a couple who will never shrink nor shun the fight. To be around them is to feel drawn into an aura of serenity and calm. You know that Christ has pleasure in the strength of their covenants (see Hebrews 10:38).

In these times, many people are starting to worry over the calamities of the last days. Fear is waxing strong, and the hearts of some men and women grow cold. To that I say as they do in Australia, "No worry, mate!" Curl up comfortably in your favorite easy chair, wrap yourself in the loving spirit of God, and read the italicized heading for the very chapter of 3 Nephi I have been quoting: "In the last days, Zion and her stakes shall be established, and Israel shall be gathered in mercy and tenderness—They shall triumph" (headnote to 3 Nephi 22).

Not long ago we experienced the worst windstorm Bountiful has seen in several decades. The wind on the freeway was gauged at 113 miles an hour. Coming out of our canyon, it seemed even more than that. Just as I was hearing news reports of semitrailer trucks—twenty of them—being blown over on the roadside, I looked out my back window down toward our creek, and I saw one of our large trees go down with a crash. A smaller one followed almost immediately.

For a moment, I confess I was truly fearful. I thought of Kosovo and Littleton, Colorado, of our own Salt Lake Family History Library, and even the great bug-a-boo Y2K. The wind became even more furious and loud.

It was very early in the morning as the worst of this was happening, and Jeff was just leaving for the office. I am a little embarrassed to admit

375

that I was scared. I said to him, "Do you think this is the end? Is it all over—or about to be?" I whispered. My husband, a man of deep faith and endless optimism, took me in his arms and said, "No, but wouldn't it be wonderful if it were? Wouldn't it be wonderful if Christ really did come and his children really were ready for him? Wouldn't it be terrific if evil was finally conquered, once and for all, and the Savior of the world came down in the midst of the New Jerusalem to wipe away *every* tear from *every* eye? Yes," my husband said, "in lots of ways I wish it were the end, but it's not. It is just a stiff windstorm in Bountiful. We have got more work to do." So, he kissed me and drove off to work, with trees falling and rafters rattling.

I was probably imagining it, but I thought I could hear him whistling a few bars of "Master, the Tempest Is Raging," especially that lovely closing refrain: "Peace, be still; peace, be still."[9]

"They mount up to the heaven, they go down again to the depths: their soul is melted because of trouble. They reel to and fro, and stagger like a drunken man, and are at their wits' end. Then they cry unto the Lord in their trouble, and he bringeth them out of their distresses. He maketh the storm a calm, so that the waves thereof are still. Then are they glad because they be quiet; so he bringeth them unto their desired haven" (Psalm 107:26–30). This is God's covenant of peace to you. His kindness shall not depart from you, and terror shall not come near you. God's covenant of peace shall not be removed, for he has so declared.

NOTES

1. Edward Le Joly, *Mother Teresa of Calcutta: A Biography* (San Francisco: Harper & Row, 1985), 321.
2. May Sarton, *Journal of a Solitude* (New York: Norton, 1973), 108.
3. *Winthrop Papers*, 6 vols. (Boston: Massachusetts Historical Society, 1929–1947), 2:84.
4. David Whyte, *Where Many Rivers Meet* (Langley, Wash.: Many Rivers Press, 1996), 35.
5. Pierre Teilhard de Chardin, *The Divine Milieu* (New York: Harper & Row, 1960), 86.
6. See T. S. Eliot, "The Hollow Men," in *Norton Anthology of American Literature*, ed. Nina Baym et al., 3d ed. (New York: W. W. Norton, 1989), 2:1291–94.
7. Martin Luther King Jr., *Strength to Love* (Cleveland, Ohio: Collins, 1963), 112.
8. *Hymns of The Church of Jesus Christ of Latter-day Saints* (Salt Lake City: The Church of Jesus Christ of Latter-day Saints, 1985), no. 27.
9. *Hymns*, no. 105.

Hope Everlasting

COLLEEN H. MAXWELL

That "we hope all things" is a basic tenet of our faith (Article of Faith 13). Is hope, then, an indicator of the depth of our faith, a measure of our hearts? What is hope, and if we have it, how are we changed? Can we earn hope, or is it given to us? Let us consider some scriptures that will help us answer these questions and one final query: What is "everlasting . . . and good hope," that hope which can light our way with "perfect brightness"? (2 Thessalonians 2:16; 2 Nephi 31:20).

News of world events could easily overcome us, if we allow it to do so. So could events closer to home. During the past few months, my husband and I have felt bombarded with one report after another of a dear friend, relative, or neighbor encountering some grave illness, a death in the family, or another particularly difficult challenge. Although I am not one to be easily disheartened or discouraged, I have found myself struggling with feelings of sadness. Yet, as members of the gospel of Jesus Christ, we have many assurances and teachings to help us assuage downhearted feelings. In 2 Corinthians 4:8 we are told, "We are troubled on every side, yet not distressed; we are perplexed, but not in despair." I hope we are not in despair.

Perhaps our first task is to determine which dimension of hope we are talking about. While we may refer at times to proximate hope, what concerns us most is ultimate hope or the eternal concept of hope. "Life's

Colleen Hinckley Maxwell is a member of the board of Primary Children's Hospital and has been a volunteer at the spina bifida clinic. She has also served on the advisory council of the Department of Family Living and Consumer Studies and the University of Utah alumni board. She and her husband, Neal A. Maxwell, a member of the Quorum of the Twelve Apostles, are the parents of four children and the grandparents of twenty-four.

disappointments often represent the debris of our failed, proximate hopes," says my favorite author and speaker (you know who that is, of course—my husband).[1]

Proximate hope, defined as immediate or imminent, is subject to the agency of other people, whereas the reasons for eternal hope, such as the Atonement and resurrection, are fixed. That is, if we use our agency wisely and faithfully, our ultimate hopes are not at the mercy of other people or of external events. Heavenly Father will give eternal rewards to the faithful. Still, we may experience the dashing of our proximate hopes, but ultimate hope gives us the spiritual energy to revise and rebuild them.

There are so many variables in our lives that we cannot control with regard to our proximate hopes. It isn't that we shouldn't plan or have hope about certain things in our daily lives, but it is most heartening to know that if we choose to do what is right, our eternal hopes are fixed. Disappointments of the day are not to affect our ultimate hopes. We must not mistake today's local cloud cover for general darkness.

"Just as doubt, despair, and desensitization go together, so do faith, hope, charity, and patience. The latter qualities must be carefully and constantly nurtured, however, whereas doubt and despair, like dandelions, need little encouragement in order to sprout and spread. Alas, despair comes so naturally."[2]

Where does faith end and hope begin? Moroni asks, "How is it that ye can attain unto faith, save ye shall have hope? . . . Wherefore, if a man have faith he must needs have hope; for without faith there cannot be any hope" (Moroni 7:40–42). To clarify, let me again quote from my favorite author: "Faith and hope are constantly interactive and not always easily or precisely distinguished. . . . Hope corresponds to faith but sometimes has an even greater circumference." Not surprisingly, then, hope is "intertwined with other gospel doctrines, especially faith and patience."[3]

Gospel hope is a very focused and particularized hope based upon justified expectations and upon our Savior, Jesus Christ. President Gordon B. Hinckley, speaking at a funeral not long ago, said: "In all these circumstances, there is only one source of comfort, one source of reassurance. That source is the Lord Jesus Christ, the Savior and Redeemer of the world. When all else fails, when our hopes and dreams are shattered, when death strikes with certainty and finality, there is the voice of the Lord speaking to the sorrowing heart and to all mankind. . . .

"None other can give such assurance."[4]

Eternal or ultimate hope always radiates from or is about Jesus Christ and his atonement. Moroni asked, "What is it that ye shall hope for? Behold I say unto you that ye shall have hope through the atonement of Christ" (Moroni 7:41). As Elder Maxwell has said, "Resurrection and the precious opportunity provided thereby for us to practice emancipating repentance makes possible what the scriptures call 'a perfect brightness of hope' (2 Nephi 31:20)."[5]

Many examples in the scriptures illustrate ultimate hope. Alma the Younger wanted "to be banished and become extinct" until he remembered his father's sermon about Jesus' atonement. He then called out in hope to God for mercy (see Alma 36:15–18). In the New Testament, sorrowing disciples rushed, full of rising hopes, to an empty garden tomb (see Mark 16:1–8; Luke 24:8–12).

Hope is born of righteousness, and Proverbs 10:28 tells us that "the hope of the righteous shall be gladness." What a promise! Hope is found through the scriptures themselves as they have been recorded in order that man "might have hope" (Romans 15:4).

In Church history, we need only to look at the earliest of Saints who exhibited profound hope, despite horrendous reasons to be downcast. In a letter from Nauvoo, dated 1 July 1844, to her family in New England, Sally Carlisle Randall describes the Saints' desolation at the martyrdom of Joseph and Hyrum Smith: "If you can imagine to yourselves how the apostles and saints felt when the Savior was crucified you can give something of a guess how the Saints felt here when they heard that their prophet and patriarch were both dead. . . . It seems that all nature mourned."[6]

Jeffrey R. Holland, then president of Brigham Young University, spoke stirringly of these times in a talk entitled "However Long and Hard the Road." After outlining the Prophet Joseph Smith's trials and persecutions, he asked, "If all this and so much more was to face the Prophet in such a troubled lifetime, . . . why didn't he just quit somewhere along the way? Who needs it?" Why not just give up?

"Why not? For the simple reason he had dreamed dreams and seen visions. Through the blood and the toil and the tears and the sweat, he had seen the redemption of Israel." He had that ultimate hope, the hope that transcends proximate calamities. "So he kept his shoulder to the wheel until God said his work was finished."

"And what of the other Saints? [After] Joseph and Hyrum [were] gone, shouldn't they [have] just quietly slipped away?" asks President Holland.

He continues: "Well, it was those recurring dreams, and compelling visions. It was spiritual strength. It was the fulfillment they knew to be ahead, no matter how faint or far away." These few Saints—so few in number—were "planning to overthrow the prince of darkness and establish the kingdom of God in all the world. . . . What presumption!"[7]

What faith, what hope!

Many of us have valiant predecessors who carried on with faith and hope to provide the empowering truths of the restored gospel to those who followed after—to us. Gail Smith, author of *Shadowfall*, expressed the Saints' ultimate hope: "My pioneer ancestors could not have endured all that they did merely on some vague hope that there was a better world beyond the harsh and dangerous and unforgiving one in which they lived."[8] As women and as modern-day pioneers, we may have different frontiers to tame than our early sister Saints had. But as one woman observed: "Our challenges are just as important as those of the past. Our testing is as crucial; our contributions may be as great."[9] It is wise for us to contemplate how we will be remembered and what contributions to society we will have made."

Bright examples of hope are seen in many areas of human endurance. Because of the "cancer network"—as my husband refers to the dozens of dear friends with various types of cancer who communicate with him—we have many very tender and heartwarming stories of courage and valor. We have been touched by the example of a returned sister missionary who, at the age of twenty-five, seriously ill with cancer herself, serves at Camp Hope in her area, courageously reaching out to other young people suffering with cancer. She says she will hold on to hope until her last breath. We have admired the example of hope and faith in the life of a young missionary who was diagnosed with leukemia while serving in the Ventura California Mission. We marvel at the caring ward in that area that raised twelve thousand dollars for a bone marrow transplant. That young elder is now completing his mission there. We were so touched and impressed with his spirit, his selflessness, and the hope that quietly but powerfully radiates from him.

Consider also the examples of hope in areas where the precious freedoms and opportunities found in America are not common. In Ukraine a few years ago, we heard a new convert leader describe his struggle with despair as his country and his life were in financial and political peril. He had written to relatives in America, explained his deplorable state, and asked their advice. "Look up the Mormon Church," they said. He was bewildered by this suggestion but followed their counsel. We heard him tearfully express the hope and joy he had discovered in the truths of the gospel of Jesus Christ—the gospel of hope, the gospel of love, the gospel of happiness. He and his wife found President Hinckley's promise to be true, "The Lord will bless us with the strength to weather every storm and continue to move forward through every adversity."[10]

Sister Julia Mavimbela from Soweto, South Africa, helped her people to become self-sufficient and rise above the bitterness of bloodshed and poverty by leading them to transform plots of neglected ground into productive gardens. She mobilized children, teenagers, and unemployed parents to industry, replacing their fear with hope for the future. She told them, "Let us dig the soil of bitterness, throw in a seed, show love, and see what fruits it can give . . . where there has been a bloodstain, a beautiful flower must grow."[11]

Inspiring examples abound of individuals who have dealt with the most extreme challenges life can mete out. To know how others have dealt with momentous difficulties can be a tremendous source of inspiration, hope, and courage. A family who have been that kind of example to me are the Joyce and Bruce Erickson family. The Ericksons had six children, all born healthy, but then two infant daughters and later a son each developed a mysterious disorder that left them completely dependent and unable to function. Inevitably, the Ericksons began to wonder why bad things happen to people who are living righteously. In their book, *When Life Doesn't Seem Fair,* the Ericksons tell of their search for peace in the midst of exceptional adversity. Through grief and sorrow, and even marital discord, the gospel of hope and the words of the Brethren brought them welcome comfort and healing. Job-like trials caused them to plumb the depth of their faith and then valiantly rise above seemingly insurmountable grief.[12] I have learned so much from them about the healing power of the gospel of hope.

Now, to a more difficult example to share. Those who have read his writings or heard my husband speak will know that for years he has spoken of trials, suffering, and submission to the Lord. He and I knew that although we have faced some challenges in our nearly fifty years of marriage, we had not experienced major trials. Knowing that part of our growth in this second estate comes from being tried and tested, we assumed when a precious little granddaughter was born four years ago with some birth defects that that would be the most significant trial in our lives. But that delightful little granddaughter is beautiful and so precocious—not the trial we anticipated. The other night after her father gave the family prayer, she praised him, "Good, you did it all by yourself."

But there was a trial yet to come. Because my husband had always been healthy, energetic, and vigorous, we weren't prepared for leukemia to sneak in on our blind side. The doctors did not predict the likely length of his life following this startling diagnosis, but through studying available information, we were able to diagram some possible time lines. We determined immediately to pursue the treatment of traditional medicine and through study and prayer to do all else that we could do nutritionally, medically, and spiritually.

Those closest to us had another concern: that he might incline to be *overly* submissive—which is his declared position, as it should be. As a family, however, we all decided that to petition the Lord for the extension of life is natural and even what the Lord expects of us, if we also humbly desire that the Lord's will, whatever it might be, will be done. Even our dear Savior prayed, "Father, . . . remove this cup from me: nevertheless not my will, but thine, be done" (Luke 22:42).

In this life, we do not know why things turn out as they do, but after two strenuous series of treatments, Elder Maxwell is in his second remission and his periodic but milder treatments are now performed at home.

We have calculated, most gratefully, that he has actually only missed six months of work in the nearly three years since he was diagnosed. How very appreciative and humble we feel for his delay en route.

He works tirelessly to lift and encourage others with similar challenges. I have frequently heard him say he's convinced he hasn't been given more time in this life simply to sightsee or to loiter.

I saw my role at the time as an encourager and lifter. Although I was fairly realistic about what we were facing, I believe many of our friends thought I had a serious case of denial. Nevertheless, being of a hopeful and an optimistic temperament, I summoned all the hope and good cheer that was in me. After all, little is lost through remaining hopeful, and much may be gained. My husband and my family needed that spirit of optimism more than ever before.

Through glorious priesthood blessings, outpourings of love, and prayers from all corners of the world, wonderful and caring doctors and nurses, heaven-sent and effective medical treatments (however grim), and most important, through the love, comfort, mercy, and kindness of our gracious Heavenly Father, we were sustained in a very real and tangible way and lifted beyond our ability to comprehend.

We knew that whether Elder Maxwell improved or not, our lives were in the hands of our dear Savior. Because of all he had suffered and experienced for us, we knew that we could count on his comfort. We knew he would lift and ease us through this trying time. The Lord truly is our Shepherd. As Thomas Moore's hymn so beautifully says:

> Come, ye disconsolate,
> . . . .
> Earth has no sorrow that heav'n cannot heal.[13]

Ironically, this has been a sweet time for us—a time of priority for each other and joy in each new day.

It is very important to be of good cheer in these times of tests and trials and also in daily life. The Savior, on numerous and often unimaginable occasions, instructed his disciples to be of good cheer. He told the Twelve to be of good cheer when, as his crucifixion approached, it appeared they had little to be cheerful about. He reassured them by telling them, "In the world ye shall have tribulation: but be of good cheer; I have overcome the world" (John 16:33).

Are these words applicable to us today? Of course they are. The Spirit of the Lord sheds forth cheerfulness and hope, but the spirit of the devil casts men into despair and despondency. Moroni emphasizes, "If ye have no hope ye must needs be in despair; and despair cometh because of iniquity" (Moroni 10:22). As Marilla expressed to Anne in *Anne of Green Gables*, "To despair is to turn your back on God."[14]

If we understand the Atonement, the plan of salvation, and the glad tidings of the gospel, then we have reason to be of good cheer. If we are of good cheer—if we portray optimism and hope—others around us will know the tilt of our soul and that it is positive. The spiritual radiance we may have can carry over to daily life. Arthur Bassett suggests that "if we are not careful in talking about the problems and tragedies of today's society, our children could get the message that the world is no good and no one is to be trusted."[15] How vital it is, then, that we convey hope to our families and a feeling that we are living in extraordinary times with many blessings and opportunities. We can let the gospel fill us with a brightness of hope in him in whom we can place our absolute trust. That is what it means to have a perfect brightness of hope, an everlasting hope.

As I consider the Savior's sacrifice and atonement for me and for those I love, I am overcome with humility and unspeakable joy. I pray that my life will ever validate this knowledge I possess. I know that he lives. I could never deny his love nor his sustaining and comforting power in my life.

NOTES

1. Neal A. Maxwell, *Ensign*, November 1998, 61.
2. Maxwell, *Ensign*, November 1998, 61.
3. Maxwell, *Ensign*, November 1998, 61.
4. Gordon B. Hinckley, quoted in R. Scott Lloyd, "'Daddy Don' Eulogized for Heroism," *Church News*, 24 April 1999, 5.
5. Maxwell, *Ensign*, November 1998, 61.
6. Quoted in *Women's Voices*, ed. Kenneth W. Godfrey, Audrey M. Godfrey, and Jill Mulvay Derr (Salt Lake City: Deseret Book, 1982), 141.
7. Jeffrey R. Holland, *However Long and Hard the Road* (Salt Lake City: Deseret Book, 1985), 119–20.

8. A. Gail Smith, *Shadowfall* (Salt Lake City: Deseret Book, 1996), 221.

9. Laurel Thatcher Ulrich, "A Pioneer Is Not a Woman Who Makes Her Own Soap," *Ensign*, June 1978, 54.

10. Gordon B. Hinckley, *Teachings of Gordon B. Hinckley* (Salt Lake City: Deseret Book, 1997), 7.

11. Julia Mavimbela in "Serving Where She Stands: Julia Mavimbela in Soweto," *This People* 19, no. 4 (Winter 1998): 31.

12. Joyce and Bruce Erickson, *When Life Doesn't Seem Fair* (Salt Lake City: Bookcraft, 1995).

13. *Hymns of The Church of Jesus Christ of Latter-day Saints* (Salt Lake City: The Church of Jesus Christ of Latter-day Saints, 1985), no. 115.

14. *Anne of Green Gables*, vol. 1, produced and directed by Kevin Sullivan, 98 minutes, Walt Disney Company, videocassette.

15. Arthur R. Bassett, "Thou Shalt Not Kill," *Ensign*, August 1994, 29.

Famous Last Words

SHERI L. DEW

As I have prayed about my talk, one impression has come again and again—Latter-day Saint women are no ordinary group of women! The Lord delights in us. He loves us. He is counting on us, for our most crucial work lies ahead. Hence the theme for my address: Famous Last Words. Obviously there's nothing famous about my words, and I hope these aren't my last words, but as we stand on the brink of an era foretold by prophets from the beginning of time, there are some famous words we ought to review.

Among them are those of Joseph who was sold into Egypt but who was reunited with his conniving brothers when famine forced them to Egypt for grain. As Joseph dispatched his brothers back to Canaan to retrieve their father, his last words to them were: "See that ye fall not out by the way" (Genesis 45:24). That advice is reminiscent of the famous last words of the apostle Paul, written at the end of his life: "I have fought a good fight, I have finished my course, I have kept the faith: Henceforth there is laid up for me a crown of righteousness, which the Lord . . . shall give me at that day" (2 Timothy 4:7–8). Paul's declaration makes me think of the hymn "Put Your Shoulder to the Wheel," which we sang frequently in our little Kansas branch because Grandma chose the music, and she loved the last verse:

> Then work and watch and fight and pray
> With all your might and zeal.

Sheri L. Dew is the second counselor in the Relief Society General Presidency. She grew up in Ulysses, Kansas, and graduated from Brigham Young University with a degree in history. A popular speaker and writer, she is vice-president of publishing at Deseret Book Company.

Push ev'ry worthy work along;
Put your shoulder to the wheel.[1]

All of these last words illuminate our goal and our challenge: to keep from falling out by the way on our mortal sojourn, to wage a good fight against the enemy of righteousness, to finish the custom-made course prepared for each of us, and to nourish our faith in Jesus Christ—all of which we will do only if we work and watch and fight and pray.

This process in which we are engaged is glorious but difficult. There are many reasons for that, one of which I learned as a 5'10" tomboy who lived and breathed sports and played whatever was in season. We had a great eighth-grade fast-pitch softball team, and as the pitcher and captain I was determined to lead our team to the championship. Everyone turned out for the deciding game, including my family.

The game was tight from the opening pitch, but as we went into the final inning we were ahead 2–1. Unfortunately, that's when things began to unravel. First, I walked the leadoff batter. Then the next hitter popped a fly ball to the shortstop, who dropped it. There were now runners on first and second. The third batter grounded to the third baseman, who let the ball get past her. The bases were loaded. The next batter hit a line drive right at the first baseman, who ducked. Two runners scored, and my vision of trophies began to vanish. Then the next hitter whacked the ball deep, and as the left fielder chased it into the corner, all of the runners scored.

You might wonder why I can still remember these details. The entire episode is engraved in my memory, because at that point something happened that I still can't explain. From the mound, I began shouting at my teammates—and they weren't the come-on-you-can-do-it kinds of words you would hope to hear from a team captain. This was a tongue-lashing in which I chewed out the entire infield. This scene went on for perhaps a minute when suddenly I realized that I was not alone on the mound. There stood Mother, who had apparently seen enough. Taking me by the arm, she escorted me off the field and motioned me into a nearby school bus.

Action on the field stopped. The umpire and coaches looked back and forth at each other and then at the school bus, where inside, and with her index finger waving in a steady beat, Mother stated what became her most famous words to me during childhood: "*You* are out of control. You have forgotten *who* you are, *where* you are, and what is really important. And if you would *ever* like to play ball again, I suggest you correct this mistake right now." I walked off the bus, apologized to everyone, and returned to the mound. We lost the game.

Mother was right. I was out of control. I had forgotten who I was and what standard of behavior was expected of me, where I was and what was appropriate on a ball diamond, and what was important—which was not only to play well but to behave well.

It seems to be easy here in mortality to do what I did—to lose sight of who we are and what we're here for and as a result to become distracted from what is really important. If we don't have a clear sense of our identity and purpose, we are much more vulnerable to Lucifer.

He of course knows that and attempts to blur our vision. He challenged even the Savior: "If thou be the Son of God, cast thyself down," Lucifer taunted, to which the Savior responded, "Thou shalt not tempt the Lord thy God," leaving no question about who he was (Matthew 4:6–7). When the adversary tried to entice the Savior to worship him, promising kingdoms he couldn't deliver, Christ made short work of him: "Get thee hence, Satan" (Matthew 4:10). There was no clever repartee or negotiation. The Lord simply rejected and banished his tempter, at which point the devil was forced to leave, because the power of Jesus Christ is *always* stronger than the power of Satan. The Savior was clear about who he was, which allowed him to neutralize and defeat the adversary.

Satan tries some variation of this approach on each of us. He lies. He shades and obscures truth. He makes evil look good and good look unenlightened and unsophisticated. He will try anything to obscure the truth about who we are, where we are, and what's really important. In President Harold B. Lee's last general conference, he stated that without an understanding of who we are, we lack "a solid foundation upon which to build [our] lives."[2]

Is it any wonder, then, that the enemy of all truth and righteousness would launch an all-out attack on Latter-day Saint women? He understands what President Joseph F. Smith articulated: "There are people fond of saying that women are the weaker vessels. I don't believe it. Physically, they may be; but spiritually, morally, religiously and in faith, what man can match a woman who is really convinced?"[3]

From the adversary's point of view, we are dangerous. Righteous women dedicated to the Lord and united in the cause of goodness threaten his work. Of course he would target and attempt to deceive us, women who have a clear understanding of who we are. As I said at the outset, we are not ordinary women.

We know that we are beloved spirit daughters of heavenly parents. We are women who seek to hear the voice of the Lord. We are women devoted to our families, women whose covenants and influence span generations, women who are not easily deceived, women of integrity, charity, and purity.

We are women who understand that to qualify for eternal life, we must deal with a full range of difficulty and disappointment here. We are free to choose how we live, where we spend our temporal, emotional, and spiritual resources, and to what and whom we devote ourselves. We are free "to choose liberty and eternal life, through the great Mediator . . . or to choose captivity and death, according to the captivity and power of the devil" (2 Nephi 2:27).

I have a friend who is a gifted teacher. During a hospital stay he learned that his nurse was taking the discussions, and one evening they talked at length about the plan of salvation. She summed up their conversation by saying, "Satan sure doesn't end up with much, does he?" No, Satan won't end up with much, and neither will those who are duped into following him. Hence our challenge to walk the straight and narrow path until the end of our probation (see 2 Nephi 9:27).

Our ability to successfully negotiate this spiritual minefield called mortality improves dramatically if we are clear about who we are and what is important. What is important is eternal life. Said President Spencer W. Kimball, "Since immortality and eternal life constitute the sole purpose of life, all other interests and activities are but incidental thereto."[4]

Does that mean there should be no ball games or barbecues or ballets? Of course not. But it does mean that we must be riveted on our goal. Anything that takes us closer to exaltation is worth our time and energy.

Anything that doesn't is a distraction. Brigham Young said it this way: "To be sealed up to the day of redemption and have the promise of eternal lives, is the greatest gift of all. The people do not fully understand these things and have them not in full vision before their minds, if they did I will tell you, plainly and in honesty, that there is not a trial which the Saints are called to pass through that they would not realize and acknowledge to be their greatest blessing."[5]

Of course our faith will be tried. Of course we will have tests of our endurance, of our desires, and of our convictions. Said President Lorenzo Snow: "The Lord . . . will try us until He knows what He can do with us. He tried His Son Jesus. Thousands of years before He came upon earth the Father had watched His course and knew that He could depend upon Him when the salvation of worlds should be at stake. . . . So . . . He will . . . continue to try us, in order that He may place us in the highest positions in life and put upon us the most sacred responsibilities."[6] It is in moments of disappointment, heartache, and loneliness that we often make decisions that forge our faith, mold our characters, and fortify our convictions about the only source of strength and solace that satisfies. And that is Jesus Christ.

It is significant that the famous last words of prophets ancient and modern inevitably point us to Christ. Ether admonished us in his last words to "seek this Jesus of whom the prophets . . . have written" (Ether 12:41). Moroni sealed the Book of Mormon with his plea that we "come unto Christ, and be perfected in him" (Moroni 10:32).

In King Benjamin's last recorded address, he bore this resounding witness of Christ: "If ye have come to a knowledge of the goodness of God, and his matchless power, and his wisdom, and his patience, . . . and also, the atonement which has been prepared from the foundation of the world . . . I say, that this is the man who receiveth salvation. . . . Believe in God; believe that he is." Then he counseled us to "always retain in remembrance, the greatness of God" (Mosiah 4:6–11).

Yet, how quickly we forget. The word *remember* is used in the Book of Mormon 136 times, which is not surprising in the story of a people with roller-coaster spirituality who experienced visions and miracles, only to forget with lightning speed what they knew and had felt. Repeatedly they were admonished to *remember* the covenants they had made, to *remember* the purpose for their existence, and to *remember* the greatness of the Holy One of Israel (see 2 Nephi 9:40). Helaman's last words to his sons included this powerful counsel: "Remember, remember that it is upon the rock of our Redeemer, who is Christ, the Son of God, that ye must build your foundation" (Helaman 5:12).

And it's no wonder. They and we face the same challenge, that of maintaining an eternal, spiritual focus in a temporary, temporal world. One of the business magazines that comes to my office publishes a special edition each summer called *The Good Life*. This summer's edition features articles about everything from exotic vacation hideaways to one-of-a-kind designer clothes. With the exception of a few scantily clad models showing off the latest in scuba gear, there is nothing offensive in the magazine—nothing, that is, except for its basic premise, which is at least a distraction if not an out-and-out lie because it suggests that the good life can be purchased with money and that material pleasures bring happiness.

It's not that there is anything wrong with enjoying the finer products this world has to offer—unless they become our object or unless we come to believe that they are the source of joy. It won't surprise you that I found no mention of the fruits of the Spirit or the Savior's healing balm in this magazine. I found myself wondering which expensive suit of clothing or which island bungalow would help you if your heart were breaking or if you longed for a feeling of peace. That is why we are counseled to "fast and pray oft" (Helaman 3:35) and to pray "continually without ceasing" (Alma 26:22), that the purpose of life and the knowledge of the Redeemer will never be far from our minds. Weekly we partake of the sacrament to renew our covenant to "always remember" the Lord (Moroni 4:3; 5:2). Imagine how our perspective and behavior would be affected if we always remembered him, because remembering the Lord and remembering who we are seem to be inseparably connected.

In *The Lion King*, the lion cub Simba forsakes his heritage and turns to riotous living after the death of his father, Mufasa. But when that lifestyle fails to satisfy his inner self, Simba turns to the heavens in a moment of desperation. His father responds by appearing to him, and after listening to Simba try to justify his behavior, Mufasa delivers profound parting words: "You have forgotten who you are, because you have forgotten me."[7]

As our testimony of God the Father and his Son Jesus Christ expands and matures, our view of ourselves and our potential does likewise, and we begin to focus more on life forever than life today. But when we forget our Father and his Son, we forget who we are, and almost inevitably our behavior disappoints us.

How then do we remember the Lord during a time when the adversary has unleashed his most potent strategies? Captain Moroni provides a model for our day. Just as he prepared his people to face an army larger and more ferocious than his, so are we at battle with a sinister strategist who is devoted to our destruction. Moroni prepared his people spiritually and temporally. His preparations were so extensive that the Lamanites were "astonished exceedingly, because of the wisdom of the Nephites in preparing their places of security" (Alma 49:5).

As recent tragic events have demonstrated in a devastating fashion, we too need places of security, places where we are safe not only physically and emotionally but spiritually. May I suggest three.

Strengthening Ourselves Spiritually

Our first place of security lies within our own testimonies, which form the foundation of our faith. A personal witness of Jesus Christ and the ability to hear his voice provide our first and most reliable line of defense against the adversary. When all else fails, the Savior will not. But his mercy, his wisdom, and his strength cannot reach us if we do not believe in him and seek him.

I am technologically impaired. I can't even make my VCR stop blinking. But I've used a computer for twenty years, and I can't imagine life without it, though frankly I only know how to do a few things well. Compared to my brother, who works in the software industry, I'm illiterate. He knows how to do much more using the same computer and the same programs than I do. At least a hundred times he has offered to show me how to work better and faster. But he always offers when I'm right in the middle of a huge deadline, and I don't have time to learn how to do things better and faster. I continue to just get by, doing what

I know how to do well but leaving a tremendous source of power untapped.

How many of us are just getting by spiritually rather than learning how to access the divine power available to those who seek for it? President Brigham Young declared that "we should learn how to take into our possession every blessing and every privilege that God has put within our reach."[8]

After a trip abroad, Eliza R. Snow said: "I have thought much since I returned, how necessary for [us] to be more of a distinct people than what [we] are, to be . . . different from the rest of the world as our privileges are more exalted—we should be a shining light to the nations of the earth. But I often say to myself, are we what we should be?"[9]

We are distinct from the women of the world not only because of what we know but because of the spiritual privileges that accompany those gifted with the Holy Ghost and endowed with power in the house of the Lord. The Lord places no limits on our access to him. But we, unfortunately, often do. We limit ourselves when we sin, when we are lazy spiritually, when we fail to ask and seek. Doctrine and Covenants 6 is a rich tutorial about our accessibility to the Spirit. We are told that if we ask, we will receive; if we inquire, the mysteries of God will be unfolded to us; and if we build our lives upon the rock of Jesus Christ, neither earth nor hell will prevail against us (see D&C 6:5, 11, 14, 23, 34). In the Sermon on the Mount the Savior promised that "*every one* that asketh receiveth; and he that seeketh findeth" (Matthew 7:7; emphasis added). He didn't say the cute ones, or the really smart ones, or those with two or more children. He said *every one* who seeks and asks.

The best way I know to strengthen our personal testimonies and protect ourselves from evil is to seek to have as many experiences with the Lord as possible. When Satan tempted Moses, he rejected him outright, saying, "I will not cease to call upon God . . . : for his glory has been upon me, wherefore I can judge between him and thee" (Moses 1:18). Moses resisted the master of evil by relying upon previous experience with God, which had taught him to discern good from evil and to treasure the fruits of the Spirit. There is nothing as exhilarating as the Spirit, and those most susceptible to Satan are those who have not tasted of its sweetness, who do not hearken to its promptings, and who are left to deal with life alone.

Having meaningful experiences with the Lord comes through earnest fasting and prayer, by repenting and obeying, and through immersing ourselves in the temple and in the words of God. They come as we submit ourselves to the Lord, for he will not force himself upon us. Among Amaleki's last words were these: "I would that ye should come unto Christ . . . and offer your whole souls as an offering unto him" (Omni 1:26).

This process of total commitment takes time and is not easy, but it is only when we yield to the enticings of the Holy Spirit that we can hope to overcome the natural man, who wants to control, is self-indulgent and self-absorbed, rarely if ever wants what is good for him, and is impatient, egotistical, and demanding. When Jesus said, "The spirit indeed is willing, but the flesh is weak" (Matthew 26:41), he was doing more than commenting on sleepy disciples.

Yielding ourselves to the Lord always requires sacrifice and often a sacrifice of our sins. How many favorite sins are we holding onto that alienate us from the Spirit and keep us from turning our lives over to the Lord? Things such as jealousy, or holding onto a grudge, or being casual about the Sabbath day, or the wearing of the garment, or what we watch or read? Imagine the rippling impact on our lives and our families if every one of us determined to sacrifice something that is dulling our spiritual senses!

Yielding ourselves to the Lord, from whom we may obtain greater strength than we will ever muster on our own, is the only source of strength in this life and happiness in the life to come. Truly, we must lose our lives to find them. Two weeks ago I met a sister missionary who was the first young woman in her Bulgarian city to be baptized. Her family has disowned her. Yet she said through her tears: "I had never heard of Jesus Christ. But when the missionaries taught me about him, it was like hearing something I already knew. I love this gospel, and now I have a great responsibility in how I live, because Jesus Christ has changed my life."

A few days ago I received a letter from a great young man and good friend who is serving a mission in Italy. He has been there for a year and has yet to see a baptism, so you can imagine the range of his emotions. In that context, consider what he wrote: "Before my mission I thought I had a testimony, but truly it was just a weak one. I have seen the Master take my life and begin to sculpt, form, and design it. It has been amazing! At times it hasn't been easy, to say the least. I have had to succumb to his will. The thing is that I know all the sculpting, forming, and designing are not finished and that the Lord has just begun. It will take more than a lifetime to get the finished product. But it will be worth it." It *will* be worth it, because if we will let him, if we will come unto him, if we will submit ourselves to him, the Lord will change our lives.

In this day and age we cannot afford to be casual about our testimonies. Satan never sleeps. Neither can we. But the promise for our diligence is magnificent. It is to us as it was to Captain Moroni's people: "Those who were faithful in keeping the commandments of the Lord were delivered at all times . . . [and] there never was a happier time among the people of Nephi" (Alma 50:22–23).

Strengthening Our Families

The second most important place of security is the family, which President Howard W. Hunter said is "the most important unit in time and in eternity and, as such, transcends every other interest in life."[10] No wonder, then, that Lucifer and his lieutenants are attacking the family on every front. Experts predict that the twenty-first century will bring a dramatic redefinition of the family, one that would almost certainly undermine what God intended it to be. The Proclamation on the Family warns that "the disintegration of the family will bring upon [us] . . . the calamities foretold by ancient and modern prophets."[11]

Our prophet, President Gordon B. Hinckley, was speaking directly to us as sisters when he declared, "The home is under siege. So many families are being destroyed. . . .

"If anyone can change the dismal situation into which we are sliding, it is you. Rise up, O women of Zion, rise to the great challenge which faces you. . . .

" . . . My challenge to you . . . is that you will rededicate yourselves to the strengthening of your homes."[12]

If the world can't look to us for a clear signal about the sanctity of marriage, motherhood, and the family, where can it look? I love President Heber J. Grant's statement that "the mother in the family far more than the father, is the one who instills in the hearts of the children, a testimony and a love for the gospel . . . and wherever you find a woman who is devoted to this work, almost without exception you will find that her children are devoted to it."[13] I cannot speak from experience about motherhood, but I can speak from observation. Whenever I am tempted to whine about my hectic life, something inevitably reminds me of those who are mothers and the exceptional load they carry. That is when I stop complaining, because I'm not sure that it's even possible for me to work as hard as they do. And I am sure that I'll never have their influence, which is a result of the billions of acts of service, compassion, and patience mothers perform as they nurture their children and nudge them towards exaltation.

Just because I have not had the privilege of bearing children does not mean that I am unconcerned about the family. I have a family that includes seventeen nieces and nephews, and I work hard at being their favorite aunt. Though I would do anything for these children, I have often wondered just who is really helping whom.

I had one such experience recently. I was assigned to speak at general conference. Such an assignment is both a privilege and a pressure, and only after several weeks of hard work did I finally complete the message I felt prompted to prepare. But then, just days before conference, I came to understand that the talk I had prepared was not the one I should deliver on Easter Sunday. It seemed inconceivable to start over, but that is what I had to do. I had three days to prepare an entirely new talk.

And after slaving day and night for weeks on the first message, I was emotionally, physically, and spiritually spent. All of this transpired on Friday, and I worked that afternoon, through the night, and all the next day. By Saturday evening I had written dozens of pages of mediocre text—none of which I could use. I was depressed. I had no ideas. And fear was gripping every cell of my body. Late Saturday evening I decided to lie down for a few hours.

Then something happened unlike anything I have experienced before. When I arose at 3:00 Sunday morning, I felt optimistic and full of energy. I turned on my computer, opened my scriptures, and began to write. Nine hours later the talk was basically done. Parting the Red Sea would have been no more miraculous to me.

Now, for the rest of the story. When my two sisters learned about my plight, they sprang into action, contacting everyone in our family and asking them to fast, beginning Saturday afternoon. I'll never forget my sister Michelle saying, "We'll get all of your nieces and nephews fasting for you. That will work."

When I felt rejuvenated Sunday morning, I was given to know that I was being strengthened because of the fasting and prayers of my family and perhaps particularly because of the willingness of my nieces and nephews to help Aunt Sheri. I have never experienced such a restoration of mind and spirit in so short a period. Once again I ask, who is really helping whom? I simply could not have done what I had to do if my family had not united to call upon the Lord in my behalf. What if our parents had not taught us to fast and pray as children? What if my siblings hadn't done the same in their homes? But everyone was ready and willing to respond when I was in need. My family provided a safety net during a time of great challenge.

The foundation of the Church and the hope of the future is the family, and there is no place of security like it. There is power in the family that we will find nowhere else, a power that spans generations and reaches across the veil. My Grandma Dew's last written words were those asking to be released from her calling because she had become ill. She wrote, "I hope the Lord does not think I have said no to him. I love the gospel so very much and also this work." Grandma died one week later. But she left behind a legacy of faith that influences me to this day. Our eternal families provide a vital place of security.

Strengthening the Church Family

The third place of security is the Church, or the Church family. As individuals and families we need additional protection from the storms of the world: "The gathering together upon the land of Zion, and upon her stakes, may be for a defense, and for a refuge from the storm, and from wrath when it shall be poured out . . . upon the whole earth" (D&C 115:6).

The tragic events at Columbine High School in Littleton, Colorado, have demonstrated how desperately we need each other's support. Within minutes after teenage gunmen began their rampage, a large number of members and leaders had gathered to search for their youth. It took the stake president some time to locate all of the bishops, who were already searching out their flock. A fundamental characteristic of followers of Christ is our willingness to take care of each other.

I have experienced this kind of care myself, for as much as I love my family, life would not be as full were it not for my Church family. I am often asked why I feel comfortable as an unmarried member of a family-oriented Church. I do not understand this question, which implies that I would be happier if I were not a member of the Church. It also implies that happiness comes only to those whose lives are ideal—which would make for a very small group of happy people. So isn't the question really, How does someone in nontraditional circumstances feel a sense of belonging in this Church?

The answer has been articulated repeatedly by President Gordon B. Hinckley as he has identified the three things each new member—and, I submit, each member—of the Church needs: "friends, a responsibility [or the opportunity to serve], and nurturing with the 'good word of God' (Moro. 6:4)."[14]

I have never felt ignored in the Church because I have had opportunities to serve that have strengthened my testimony and blessed me with my dearest friends. I will ever be grateful to the stake president who called me to serve as the Relief Society president in a married stake. In my call he sent a message that what we have in common is far more important than any differences we may have. If there is anyplace in the world where every one of us, regardless of our personal circumstances, should feel accepted, needed, valued, and loved, it is within our Church family. And every one of us can reach out to others and help them feel a sense of belonging.

Such inclusiveness thwarts Lucifer's purposes, for he despises a united people. Said President George Q. Cannon: "[The devil] hates the Latter-day Saints because they act together. . . . If we would split up and divide, . . . then the devil . . . would rejoice."[15] No wonder Satan delights when we cluster ourselves based on social standing, ethnicity, and a host of other superficial criteria. Among his most divisive tactics is his campaign to polarize us according to gender and to confuse us about the distinctive nature and supernal value of our respective assignments as men and women. This tactic, left unchecked, threatens the unity of our Church family.

When our general presidency is interviewed by the press, we invariably field questions that imply that Latter-day Saint women are dominated and ignored. I find this curious, for I have been unable to identify any organization anywhere in the world where women have more influence than in this Church. Not long ago our presidency had the privilege of hosting Madame Jehan Sadat, the widow of the former president of Egypt, Anwar Sadat. One of her first comments to us was, "The women in your Church have such great leadership opportunities. It is wonderful!" Hundreds of thousands of us in more than 160 nations have the rights and responsibilities of presidency, and thousands more are called to teach men, women, youth, and children. Where else do women bear such weighty responsibility and enjoy such respect? There is no other organization for women that rivals the Relief Society, which is the only such organization founded by a prophet of God.

Though the Prophet Joseph Smith organized the Relief Society "after the pattern of the priesthood" and stated that the Church "was never perfectly organized until the women were thus organized,"[16] there are some who cite the fact that sisters are not ordained to the priesthood as evidence that our work is less significant than that of men. But such a view of the Lord's plan is incomplete and narrow, for the gospel of Jesus Christ embraces an ennobling doctrine regarding women. Said Elder Bruce R. McConkie, "In all matters that pertain to godliness and holiness and which are brought to pass as a result of personal righteousness . . . men and women stand in a position of absolute equality before the Lord."[17]

From an eternal perspective we know little about the reasons specific assignments were given to men and women. Because of that, the adversary seeks to create confusion about something that need not be confusing. What we do know is that the Lord has declared his will on this matter, and for reasons known to him, our assignments as sisters do not require that we be ordained to the priesthood, though the assignments of worthy men do require ordination. This difference in the stewardship between the sons and daughters of God need not concern us. We should feel secure about the manner in which the Lord administers his kingdom.

I do. I feel secure because I trust the Lord, and this is an issue of faith. This is his Church. He stands at its head. And it is inconsistent within his divine character to undermine or diminish the contribution or value of any of us.

Regrettably, some priesthood bearers treat women inappropriately and live beneath the privileges they hold. But on this issue President Hinckley has been clear: "I believe that any man who offends a daughter of God will someday be held accountable, and the time will come when he will stand before the bar of judgment with sorrow and remorse."[18] Gratefully, the abuses of a relative few do not negate the blessings of the priesthood, which are eternal and make anything this world has to offer pale by comparison. The Lord's plan assures that all our Father has is available to all who qualify.

President Joseph Fielding Smith explained that "the Lord offers to his daughters every spiritual gift and blessing that can be obtained by his sons."[19] Elder James E. Talmage stated that "in the sacred endowments associated with the ordinances [of] the House of the Lord, [it is clear how dramatically] woman shares with man the blessings of the Priesthood."[20]

All of us, men and women alike, receive the gift and gifts of the Holy Ghost and are entitled to personal revelation. We may all take upon us the Lord's name, become sons and daughters of Christ, partake of ordinances in the temple from which we emerge armed with power (D&C 109:22), receive the fulness of the gospel, and achieve exaltation in the celestial kingdom. These spiritual privileges derive from the Melchizedek Priesthood, which holds the "keys of all the spiritual blessings of the Church" (D&C 107:18).

As sisters we are not diminished by priesthood power; we are magnified by it. When respected and exercised righteously, this power unites rather than separates us. Elder James E. Talmage stated that "the world's greatest champion of woman and womanhood is Jesus the Christ."[21] I believe it, and in his plan I have complete trust.

A penetrating question related to the blessings of the priesthood is why more of us, both men and women, don't more earnestly seek the blessings available by virtue of this transcendent power. Throughout the Doctrine and Covenants the word *receive* is used to mean having faith in, or accepting as true. All of us, including those who are not ordained, *receive* or activate the blessings of the priesthood in our lives by first believing the priesthood to be the power of God and having faith in its governance, by seeking those blessings and keeping sacred covenants, and by sustaining those who are ordained and called to lead us.

As President Brigham Young taught, "The Priesthood is given to the people . . . and, when properly understood, they may actually unlock the treasury of the Lord, and *receive* to their fullest satisfaction."[22] It is the power of the priesthood that unlocks the door to heaven and allows us to understand the mysteries of God. The question we might therefore ask ourselves is, Are we *receiving* the privileges and unspeakable blessings associated with the gift of priesthood power?

Sister Carol Thomas of the Young Women General Presidency and I had an unforgettable experience in Cali, Colombia. After a long evening of meetings, because we were to catch a predawn flight, the presiding stake president asked the large congregation to remain seated while we departed. But upon the final "amen," several dozen priesthood leaders jumped to their feet and formed two lines, creating a pathway from the chapel outside to a waiting van. As we walked through this sheltered passageway, I was deeply moved. In that setting, there was no need to protect us, but the metaphor was clear. Priesthood leaders were symbolic of priesthood power. It is the power of the priesthood that marks the path leading to eternal life, clears the path, and protects the path. Within the priesthood is the power to separate and safeguard us from the world; the power to subdue the adversary and surmount obstacles; the power to comfort, bless, and heal; the power to enlarge our capacity and enable us to hear the voice of the Lord; the power to strengthen marriages and families and bind us to each other; and the power to triumph over mortality and come unto him. These blessings may be received by every righteous, seeking son or daughter of God. As President Harold B. Lee taught, "Through the priesthood and only the priesthood may we . . . find our way back home."[23]

After years of seeking understanding in the scriptures and in the temple, I have come to know for myself that the priesthood is the power of God to bless and exalt every one of us if we live worthily and seek its blessings. I believe it is imperative that we understand these blessings and how to activate them, for they will be a vital source of strength and protection in the days ahead. Truly, the priesthood of God distinguishes the Lord's Church from any other, and wherever and whenever its power and blessings are exercised and called upon righteously, there results a tremendous place of security.

Regardless of our personal circumstances as we march forward to fulfill our foreordained missions in the next millennium, it is in our places of security that we will be reminded of who we are, where we are, and what is really important. Such places of refuge are essential in a world that is increasingly hostile to followers of Christ.

Among the adversary's pawns during this century was Hitler, whose evil designs wreaked havoc on the entire world. Early on, Winston Churchill attempted to warn fellow countrymen about this German madman. But Churchill was labeled a warmonger, and while England slept, Hitler amassed a huge army and began to put his diabolical scheme into motion. The young Elder Gordon B. Hinckley was serving a mission in England at the time, and he heard Churchill's speeches of warning. Upon his release, Elder Hinckley toured the European continent. Throughout Germany he watched spit-and-polish Nazi troops goose-step through the streets. He noticed a dramatic difference in other countries, where troops were undisciplined in demeanor and dress. He later reflected that Hitler had identified his object and knew exactly what he was doing, but the rest of Europe was asleep. Young Elder Hinckley sensed that he was "sitting on a front row in the bleachers of history."[24]

We have a front-row seat on the bleachers of an era in which Satan is moving about largely uncontrolled and unchecked. As brutal as Hitler was, our opponent is far more threatening, for what we have to lose is not only our happiness and peace of mind here but also eternal life in the world to come. Satan knows exactly what he is doing. But do we? Are we sleeping, or are we creating places of security where we may insulate ourselves from his advances?

If there was ever a time when the Lord needed righteous, determined women who can distinguish between the adversary's deceptions and the voice of the Lord, it is now. If there were ever a time when the Lord needed women who stand committed and consecrated, it is now. If there were ever a time when the Lord needed women of integrity and purity who live in the world but rise above it, it is now. If there were ever a time when the Lord needed his daughters to be alert to what is happening in society and to defend the sanctity of the home and family, it is now. If there were ever a time when the Lord needed us to have a clear vision of who we are, where we are, and what is important, it is now. We are a sleeping giant ready to awake, for the sisters of Relief Society will increasingly become an anomaly in this world. And because of our cheerful and righteous differences, we will become a beacon and a magnet for countless good women everywhere who are looking for female role models who exhibit compassion and strength, charity and conviction—and who do so while remaining unsullied by the world.

Might we therefore covenant this very hour to work and watch and fight and pray. To work to strengthen ourselves spiritually every week of every month of every year. To watch over and fortify our families and our Church family so that within the stakes of Zion will exist the strength and unity to help us withstand Lucifer's minions. To fight the adversary in every arena. And to pray with increasing strength and confidence and faith. The Lord has never expected more of faithful women than he does now. But we would not be here if we were not up to the challenge.

The historian Wallace Stegner concluded his introduction to *The Gathering of Zion: The Story of the Mormon Trail* with these words: "That I do not accept the faith that possessed [the Mormons] does not mean I doubt their . . . devotion and heroism. . . . Especially their women. Their women were incredible."[25] Our sister forebears *were* incredible. And so are we, with foreordained missions that only we can fulfill.

Captain Moroni raised a title of liberty and invited all who would maintain it to "come forth in the strength of the Lord" (Alma 46:20). President Gordon B. Hinckley has done likewise: "We have work to do, . . . so very much of it. Let us roll up our sleeves and get at it, with a new commitment, putting our trust in the Lord. . . . We can do better than we have ever done before."[26]

Mormon's last words to his son Moroni were these: "Let us labor diligently; . . . for we have a labor to perform whilst in this tabernacle of clay, that we may conquer the enemy of all righteousness, and rest our souls in the kingdom of God" (Moroni 9:6).

May our faith and our works qualify us for the exaltation of which Mormon wrote. May we come to know that Jesus Christ stands ready to encircle and strengthen and comfort and change every one who seeks after him. And may we come to testify as did the Prophet Joseph, "And now, after the many testimonies which have been given of him, this is the testimony, last of all, which we give of him: That he lives!" (D&C 76:22). For in a coming day, perhaps sooner than later, the most famous last words of all will be fulfilled, when every knee will bow and every tongue confess that Jesus is the Christ. I so testify, adding my witness that we are his daughters, that we are beloved of him, and that he is our Savior, our Protector, and our Redeemer.

NOTES

1. *Hymns of The Church of Jesus Christ of Latter-day Saints* (Salt Lake City: The Church of Jesus Christ of Latter-day Saints, 1985), no. 252.
2. Harold B. Lee, Conference Report, October 1973, 5.
3. As quoted in John A. Widtsoe, *Priesthood and Church Government* (Salt Lake City: Deseret Book, 1939), 86.
4. Spencer W. Kimball, *The Miracle of Forgiveness* (Salt Lake City: Bookcraft, 1969), 2.
5. Brigham Young, *Journal of Discourses*, 26 vols. (London: Latter-day Saints' Book Depot, 1854–86), 2:301.
6. Lorenzo Snow, *Millennial Star* 61 (24 August 1899): 532.
7. *The Lion King*, Disney Company, 88 minutes, videocassette.
8. Brigham Young, *Discourses of Brigham Young*, sel. John A. Widtsoe (Salt Lake City: Deseret Book, 1954), 53.
9. Eliza R. Snow, *Woman's Exponent* (15 September 1873): 62.
10. Howard W. Hunter, *Ensign*, November 1994, 50.
11. First Presidency and Quorum of the Twelve Apostles of The Church of Jesus Christ of Latter-day Saints, "The Family: A Proclamation to the World," *Ensign*, November 1995, 102.
12. Gordon B. Hinckley, *Ensign*, November 1998, 99–100.
13. Heber J. Grant, *Gospel Standards* (Salt Lake City: Improvement Era, 1969), 150.
14. Gordon B. Hinckley, *Ensign*, May 1997, 47.
15. George Q. Cannon, *Gospel Truth*, comp. Jerreld L. Newquist, 2 vols. (Salt Lake City: Deseret Book, 1974), 1:210.
16. Joseph Smith, *Woman's Exponent* 12 (1 September 1883): 51.

17. Bruce R. McConkie, *Ensign*, January 1979, 61.
18. Gordon B. Hinckley, *Ensign*, November 1989, 95.
19. Joseph Fielding Smith, *Improvement Era*, June 1970, 66.
20. James E. Talmage, *Young Woman's Journal* (October 1914): 602.
21. James E. Talmage, *Jesus the Christ* (Salt Lake City: Deseret Book, 1972), 475.
22. Young, *Discourses of Brigham Young*, 131; emphasis added.
23. Harold B. Lee, *Be Loyal to the Royal within You*, Brigham Young University Speeches of the Year (Provo, 20 October 1957), 2.
24. Sheri L. Dew, *Go Forward with Faith: The Biography of Gordon B. Hinckley* (Salt Lake City: Deseret Book, 1996), 80.
25. Wallace Stegner, *The Gathering of Zion: The Story of the Mormon Trail* (Lincoln: University of Nebraska Press, 1964), 13.
26. Gordon B. Hinckley, *Ensign*, May 1995, 88.

Index